D1626197

EUROPE UNITED

A HISTORY OF THE EUROPEAN CUP/ CHAMPIONS LEAGUE

ANDREW GODSELL

SPORTS BOOKS

Published in Great Britain by
SportsBooks Limited
PO Box 422
Cheltenham
GL50 2YN
Tel: 01242 256755
Fax: 01242 254694
www.sportsbooks.ltd.uk

© Andrew Godsell 2005
First Published September 2005

All rights reserved. No part of this publication may be produced or transmitted in any form or by any means, including photocopying and recording, without written permission of the publishers. Such written permission must also be obtained before any part of the publication is stored in any retrieval system of any nature.

Front cover designed by Kath Northam.

All photographs, except those on the cover, by Actionimages

A catalogue record for this book is available from
the British Library.
ISBN 1 899807 30 6

Printed in Malta on behalf of Compass Press Limited.

Contents

Preface

The season-by-season narrative and statistical material, which forms the core of this history of the first 50 years of the European Cup/Champions League, is complemented by biographical sketches of players and managers, plus features, liking the competition to the wider football context. I have followed the competition since becoming a football fan as a child in the early 1970s, and recalled many happy memories in the course of writing. Back in the 1970s, the European Cup final was one of the few football matches shown live on television. Recent years have seen the vast expansion of the new Champions League, building upon the long-established position of the European Cup as the world's leading competition for club teams. Amid the virtually daily diet of contemporary football, the Champions League retains a massive reputation.

The writing of a detailed factual book necessarily involves the accumulation of information from a series of sources, before the author's selection and interpretation of events can see the light of day. I have built an extensive collection of football books, magazines, match programmes, and videos across many years, and made good use of the archive. I wish to acknowledge the wealth of detail provided by three previous books about the competition, *The European Cup 1955-1980* by John Motson and John Rowlinson (1980), *Champions of Europe: The History, Romance and Intrigue of the European Cup* by Brian Glanville (1991), and *The European Cup: An Illustrated History* by Rab MacWilliam (2000). These have been supplemented by excellent material in *The Guinness Book of World Soccer* by Guy Oliver (second edition 1995) and *Rothmans Football Yearbook* (*Sky Sports Football Yearbook* from 2003). World Soccer is a magazine that provides unrivalled coverage of the global game, while *Champions: The Official Magazine of the UEFA Champions League* revolves around the specific competition. The websites of UEFA and the Rec Sport Soccer Statistics Foundation have chronicled the European competitions for several years, and provided a framework for the statistics included in the book. Television coverage by both the BBC and ITV has allowed myself and millions of others to follow events in the competition as they have happened.

I received advice and encouragement from many people. My parents, Phil and Jill Godsell, sparked my interest in football as a child. One of my earliest football memories is being allowed to stay up later than usual, at the age of seven, to watch the first half of the 1972 European Cup final live on TV. My father was a good amateur footballer, who recalls playing in a RAF team in the 1950s, with the opposition including Ron Flowers, who would appear for Wolves in the European Cup a few years later. I followed him in becoming a supporter of Manchester United, enthralled by stories of the 'Busby Babes', and the team that won the European Cup in 1968. In recent years I have followed United's campaigns in the Champions League, the highlight being their unforgettable triumph in 1999. Roy and Linda Roberts, my father-in-law and mother-in-law, have also been loyal supporters of the book. Simon Clarke, Brendan Hosey, Dan Parker, and Mark Tong all read substantial excerpts from the draft manuscript, and provided feedback that was greatly appreciated. Harry Sykes, my godson, has an enthusiasm for football that mirrors mine as a child. Harry is a Liverpool fan, and I am delighted that his team won the 2005 final with a famous performance.

Jeannette, my wife, and Anna, our daughter, have been a wonderful support to my writing in many ways over the years.

Andrew Godsell

I dedicate this book to Jeannette and Anna, with love and thanks.

Chapter 1

Early Years
Real Madrid Quintet 1955-1960

The Birth of the Competition

THE PRESENT day UEFA Champions League developed during the 1990s out of the competition which was officially called the European Champion Clubs' Cup from its inauguration in 1955, but was generally known as the European Cup. With the basic concept of the competition remaining the same, traditionalists still call the UEFA Champions League by the old European Cup name. The Union of European Football Associations (UEFA) refer to the combined competition as the European Cup/Champions League. Whichever name, or set of names, is used, this is recognisably a continuous competition, that has now stretched across half a century. With Europe being the dominant continent in the football world, while the new FIFA Club World Championship has yet to fulfil its potential, the European Cup/Champions League is clearly the world's leading club football competition.

The birth of the European Cup sprang, in part, from creative tension between England and France, with traditional political and cultural rivalry between the two countries having an impact on football. Britain gave football to the world. The game was developed in England in the middle of the 19th century, and the Football Association, formed in 1863, provided a framework for its growth. The FA Cup was launched as a national knock-out competition in 1871, and this was followed by the inauguration of the Football League, by the body of that name, in 1888. The international spread of the game, largely influenced by British trading links, during the late 19th century, and early 20th century, led to the spawning of clubs, football authorities, plus knock-out and league competitions, throughout the world. Unfortunately British football also developed a superiority complex, and an insular attitude, believing that it alone should dominate the game.

France did not match Britain in the development of football, but during the 20th century it was the French who led the way in the international organisation of the game. Building upon the foundations laid by the British, the French launched FIFA, the World Cup, the European Cup, and the European Championship. In each case, French initiative was met by disinterest from the English. At the start of the 20th century, Robert Guerin, a member of the French Sports Federation, suggested that England take the lead in forming an international governing body for the game, but the Football Association declined to take up the challenge. Undeterred, Guerin and the French convened the meeting in Paris, on May 21 1904, at which the Federation Internationale de Football Association (FIFA) was formed.

A quarter of a century later, the impetus for the establishment of the World Cup was provided by two Frenchmen, namely Jules Rimet, the President of FIFA, and Henri Delauney, the Secretary of the French Football Federation. The first World Cup was played in Uruguay in 1930, and won by the host nation, but England were not among the participants, being ineligible as they were not members of FIFA. England had joined FIFA in 1905, but withdrew in 1920, in order to avoid association with nations they had fought against in the First World War, before rejoining in 1924, and then breaking from FIFA again in 1928, in a dispute over the nature of amateurism. England remained outside the fold as the 1934 and 1938 World Cups, hosted by Italy and France respectively, were both won by Italy.

England even declined a special invitation from FIFA to compete in the 1938 finals, as a replacement for Austria, following the annexation of that country by Germany. England rejoined FIFA in 1946, and qualified for the 1950 World Cup finals in Brazil, but suffered a humiliating 1-0 defeat against the USA, and an early exit, while Uruguay regained the world title. Despite the setback, English football continued to regard itself as the best in the world.

Further embarrassment followed for England, in the shape of two heavy defeats against Hungary, who won 6-3 at Wembley in 1953, and 7-1 in Budapest the following year. At the 1954 World Cup finals, staged in Switzerland, England again struggled, and lost to Uruguay in the quarter-finals, while West Germany emerged as the surprise winners, beating Hungary 3-2 in the final.

The battering suffered by England's pride at international level was offset by some clutching at the straws offered by a victory in a friendly match between two club sides. On December 13 1954 Wolverhampton Wanderers won 3-2 against Honved, the club side around which the Hungarian national team was built, at Molineux. Honved had taken a two goal lead early in the match, but Wolves, cheered on by a crowd of 54,998, stormed back with three goals in the second half, as heavy rain fell on a muddy pitch. Stan Cullis, the Wolves manager, pointed to his players after the match, and exclaimed to onlookers, "There they are, the champions of the world". The illusion of English footballing pre-eminence was instantly restored, as the national press took up the refrain of Cullis the following day.

The continental antidote to this fever appeared in *L'Equipe*, the French sports newspaper, on December 16. Gabriel Hanot, the football editor, wrote: "We must wait for Wolves to visit Budapest and Moscow before we proclaim their invincibility. There are other clubs of international prowess, like Milan and Real Madrid. There is a strong case for starting a European championship for clubs".

Hanot and a colleague, Jacques Ryswick, put forward a plan for a European midweek league, bringing together 14 or 16 of the continent's leading clubs. The plan attracted support as *L'Equipe* canvassed clubs who would be potential participants over the next few weeks, although it soon became clear that the clubs would prefer a knock-out competition to a league, to avoid fixture congestion. On March 2 1955 a delegation from *L'Equipe* presented their plan to a UEFA congress in Vienna. Having received further encouragement, *L'Equipe* convened a meeting of interested clubs at the Ambassador Hotel in Paris, on April 2. The meeting agreed rules for a knock-out competition, a list of 16 clubs to participate in the inaugural 1955-56 season, and the composition of a committee to oversee the tournament.

The competition planned by *L'Equipe*, along with other proposals, was considered at a series of meetings during May 1955. On May 7 a FIFA meeting in London approved the new competition, subject to UEFA agreeing to organise it. Ten days later, in Madrid, the committee for the new competition met for the first time, and accepted the guidance of FIFA. A joint meeting between UEFA and the committee rapidly followed on May 21, in Paris – 51 years to the day after FIFA was founded in the same city. At this meeting it was agreed that UEFA would organise the new competition, which was given the name the European Champion Clubs' Cup, on the lines already agreed for the 1955-56 season by *L'Equipe* and the competing clubs. UEFA and *L'Equipe* agreed that from the 1956-57 season onwards the competition would be reserved for national champions.

At the same time, UEFA decided to press ahead with another competition, the International Industries Fairs Inter-Cities Cup, which would be open to teams from cities that staged international trade fairs. A third European club competition was also set up in 1955, but independently of UEFA, as the Mitropa Cup was revived. This competition, which had provided a model for Hanot's recent proposal, had previously been staged on an annual basis from 1927 to 1939, before being abandoned due to the outbreak of the Second World War.

The Mitropa Cup brought together clubs of several nations from Mittel Europa (the centre of Europe) – namely Austria, Czechoslovakia, Hungary, Italy, Romania, Switzerland, and Yugoslavia. Initially open to the national champions, the competition was extended to include other leading clubs – an anticipation of the development of the Champions League. The new Mitropa Cup, however, paled into insignificance compared with the European Cup and Fairs Cup.

The establishment of the European Cup, and the related club competitions, was seen by many as part of the positive moves towards a Europe united by sporting, cultural, and trading links, in contrast to the political division hanging over the continent. The 1950s saw the development of trading agreements, which were to lead to the establishment of the European Economic Community in 1958. On the other hand, a decade after the end of the Second World War, west and east faced each other in a Cold War. Indeed on May 14 1955, while the football authorities were agreeing the establishment of the European Cup, the Warsaw Pact was concluded between the Soviet Union and several of its east European allies, as a military rival to the North Atlantic Treaty Organisation.

Coincidentally Gwardia Warsaw were to feature in the first European Cup, arriving as a late replacement for Chelsea. The new English champions withdrew during July 1955, being persuaded to do so by the Football League. In an unfortunate re-surfacing of England's insular attitude, the Football League saw the new competition as a distraction from domestic football, which should be avoided to prevent fixture congestion. During the summer of 1955, UEFA finalised the rules and arrangements for the European Cup. The competition would be played on a knock-out basis, with ties prior to the final having two legs – each team playing once on their own ground – and the winner being decided on aggregate score. Where the aggregate score was level, a single play-off match would follow. The final would be staged as a single match, with Paris being selected in advance as the venue for the first final, in honour of the leading role of the French in the founding of the competition. Within a few months of Hanot's proposal, the European Cup was ready to begin.

1955-56

The European Cup began with entertainment and goals, as Sporting Lisbon drew 3-3 at home to Partizan Belgrade, on September 4 1955. Joao Martins of Sporting Lisbon scored the first goal after 14 minutes. Partizan won the return 5-2 on October 12, to take the tie 8-5 on aggregate. Milos Milutonovic, who scored twice for Partizan in the first leg, and four times in the second leg, was to emerge as the tournament's leading scorer, with eight goals this season. Neither Sporting Lisbon or Partizan Belgrade were their nation's reigning champions. With the 16 participants in the inaugural European Cup having been selected by invitation, only half of the entrants were actually current national champions.

In the absence of Chelsea, the sole British representative was Hibernian, who had finished fifth in the Scottish league the previous season. Hibernian, with support from British soldiers based in Germany, began with a 4-0 win away to Rot Weiss Essen, before drawing the return 1-1. One of Hibernian's goals in the first leg was scored by Willie Ormond, who had played for Scotland in the 1954 World Cup finals, and was to manage them in the 1974 finals. Stade de Reims, the French representative, beat Aarhus 4-2 on aggregate.

Real Madrid opened with a pair of victories against Servette Geneva, winning 2-0 away and 5-0 at home, with the legendary Alfredo Di Stefano scoring twice in the second leg to open his European Cup goal tally. Saarbrucken made the single European Cup appearance by a team representing Saar – a country that was to be incorporated within West Germany at the start of 1957, as the result of a referendum. After unexpectedly winning 4-3 against Milan in the first leg, Saarbrucken lost the return 4-1, which meant Milan advanced with a 7-5 aggregate win.

The first round matches stretched across September, October, and November, following which the quarter-finals were also played at a leisurely pace, between November 1955 and February 1956. The first leg of the tie between Real Madrid and Partizan Belgrade was surprisingly played on Christmas Day. Real gave their fans a great Christmas present by winning 4-0 – Castanos leading the way with two goals in the first 23 minutes, following which Francisco Gento and Di Stefano completed the scoring. This meant that a 3-0 defeat in the return leg did not prevent Real from taking the tie. Hibernian were again impressive, beating Djurgardens twice. Milan drew away to Rapid Vienna, before thrashing them 7-2 in the second leg. Stade de Reims beat Voros Lobogo 4-2, and then drew 4-4, to take the tie 8-6 on aggregate.

Hibernian's progress was halted by Stade de Reims in the semi-finals, which took place during April and May. The French club won 2-0 at home, with goals from Leblond and Bliard, and 1-0 away, with Glovacki being the scorer. A possible place in the final had proved beyond Hibernian, but reaching the last four was a creditable achievement, and a fine start to the British challenge in Europe. Hibernian also increased their income for the season by £25,000 due to extra gate receipts. This was an impressive sum at the time – although dwarfed by the earnings available to clubs from the European Cup/Champions League in more recent years. In the other semi-final, Real Madrid beat Milan 4-2 in Spain, following which Milan won their home leg 2-1 – both of Milan's goals in the second match were penalties by Dal Monte. Real therefore took the tie 5-4 on aggregate.

Real Madrid and Stade de Reims contested the first European Cup final, on June 13 1956, at the Parc des Princes in Paris, before a crowd of 38,239 with gate receipts of around £20,000. The figure for the final boosted the combined attendance for the 29 matches in the inaugural competition to 912,000 – giving an encouraging average of more than 31,000 per game. The advance selection of the venue had the effect of benefiting Reims, who were playing in their home country. Despite the absence of an English club in the tournament, Arthur Ellis, an Englishman, was selected as referee. Meanwhile the second half of the match was to be broadcast live to British television viewers, by the BBC. It was fitting the final brought together two clubs who were among the reigning national champions taking part. Stade de Reims were the leading French club side of the era, with all six of their national titles being won between 1949 and 1962. They had been managed since 1950 by Albert Batteux, who was previously a player for Reims. He also managed the national team from 1955 to 1962.

His line-up included Michel Hidalgo, who was to be manager of France from 1976 to 1984, leading the country through a golden era, which included third place in the 1982 World Cup, and victory in the 1984 European Championship. After many years in the doldrums, Real Madrid had won the Spanish title in 1954 – for the first time since 1933 – and repeated the success in 1955. Real had a fine manger in Jose Villalonga, but the revival of the club was largely due to the influence of two other men.

Di Stefano, an Argentinian by birth, was the team's centre forward, and a great motivator. Santiago Bernabeu, who became president in 1943, launched a membership scheme for the club's supporters – a novelty in those days – and used the proceeds to build a massive arena. This was opened in 1947, and renamed the Santiago Bernabeu Stadium in 1955. The investment paid off, with the revenues from large crowds financing the further development of the club, and fulfilling the dreams Bernabeu had for Real Madrid. In 1955, Bernabeu was one of the enthusiasts who did much to turn the idea of a European Cup into reality. Jacques Ferran, editor in chief of *L'Equipe*, regarded Bernabeu as a major positive influence in the meeting at Paris in April 1955. Ferran said of Bernabeu: "His sometimes shaky French was good enough for all of us to understand. His friendliness and courtesy hid a strong and forceful personality. This, and the importance of his great club, were vital factors in the way the meeting went".

Real Madrid and Reims had featured in a series of high scoring matches on their way to the final, and continued this trend in the final. Reims took the lead after just six minutes, as a free kick from Raymond Kopa was headed on by Michel Leblond. Ellis awarded the goal despite protests from Real that the ball had not crossed the goal-line. Four minutes later Jean Templin put Reims 2-0 ahead. Real Madrid got back into the game on the quarter of an hour mark, courtesy of a great goal from Di Stefano, who beat two opponents in midfield, exchanged passes with Marsal, and then scored with a powerful shot.

On the half hour Real pulled level at 2-2, as a corner was met by a header from Hector Rial. Real Madrid thought they had taken the lead shortly after the interval, but Joseito's effort was disallowed for offside. Seventeen minutes into the second half Reims regained the lead, with a goal similar to their first, except that this time it was Michel Hidalgo who headed in a free kick from Kopa. Reims looked to be back on course for victory, but Real Madrid thwarted them with another fight back. Marquitos equalised with an excellent solo effort only five minutes after Hidalgo's goal. Following this Rial scored his second with ten minutes left to play, to put Real Madrid ahead for the first time. In the closing minutes Templin struck the crossbar, as Reims came close to equalising, and forcing extra time, but Real Madrid held on to win 4-3. The match was followed by the presentation of the European Cup trophy to Miguel Munoz, the Real Madrid captain, by Ebbe Schwartz, the Danish President of UEFA.

Ironically Real Madrid's victory in the first European Cup final owed much to the performances of two Argentinians. Rial scored twice, while Di Stefano scored once, as well as inspiring his team's recovery. Both had scored five times during the course of Real's victorious campaign. On the day after the final, the success of the first European Cup was marked by a banquet at the Eiffel Tower. Real Madrid's victory against Reims, in a seven goal thriller, appeared to be the icing on the cake, but it also proved to be the start of a wonderful run of victories for the Spanish club.

1955-56

First round

		1st leg	2nd leg	agg
Servette Geneva	Real Madrid	0-2	0-5	0-7
Sporting Lisbon	Partizan Belgrade	3-3	2-5	5-8
Rapid Vienna	PSV Eindhoven	6-1	0-1	6-2
Milan	Saarbrucken	3-4	4-1	7-5
Rot Weiss Essen	Hibernian	0-4	1-1	1-5
Djurgardens	Gwardia Warsaw	0-0	4-1	4-1
Voros Lobogo	Anderlecht	6-3	4-1	10-4
Aarhus	Stade de Reims	0-2	2-2	2-4

Quarter-finals

		1st leg	2nd leg	agg
Real Madrid	Partizan Belgrade	4-0	0-3	4-3
Rapid Vienna	Milan	1-1	2-7	3-8
Djurgardens	Hibernian	1-3	0-1	1-4
Stade de Reims	Voros Lobogo	4-2	4-4	8-6

Semi-finals

		1st leg	2nd leg	agg
Real Madrid	Milan	4-2	1-2	5-4
Stade de Reims	Hibernian	2-0	1-0	3-0

Final

June 13 1956 Paris

Real Madrid 4	Stade de Reims 3
Di Stefano	Leblond
Rial 2	Templin
Marquitos	Hidalgo

Real Madrid: Alonso, Atienza, Marquitos, Lesmes, Munoz, Zarraga, Joseito, Marsal, Di Stefano, Rial, Gento
Stade de Reims: Jacquet, Zimny, Jonquet, Giraudo, Leblond, Siatka, Hidalgo, Glovacki, Kopa, Bliard, Templin
HT: 2-2
Referee: Ellis (England)
Attendance: 38,239

1956-57

The success of the first European Cup prompted an increased entry of 22 teams for the second tournament. All were reigning national champions, apart from Real Madrid, third in the Spanish league the previous season, but invited as defending champions. Manchester United, who had won the First Division in 1955-56, became the first English club to enter. Matt Busby, United's manager, was a powerful advocate for the new competition, having been influenced by the positive experience the previous season of his friend Harry Swan, the chairman of Hibernian. Busby told United's board of directors: "Football has become a world game. It no longer exclusively belongs to England, Scotland, and the British Isles. This is where the future of the game lies".

The Football League tried to persuade them not to enter, but United refused to buckle. They were one of the 12 clubs drawn into the preliminary round, which was required to reduce the field to 16 teams for the first round. United's youthful team, nicknamed the 'Busby Babes', began with a 2-0 win away to Anderlecht, with goals from Dennis Viollet and Tommy Taylor, and then ran up a 10-0 win in the return match – which was played at the Maine Road ground of Manchester City, as floodlights had not yet been installed at United's Old Trafford home. Viollet scored four times in the second leg and Taylor notched up a hat-trick, while Liam Whelan scored twice, and Johnny Berry once.

United's opponents in the first round were Borussia Dortmund, who had been held to a 5-5 aggregate draw by Spora Luxembourg in their previous tie, before winning the play off 7-0. The first leg of that tie had been played on August 1, just seven weeks after the previous season's final. United beat Borussia Dortmund 3-2 before a crowd of 75,598 at Maine Road, with Viollet scoring twice, and then drew the return 0-0. The second leg was followed by a banquet for the two teams, at which Bert Trautmann, a German, and former prisoner of war, acted as interpreter. Trautmann was goalkeeper for Manchester City, and had recently played part of their 3-1 win against Birmingham City in the FA Cup final with a broken neck, being unaware of the seriousness of his injury.

Rangers failed to emulate Hibernian's progress to the previous season's semi-finals, losing to Nice in a play off. Fiorentina, who had won the Italian title for the first time the previous season, with only a single defeat in their 34 matches, struggled to beat Norrkoping 2-1 on aggregate. Real Madrid required a play off to dispose of Rapid Vienna, winning 2-0 after a 5-5 scoreline over the first two matches – Ernst Happel scored a hat-trick for the Austrians in the second leg. Meanwhile Athletic Bilbao, the Spanish title-holders, beat Honved 6-5 on aggregate. A tour by Honved, in preparation for this tie, coincided with the crushing of the Hungarian government by an invasion from the Soviet Union. The upheaval at home caused three of Honved's star players, namely Zoltan Czibor, Sandor Kocsis, and Ferenc Puskas, to decide against returning to Hungary. Each was to make a new career in the west.

In the quarter-finals, Athletic Bilbao ran up a 3-0 half time lead at home to Manchester United in the first leg, played on a muddy pitch in a blizzard, but United fought back to reduce the deficit to 5-3 at full time. United completed the fight back with a 3-0 win in the return, with goals from Viollet, Taylor, and Berry, to take the tie 6-5 on aggregate. Real Madrid continued to fly the flag for Spain, beating Nice 6-2 on aggregate.

United's next challenge was another meeting with a Spanish team, Real Madrid providing the opposition in the semi-finals. Real outplayed United in the first leg, and won 3-1 with goals from Rial, Di Stefano, and Mateos, while Taylor scored for United. The second leg was United's first European match at Old Trafford. Real extended their aggregate lead with goals from Kopa and Rial, but United fought back, with Taylor and Bobby Charlton scoring to level the score on the night at 2-2. United, like Hibernian a year earlier, had proved themselves to be among the best teams in the competition, only to be eliminated one step short of the final. For Viollet there was the personal consolation of being the season's leading scorer, with nine goals.

Real Madrid's opponents in the final were Fiorentina, whose progress to the final was completed by a single goal victory against Red Star Belgrade in their semi-final. Real had the great advantage that their stadium had been chosen in advance as the venue for the final, in honour of the club winning the inaugural European Cup. Jose Villalonga, the Real manager, retained eight players from the victory in the 1956 final – Juanito Alonso, Di Stefano, Gento, Rafael Lesmes, Marquitos, Munoz, Rial, and Zarraga. The newcomers included Raymond Kopa, a Frenchman who had played for Reims in the previous final. Kopa finished in the top ten for each of the first five European Footballer of the Year polls, and won the award in 1958. Fiorentina were a solid team, whose defensive strength outweighed that of an attack that was built around two South Americans – Julinho from Brazil, and Miguel Montouri from Argentina.

Despite being cheered on by a crowd of 124,000, Real Madrid made heavy weather of their 2-0 win against cautious opponents. They did not open the scoring until 20 minutes from time, when they were fortunate to be awarded a penalty by Dutch referee Leo Horn. Fiorentina's Ardico

Magnini fouled Enrique Mateos, but the latter player had been flagged as offside by a linesman when he began his run towards goal. Di Stefano scored from the penalty, despite Guiliano Sarti, the Fiorentina goalkeeper, dashing forward from the goal-line before the kick was taken. Six minutes later Kopa set up a chance from which Francisco Gento scored the second goal. The 1957 final had lacked the quality of Real's win against Reims, but the home crowd were delighted to see Real retain the trophy, which was presented to Miguel Munoz by General Franco, the fascist dictator of Spain, who was a supporter of the victorious club.

1956-57

Preliminary round

		1st leg	2nd leg	agg
Aarhus	Nice	1-1	1-5	2-6
Porto	Athletic Bilbao	1-2	2-3	3-5
Anderlecht	Manchester United	0-2	0-10	0-12
Borussia Dortmund	Spora Luxembourg	4-3	1-2	5-5

Play off
Borussia Dortmund 7 Spora Luxembourg 0 (Dortmund)

		1st leg	2nd leg	agg
Dynamo Bucharest	Galatasaray	3-1	1-2	4-3
Slovan Bratislava	CWKS Warsaw	4-0	0-2	4-2

First round

		1st leg	2nd leg	agg
Real Madrid	Rapid Vienna	4-2	1-3	5-5

Play off
Real Madrid 2 Rapid Vienna 0 (Madrid)

		1st leg	2nd leg	agg
Rangers	Nice	2-1	1-2	3-3

Play off
Nice 3 Rangers 1 (Paris)

		1st leg	2nd leg	agg
Athletic Bilbao	Honved	3-2	3-3	6-5
Manchester United	Borussia Dortmund	3-2	0-0	3-2
Rapid Heerlen	Red Star Belgrade	3-4	0-2	3-6
CDNA Sofia	Dynamo Bucharest	8-1	2-3	10-4
Slovan Bratislava	Grasshoppers	1-0	0-2	1-2
Fiorentina	Norrkoping	1-1	1-0	2-1

Quarter-finals

		1st leg	2nd leg	agg
Real Madrid	Nice	3-0	3-2	6-2
Athletic Bilbao	Manchester United	5-3	0-3	5-6
Red Star Belgrade	CDNA Sofia	3-1	1-2	4-3
Fiorentina	Grasshoppers	3-1	2-2	5-3

Semi-finals

		1st leg	2nd leg	agg
Real Madrid	Manchester United	3-1	2-2	5-3
Red Star Belgrade	Fiorentina	0-1	0-0	0-1

Final

May 30 1957 Madrid
Real Madrid 2   Fiorentina 0
Di Stefano (penalty)
Gento
Real Madrid: Alonso, Torres, Marquitos, Lesmes, Munoz, Zarraga, Kopa, Mateos, Di Stefano, Rial, Gento
Fiorentina: Sarti, Magnini, Orzan, Cervato, Scaramucci, Segato, Julinho, Gratton, Virgili, Montuori, Bizzarri
HT: 0-0
Referee: Horn (Netherlands)
Attendance: 124,000

1957-58

This season's competition will always be remembered for the tragedy of the Munich air crash, which decimated the Manchester United team as it returned home from their quarter-final against Red Star Belgrade. Seven players were killed instantly, and Duncan Edwards, their greatest player, died 15 days later as a result of his injuries. The deaths of several members of a team, famed as the 'Busby Babes', cast a huge shadow over the European Cup, while also prompting a great deal of sympathy for the club.

United's second campaign had begun with a 9-2 aggregate win against Shamrock Rovers in the preliminary round, with David Pegg, Tommy Taylor, Dennis Viollet, and Liam Whelan each scoring twice. Shamrock were the first club from the Republic of Ireland to appear in the competition. Northern Ireland were also represented for the first time this season, with Glenavon losing to Aarhus. Red Star Belgrade thrashed Stade Dudelange 14-1 on aggregate, with Borivoje Kostic scoring twice in the first leg, and four times in the return. By contrast Wismut Karl-Marx-Stadt and Gwardia Warsaw drew 4-4 on aggregate and then 1-1 in a play-off, and could only be separated by the toss of a coin, with the East German club being the first in the history of the European Cup to progress by this dubious method. In the first round, Manchester United beat Dukla Prague 3-1 on aggregate, but Rangers, who had previously eliminated Saint-Etienne, succumbed to Milan. Rangers lost 4-1 at home, with all of Milan's goals being scored in the last quarter of an hour, and then 2-0 in Milan, with the latter match attracting a crowd of only 2,000 people.

The tragedy struck following United's 3-3 draw in Belgrade, after they had won 2-1 in the first leg. The return was a fascinating encounter, in which United built up a three goal lead in the first 20 minutes, with Viollet scoring once and Bobby Charlton twice. The United party's flight home the following day included a stop for re-fuelling at Munich, where the plane crashed as it attempted to take-off. The tragedy shocked the world football community. Red Star sportingly suggested that the season's European Cup be abandoned, and the trophy awarded to Manchester United, but UEFA decided the competition should continue as scheduled.

In the weeks after the crash, a depleted United team managed to reach the FA Cup final, where they lost 2-0 against Bolton Wanderers. A few days later United faced Milan in the first leg of their European Cup semi-final, at Old Trafford, and achieved a 2-1 victory. At the San Siro, however, Milan's experience proved too much for United, and the Italian team won 4-0, with two of the goals being scored by Juan Schiaffino. It was a sad end to Manchester United's tragic campaign.

Milan's opponents in the final would be Real Madrid. After a bye through the preliminary round, Real had opened their defence of the trophy with an 8-1 aggregate demolition of Royal Antwerp, which included a second leg hat-trick from Hector Rial. This set up an all-Spanish quarter-final between Real Madrid and Seville. UEFA had allowed Seville to enter despite their being runners-up in the Spanish league the previous season, as Real Madrid had won both the European Cup and the Spanish title. Real won the first leg 8-0, four of the goals coming from Alfredo Di Stefano, and drew the return 2-2. In the semi-finals Real Madrid beat Vasas Budapest 4-0 at home, with a hat-trick from Di Stefano, before losing 2-0 in the second leg.

The final was played at the Heysel Stadium in Brussels – sadly destined to be the scene of another European Cup tragedy 27 years and one day later – and for the second successive season, Real faced Italians. Now managed by Luis Carniglia, who had coached the Nice team which lost to Real in the previous season's quarter-finals, Real fielded nine players who had appeared in either, or both, of the previous finals, the newcomers being José Santamaria and Juan Santisteban. Santamaria had represented Uruguay, the country of his birth, in the 1954 World Cup finals, but as a naturalised Spaniard was to play for his adopted country in the 1962 finals. He would go on to manage Spain when they hosted the 1982 World Cup finals. Santisteban was also destined for a managerial role with Spain, becoming assistant coach – a role he performed at the Euro 2004 finals. Milan featured Juan Schiaffino, who had scored for Uruguay in the 2-1 win against Brazil that won the 1950 World Cup, before re-appearing in the 1954 finals. Milan's team also included Ernesto Grillo, an Argentinian, and Nils Liedholm, from Sweden.

The match developed into an exciting contest, but only after a nervous, and goalless, first half. The deadlock was broken when Schiaffino, fed by Liedholm, gave Milan the lead 14 minutes into the second half. Real, starting to face the prospect of defeat, were rallied by Di Stefano, who led a fightback, and equalised with 16 minutes remaining. This was Di Stefano's 10th goal in this season's competition, which made him the leading scorer. Four minutes later Milan regained the lead, through Ernesto Grillo. Real's response was to score again a minute later, with a goal from Rial. With the score still level at 2-2 after 90 minutes, half an hour of extra time was played. Milan nearly regained the lead during this added period, as a shot from Tito Cucchiaroni hit the crossbar. With 13 minutes of extra time remaining, Gento scored a fortuitous goal, to put Real ahead for the first time in the match. After his initial shot was blocked, Gento's second strike travelled through a crowd of players, who obscured the view of Narciso Soldan, the Milan goalkeeper. Gento's goal, the only one not scored by a player born in South America, secured a 3-2 win for Real Madrid, to complete their third European Cup triumph. Di Stefano subsequently recalled this match as "the toughest test of all" faced by Real Madrid in the early European Cups.

1957-58

Preliminary round

		1st leg	2nd leg	agg
Seville	Benfica	3-1	0-0	3-1
Aarhus	Glenavon	0-0	3-0	3-0
CDNA Sofia	Vasas Budapest	2-1	1-6	3-7
Gwardia Warsaw	Wismut Karl-Marx-Stadt	3-1	1-3	4-4

Play off
Wismut Karl-Marx-Stadt 1 Gwardia Warsaw 1 (East Berlin)
Wismut Karl-Marx-Stadt won on the toss of a coin

Shamrock Rovers	Manchester United	0-6	2-3	2-9
Stade Dudelange	Red Star Belgrade	0-5	1-9	1-14
Rangers	Saint-Etienne	3-1	1-2	4-3
Milan	Rapid Vienna	4-1	2-5	6-6

Play off
Milan 4 Rapid Vienna 2 (Zurich)

First round

		1st leg	2nd leg	agg
Royal Antwerp	Real Madrid	1-2	0-6	1-8
Seville	Aarhus	4-0	0-2	4-2
Wismut Karl-Marx-Stadt	Ajax	1-3	0-1	1-4
Young Boys Berne	Vasas Budapest	1-1	1-2	2-3
Manchester United	Dukla Prague	3-0	0-1	3-1
Norrkoping	Red Star Belgrade	2-2	1-2	3-4
Borussia Dortmund	CCA Bucharest	4-2	1-3	5-5

Play off
Borussia Dortmund 3 CCA Bucharest 1 (Bologna)

Rangers	Milan	1-4	0-2	1-6

Quarter-finals

		1st leg	2nd leg	agg
Real Madrid	Seville	8-0	2-2	10-2
Ajax	Vasas Budapest	2-2	0-4	2-6
Manchester United	Red Star Belgrade	2-1	3-3	5-4
Borussia Dortmund	Milan	1-1	1-4	2-5

Semi-finals

		1st leg	2nd leg	agg
Real Madrid	Vasas Budapest	4-0	0-2	4-2
Manchester United	Milan	2-1	0-4	2-5

Final

May 28 1958 Brussels
Real Madrid 3   Milan 2 (after extra time)
Di Stefano   Schiaffino
Rial   Grillo
Gento

Real Madrid: Alonso, Atienza, Santamaria, Lesmes, Santisteban, Zarraga, Kopa, Joseito, Di Stefano, Rial, Gento
Milan: Soldan, Fontana, Maldini, Beraldo, Bergamaschi, Radice, Danova, Liedholm, Schiaffino, Grillo, Cucchiaroni
HT: 0-0
FT: 2-2
Referee: Alsteen (Belgium)
Attendance: 67,000

The Munich Air Crash

The decimation of the Manchester United team in the crash at Munich airport in 1958 was the first tragedy to hit the European Cup. Nearly half a century later, it still ranks as one of the darkest days in the history of the competition, equalled only by the deaths caused by mindless hooliganism at the Heysel stadium in 1985. Eight of United's players were killed by the crash, which claimed a death toll of 23 people – there were 20 survivors.

United's 3-3 draw with Red Star Belgrade, in the quarter-finals, had been followed by a banquet, shared by the players and officials of the two clubs. On the following morning, the United party began the journey home from Belgrade, flying in an Elizabethan airliner. During the early afternoon the plane landed for re-fuelling, at a snowy Munich airport. At 2.31pm the plane set off down the runway, but the flight captains, James Thain and Ken Rayment, aborted the take-off, due to apparent over-acceleration in one of the engines – this was a known problem in Elizabethans. A second attempt at take-off, three minutes later, was also abandoned in the same circumstances. The crew and passengers returned to the terminal, where the United party considered the possibility of travelling by land to the Hook of Holland, and then catching a boat back to England. The pilots decided against an overnight stay at Munich to re-tune the engine, believing that take-off, and the flight, was still safe. As the passengers returned to the plane, some of them expressed the fear that a crash was possible. On the third attempt, the plane failed to take-off, crashing into a fence, and then a house, on the perimeter of the airfield, as a result of which it broke up. The time was 3.04 in the afternoon of February 6 1958 – a moment forever to be remembered at Old Trafford, where a clock and plaque commemorate the tragedy.

The impact of the collisions caused the immediate deaths of about half of those on board the flight. Those who remained alive were quickly able to leave the plane, some of them being rescued by Harry Gregg, the United goalkeeper, who bravely fought his way through burning wreckage several times.

Among the people rescued by Gregg were Vera Lukic, a Yugoslav woman, and her baby daughter. Seven United players had been killed, namely Geoff Bent, Roger Byrne, Eddie Colman, Mark Jones, David Pegg, Tommy Taylor, and Liam Whelan. The club also lost Walter Crickmer, the secretary, Bert Whalley, a coach, and Tom Curry, a trainer. The dead also included several English journalists who had covered the match in Belgrade.

News of the tragedy reached England as evening fell. The mood was later captured by H E Bates, a novelist whose most famous work, The Darling Buds of May, was published in 1958. Writing in the FA Year Book for the 1958-59 season, Bates recalled: "At six o'clock, out of pure curiosity, I turned on my television set. As the news came on, the screen seemed to go black. The normally urbane voice of the announcer seemed to turn into a sledge hammer. My eyes went deathly cold and I sat listening with a frozen brain to that cruel and shocking list of casualties that was now to give the word Munich an even sadder meaning than it had acquired on a day before the war, after a British Prime Minister had come home to London waving a pitiful piece of paper and most of us knew that new calamities of war were inevitable".

The black and white film, and photographs, of the smouldering wreckage of the Elizabethan, laying amidst the darkness and snow a few hours after the crash, have captured the desolation of the tragedy. The injured were taken to Munich's Rechts der Isar hospital. Jimmy Murphy, who combined the role of Matt Busby's assistant at United with being manager of Wales, had missed the trip to Belgrade, as it coincided with the match in which Wales qualified for the 1958 World Cup finals. Murphy flew to Munich the following day, to meet the survivors. Duncan Edwards was in a critical condition, with multiple injuries, but managed to ask Murphy what was the time of kick-off. Edwards had established himself as one of the greatest players in England, despite being only 21. He had made his England debut at the age of 18, and scored five goals in 18 appearances for his country, playing most of his games at left half. After fighting for life with the strength he normally put into his football, Edwards sadly died of kidney failure on February 21, 15 days after the crash. Many people still regard him as United's greatest ever player. Bobby Charlton has said of his team-mate "Awesome is a word that is a bit over-used, but it was appropriate in Duncan's case. He had such presence, strength, an aura".

Besides killing eight players, the disaster ended the playing careers of Johnny Berry and Jackie Blanchflower, both of whom were forced to retire prematurely due to their injuries. Busby's life also hung in the balance as he was treated in hospital. He was twice read the last rites, yet managed to survive, although he did not leave the hospital until mid-April. During the remainder of the season, Murphy was acting manager for a patched-up team, in which a few of the previous regulars were joined by reserves, youth team players, and new signings. On February 19, just 13 days after the crash, United beat Sheffield Wednesday 3-0 in an FA Cup match. The match programme featured a blank team-sheet for United, as it was not known in advance who would be playing. United impressively went on to reach the FA Cup final, but lost 2-0 against Bolton Wanderers. This was followed by defeat against Milan in the European Cup semi-final. Five days before the crash, United had beaten Arsenal 5-4 in a brilliant League game at Highbury. United had hoped to win the title for a third successive season, but after the disaster their League record was one win, five draws, and eight defeats, as a result of which they slumped to ninth place.

The average age of the eight players killed at Munich was only 23. The crash prevented Manchester United from fulfilling the potential of a team that could have dominated English football for a decade, and been serious rivals to Real Madrid in the European Cup. The sympathy felt for Manchester United *in the wake of the disaster, and the way in which it recovered to start winning trophies again over the next few years, led to its legendary place among the greatest football clubs in the world. Ten years would pass between the Munich disaster and United's triumph, when they finally won the European Cup that was denied to the 'Busby Babes'.*

1958-59

Manchester United were offered a special invitation to compete in the 1958-59 European Cup by UEFA, despite having finished ninth in the English League the previous season, in a gesture of sympathy following the Munich disaster. United initially accepted the invitation, but were subsequently forced to decline by the Football Association and Football League, who argued insensitively that United should not participate in the competition, as they were not the reigning English champions. This was an unfortunate echo of the negative response of the English football authorities to the wishes of Chelsea and Manchester United to enter the 1955-56 and 1956-57 competitions respectively.

The reluctant withdrawal of Manchester United gave Young Boys Berne a walkover through the preliminary round. Heart of Midlothian lost 5-1 away to Standard Liege in their opener, which meant a 2-1 win in the return could not prevent the immediate elimination of a team who had been runaway winners of the Scottish league the previous season – they finished 13 points clear of runners-up Rangers.

The sensation of the round was provided by Wiener Sport Club, who recovered from a 3-1 defeat in their first leg against Juventus, to win the return 7-0. Omar Sivori, an Argentinian bought from River Plate for a world record transfer of £91,000, scored a hat-trick for Juventus in the first leg. The Juventus team also included John Charles, the 'Gentle Giant' who ranks as Wales' greatest ever footballer. Within a few years Juventus established themselves among the masters of *catenaccio* defence, making seven goal defeats unthinkable. Wolverhampton Wanderers, the club whose supposed claim to be the best in the world had been a catalyst for the European Cup, entered the fray for the first time, only to depart upon a 4-3 aggregate defeat against Schalke 04 in the first round. This was the only time in the first six seasons of English participation in the European Cup that the national champions failed to reach the quarter-final stage.

Real Madrid opened their campaign with a 3-1 aggregate success against Besiktas, despite having Alfredo Di Stefano sent off in their home leg. In the quarter-finals Real Madrid were held to a 0-0 draw away to Wiener Sport Club, with Ferenc Puskas, who had recently joined the club, being sent off, but won the return 7-1, with Alfredo Di Stefano scoring four times. Meanwhile Atletico Madrid, allowed into the competition as runners-up in the Spanish League to Real Madrid the previous season, disposed of Schalke 04. The Atletico Madrid team included Vava, who had scored twice for Brazil when they beat Sweden 5-2 in the recent World Cup final, at Stockholm. Despite the dominance of Real Madrid at club level, Spain had failed to reach the 1958 World Cup finals, being eliminated by Scotland.

The World Cup finals were followed, in September 1958, by the commencement of the European Nations' Cup. In a familiar pattern, the French devised the competition, while the British were disinterested – the Republic of Ireland being the only team from the British Isles among the 17 entrants.

The two Madrid clubs met in the semi-finals. Real won 2-1 at the Bernabeu stadium, but lost

1-0 in the return. They then moved to Zaragoza for a play–off, which Real won 2-1, with goals from Di Stefano and Puskas. In the other semi-final, Stade de Reims met Young Boys Berne. After their walkover against Manchester United, Young Boys had eliminated MTK Budapest and Wismut Karl-Marx-Stadt, the latter after a play-off. Reims had begun with a 10-3 aggregate win against Ards, from Northern Ireland – Just Fontaine scoring all four of their goals in the first leg, and two in the second leg. Following this Reims beat HPS Helsinki, who were the first Finnish club to appear in the European Cup, and Standard Liege. Young Boys won their home leg in the semi-final by a single goal, but Reims took the return 3-0.

The 1959 final, played at Stuttgart on June 3, brought together Real Madrid and Stade de Reims, in a repeat of the 1956 decider. Real Madrid retained five players who had appeared in 1956 – Di Stefano, Francisco Gento, Marquitos, Hector Rial, and Zarraga. Meanwhile Raymond Kopa, who had played for Reims three years earlier, appeared for Real. Real were, however, without the injured Ferenc Puskas. Four players featured for Reims in both finals – Rene Bliard, Raoul Giraudo, Robert Jonquet, and Michel Leblond.

One of the newcomers for Reims was Just Fontaine, the competition's leading scorer this season, with ten goals. Fontaine had been the leading marksman at the 1958 World Cup finals, with 13 goals – which still remains the best in any World Cup finals. Moroccan born Fontaine gained a place in the French team that took third place in the 1958 finals only because Bliard was injured in training shortly before the tournament began. Bliard was now in the Reims team, along with Roger Piantoni, who had scored three times for France in the 1958 finals. Reims were still coached by Albert Batteux, who had led them to the 1956 final – their only previous appearance in the European Cup. Real Madrid were managed by Luis Carniglia, as in the 1958 final.

The match proved to be a disappointing contrast to the excitement of the 1956 contest. Real Madrid won 2-0, but neither team played to their potential. Enrique Mateos gave Real the lead in the second minute, with a fine shot. After quarter of an hour a foul on Mateos by Giraudo gave Real a penalty. Mateos took the penalty, but Colonna saved it. Reims produced some attacks but Di Stefano doubled the lead a couple of minutes into the second half, exchanging passes with Gento before shooting.

Real Madrid controlled the remainder of the match, but without showing much flair, partly because Kopa was struggling with an injury caused by a rash challenge by Jean Vincent in the first half. Vincent, who had played for France in both the 1954 and 1958 World Cup finals, would later manage the Cameroon team, one of the brightest sparks of the 1982 finals in Spain. As for Kopa, he was to be sold back to Reims after the 1959 final. The manner of Real Madrid's victory in this match was not spectacular, but they had maintained their dominance of the European Cup, with a fourth successive title.

1958-59

Preliminary round

		1st leg	2nd leg	agg
Juventus	Wiener Sport-Club	3-1	0-7	3-8
Dynamo Zagreb	Dukla Prague	2-2	1-2	3-4
KB Copenhagen	Schalke 04	3-0	2-5	5-5
Play off				
Schalke 04 3 KB Copenhagen 1 (Enschede)				
Atletico Madrid	Drumcondra	8-0	5-1	13-1
Wismut Karl-Marx-Stadt	Petrolul Ploiesti	4-2	0-2	4-4

Play off
Wismut Karl-Marx-Stadt 4 Petrolul Ploiesti 0 (Kiev)

		1st leg	2nd leg	agg
Jeunesse D'Esch	IFK Gothenburg	1-2	1-0	2-2

Play off
IFK Gothenburg 5 Jeunesse D'Esch 1 (Gothenburg)

Polonia Bytom	MTK Budapest	0-3	0-3	0-6
DOS Utrecht	Sporting Lisbon	3-4	1-2	4-6
Standard Liege	Heart of Midlothian	5-1	1-2	6-3
Ards	Stade de Reims	1-4	2-6	3-10

Besiktas walked over, Olympiakos withdrew
Young Boys Berne walked over, Manchester United withdrew

First round

		1st leg	2nd leg	agg
Real Madrid	Besiktas	2-0	1-1	3-1
Wiener Sport-Club	Dukla Prague	3-1	0-1	3-2
Wolverhampton Wanderers	Schalke 04	2-2	1-2	3-4
Atletico Madrid	CDNA Sofia	2-1	0-1	2-2

Play off
Atletico Madrid 3 CDNA Sofia 1 (Geneva)

MTK Budapest	Young Boys Berne	1-2	1-4	2-6
IFK Gothenburg	Wismut Karl-Marx-Stadt	2-2	0-4	2-6
Sporting Lisbon	Standard Liege	2-3	0-3	2-6
Stade de Reims	HPS Helsinki	4-0	3-0	7-0

Quarter-finals

		1st leg	2nd leg	agg
Wiener Sport-Club	Real Madrid	0-0	1-7	1-7
Atletico Madrid	Schalke 04	3-0	1-1	4-1
Young Boys Berne	Wismut Karl-Marx-Stadt	2-2	0-0	2-2

Play off
Young Boys Berne 2 Wismut Karl-Marx-Stadt 1 (Amsterdam)

Standard Liege	Stade de Reims	2-0	0-3	2-3

Semi-finals

		1st leg	2nd leg	agg
Real Madrid	Atletico Madrid	2-1	0-1	2-2

Play off
Real Madrid 2 Atletico Madrid 1 (Zaragoza)

Young Boys Berne	Stade de Reims	1-0	0-3	1-3

Final

June 3 1959 Stuttgart
Real Madrid 2   Stade de Reims 0
Mateos
Di Stefano
Real Madrid: Dominguez, Marquitos, Santamaria, Zarraga, Santisteban, Ruiz, Kopa, Mateos, Di Stefano, Rial, Gento
Stade de Reims: Colonna, Rodzik, Jonquet, Giraudo, Penverne, Leblond, Lamartine, Bliard, Fontaine, Piantoni, Vincent
HT: 1-0
Referee: Dusch (West Germany)
Attendance: 72,000

Alfredo Di Stefano

Alfredo Di Stefano was the first superstar of the European Cup, scoring for Real Madrid in each of the first five finals. Ironically Di Stefano was not a European, being Argentinian by birth, although he took Spanish nationality. Di Stefano's name is perhaps the one mentioned most often as a rival to the claim that Pele was the greatest ever footballer. Besides prolific goalscoring – his career total was more than 800 goals in first class matches – the strength of Di Stefano's game was the enormous scope of his play. Although he may be categorised as a deep-lying centre forward, Di Stefano ranged across the pitch. Helenio Herrera summed up the stature of the player with the following analogy: "Di Stefano was the greatest player of all time. People used to say to me 'Pele is the first violinist in the orchestra', and I would answer 'Yes, but Di Stefano is the whole orchestra'. He was in defence, in midfield, in attack. He would never stop running, and he would shout at the other players to run too".

Di Stefano had explained his role in more prosaic, but equally enlightening, terms. He anticipated the theory of 'Total Football', which was to emerge a few years after his retirement as a player, with the following thoughts: "As a centre forward I am always on the move. Up, back, and across, trying not to be fixed in one position and so allowing the defender to see too much of me. Or I may be trying to avoid bunching with other forwards. Or I may be reading what is to come, and be moving quickly to help the next man on the ball. Forwards should accept it as part of their job that they should help the defence. When the opposing attack is in possession, you obviously are out of the game. What do you do? Just accept that position, while the defence tries to come through a difficult time? If the defence fails, the forward's job becomes that much harder. He has to score more goals. So the obvious thing is to get back quickly and help the defence. It eases your own job over the game. I think nothing of popping up at centre half or full back, to cover a colleague who has had to leave his position. We are all footballers, and as such should be able to perform competently in all 11 positions".

Di Stefano was born on July 4 1926, at Buenos Aires, into a family of Italian immigrants. He had to work on the family farm as a youth, but this had the effect of building his strength and stamina. He joined River Plate, a club his father had played for, and made his first team debut at the age of 16. During his early years, before he established a regular place in the team, Di Stefano was loaned to Huracan, but he soon returned to River Plate, whose fans nicknamed him 'the Blond Arrow', for his ability to dart around the field. Di Stefano helped River Plate to win the Argentinian title in 1947. In that year he also starred for Argentina, as they won the South American championship, which was staged in Ecuador, scoring six goals in six appearances. This tournament apart, Di Stefano played only one other match for Argentina.

In 1949 he moved to Los Millionarios, the Colombian club whose very name was chosen to symbolise its wealth. The Colombians had set up a rebel league, beyond the auspices of FIFA. The clubs refused to pay transfer fees, but offered high pay which led many South American footballers, plus some from England, to join them. Los Millionarios dominated the new league, while Di Stefano was even selected to play twice for Colombia's national team, on the basis of his short residence there.

Real Madrid arranged to buy Di Stefano from Los Millionarios in 1953, but at the same time Barcelona agreed a transfer with River Plate, who officially still held the player's registration. With Real and Barcelona in dispute over which club Di Stefano now belonged to, the Spanish football *authorities arranged a compromise whereby he would play alternate seasons for the two clubs. Barcelona's enthusiasm for the player soon waned, and they agreed to sell their rights in return for Real reimbursing the paltry fee of US $27,000 they had paid to River Plate. Di Stefano soon emphasised his real value, by scoring four goals as Real beat Barcelona 5-0.*

The arrival of Di Stefano helped transform Real Madrid from one of Spain's leading clubs into a team that dominated the domestic, and then the European, game. During the 11 seasons Di Stefano played for them, Real Madrid won the Spanish league eight times – 1954, 1955, 1957, 1958, 1961, 1962, 1963, and 1964. They also won the Spanish cup in 1962. Towering over these achievements, however, was Real Madrid's record in the European Cup. They won the first five competitions, and were the runners-up in 1962 and 1964. Real also won the inaugural World Club Championship in 1960. Di Stefano scored in each of the first five European Cup finals, and accumulated a total of 49 goals in the competition between 1955 and 1964. Di Stefano's brilliance was twice recognised with the European Footballer of the Year award – in 1957 and 1959.

Having become a naturalised Spaniard, Di Stefano was cleared by FIFA to play for Spain, despite his having already appeared for both Argentina and Colombia. Di Stefano is one of only two players to have represented three different countries in international football, the other being Ladislav Kubala. Di Stefano scored 23 goals in 31 matches for Spain between 1957 and 1961, thereby taking his international total to 29 goals in 40 games.

He was included in the Spanish squad for the 1962 World Cup finals, but did not play, due to the combination of a pulled muscle and strained relations with Spain's manager Helenio Herrera.

Di Stefano left Real Madrid in 1964, moving to Espânol, with whom he played for a couple of seasons, before injury forced his retirement in 1966. He went on to be a successful coach, winning the Argentinian title with Boca Juniors in 1970 and River Plate in 1981. In between Di Stefano led Valencia to the Spanish title in 1971, and the European Cup-Winners Cup trophy in 1980.

He also twice acted as caretaker manager for Real Madrid, during the 1982-83 and 1990-91 seasons. Half a century after joining the club as a player, Di Stefano continues to be a father figure at Real Madrid, in the role of honorary president of the club.

1959-60

In 1960 Real Madrid won the European Cup for a fifth successive time, beating Eintracht Frankfurt 7-3 in a final which ranks as the greatest match in the history of the tournament – indeed it remains among the most brilliant games in any competition. This final was the fitting culmination to a thrilling tournament, in which several great teams produced a series of outstanding matches. The 52 matches drew a combined attendance of 2,780,000, and the average attendance of more than 53,000 per match remains the record for the European Cup/Champions League.

Real Madrid, as reigning European title-holders, were joined by the champions of 26 countries – including Barcelona, who had beaten them in the Spanish title-race the previous season. Wolverhampton Wanderers, appearing for a second successive season, featured five England internationals – Peter Broadbent, Eddie Clamp, Norman Deeley, Ron Flowers, and Bill Slater. They began in the preliminary round with a 2-1 defeat away to Vorwarts Berlin, but won the return leg 2-0 to progress to the next stage. Rangers had a much smoother passage, beating Anderlecht 5-2 and 2-0. Linfield, of Northern Ireland, unexpectedly beat IFK Gothenburg 2-1 in their opening match, but a 6-1 reverse in Sweden – including an amazing five goal haul for Ohlsson – left them with a 7-3 aggregate defeat. Shamrock Rovers, of the Republic of Ireland, fared a bit better, but lost to Nice 4-3 on aggregate. Barcelona made an early impact, beating CDNA Sofia 6-2 – with hat-tricks from both Ladislav Kubala and Evaristo – after a 2-2 draw in the first leg. The surprise of the round was provided by Jeunesse D'Esch, who registered a rare success for Luxembourg, with a 6-2 aggregate win over LKS Lodz.

In the first round, Jeunesse D'Esch were thrashed 12-2 on aggregate by Real. Ferenc Puskas scored four times in the tie – including a first leg hat-trick – while Matteos accounted for three more. Barcelona beat Milan – runners-up in 1958 – by the surprisingly large margin of 7-1, as Kubala chalked up a second leg hat-trick. Wolves enjoyed a fine success, drawing 1-1 away to Red Star Belgrade, before winning the return 3-0. Rangers also progressed, with a 5-4 win over CH Bratislava.

Wolves' campaign was ended dramatically by Barcelona in the quarter-finals, as the Spaniards won 4-0 and 5-2. In the second leg Barcelona produced a great display on a muddy pitch at Molineux, led by Sandor Kocsis who scored four times. Wolves enjoyed their best ever spell during the managership of Stan Cullis, which stretched from 1948 to 1964. They had won the League in 1954, 1958, and 1959, and been runners-up in 1950 and 1955. They were prolific goalscorers, notching up more than 100 goals in each of four successive League campaigns – 103 in 1957-58, 110 in 1958-59, 106 in 1959-60, and 103 in 1960-61. At the end of the 1959-60 season, Wolves won the FA Cup – a trophy they had also taken in 1949 – and finished as runners-up in the League. But they have not played in the European Cup since that season. Rangers had to play a European Cup match in England, with Arsenal's Highbury ground staging the play-off in which they squeezed past Sparta Rotterdam. Real Madrid lost 3-2 in Nice – a hat-trick from Nurembourg giving the French a surprise win, after they had trailed by two goals at half time – but a 4-0 win in the return saw the European champions through to the last four.

The semi-final draw paired Real Madrid with Barcelona. The clash has always gone beyond the confines of football, with a political dimension to the long-established rivalry between the clubs. General Franco's Fascist dictatorship associated itself actively with the success of Real Madrid. By contrast Barcelona represented Catalan nationalism, and the democratic spirit which had made their city a centre of resistance to Franco during the Civil War of 1936-39. The wish to emerge from the shadows of Real was a great motivating factor for Barcelona.

Having won the Spanish league in 1959 for the first time in six years, this was Barcelona's first campaign in the European Cup. Before their matches Helenio Herrera, Barcelona's eccentric Argentinian manager, insisted that each player place a hand on a football, and chant "The European Cup, we shall have it, we shall have it". Both legs of the semi-final were excellent contests, and each time Real Madrid won 3-1. Alfredo Di Stefano scored twice in the first leg – Puskas did likewise in the return. Barcelona took the defeat hard, with much of the blame being placed unfairly upon Herrera, who was rapidly sacked. Barcelona gained compensation for their European elimination at the hands of Real by pipping their rivals to the Spanish title, on goal average. Ironically Barcelona also won a European trophy in 1960, by beating Birmingham City – neighbours of Wolves – in the final of the second Fairs Cup, a competition that stretched across two seasons. After drawing 0-0 in Birmingham, Barcelona won the return 4-1 – the two matches being played either side of Barcelona's European Cup semi-final.

The other semi-final brought together Rangers – whose steady progress had made them the first Scottish team to reach this stage since Hibernian in the inaugural competition – and Eintracht Frankfurt. The Germans had progressed quietly, beating Young Boys Berne and Wiener Sport-Club, after a withdrawal had given them a walkover in the preliminary round. Eintracht showed their true quality, by beating Rangers 12-4 on aggregate. The score was 1-1 at half time in the first leg, but the Germans crushed the Scots in the second half, scoring five times without reply – Dieter Lindner scored a hat-trick, and Alfred Pfaff netted twice. Proving this had not been a freak result, Eintracht won the return, in Glasgow, 6-3 – Pfaff again scoring two.

Eintracht Frankfurt returned to Glasgow for the final, played on May 18, just 13 days after their second meeting with Rangers. Eintracht had won the championship of West Germany the previous year, which remains their only national title. They have the distinction of being the only club from outside Spain, France, Italy, and Portugal to reach the final in the first ten seasons of the European Cup. Their amazing defeat of Rangers suggested they were potential European title winners, but now they faced the mighty Real Madrid. The stars of the Eintracht team were two veterans, Richard Kress, aged 35, and Pfaff, who was 33. Pfaff had played a single game for West Germany in the 1954 World Cup finals, this being the 8-3 defeat against Hungary in the group stage, which was dramatically reversed by the Germans' 3-2 win in the final. Real Madrid's team included three players who were appearing in a fifth European Cup final – Francisco Gento, Alfredo Di Stefano, and Zarraga. On the other hand, five of the team were making their first appearance in a final – Canario, Luis Del Sol, Enrique Pachin, Puskas, and Jose Maria Vidal. Ferenc Puskas, the 'Galloping Major', was now aged 34, and enjoying a wonderful twilight to the career in which he had inspired both Honved and Hungary's 'Magic Magyars'. The national team had won the Olympic title in 1952, and thrashed England twice during the 1953-54 season, before falling just short of an expected World Cup victory – Puskas scored in both of the matches against the Germans, but an injury he picked up in the first meeting hampered the team in the final. Puskas was now developing a devastating striking partnership with Di Stefano who, at the age of 33 remained the brightest star in the Real Madrid constellation. The Real team was now managed by Miguel Munoz, who had recently been one of the players, having appeared for them in the 1956 and 1957 finals. Munoz had been appointed between this season's quarter-finals and semi-finals, replacing Fleitas Solich, a Paraguayan coach who had been sacked.

The final has become legendary for several reasons. Real and Eintracht each played outstanding football, to produce constant excitement and ten goals. There could have been several more goals, as each team hit the woodwork three times. Besides this the match was played in a sporting spirit, with few serious fouls, little dissent, and only one booking. The football was almost uninterrupted, as the trainers were on the pitch for injuries only twice, and each time just briefly, while the skill of the teams led to a single instance of a player being caught offside. This spectacle was played out on a sunny evening in late spring, before an appreciative crowd of 134,0000 – the highest ever for a European Cup final – who had paid ticket prices ranging from 5 shillings (now 25 pence) to 50 shillings (now £2.50). The receipts of £55,000 set a new European record for a football match.

The Real players had been offered a bonus of about £650 per player to win the final, while Eintracht's players were offered around one tenth of this by a rather frugal management. It all seems very small money compared to the multi-million pound Champions League we are accustomed to in the present day.

In the first minute Erich Meier hit the crossbar with a shot from near the corner flag and this set the tone with Eintracht taking the lead after 18 minutes. Erwin Stein's cross was met with a controlled volley by Richard Kress at the near post.

The goal prodded Real into action, particularly Di Stefano, who single-handedly took control of midfield, and directed the team's attacks. Off the pitch, a power cut interrupted BBC television's live coverage of the game, but normal service was fortunately resumed after a break of only four minutes, allowing film of almost the whole of this brilliant match to be preserved forever. After 26 minutes Canario swiftly beat a defender to pull the ball back across the goalmouth and Di Stefano, falling, met it on the six yard line towards the far post to sweep the ball into the net. He thus maintained his record of scoring in each European Cup final. He scored his second on the half hour with Canario again being the provider. The Brazilian's powerful shot along the ground from the edge of the penalty area was only parried by Egan Loy, whereupon the Argentinian thrashed the ball into the roof of the net from three yards. Real went further in front on the stroke of half time when Puskas scored with a powerful shot from a narrow angle.

Eintracht hit the post through Meier four minutes after the restart but any hopes Eintracht might have retained of winning the match were ended five minutes later when Puskas scored from a penalty, harshly awarded by Scottish referee Jim Mowat – after consulting with a linesman – for what appeared to be an innocuous challenge on Gento. A minute before the hour mark, Real cleared an Eintracht corner, and produced a breakaway attack down the left, led by Gento, whose cross was met by Puskas, with a stooping header, that completed his hat-trick, and put Real 5-1 ahead.

On 69 minutes Puskas scored his fourth, with a piece of magic. Receiving a pass from Del Sol with his back facing goal, about 15 yards from the target, the Hungarian trapped the ball with his right foot, turned, and hit a ferocious shot with his left that flew into the top left corner of the net.

Stein deservedly pulled a goal back for Frankfurt, linking well with Pfaff before shooting across Rogelio Dominguez into the top right-hand corner but Real's response was spectacular. From the restart Di Stefano led an exchange of passes, ran through the Eintracht defence, and drove a shot from 20 yards that sped into the bottom right-hand corner of the net. Di Stefano had now scored a hat-trick. Frankfurt were heading for a heavy defeat, but kept up the hunt for goals, and were soon rewarded, with Stein again the scorer, as he seized upon a short back pass from Vidal which did not reach the goalkeeper. This was the fourth goal in the space of five minutes. The outcome of the scoring spree, in which the teams had alternated goals, was that Real Madrid led 7-3, with 74 minutes played.

The final surprise of the match was that no more goals were scored in the last quarter of an hour, just as the first quarter of an hour had been goalless. By contrast, ten goals had been packed into the middle hour of the match. During the closing stage the crowd were delighted by a display of tricks from Real, while Eintracht continued to press, and create chances. Puskas emerged as the leading scorer in this season's competition, with 12 goals, ahead of Di Stefano, who scored eight times.

Gento later recalled Real's thoughts on the match: " We were aware that the day was something special, even for us. I do not think any of us wanted the referee to end the match, and I think that was true of the crowd also. I think it was our best display, because of the quality of the goals. You must also remember that Eintracht played very correctly, and that it was a friendly game".

As the match ended the enormous crowd – most of them Scottish – rose to acclaim the efforts of both teams. Those lucky enough to be present knew they had witnessed a game almost without equal. The crowd's appreciation continued for a quarter of an hour, as Zarraga, the Real captain, collected the trophy, following which the players received their medals, and Real ran a lap of honour. Real Madrid had won the European Cup for a fifth successive time with a golden performance that immortalised the exploits of a team that ranks among the greatest in the history of football. Their spectacular football also gave a great boost to the standing of the European Cup, helping to secure the prominence the competition has always deserved. A few weeks after the 1960 final, Real moved beyond the confines of Europe to assert their place in the global game, by winning the inaugural World Club Championship.

1959-60

Preliminary round

		1st leg	2nd leg	agg
Jeunesse D'Esch	LKS Lodz	5-0	1-2	6-2
Fenerbahce	Csepel	1-1	3-2	4-3
Nice	Shamrock Rovers	3-2	1-1	4-3
Vorwarts Berlin	Wolverhampton Wanderers	2-1	0-2	2-3
Olympiakos	Milan	2-2	1-3	3-5
CDNA Sofia	Barcelona	2-2	2-6	4-8
Rangers	Anderlecht	5-2	2-0	7-2
CH Bratislava	Porto	2-1	2-0	4-1
Linfield	IFK Gothenburg	2-1	1-6	3-7
Wiener Sport-Club	Petrolul Ploiesti	0-0	2-1	2-1

Eintracht Frankfurt walkover, KuPS Kuopio withdrew

First round

		1st leg	2nd leg	agg
Real Madrid	Jeunesse D'Esch	7-0	5-2	12-2
Fenerbahce	Nice	2-1	1-2	3-3

Play Off
Fenerbahce 1 Nice 5 (Geneva)

		1st leg	2nd leg	agg
Red Star Belgrade	Wolverhampton Wanderers	1-1	0-3	1-4
Milan	Barcelona	0-2	1-5	1-7
Rangers	CH Bratislava	4-3	1-1	5-4
Sparta Rotterdam	IFK Gothenburg	3-1	1-3	4-4

Play off
Sparta Rotterdam 3 IFK Gothenburg 1 (Bremen)

		1st leg	2nd leg	agg
B1909 Odense	Wiener Sport-Club	0-3	2-2	2-5
Young Boys Berne	Eintracht Frankfurt	1-4	1-1	2-5

Quarter-finals

		1st leg	2nd leg	agg
Nice	Real Madrid	3-2	0-4	3-6
Barcelona	Wolverhampton Wanderers	4-0	5-2	9-2
Sparta Rotterdam	Rangers	2-3	1-0	3-3

Play off
Sparta Rotterdam 2 Rangers 3 (London)

		1st leg	2nd leg	agg
Eintracht Frankfurt	Wiener Sport-Club	2-1	1-1	3-2

Semi-finals

		1st leg	2nd leg	agg
Real Madrid	Barcelona	3-1	3-1	6-2
Eintracht Frankfurt	Rangers	6-1	6-3	12-4

Final

May 18 1960 Glasgow

Real Madrid 7	Eintracht Frankfurt 3
Di Stefano 3	Kress
Puskas 4 (1 penalty)	Stein 2

Real Madrid: Domínguez, Marquitos, Santamaria, Pachin, Vidal, Zarraga, Canario, Del Sol, Di Stefano, Puskas, Gento
Eintracht Frankfurt: Loy, Lutz, Eigenbrodt, Hofer, Weilbacher, Stinka, Kress, Lindner, Stein, Pfaff, Meier
HT: 3-1
Referee: Mowat (Scotland)
Attendance: 134,000

Chapter 2

Southern European Dominance 1960-1966

1960-61

The dominance of Real Madrid in the early seasons of the European Cup made Spain one of the favourites to win the inaugural European Nations' Cup. They were scheduled to meet the Soviet Union in the quarter-finals, during May 1960 – the month in which Real beat Eintracht Frankfurt – but the government of General Franco, steeped in the hostility between fascism and communism, refused to allow the team to travel to Moscow. Spain therefore withdrew. The finals were held in France during July, with the Soviet Union beating Yugoslavia 2-1 at the Parc des Princes in Paris – previously the venue for the first European Cup final. Surprisingly the Soviet Union had not yet entered teams in the European Cup.

Besides the conclusion of the first European Nations' Cup, 1960 brought the establishment of two new club competitions, namely the World Club Championship and the European Cup-Winners' Cup. Meanwhile the 1960-61 season marked the beginning of a new era in the history of the European Cup, as the reign of Real Madrid came to an end, Benfica replacing them. On the other hand, a similar dominance was to unfold, as 11 of the 12 teams which competed in the finals between 1961 and 1966 came from just three nations in southern Europe – namely Italy, Portugal, and Spain. The exception was Partizan Belgrade, who in 1966 became the first team from eastern Europe to reach the final.

Real Madrid's downfall came against Barcelona, in a first round tie that has achieved the enduring fame normally reserved for a European Cup final. Real had been given a bye through the preliminary round as reigning champions, while Barcelona, the Spanish title-holders, had warmed up with two victories over Lierse. The first leg at the Bernabeu finished 2-2, with both Barcelona goals scored by Luis Suarez, soon to be voted European Footballer of the Year for 1960, thus ending Real's record of having won every European Cup match they had played on their home ground – there had been 17 between 1955-56 and 1959-60. Surprisingly Barcelona won the return 2-1, with goals from Martin Verges and Evaristo .And so after winning the first five European Cups, Real Madrid had fallen at the start of their sixth campaign and to add to the disappointment they had been eliminated by their greatest rivals.

Benfica's tournament opened with a 5-1 aggregate win in the preliminary round against Heart of Midlothian, who were representing Scotland for a second time – José Aguas scoring three of the Portuguese team's goals. They followed this with a 7-4 aggregate win against Ujpest Dozsa. Back in the preliminary round, Fredrikstad, becoming the first Norwegian club to appear in the European Cup, beat Ajax 4-3, and then drew the return 0-0, while Stade de Reims thrashed Jeunesse D'Esch 11-1 on aggregate. In their next tie, Reims fell against Burnley, the English champions for the first time since 1921, who achieved a fine 4-3 aggregate win.

Burnley's interest in the competition was ended by Hamburg in the quarter-finals. Burnley won their home leg 3-1, but a 4-1 reverse in the return, in which Uwe Seeler scored twice for Hamburg, left them 5-4 losers on aggregate. The main reason for Burnley's collapse in the second leg was the fatigue caused by fixture congestion, as the club chased success in several competitions. The season ended in disappointment for Burnley, as they lost in the semi-finals of both the FA Cup and League Cup, while coming fourth in the League. In the other quarter-finals, Barcelona brushed aside Spartak Kralove, Benfica thrashed Aarhus 7-2 on aggregate – Aguas and José Augusto each scoring three times – and Rapid Vienna accounted for Malmo.

In the semi-finals, Benfica beat Rapid Vienna 3-0 in Lisbon. Late in the second leg, with the teams level on the day at 1-1, Rapid had a penalty appeal declined by Reg Leafe, the English referee. This sparked a disturbance, in which spectators invaded the pitch, and fought with players. Leafe abandoned the match, in the face of this hooliganism – the first to afflict the European Cup. UEFA decided that the result should stand, enabling Benfica to take their deserved place in the final, and banned Rapid Vienna from playing European matches on their ground for a period of three years. In the other tie, Barcelona beat Hamburg 1-0 at home, but lost 2-1 away. With the aggregate score 2-2, a play off was staged in Brussels, which Barcelona won with a single goal from Evaristo.

The final was played at the Wankdorf Stadium in Berne. In 1954 a crowd of 60,000 had gathered in the stadium to see West Germany beat Hungary 3-2 in a World Cup final. Seven years later only 26,732 people saw this European Cup final, which was refereed by Gottfried Dienst, from Switzerland, who would later control the 1966 World Cup final. Barcelona were managed by Enrique Orizaola, who until a few weeks earlier had been assistant to the previous manager Ljubisa Brocic. Barcelona had sacked Brocic due to the team's weak domestic record, despite their success in Europe. Barcelona's team included two players who had appeared for Hungary in the 1954 World Cup final, Zoltan Czibor and Sandor Kocsis. They also fielded Ladislav Kubala, who had played international football for Hungary, Czechoslovakia, and Spain. Kubala would later manage Spain at the 1978 World Cup finals. Benfica were managed by Bela Guttmann, a former Hungarian international player. The Benfica team he selected for the final included three players born in Africa. Jose Aguas and Joaquim Santana were from Portuguese West Africa (now Angola) while Mario Coluna came from Portuguese East Africa (now Mozambique). Coluna, one of the finest midfielders of the time, was the captain. Guttmann encouraged Benfica to play attacking football, and later recalled the approach by saying: "I always wanted to give the public their money's worth. I believed in defending only if my team were ahead with five minutes to go. I never subscribed to the Italian approach of stopping other teams from playing. In my time at Benfica, I think we only ever had one goalless draw. We nearly always scored first, and I never minded that much if the opposition scored, because I always felt we could score one more than them".

Barcelona, as conquerors of Real Madrid, began as favourites. The Spaniards got off to the better start, and Kocsis gave them the lead with a diving header after 19 minutes. Benfica equalised on the half hour mark, Aguas scoring as Antonio Ramallets, the Barcelona goalkeeper, made a positional error. Two minutes later a headed backpass by Barcelona's Enrique Gensana caught out Ramallets, who punched the ball against a post, from where it dropped into the net. For both goals it appeared that the goalkeeper's view had been affected by the sun. Benfica were suddenly 2-1 ahead. They extended the lead ten minutes after the restart, as a cross from Domiciano Cavem was volleyed in by Coluna. Barcelona responded with concerted pressure, during which Kocsis and Kubala each hit a post, while Costa Pereira, the Benfica goalkeeper, made several fine saves. Eventually Barcelona's efforts brought a goal, scored by Czibor a quarter-of-an-hour from time. A few minutes later Czibor became the third Barcelona player to hit a post, as Benfica held on for a 3-2 victory.

Benfica's success was unexpected. No Portuguese club had previously advanced beyond the first round, while Benfica had been eliminated in the preliminary round on their sole previous appearance – losing to Seville in 1957-58. Benfica had been favoured by fortune in the final, but had defeated Barcelona in an excellent contest, and established themselves as worthy successors to Real Madrid in the role of champions of Europe. During their nine matches in this season's competition, Benfica had achieved seven wins, while they drew one match, and lost the other. They had also scored 26 goals, 11 of them from Jose Aguas, who was the leading scorer in the tournament, during a series of exciting, attacking, displays.

1960-61

Preliminary round

		1st leg	2nd leg	agg
Heart of Midlothian	Benfica	1-2	0-3	1-5
Red Star Belgrade	Ujpest Dozsa	1-2	0-3	1-5
Fredrikstad	Ajax	4-3	0-0	4-3
Aarhus	Legia Warsaw	3-0	0-1	3-1
Juventus	CDNA Sofia	2-0	1-4	3-4
HIFK Helsinki	Malmo	1-3	1-2	2-5
Rapid Vienna	Besiktas	4-0	0-1	4-1
Limerick	Young Boys Berne	0-5	2-4	2-9
Stade de Reims	Jeunesse D'Esch	6-1	5-0	11-1
Barcelona	Lierse	2-0	3-0	5-0

Wismut Karl-Marx-Stadt walked over, Glenavon withdrew
Spartak Kralove walked over, CCA Bucharest withdrew

First round

		1st leg	2nd leg	agg
Benfica	Ujpest Dozsa	6-2	1-2	7-4
Aarhus	Fredrikstad	3-0	1-0	4-0
Malmo	CDNA Sofia	1-0	1-1	2-1
Rapid Vienna	Wismut Karl-Marx-Stadt	3-1	0-2	3-3

Play off
Rapid Vienna 1 Wismut Karl-Marx-Stadt 0 (Basle)

		1st leg	2nd leg	agg
Young Boys Berne	Hamburg	0-5	3-3	3-8
Burnley	Stade de Reims	2-0	2-3	4-3
Spartak Kralove	Panathinaikos	1-0	0-0	1-0
Real Madrid	Barcelona	2-2	1-2	3-4

Quarter-finals

		1st leg	2nd leg	agg
Benfica	Aarhus	3-1	4-1	7-2
Rapid Vienna	Malmo	2-0	2-0	4-0
Burnley	Hamburg	3-1	1-4	4-5
Barcelona	Spartak Kralove	4-0	1-1	5-1

Semi-finals

		1st leg	2nd leg	agg
Benfica	Rapid Vienna	3-0	1-1	4-1

Second leg abandoned with the score at 1-1 – the result stood

| Barcelona | Hamburg | 1-0 | 1-2 | 2-2 |

Play off

Barcelona 1 Hamburg 0 (Brussels)

Final

May 31 1961 Berne

Benfica 3	Barcelona 2
Aguas	Kocsis
Ramallets (own goal)	Czibor
Coluna	

Benfica: Costa Pereira, Joao, Germano, Angelo, Neto, Cruz, Augusto, Santana, Aguas, Coluna, Cavem

Barcelona: Ramallets, Foncho, Gensana, Gracia, Verges, Garay, Kubala, Kocsis, Evaristo, Suarez, Czibor

HT: 2-1

Referee: Dienst (Switzerland)

Attendance: 26,732

1961-62

The 1961-62 competition brought another triumph for Benfica, for whom Eusebio emerged as an overnight sensation, culminating in a 5-3 victory against a revived Real Madrid, in one of the greatest ever European Cup finals. Prior to this, Benfica eliminated Tottenham Hotspur, who had won the English League and FA Cup double the previous season. 'Super Spurs', as they were nicknamed, won the double with a team that played attractive and excellent football, directed by their manager, Bill Nicholson, who had played in the Tottenham team which won the League in 1951 with a 'push and run' game. As a manager, Nicholson – who would lead Spurs to victory in the European Cup-Winners' Cup final the following season – found that fixture congestion was a major issue for an English team during a European campaign. He later recalled: "In those early years, UEFA would set a time limit by which the ties had to be played, but actual dates were agreed between the clubs. Fixing dates for European matches was my biggest headache. We had so many commitments, with League games, cup ties, and a lot of our players being required for internationals – the home internationals were fitted in during the season in those days. I used to go to the European Cup draw, and show the other team our fixture list, and they just would not believe me. Eventually UEFA fixed specific dates, and these were incorporated into the programme in England. It was the best thing that ever happened for our clubs in Europe".

Tottenham's campaign opened in the preliminary round, with a tie against Gornik Zabrze that became a festival of goalscoring. The Poles led 4-0 early in the second half of the first leg, but Tottenham gave themselves hope by reducing the margin of their defeat to 4-2. The fight-back became a rout at White Hart Lane, as Spurs stunned Gornik with an 8-1 win, in which Cliff Jones scored a first half hat-trick, to take the tie 10-5 on aggregate. Rangers twice beat Monaco 3-2, with Alex Scott scoring three of their six goals. Linfield lost 3-0 away to Vorwarts Berlin, and then sportingly conceded the tie when – following the construction of the Berlin Wall in August 1961 – the East German team were refused visas to enter Northern Ireland. Drumcondra, from the other part of Ireland, lost 9-1 on aggregate to Nuremberg, from West Germany. Other large victories were run up by B1913 Odense (15-2 against Spora Luxembourg, with five of their goals in the second leg being scored by Lofquist) and Feyenoord (11-2 against IFK Gothenburg, as

Bouwmeester scored four times in the second leg). Hibernians, the first Maltese participant in the competition, lost 7-1 to Servette Geneva.

Real Madrid began their attempt to regain the European crown with a straightforward 5-1 aggregate win against Vasas. In a repeat of the first ever European Cup tie, Partizan Belgrade eliminated Sporting Lisbon. The Portuguese club had been runners-up in their domestic league the previous season, but were allowed into the European Cup, as Benfica had won both the European Cup and the Portuguese title in 1961. Sporting Lisbon were the third and last club to benefit from this dispensation – the others being Seville in 1957-58 and Atletico Madrid in 1958-59 – as the relevant rule was scrapped from the 1965-66 European Cup.

Most of the preliminary round matches were played in September 1961, a month during which Benfica, who received a bye, participated in the second instalment of the World Club Championship. They beat Penarol 1-0 in Lisbon, with a goal from Coluna, but were thrashed 5-0 in the return match. Benfica hurriedly flew Eusebio out to Uruguay to play in the decider, and he scored an excellent goal, but home advantage helped Penarol to a 2-1 victory. At least justice was done, given the margin of the Uruguayans' victory in the second leg. Benfica opened their defence a few weeks later, with a 6-2 aggregate win against FK Austria in the first round. With Vorwarts Berlin still denied visas for entry into the United Kingdom, the away leg of their tie against Rangers was played at Malmo, in Sweden. The initial attempt to play in Malmo was thwarted by fog, causing the abandonment of the match at half time, but the following day Rangers won 4-1, to add to a 2-1 win from the previous leg. In Real Madrid's 12-0 aggregate win over B1913 Odense, Alfredo Di Stefano and Ferenc Puskas each scored three times, while Francisco Gento and Luis Del Sol both netted twice.

Tottenham were the first English club to reach the semi-finals since Manchester United in 1958 and for their tie against Benfica were strengthened by the inclusion of Jimmy Greaves, recently returned to England after a difficult spell with Milan. Spurs paid Milan £99,999, breaking the British transfer record, but avoiding putting the player under the pressure of being the first to cost £100,000. But Greaves could not breach the Benfica defence as the Portuguese champions won 3-1 in Lisbon, with Augusto scoring twice, following which Spurs won 2-1 in London. Spurs were unlucky to be eliminated, having a goal disallowed in each leg, and hitting the woodwork three times during a stirring performance at White Hart Lane.

So for the second successive season, Benfica met Spanish opponents in the final. In 1961 it had been Barcelona, now it was a Real Madrid team hoping to resume the winning ways that had brought five European titles. The match was played at Amsterdam's Olympic Stadium, before a crowd of 61,257, and controlled by a Dutch referee, Leo Horn. Benfica's coach, Bela Guttmann, retained nine members of the team which had won the previous year's final – José Aguas, Angelo, Jose Augusto, Cavem, Coluna, Costa Perreira, Fernando Cruz, Germano, and Mario Joao. Real Madrid, managed by Miguel Munoz, who led them to victory in the 1960 final, selected six players who featured in that triumph – Del Sol, Di Stefano, Gento, Enrique Pachin, Puskas, and José Santamaria.

Real Madrid had conceded the first goal in three of their previous appearances in the final, but in 1962 they struck first. After 17 minutes a Benfica free kick was cleared by the Real defence as far as Di Stefano, who volleyed the ball into the path of Puskas, who out-paced the Benfica defence, before driving the ball beyond goalkeeper Pereira and into the bottom right-hand corner of the net. Six minutes later Puskas scored again, with a 30 yard shot, catching the Benfica defence napping as he received the ball from a midfield free kick. Benfica soon fought back, and scored after 25 minutes. Coluna tapped a free kick to Eusebio, whose 20 yard shot cannoned against a post, for Aguas to score from the rebound. Nine minutes later a 25 yard shot by Cavem, following a scramble on the

Ten of the 1958 Manchester United team. (top left to right) Bert Whalley (chief coach), Duncan Edwards, Mark Jones, Ray Wood, Bobby Charlton, Bill Foulkes, Matt Busby (manager). (front) Johnny Berry, Liam Whelan, Roger Byrne, David Pegg, Eddie Colman.

The wreckage of the Elizabethan aircraft carrying the Manchester United party home from Belgrade. The death toll from the crash was 23, including eight players.

Alfredo Di Stefano scores against Eintracht Frankfurt in Glasgow in 1960.

Altafini scores for Milan against Benfica at Wembley in 1962.

Celtic, the first British winners, parade the trophy back home in 1967.

Steve Chalmers takes on the Dukla Prague defence in the semi-final.

The Manchester United squad with the trophy in 1968. (back row, left to right) Bill Foulkes, John Aston, Jimmy Rimmer, Alex Stepney, Alan Gowling, David Herd. (middle row) David Sadler, Tony Dunne, Shay Brennan, Paddy Crerand, George Best, Francis Burns, Crompton (trainer), (front row) Jimmy Ryan, Nobby Stiles, Denis Law, Matt Busby (manager), Bobby Charlton, Brian Kidd, John Fitzpatrick,

"We won." Nobby Stiles (left) and Bobby Charlton celebrate after Manchester United beat Benfica in 1968.

Ajax's Dick Van Dijk wheels away after scoring their first in their victory over Panathiniakos at Wembley in 1971.

Bayern Munich's Franz Beckenbauer bloodied but victorious after the 1975 final against Leeds in Paris.

Liverpool manager, the late Bob Paisley, watches impassively during their first European Cup victory, over Borussia Moenchengladbach in 1977.

edge of the penalty area, levelled the score. Parity was short-lived, as Puskas completed a hat-trick on 38 minutes, with a powerful shot following a fine passing move, to give Real a 3-2 lead. Real went close to extending the lead before half time, as a cross from Gento on the right found Justo Tejada, but the latter's fine header hit the crossbar.

Benfica equalised again five minutes into the second half, as Puskas failed to control a bouncing ball, and Coluna took advantage with a shot from 30 yards. Although Puskas had scored three times in the first half, the decisive contribution was to come from Eusebio midway through the second half. With 25 minutes remaining he received the ball on the right wing, 20 yards inside the Benfica half, and set off on a powerful run, which took him into the Real penalty area, where he was fouled by Pachin. Eusebio scored from the penalty, to put Benfica ahead for the first time. Three minutes later Coluna rolled a free kick to Eusebio, and the latter's shot from 25 yards deflected off Real's defensive wall, and out of the reach of goalkeeper Jose Araquistain.

Benfica controlled the play to hold on to a 5-3 victory, with Real Madrid suffering collective fatigue, due to over-reliance on veterans. The eight goals meant that the first seven European Cup finals had produced 39 goals – an average of 5.57 goals per game. In five of the seven finals, the winning team had scored three or more goals, while the losers had scored two or more – the exceptions being a couple of 2-0 scorelines.

Benfica had retained the trophy by beating Real Madrid in a brilliant game of football, that was a closer contest than the 1960 final, although it did not quite match it for quality. Puskas was unlucky to finish on the losing side, having scored a hat-trick. Di Stefano, on the scoresheet in each of Real Madrid's five previous finals, had been unable to maintain that record. Puskas, Di Stefano, and their team-mate Tejada, were joint leading scorers in this season's competition, with seven goals each, but Real Madrid had been eclipsed by Benfica, and Eusebio, a player who had turned 20 midway through the season. The changing order was symbolised at the end of the final, as Di Stefano swapped shirts with Eusebio. Years later, Eusebio would recall this as the proudest moment of his career.

1961-62
Preliminary round

		1st leg	2nd leg	agg
CCA Bucharest	FK Austria	0-0	0-2	0-2
Nuremberg	Drumcondra	5-0	4-1	9-1
Servette Geneva	Hibernians	5-0	2-1	7-1
CDNA Sofia	Dukla Prague	4-4	1-2	5-6
IFK Gothenburg	Feyenoord	0-3	2-8	2-11
Gornik Zabrze	Tottenham Hotspur	4-2	1-8	5-10
Standard Liege	Fredrikstad	2-1	2-0	4-1
Vorwarts Berlin	Linfield	3-0		
Vorwarts Berlin walked over, Linfield withdrew				
Monaco	Rangers	2-3	2-3	4-6
Sporting Lisbon	Partizan Belgrade	1-1	0-2	1-3
Panathinaikos	Juventus	1-1	1-2	2-3
Spora Luxembourg	B1913 Odense	0-6	2-9	2-15
Vasas Budapest	Real Madrid	0-2	1-3	1-5

First round

		1st leg	2nd leg	agg
FK Austria	Benfica	1-1	1-5	2-6
Fenerbahce	Nuremberg	1-2	0-1	1-3
Servette Geneva	Dukla Prague	4-3	0-2	4-5

		1st leg	2nd leg	agg
Feyenoord	Tottenham Hotspur	1-3	1-1	2-4
Vorwarts Berlin	Rangers	1-2	1-4	2-6
Standard Liege	Haka Valkeakoski	5-1	2-0	7-1
Partizan Belgrade	Juventus	1-2	0-5	1-7
B1913 Odense	Real Madrid	0-3	0-9	0-12

Quarter-finals

		1st leg	2nd leg	agg
Nuremberg	Benfica	3-1	0-6	3-7
Dukla Prague	Tottenham Hotspur	1-0	1-4	2-4
Standard Liege	Rangers	4-1	0-2	4-3
Juventus	Real Madrid	0-1	1-0	1-1

Play off
Real Madrid 3 Juventus 1 (Paris)

Semi-finals

		1st leg	2nd leg	agg
Real Madrid	Standard Liege	4-0	2-0	6-0
Benfica	Tottenham Hotspur	3-1	1-2	4-3

Final

May 2 1962 Amsterdam
Benfica 5   Real Madrid 3
Aguas   Puskas 3
Cavem
Coluna
Eusebio 2 (1 penalty)
Benfica: Costa Pereira, Joao, Germano, Angelo, Cavem, Cruz, Augusto, Eusebio, Aguas, Coluna, Simoes
Real Madrid: Araquistain, Casado, Santamaria, Miera, Felo, Pachin, Tejada, Del Sol, Di Stefano, Puskas, Gento
HT: 2-3
Referee: Horn (Netherlands)
Attendance: 61,257

1962-63

In 1963 the European Cup final was staged at Wembley for the first time, and Milan became the first Italian club to take the trophy when they beat Benfica. On their way to the final, Milan had eliminated both the English and Scottish champions. England's representatives were Ipswich Town, managed by Alf Ramsey. Having taken over at Ipswich in 1955, Ramsey led them out of the Third Division in 1957, following which they gained promotion from the Second Division in 1961, and took the First Division title at the first attempt in 1962. This catalogue of success helped him become England manager in 1963, a role in which he masterminded the nation's win in the 1966 World Cup. Ramsey's stewardship of Ipswich in the European Cup was less successful. They began with a 14-1 aggregate win against Floriana, from Malta, in which Ray Crawford scored twice in the first leg, and five times in the return, but in the next round, they failed against Milan, losing the opener 3-0, with Paolo Barison scoring twice, before winning the second leg 2-1.

Dundee had won the Scottish League for the only time in their history in 1961-62, under the managership of Bob Shankly, whose more famous brother Bill held the equivalent post at Liverpool. The Dundee team included the veteran Gordon Smith, who had previously appeared in the European Cup for both Hibernian and Heart of Midlothian, plus Alan Gilzean and Ian Ure, promising young players destined for moves to Tottenham Hotspur and Arsenal respectively. A lop-sided preliminary round encounter saw the Scots beat Cologne 8-1, with Gilzean scoring a hat-trick, but then lose the return 4-0 – an 8-5 aggregate victory. In the next round Dundee lost 1-0 away to Sporting Lisbon, before recovering with a 4-1 win at home, as Gilzean scored another hat-trick. In the quarter-final Dundee achieved consistency, winning both legs against Anderlecht. The semi-finals saw a return to old ways, as Dundee were thrashed 5-1 by Milan in the San Siro, where Barison and Mora each scored twice, but won the return 1-0. Unfortunately the overall outcome this time was an aggregate defeat for Dundee. Gilzean had a mixed second leg, scoring Dundee's goal, to take his total for this European Cup campaign to nine, and being sent off.

The big surprise of the season was the elimination of Real Madrid in the preliminary round, as they lost 4-3 on aggregate to Anderlecht. Elsewhere Partizan Tirana became the first club from Albania to appear in the European Cup, breaking with that country's Stalinist isolation, but immediately losing to Norrkoping. Stade de Reims, who fell to Feyenoord in the quarter-finals, were making what proved to be their last appearance in the European Cup. Reims were runners-up in 1956 and 1959, but the following years brought rapid decline. After a bankruptcy, the club was re-formed, but slumped to the lower leagues in France.

When not eliminating Ipswich and Dundee, Milan were practising scoring goals on the way to the final. Jose Altafini scored eight in the 14-0 aggregate win over Union Luxembourg and followed with a hat-trick in the second leg against Galatasaray. Altafini had been a member of the Brazilian team that won the World Cup in 1958, at which point he was known by the nickname Mazzola, due to his physical likeness to Valentino Mazzola, an Italian international who had died in the Superga air crash, which killed the entire Torino team in 1949. In Italy, however, Altafini was known by his real name, to avoid confusion with Sandro Mazzola, the son of Valentino.

Fernando Riera, who coached his native Chile to third place in the 1962 World Cup finals, when they were host nation, subsequently became manager of Benfica, replacing Bela Guttmann. Riera moved Benfica away from their attacking style to a more cautious set-up, and their route to the 1963 final was far from spectacular.

The staging of a European Cup final in the home of football unfortunately did not capture the imagination of the English public, and Wembley was less than half full with an attendance of 45,715, a low turnout not helped by the match being staged on a Wednesday afternoon. Benfica retained most of the team that had won the 1961 and 1962 finals, with eight players from either, or both, of those victories re-appearing – Jose Augusto, Cavem, Coluna, Costa Pereira, Fernando Cruz, Eusebio, Joaquim Santana, and Mario Simoes. Milan, managed by Nereo Rocco, a defensively-minded and disciplinarian coach, featured only one player from their defeat in the 1958 final, Cesare Maldini, later to become Italian manager. Paolo Barison, a striker who had scored several vital goals on the way to the final, was dropped, but Gianni Rivera, Milan's 19-year-old 'Golden Boy', played.

The match was a disappointing encounter between two teams playing cautious football for much of the time. Eusebio gave Benfica the lead after 18 minutes, running half the length of the field with the ball, before hitting a shot that went in via the inside of a post. Milan had the better of the remainder of the first half, but were let down by some poor finishing by Altafini. Early in the second half Jose Torres wasted a chance to put Benfica further ahead. Altafini then regained his goalscoring form, equalising 13 minutes after the re-start, with a shot from the edge of the penalty area. Immediately after the goal Coluna was injured when fouled by Gino Pivatelli, an incident which turned the tide against Benfica. With 20 minutes left to play, Milan broke out of defence, and found Altafini, who ran from the half-way line towards the Benfica goal, had a shot parried by Costa Pereira, and then put in the rebound. Altafini's second goal took his tally for the season to a massive 14, the most any player had scored in the European Cup, and completed a 2-1 win for Milan, which ended Benfica's hopes of a hat-trick of trophies.

1962-63

Preliminary round

		1st leg	2nd leg	agg
Milan	Union Luxembourg	8-0	6-0	14-0
Floriana	Ipswich Town	1-4	0-10	1-14
Dynamo Bucharest	Galatasaray	1-1	0-3	1-4
Polonia Bytom	Panathinaikos	2-1	4-1	6-2
CDNA Sofia	Partizan Belgrade	2-1	4-1	6-2
Real Madrid	Anderlecht	3-3	0-1	3-4
Shelbourne	Sporting Lisbon	0-2	1-5	1-7
Dundee	Cologne	8-1	0-4	8-5
Servette Geneva	Feyenoord	1-3	3-1	4-4

Play off
Feyenoord 3 Servette Geneva 1 (Dusseldorf)

		1st leg	2nd leg	agg
Fredrikstad	Vasas Budapest	1-4	0-7	1-11
FK Austria	HIFK Helsinki	5-3	2-0	7-3
Vorwarts Berlin	Dukla Prague	0-3	0-1	0-4
Linfield	Esbjerg	1-2	0-0	1-2
Norrkoping	Partizan Tirana	2-0	1-1	3-1

First round

		1st leg	2nd leg	agg
Milan	Ipswich Town	3-0	1-2	4-2
Galatasaray	Polonia Bytom	4-1	0-1	4-2
CDNA Sofia	Anderlecht	2-2	0-2	2-4
Sporting Lisbon	Dundee	1-0	1-4	2-4
Feyenoord	Vasas Budapest	1-1	2-2	3-3

Play off
Feyenoord 1 Vasas Budapest 0 (Antwerp)

		1st leg	2nd leg	agg
FK Austria	Stade de Reims	3-2	0-5	3-7
Esbjerg	Dukla Prague	0-0	0-5	0-5
Norrkoping	Benfica	1-1	1-5	2-6

Quarter-finals

		1st leg	2nd leg	agg
Galatasaray	Milan	1-3	0-5	1-8
Anderlecht	Dundee	1-4	1-2	2-6
Stade de Reims	Feyenoord	0-1	1-1	1-2
Benfica	Dukla Prague	2-1	0-0	2-1

Semi-finals

		1st leg	2nd leg	agg
Milan	Dundee	5-1	0-1	5-2
Feyenoord	Benfica	0-0	1-3	1-3

Final

May 22 1963 Wembley

Milan 2	Benfica 1
Altafini 2	Eusebio

Milan: Ghezzi, David, Maldini, Trebbi, Benitez, Trapattoni, Pivatelli, Dino Sani, Altafini, Rivera, Mora
Benfica: Costa Pereira, Cavem, Cruz, Humberto, Raul, Coluna, Santana, Augusto, Torres, Eusebio, Simoes
HT: 0-1
Referee: Holland (England)
Attendance: 45,715

Eusebio

Eusebio, one of the greatest stars in the history of the European Cup, and Portugal's finest ever footballer, was born in Africa. To be precise he was born at Lourenco Marques in the colony of Portuguese East Africa – now Maputo in Mozambique – on January 25 1942. His full name is Eusebio da Silva Ferreira, but he has always simply been Eusebio to the footballing world. Given the nickname 'the Black Pearl', he was a prolific goalscorer, with a career record of 727 goals in 715 games. His ability as a striker combined acceleration, and great dribbling, with a powerful right foot shot. Besides being the star of the Benfica team which reached a series European Cup finals in the 1960s, he shone for the Portuguese national team.

His career began with the Sporting Club of Lourenco Marques, for whom he starred from the age of 16 in 1958. The club acted as a nursery for Sporting Lisbon, and it was expected that Eusebio would move to them, but on arriving in Portugal he was quickly acquired by Benfica. After a legal dispute with their Lisbon rivals that stretched over several months, Eusebio made his debut for Benfica, and helped them to win the Portuguese championship of 1960-61, but did not participate in their victorious European Cup campaign. This was the first of ten championships won by Benfica over the 14 seasons in which Eusebio featured in their team.

In September 1961 Eusebio scored for Benfica in the World Club Championship play-off against Penarol, but ended up on the losing side. At the end of the 1961-62 season Benfica retained the European Cup, with an amazing 5-3 win against Real Madrid in the final, in which Eusebio scored twice. Benfica won the Portuguese Cup in 1962, but in the Autumn of that year they were beaten in the World Club Championship for the second successive season, losing 3-2 and 5-2 against Santos. Pele scored five times in the tie for the Brazilian club, whereas Eusebio only found the net once.

In 1963 Benfica reached the European Cup final for the third successive season, but lost 2-1 against Milan – Eusebio scored Benfica's goal. Benfica also won the Portuguese league that year. The following year Benfica won the league and cup double, thrashing Porto 6-2 in the cup final. They retained the league title in 1965, and also reached the European Cup final, only to lose 1-0 against Internazionale. Eusebio's central role in Benfica's consistent success was now recognised with his winning the European Footballer of the Year title. The quality of his play saw Eusebio into the top ten when votes were counted for this award each year from 1962 to 1968.

Eusebio reached the pinnacle of his career in 1966, being one of the outstanding players in the World Cup finals, with Portugal having qualified for the first time. He emerged as the leading goalscorer, with nine goals in six matches. Four of the goals were scored in the famous quarter-final, as Eusebio led a Portuguese fight back against North Korea, which turned an early 3-0 deficit into a 5-3 victory. Eusebio then suffered the bitter disappointment of his team's 2-1 defeat against England in the semi-final – and memorably broke down in tears after the final whistle. Eusebio played 64 times for Portugal between 1961 and 1973, scoring 41 goals, but 1966 was his only appearance in a major international tournament.

Internazionale tried to buy Eusebio from Benfica in 1966, but the idea was blocked by Antonio Salazar, the Portuguese dictator, on the grounds that the export of Eusebio would undermine national pride. Benfica failed to win either the Portuguese league or cup that year, but Eusebio was the leading scorer in the league in 1965-66. Indeed Eusebio emerged as the Portuguese league's leading scorer in seven seasons – 1963-64, 1964-65, 1965-66, 1966-67, 1967-68, 1969-70 and 1972-73. In two of these seasons Eusebio was the European leading scorer, with 42 goals in 1967-68 (six of them in the 8-0 win against Varzim which secured the league title for Benfica) and 40 goals in 1972-73. Another measure of Eusebio's prolific goalscoring was his performance in the European Cup. He scored 46 goals in Benfica's European Cup matches, and was leading scorer in the 1967-68 competition (with 6 goals) and joint leading scorer in 1965-66 (with 7).

After the blip in 1966, Benfica soon returned to winning ways, taking the Portuguese title in both 1967 and 1968. In the latter year they also reached the European Cup final, but lost 4-1 to Manchester United, after extra time. Eusebio nearly won the match for Benfica in the closing minutes of normal time, but was denied by a save from Alex Stepney. The striker congratulated the goalkeeper on the quality of the save, a famous example of the great sportsmanship for which Eusebio was revered.

Benfica continued to win titles over the next few years, taking the league and cup double in 1969, the cup in 1970, the league in 1971, and then the league and cup double – for the third time in less than a decade – in 1972, but Eusebio's contribution was hampered by a recurring knee injury.

He would not regain the heights of the 1960s, but in 1973 he enjoyed a brief swan song. Benfica won the league that year, with Eusebio being Europe's leading scorer. He was also placed seventh in the European Footballer of Year award that year – his first appearance in the top ten since 1968. The 1973-74 season, however, brought the end of his playing career with Benfica, as he finally succumbed to the knee injury.

He left Portugal, for a short career in the North American Soccer League, where he played successively for Boston Minutemen, Toronto Metros-Croatia, and Las Vegas Quicksilver. When his playing days ended, Eusebio returned to Portugal, remaining involved with Benfica in a variety of roles – a spell as assistant manager including the defeat against PSV Eindhoven in the 1988 European Cup final. His statue now adorns the entrance to the club's Stadium of Light.

He has also been given a role as an ambassador for Portuguese football, and he was one of the figureheads when the nation staged the European Championship finals in 2004. During that year, when asked to comment upon his legendary status, Eusebio reflected: "It has been said that I am a legend, but I have never considered myself greater than others. I must say that getting to the top is hard, but staying there for a long time is much more difficult. It is still nice to be recognised nowadays, and I love signing autographs for kids, even though they are far too young to have seen me play. Many of them are not even Benfica supporters. Each night before I go to bed, I sign photographs to give to fans the next day. I always put the date on them. I started with 'Eusebio 1961' and now I am up to 'Eusebio 2004'."

1963-64

All four British teams were eliminated in the preliminary round this season. Everton lost to Internazionale, for whom Brazilian winger Jair scored the only goal of the tie. Rangers were thrashed 7-0 on aggregate by Real Madrid, with Ferenc Puskas scoring four. Distillery managed to enjoy a moment of glory by holding Benfica to a 3-3 draw, having tempted Tom Finney, the former England international, out of retirement for the match. The second leg reverted to form, with Benfica winning 5-0. Dundalk fell to FC Zurich.

Milan, who received a bye through the preliminary round as holders of the trophy, opened their campaign with Jose Altafini scoring a second leg hat-trick against Norrkopping. Following this the Italians were narrowly beaten by Real Madrid in a quarter-final meeting that echoed the 1958 final. Benfica, runners-up the previous season, crashed out of the tournament in the first round.

They won 2-1 at home to Borussia Dortmund, but lost the return 5-0. The Germans were to reach the semi-finals, where they lost to Inter. The defeat triggered an extraordinary series of events at Borussia Dortmund. The committee tried to fire coach Hermann Eppenhoff for disrespectful remarks only to be told by his lawyer that committee president, Kurt Schönherr, was never legally in control of the office and thus Eppenhoff's dismissal was completely null and void. The committee resigned en bloc and Eppenhoff was reinstated.

Real Madrid, still managed by Miguel Munoz, fielded six players who had appeared for them in previous finals – Alfredo Di Stefano, Felo, Francisco Gento, Enrique Pachin, Ferenc Puskas, and José Santamaria. Inter featured Luis Suarez, a brilliant Spanish midfielder who had played for Barcelona in the 1961 final, Giacinto Facchetti, the embodiment of Italian defensive strength, and Guiliano Sarti, a goalkeeper who had played for Fiorentina in the 1957 final. Internazionale were coached by Helenio Herrera, giving him an opportunity to reverse the defeat at the hands of Real he had suffered as manager of Barcelona in the 1960 semi-finals.

Herrera's Barcelona had been an attacking team, but at Inter he had instilled the negative philosophy of the *catenaccio* system, in which a sweeper played behind a row of four other defenders, each of whom concentrated on man-marking. Whereas football had always previously been played on the basis that a team should aim to win by scoring more goals than the opposition, *catenaccio* started from the reverse viewpoint that a team which did not concede a goal could not lose.

The final developed into a tussle between Real Madrid's consistent attacking football, and Inter's reliance on defence plus counter-attack. Two minutes before the close of a quiet first half, Sandro Mazzola gave the Italians the lead with a shot from 20 yards. The second half started with Real's Puskas hiting a post but Inter doubled their lead on the hour mark, through Aurelio Milani, as Real Madrid goalkeeper Vicente misjudged the bounce.

Ten minutes later Felo pulled a goal back for the Spaniards, heading in a corner. Real's hopes were ended, however, with fourteen minutes remaining, as a poor clearance by Santamaria only reached Mazzola, who advanced to score his second, securing a 3-1 win. Real Madrid had been outplayed, in what proved to be Di Stefano's final European Cup match, as he moved to Espônol in the summer .

So, a year after Milan had won the European Cup, their neighbours succeeded them. Inter won the competition in their first campaign, becoming the first team to win without losing a game, but they were not a breath of fresh air. Their record of conceding only five goals in nine matches showed a defensive nature, and there were suggestions that bribery of referees contributed to their victories.

1963-64

Preliminary round

		1st leg	2nd leg	agg
Everton	Internazionale	0-0	0-1	0-1
Monaco	AEK Athens	7-2	1-1	8-3
Haka Valkeakoski	Jeunesse D'Esch	4-1	0-4	4-5
Partizan Belgrade	Anorthosis	3-0	3-1	6-1
Gornik Zabrze	FK Austria	1-0	0-1	1-1
Play off				
FK Austria 1 Gornik Zabrze 2 (Vienna)				
Dukla Prague	Valletta	6-0	2-0	8-0
Distillery	Benfica	3-3	0-5	3-8
SOFK Lyn Oslo	Borussia Dortmund	2-4	1-3	3-7

Dundalk	FC Zurich	0-3	2-1	2-4
Galatasaray	Ferencvaros	4-0	0-2	4-2
Partizan Tirana	Spartak Plovdiv	1-0	1-3	2-3
Esbjerg	PSV Eindhoven	3-4	1-7	4-11
Standard Liege	Norrkoping	1-0	0-2	1-2
Dynamo Bucharest	Motor Jena	2-0	1-0	3-0
Rangers	Real Madrid	0-1	0-6	0-7

First round

		1st leg	2nd leg	agg
Internazionale	Monaco	1-0	3-1	4-1
Jeunesse D'Esch	Partizan Belgrade	2-1	2-6	4-7
Gornik Zabrze	Dukla Prague	2-0	1-4	3-4
Benfica	Borussia Dortmund	2-1	0-5	2-6
FC Zurich	Galatasaray	2-0	0-2	2-2

Play off
FC Zurich 2 Galatasaray 2 FC Zurich won on the toss of a coin (Rome)

Spartak Plovdiv	PSV Eindhoven	0-1	0-0	0-1
Norrkoping	Milan	1-1	2-5	3-6
Dynamo Bucharest	Real Madrid	1-3	3-5	4-8

Quarter-finals

		1st leg	2nd leg	agg
Partizan Belgrade	Internazionale	0-2	1-2	1-4
Dukla Prague	Borussia Dortmund	0-4	3-1	3-5
PSV Eindhoven	FC Zurich	1-0	1-3	2-3
Real Madrid	Milan	4-1	0-2	4-3

Semi-finals

		1st leg	2nd leg	agg
Borussia Dortmund	Internazionale	2-2	0-2	2-4
FC Zurich	Real Madrid	1-2	0-6	1-8

Final

May 27 1964 Vienna

Internazionale 3	Real Madrid 1
Mazzola 2	Felo
Milani	

Internazionale: Sarti, Burgnich, Guarneri, Facchetti, Tagnin, Picchi, Jair, Mazzola, Milani, Suarez, Corso
Real Madrid: Vicente, Isidro, Santamaria, Pachin, Zoco, Muller, Amancio, Felo, Di Stefano, Puskas, Gento
HT: 1-0
Referee: Stoll (Austria)
Attendance: 71,333

1964-65

Inter retained the European Cup this season, beating both the English and Scottish champions on the way to the final – just as their neighbours, Milan, had done in 1962-63. Following their dismal showing the previous season, British teams fared better in 1964-65.

Liverpool, appearing for the first time, twice drew 0-0 with Cologne in the quarter-finals. The play-off was a 2-2 draw, in which Ian St John and Roger Hunt scored for Liverpool. The tie therefore had to be decided on the toss of a coin, which favoured Liverpool. This was one of three ties in 1964-65 which were settled in this way. Rangers now departed, losing 3-2 on aggregate to Internazionale. In the semi-finals, it was Liverpool's turn to meet Internazionale.

A 3-1 win at Anfield – with goals from Roger Hunt, Ian Callaghan, and Ian St John – put Liverpool on the verge of the final. At the end of the match, Helenio Herrera told their manager Bill Shankly

"We have been beaten before, but never defeated – tonight we were defeated". Inter recovered to take the tie with a 3-0 victory in the return, including two goals that stemmed from bad decisions by Jose Maria Ortiz de Mendibil, the Spanish referee. This fuelled speculation that the Italian club were bribing match officials.

In Benfica's 5-0 win over La Chaux-de-Fonds Eusebio scored what he considers the greatest goal of his career: "I took a pass from Simoes, dribbled past three defenders, lifted the ball past another, and then smashed it into the net before it hit the ground. As I turned away, I heard the keeper shouting "Eusebio Eusebio" behind me, and I thought maybe he was going to hit me. He just wanted to congratulate me, and say that by the time he had got his hands up to try to save the shot, the ball was already in the back of the net".

Benfica surprisingly thrashed Real Madrid 5-1 in the first leg of the quarter-finals, with Eusebio scoring twice. Real won the return but only 2-1. Jose Torres, a giant striker who scored four times in the first leg against Aris Bonnevoie, was to be the leading scorer in this season's European Cup, with nine although he did not score against Madrid. But he did get two as did Eusebio in the 4-0 home semi-final second leg against Vasas Gyor, who were managed by Nandor Hidegkuti, a member of the Hungarian team at the 1954 and 1958 World Cup finals, and scorer of a hat-trick in the 6-3 win against England in 1953.

San Siro in Milan had been chosen as the venue for the final before the protagonists were known. Benfica protested to UEFA about having to meet Inter on the latter's home ground, but without success. Helenio Herrera selected nine members of the team which had won in 1964 – Burgnich, Corso, Facchetti, Guarneri, Jair, Mazzola, Picchi, Sarti, and Suarez. This was Benfica's fourth final in five seasons and all of their team had appeared in one or more of the club's previous finals; five playing in their fourth final – Jose Augusto, Cavem, Coluna, Costa Pereira, and Cruz.

With Benfica having scored 27 goals in eight European Cup matches this season, while Internazionale had managed 14 goals in their six matches, there was reason to hope for goals. Unfortunately the match proved to be one of the most forgettable of all European Cup finals. The match was played on a very wet pitch, in pouring rain but while the conditions worked against skilful football Inter's defensive attitude was equally to blame.

Jair scored the only goal three minutes before half time, as Costa Pereira let a shot slip from his grasp. On the hour Costa Pereira was injured and Benfica had to play the remainder of the match with ten men with Germano a stand-in goalkeeper. Despite this, Inter concentrated on defending the lead, although an effort from Peiro hit a post, and thereby held on to a 1-0 victory. In this unsatisfactory manner, Internazionale retained the trophy they had won a year earlier.

1964-65

Preliminary round

		1st leg	2nd leg	agg
Sliema Wanderers	Dynamo Bucharest	0-2	0-5	0-7
Rangers	Red Star Belgrade	3-1	2-4	5-5
Play off				
Rangers 3 Red Star Belgrade 1 (London)				
Rapid Vienna	Shamrock Rovers	3-0	2-0	5-0
Glentoran	Panathinaikos	2-2	2-3	4-5
Partizan Tirana	Cologne	0-0	0-2	0-2
Anderlecht	Bologna	1-0	1-2	2-2
Play off				
Anderlecht 0 Bologna 0 Anderlecht won on the toss of a coin (Barcelona)				
KR Reykjavik	Liverpool	0-5	1-6	1-11

Chemie Leipzig	Vasas Gyor	0-2	2-4	2-6
Lokomotiv Sofia	Malmo	8-3	0-2	8-5
DWS Amsterdam	Fenerbahce	3-1	1-0	4-1
Reipas Lahti	SOFK Lyn Oslo	2-1	0-3	2-4
B1909 Odense	Real Madrid	2-5	0-4	2-9
Dukla Prague	Gornik Zabrze	4-1	0-3	4-4

Play off
Dukla Prague 0 Gornik Zabrze 0 Dukla Prague won on the toss of a coin (Duisburg)

| Saint-Etienne | La Chaux-de-Fonds | 2-2 | 1-2 | 3-4 |
| Aris Bonnevoie | Benfica | 1-5 | 1-5 | 2-10 |

First round

		1st leg	2nd leg	agg
Internazionale	Dynamo Bucharest	6-0	1-0	7-0
Rangers	Rapid Vienna	1-0	2-0	3-0
Panathinaikos	Cologne	1-1	1-2	2-3
Liverpool	Anderlecht	3-0	1-0	4-0
Vasas Gyor	Lokomotiv Sofia	5-3	3-4	8-7
DWS Amsterdam	SOFK Lyn Oslo	5-0	3-1	8-1
Real Madrid	Dukla Prague	4-0	2-2	6-2
La Chaux-de-Fonds	Benfica	1-1	0-5	1-6

Quarter-finals

		1st leg	2nd leg	agg
Internazionale	Rangers	3-1	0-1	3-2
Cologne	Liverpool	0-0	0-0	0-0

Play off
Liverpool 2 Cologne 2 Liverpool won on the toss of a coin (Rotterdam)

| DWS Amsterdam | Vasas Gyor | 1-1 | 0-1 | 1-2 |
| Benfica | Real Madrid | 5-1 | 1-2 | 6-3 |

Semi-finals

		1st leg	2nd leg	agg
Liverpool	Internazionale	3-1	0-3	3-4
Vasas Gyor	Benfica	0-1	0-4	0-5

Final

May 27 1965 Milan
Internazionale 1   Benfica 0
Jair
Internazionale: Sarti, Burgnich, Guarneri, Facchetti, Bedin, Picchi, Jair, Mazzola, Peiro, Suarez, Corso
Benfica: Costa Pereira, Cavem, Cruz, Germano, Raul, Neto, Coluna, Augusto, Eusebio, Torres, Simoes
HT: 1-0
Referee: Dienst (Switzerland)
Attendance: 89,000

Helenio Herrera

Helenio Herrera was one of the most colourful characters to play a role in the European Cup, but the height of his success came as the coach of an Internazionale team that won the trophy in two successive years by playing dour football. This irony is symptomatic of the complexities inherent in Herrera's long career. An Argentinian who became a naturalised citizen of France, the country in which he played professional football, Herrera went on to manage club teams in France, Spain, Portugal, and Italy. He also had spells as the national manager of France, Italy, and Spain. Like the proverbial sailor with a woman in every port, Herrera successively married a Frenchwoman, a Spaniard, and an Italian.

He perfected the catenaccio system, brought new ideas to man management, and frequently became embroiled in controversy. Bill Shankly, whose Liverpool team were beaten – and probably cheated – by Internazionale in the 1965 European Cup semi-finals, said that Herrera was "a remarkable little fellow, a cut-throat man who wanted to win". Herrera would doubtless have accepted this view, but his opinion of himself was rather higher. When asked where he would feature in an Italian popularity contest, Herrera replied "Behind Sophia Loren, but only because she has a better figure".

Herrera was born at Buenos Aires in Argentina, on April 17 1916, the son of a Spaniard. The wanderings that would characterise his life began at the age of four, when his family emigrated to Casablanca, in Morocco. As an adult, Herrera moved to France, appearing as a full back for Club Francais, from Paris. After coaching in France, Herrera managed a succession of Spanish and Portuguese clubs in the 1950s. He led Atletico Madrid to the Spanish title in both 1950 and 1951. He also took Seville to runners-up spot in the league in 1956-57, but departed before their European Cup campaign the following season. In April 1958 he became the coach of a Barcelona team that played attacking football, and began to rival the dominance of Real Madrid, having arrived between the two legs of the first Fairs Cup final, the second leg of which saw Barcelona beat London 6-0 to take the trophy. In 1958-59 Herrera led Barcelona to a Spanish league and cup double. The following season they retained the league title, and also won the second instalment of the Fairs Cup, but Herrera was unable to see the club through to the culmination of these successes, as their defeat against Real Madrid in the 1960 European Cup semi-final brought about his departure.

Within a few months of leaving Barcelona, Herrera moved to Italy, becoming the coach of Internazionale. In contrast to the positive football of Barcelona, Herrera made Inter into tough exponents of catenaccio, the system based on defensive strength. His influence was negative in other ways. A tough disciplinarian, he ruled his players by fear, while gamesmanship was used to intimidate opponents, and bribery of match officials also appeared to contribute to Internazionale's victories. On a more positive note, Herrera got the players to bond with each other at regular training camps. His success at Internazionale led to him being nicknamed 'Il Mago' (the magician), and he was rewarded with a reputed salary of £50,000 a year – higher earnings than any manager had commanded in the past.

During his time at Inter, Herrera doubled as assistant manager of Italy until his enforced resignation, as Italians disliked his obvious glee when Juventus, rivals of Internazionale, were eliminated from the 1961-62 European Cup. He would later coach Italy again, as joint manager with Ferruccio Valcareggi during 1966 and 1967. His initial departure from the Italian role allowed him to manage Spain at the 1962 World Cup finals in Chile – across the border from Argentina, the country he had left far behind.

Herrera's first trophy with Internazionale was the Italian championship, won in 1962-63. In 1964 Internazionale won the European Cup for the first time, beating Real Madrid 3-1 in the final. In September of that year Internazionale took the World Club Championship, beating Independiente in a play-off. The height of Inter's success was reached in 1965, as they won the Italian title, and retained both the European and World titles. Benfica were beaten by a single goal in the European Cup final, and another win over Independiente secured the World Club Championship. In 1966 Serie A was won for the third time in four seasons. A year later Internazionale reached their third European Cup final, but lost 2-1 to Celtic.

In 1968 Herrera departed from Internazionale, and moved to Roma. Herrera immediately antagonised many at Roma by suggesting that the club's single Italian title, won back in 1942, had been achieved "only because Mussolini was the manager". Herrera's salary at Roma was even bigger *than it had been at Internazionale – money was always a major motivator for Herrera – but he was largely unable to repeat his past successes. Herrera remained at Roma until 1973, but only led the club to one trophy, this being the Italian cup, which was won in 1968-69. Roma reached the European Cup-Winners' Cup semi-finals the following season, but lost to Gornik Zabrze on the toss of a coin, after a drawn play-off.*

Herrera's final spell in the managerial limelight saw an unexpected return to Barcelona, two decades after his abrupt departure. Indeed it was a double return, as Herrera had two short spells as caretaker manager of the club in 1980 and 1981. During his retirement from management, Herrera lived in Italy – the last, and apparently the favourite, of his adopted homelands. He retained an active interest in football, and was still working as a pundit for Italian television during his seventies. Ironically Herrera was now employed by Canale 5, which was owned by Silvio Berlusconi, president of Milan, the great rivals of Internazionale. Herrera died from heart failure, on November 9 1997, at Venice, aged 81. It was the end of a remarkable football odyssey.

1965-66

Manchester United returned to the European Cup, appearing in the competition for the first time since 1957-58, when the 'Busby Babes' had fallen victims of the Munich air crash. During the intervening years, Matt Busby had rebuilt the team, and they had regained the English League title in 1965. The main strength of this team was the legendary forward trio of George Best, Denis Law, and Bobby Charlton although it was England international right winger John Connelly who scored a hat-trick in the second leg as United began their campaign with 3-2 and 6-0 victories over HJK Helsinki.

Derry City became the first club from Northern Ireland to win a European Cup tie, beating SOFK Lyn Oslo 8-6 on aggregate. But at the next stage they lost 9-0 away to Anderlecht, and then withdrew because of doubts about the suitability of their ground for European football.

In the preliminary round Benfica (appearing in the competition for a sixth successive season) beat Stade Dudelange 8-0 and 10-0 to set a record for the largest ever aggregate victory. Eusebio scored five times. Florian Albert, the great Hungarian centre forward also scored five (in the second leg) as Ferencvaros beat IBK Keflavik 13-2 on aggregate. Eusebio and Albert were to emerge as the joint-leading scorers this season, with seven goals each.

In a quarter-final tie, justly celebrated, Manchester United met Benfica. After a 3-2 win at Old Trafford, United appeared likely to face a tough test at the Stadium of Light, where Benfica's European Cup record was won 17, drew one, and lost none. United produced a brilliant display of attacking football, building up a three goal lead in the first quarter of an hour, and going on to win 5-1 on the night – thereby completing an 8-3 aggregate victory. United were inspired by George Best who scored twice, the latter goal being a brilliant solo effort. After the match, the Portuguese fans saluted Best, who they nicknamed 'El Beatle' – seeing him, with his long hair, as a superstar on a par with the legendary pop group. After spending the day following the match in Lisbon, United flew home to Manchester with Best wearing an enormous sombrero. Elsewhere at this stage, Real Madrid eliminated Anderlecht, winning 4-3 on aggregate – the exact reverse of the outcome in the 1962-63 season – and Internazionale beat Ferencvaros 5-1. Partizan Belgrade gave notice of their ability by recovering from a 4-1 defeat against Sparta Prague, to win the return 5-0.

Manchester United, becoming the third English club in five seasons to appear in the semi-finals, met the Yugoslavs. After the defeat of Benfica, United were favourites, but Partizan surprised them by winning 2-0 in Belgrade. United won the second leg 1-0 thanks to a rare goal from Nobby Stiles, but it was the Yugoslavs who progressed to the final. As in 1957 and 1958, Manchester United's European Cup campaign had ended in a semi-final defeat. The other semi-final saw Real Madrid again reverse a previous defeat, this time that in the 1964 final, as they disposed of Internazionale.

The final brought together Real Madrid, appearing in their eighth final, and Partizan Belgrade, the first team from eastern Europe to reach this stage. The match was played at the Heysel Stadium in Brussels, the first ground to stage a second European Cup final, having been the scene of Real's win against Milan in 1958. Partizan had made four previous appearances in the European Cup, but had not previously progressed beyond the quarter-finals. Miguel Munoz, now in charge of Real Madrid for the fourth time in a European Cup final, had rebuilt the team in recent years. This line-up comprised 11 Spaniards, while only Enrique Pachin and Francisco Gento remained from the 1960 winning team. The first leg of the tie against Kilmarnock had proved to be last European Cup outing for both Ferenc Puskas and Jose Santamaria.

Real were favourites, but Partizan matched them in a scrappy first half, and took the lead ten minutes into the second half, when Velibor Vasovic met a cross from Josip Pirmajer with a header. Real responded with concerted attack, and equalised through Amaro Amancio with 20 minutes remaining. Real now held the initiative, and six minutes later Fernando Serena scored with an excellent long-range shot, to put them ahead. The match was refereed by Rudolf Kreitlein, the German who a few weeks later would become famous for sending off Argentina's captain Rattin in England's 1-0 World Cup quarter-final victory. In the final minute of the European Cup final, a whistle from Kreitlein prompted some people to run on to the pitch, thinking it was all over. The pitch was cleared, and play concluded, with Real Madrid holding on to win 2-1.

So Internazionale's defensive dominance of the European Cup had been halted, as Real Madrid regained their earlier glory, by winning the trophy for a sixth time. Real were now given permanent possession of the original trophy by UEFA. Much of the acclaim for the great Real Madrid teams went to Alfredo Di Stefano, Raymond Kopa, Ferenc Puskas, and Miguel Munoz, but only one man gained six winners' medals. He was Francisco Gento, the team's left winger, who was to play in a total of 88 European Cup matches – including eight finals – for Real Madrid between 1955-56 and 1969-70, and score 31 goals. As the European Cup reached its silver jubilee in 1980, Gento reflected with appreciation, and modesty, upon his contribution: "When we first played in the European Cup, nobody thought it would be important. Now when I think of all the great names who have taken part, it makes me proud. To have been part of the story of the European Cup, that is something to tell your children".

1965-66

Preliminary round

		1st leg	2nd leg	agg
Feyenoord	Real Madrid	2-1	0-5	2-6
17 Nentori Tirana	Kilmarnock	0-0	0-1	0-1
Fenerbahce	Anderlecht	0-0	1-5	1-5
SOFK Lyn Oslo	Derry City	5-3	1-5	6-8
Panathinaikos	Sliema Wanderers	4-1	0-1	4-2
IBK Keflavik	Ferencvaros	1-4	1-9	2-13
Dynamo Bucharest	B1909 Odense	4-0	3-2	7-2
HJK Helsinki	Manchester United	2-3	0-6	2-9

		1st leg	2nd leg	agg
Drumcondra	Vorwarts Berlin	1-0	0-3	1-3
Stade Dudelange	Benfica	0-8	0-10	0-18
Djurgaardens	Levski Sofia	2-1	0-6	2-7
Lausanne-Sports	Sparta Prague	0-0	0-4	0-4
Linzer ASK	Gornik Zabrze	1-3	1-2	2-5
Apoel Nicosia	Werder Bremen	0-5	0-5	0-10
Partizan Belgrade	Nantes	2-0	2-2	4-2

First round

		1st leg	2nd leg	agg
Kilmarnock	Real Madrid	2-2	1-5	3-7
Anderlecht	Derry City	9-0		

Anderlecht walked over, Derry City withdrew after the first leg

		1st leg	2nd leg	agg
Ferencvaros	Panathinaikos	0-0	3-1	3-1
Dynamo Bucharest	Internazionale	2-1	0-2	2-3
Vorwarts Berlin	Manchester United	0-2	1-3	1-5
Levski Sofia	Benfica	2-2	2-3	4-5
Sparta Prague	Gornik Zabrze	3-0	2-1	5-1
Partizan Belgrade	Werder Bremen	3-0	0-1	3-1

Quarter-finals

		1st leg	2nd leg	agg
Anderlecht	Real Madrid	1-0	2-4	3-4
Internazionale	Ferencvaros	4-0	1-1	5-1
Manchester United	Benfica	3-2	5-1	8-3
Sparta Prague	Partizan Belgrade	4-1	0-5	4-6

Semi-finals

		1st leg	2nd leg	agg
Real Madrid	Internazionale	1-0	1-1	2-1
Partizan Belgrade	Manchester United	2-0	0-1	2-1

Final

May 11 1966 Brussels
Real Madrid 2   Partizan Belgrade 1
Amancio   Vasovic
Serena
Real Madrid: Araquistain, Pachin, De Felipe, Zoco, Sanchis, Pirri, Velazquez, Serena, Amancio, Grosso, Gento
Partizan Belgrade: Soskic, Jusufi, Rasovic, Vasovic, Mihailovic, Kovacevic, Becejac, Bajic, Hasanagic, Galic, Pirmajer
HT: 0-0
Referee: Kreitlein (West Germany)
Attendance: 46,745

Chapter 3

Northern Challenge 1966-1970

1966-67

A decade of Latin dominance of the European Cup was suddenly ended, as Celtic became the first British club to win the competition. Both Scottish and English clubs had regularly reached the semi-finals, but Celtic were the first to reach the final. Remarkably Celtic's triumph occurred in their first campaign in the competition, as they had won the Scottish League in 1965-66 for the first time since 1953-54. Celtic's success heralded a shift in the European Cup's balance of power from the south to the north of the continent over the next few seasons.

Their European adventure began with an easy 5-0 aggregate win in the first round against FC Zurich, for whom Ladislav Kubala featured as a player-manager, at the age of 41. Liverpool had won the English title the previous season with an amazingly consistent team, as Bill Shankly selected a total of only 14 players across their 42 matches, but in their first tie of this season they needed a play-off to defeat Petrolul Ploiesti. Linfield achieved a notable success, beating Aris Bonnevoie 9-4 on aggregate.

This season brought the first appearance by a team from the Soviet Union in the European Cup, surprising given that they had won the inaugural European Nations' Cup in 1960, and been runners-up in 1964. Torpedo Moscow's campaign was short-lived, however, as they lost to Inter in the first round. Anderlecht's 12-1 aggregate win against Haka Valkeakoski owed a great deal to Paul Van Himst, who scored five goals in the first leg, and one in the second leg.

Despite not scoring in the remainder of the tournament, Van Himst emerged as the joint leading scorer this season. The other player to score six was Jurgen Piepenburg, of Vorwarts Berlin, who found the net five times during his team's 12-1 aggregate thrashing of Waterford in the preliminary round. In the second round Liverpool came up against an emerging Ajax team, losing 7-3 on aggregate. Three of Ajax's goals were scored by Johan Cruyff – a player destined to make a great mark upon the European Cup. Real Madrid's defence of their title opened with a 1-0 defeat away to Munich 1860, but they won the return 3-1.

Celtic lost 1-0 away to Vojvodina Novi Sad but won 2-0 in Glasgow to reach the last four – with Billy McNeil, the Celtic captain, scoring the decisive goal in the final minute. Linfield drew 2-2 at home to CSKA Sofia, but lost the return 1-0. Their narrow aggregate defeat was an honourable end to Linfield's campaign, which had seen them become the only club from Northern Ireland to reach the last eight of the European Cup. Elsewhere Real Madrid lost 3-0 on aggregate to Internazionale, in a repeat of the 1964 final, while Dukla Prague beat Ajax. In the semi-finals Celtic beat Dukla Prague 3-1 at home, with Willie Wallace scoring twice, and then booked a place in the final with a cautious 0-0 draw in the return. Thus did Celtic break a run of defeats for British teams in the European Cup semi-finals. Manchester United on three occasions, plus Hibernian, Rangers, Tottenham Hotspur, Dundee, and Liverpool had each reached this stage, only to fail to progress – a series of eight reverses in the 11 seasons of the competition prior to the 1966-67.

The crowd of 45,000 for the final included about 12,000 Celtic fans. Inter were favourites, having won the competition in both 1964 and 1965. Their team included Bedin, Burgnich, Corso, Facchetti, Guarneri, Mazzola, Picchi, and Sarti, each of whom had played in the 1965 final. Seven of these players had also featured in the 1964 final – Bedin being the odd one out.

Still managed by Helenio Herrera, Inter retained their defensive mentality, and a reputation as difficult opponents to beat. Years later Celtic's Jimmy Johnstone jokingly recalled the contrast between the two teams as they stood in the tunnel before the match: "There they were, Facchetti, Domenghini, Mazzola, Cappellini. All six footers with Ambre Solaire suntans, Colgate smiles, and slicked-back hair. They even smelt beautiful. There's us lot – midgets. I have got no teeth, Bobby Lennox has not any, and 'old Ronnie' has got the full monty – no teeth top and bottom. The Italians are staring down at us, and we are smiling back up at them with our great gumsy grins. We must have looked like something out of the circus".

Johnstone, nicknamed 'Jinky', was a dazzling right-winger, and Celtic's most talented player. 'Old Ronnie' was Ronnie Simpson, the goalkeeper, who had made his debut for Queen's Park at the age of 14, and played for the British amateur team in the 1948 Olympics. A few weeks before the European Cup final, Simpson had made his full international debut against England, aged 36 – becoming Scotland's oldest debutant. He took his false teeth with him on to the pitch in order to improve his appearance in the post-match photos.

Celtic soon faced an uphill struggle, as Inter took the lead after six minutes, Sandro Mazzola scoring from a penalty dubiously awarded by West German referee Kurt Tschenscher as Renato Cappellini fell when apparently challenged fairly by Jim Craig. Having taken the lead, Inter resorted to massed defence.

Before the game Jock Stein, the Celtic manager, had told his players that an attacking game was the best hope of winning. Now Celtic had to take the game to their opponents. They attacked consistently, and with invention, during the remainder of the first half, and came closest to equalising when a shot from Bertie Auld hit the bar. The early part of the second half saw them still on the offensive, and persistence was finally rewarded 17 minutes after the re-start when Tommy Gemmell scored with a powerful shot from the edge of the penalty area. They continued to attack and Gemmell nearly scored again, as his cross from the left sailed over both team-mates and opponents, before hitting the bar. With seven minutes remaining Gemmell, on the left-side of the penalty area, pulled the ball back to Bobby Murdoch, whose drive towards goal was diverted by Steve Chalmers, from the six yard line, past Giuliano Sarti and into the net. Celtic had completed a well-deserved 2-1 victory. At the final whistle thousands of Celtic fans staged a good-natured pitch invasion, joining the players' celebrations, and 25 minutes passed before Billy McNeill could collect the new trophy, which replaced that awarded to Real Madrid on a permanent basis the previous season.

The victory gave Celtic the opportunity to challenge for the World Club Championship in the autumn of 1967. This supposed honour became a travesty, as Celtic lost to Racing Club, from Buenos Aires, in a violent encounter. After each team had won their home leg, the simmering conflict exploded in the play-off, staged in Montevideo. Racing Club won the decider with a single goal, but six players were sent off, four from Celtic. Having hacked their way to victory, the Argentinian players were rewarded by their club, which bought each of them a new car. Celtic had the decency to fine each of their players £250. It was a sorry episode, but could not detract from Celtic's amazing record in the 1966-67 season.

They had achieved a quadruple triumph, winning the European Cup, the Scottish League, the Scottish Cup, and the Scottish League Cup – scoring 200 goals in 64 matches. A great deal of Celtic's success was due to the intense pride of the team, all of whom had been born in either Glasgow or the surrounding area.

1966-67
Preliminary round

		1st leg	2nd leg	agg
Sliema Wanderers	CSKA Sofia	1-2	0-4	1-6
Waterford	Vorwarts Berlin	1-6	0-6	1-12

First round

		1st leg	2nd leg	agg
Celtic	FC Zurich	2-0	3-0	5-0
KR Reykjavik	Nantes	2-3	2-5	4-8
Malmo	Atletico Madrid	0-2	1-3	1-5
Admira Vienna	Vojvodina Novi Sad	0-1	0-0	0-1
Liverpool	Petrolul Ploiesti	2-0	1-3	3-3

Play off
Liverpool 2 Petrolul Ploiesti 0 (Brussels)

		1st leg	2nd leg	agg
Ajax	Besiktas	2-0	2-1	4-1
Haka Valkeakoski	Anderlecht	1-10	0-2	1-12
Esbjerg	Dukla Prague	0-2	0-4	0-6
Aris Bonnevoie	Linfield	3-3	1-6	4-9
Gornik Zabrze	Vorwarts Berlin	2-1	1-2	3-3

Play off
Gornik Zabrze 3 Vorwarts Berlin 1 (Budapest)

CSKA Sofia	Olympiakos	3-1	0-1	3-2
Munich 1860	Omonia Nicosia	8-0	2-1	10-1
Vasas Budapest	Sporting Lisbon	5-0	2-0	7-0
Internazionale	Torpedo Moscow	1-0	0-0	1-0

Valerenga walked over, 17 Nentori Tirana withdrew

Second round

		1st leg	2nd leg	agg
Nantes	Celtic	1-3	1-3	2-6
Vojvodina Novi Sad	Atletico Madrid	3-1	0-2	3-3

Play off
Atletico Madrid 2 Vojvodina Novi Sad 3 (Madrid)

Ajax	Liverpool	5-1	2-2	7-3
Dukla Prague	Anderlecht	4-1	2-1	6-2
CSKA Sofia	Gornik Zabrze	4-0	0-3	4-3
Valerenga	Linfield	1-4	1-1	2-5
Munich 1860	Real Madrid	1-0	1-3	2-3
Internazionale	Vasas Budapest	2-1	2-0	4-1

Quarter-finals

		1st leg	2nd leg	agg
Vojvodina Novi Sad	Celtic	1-0	0-2	1-2
Ajax	Dukla Prague	1-1	1-2	2-3
Linfield	CSKA Sofia	2-2	0-1	2-3
Internazionale	Real Madrid	1-0	2-0	3-0

Semi-finals

		1st leg	2nd leg	agg
Celtic	Dukla Prague	3-1	0-0	3-1
Internazionale	CSKA Sofia	1-1	1-1	2-2

Play off

Internazionale 1 CSKA Sofia 0 (Bologna)

Final

May 25 1967 Lisbon

Celtic 2	Internazionale 1
Gemmell	Mazzola (penalty)
Chalmers	

Celtic: Simpson, Craig, McNeill, Gemmell, Murdoch, Clark, Johnstone, Wallace, Chalmers, Auld, Lennox
Internazionale: Sarti, Burgnich, Guarneri, Facchetti, Bedin, Picchi, Domenghini, Mazzola, Cappellini, Bicicli, Corso
HT: 0-1
Referee: Tschenscher (West Germany)
Attendance: 45,000

Jock Stein

When Celtic became the first British team to win the European Cup, beating Internazionale 2-1 in the 1967 final, only two British managers were present at the game. One was Jock Stein, who led the Celtic team, and the other was Bill Shankly, the Scottish manager of Liverpool. Shankly congratulated Stein after match, saying "Jock, you will be immortal now". Stein had indeed become a giant figure in British football, through an unexpected rise to the top.

Born on October 5 1922, at Burnbank, in Lanarkshire, he began his playing career as a centre half with Albion Rovers, while continuing to work as a miner, before moving to Llanelli, a Welsh non-league club. In 1951 Celtic bought Stein for £1,200 and he soon became a regular, captaining them to the League and Cup double in 1954.

His playing career was ended by an ankle injury in 1956, but he stayed with the club, as coach to the reserves. In 1960 he moved to Dunfermline Athletic as manager and after helping the club avoid relegation during his first few weeks in charge, he led them to victory in the Scottish Cup in 1961. In 1963 Stein and Willie Waddell, the manager of Kilmarnock, made a visit to an Internazionale training camp, where they met Helenio Herrera, and learned from his methods. After a brief spell as manager of Hibernian, starting in 1964, Stein took the same position with Celtic the following year, becoming the first non-Catholic to manage the club. He also doubled as manager of the Scottish national team during 1965.

When Stein became their manager, Celtic had not won the Scottish title since 1954, when he had been one of the players. This soon changed, as Celtic won nine successive league titles between 1965-66 and 1973-74, and also won the title in 1976-77. Stein also led Celtic to victory in the Scottish Cup eight times – in 1965, 1967, 1969, 1971, 1972, 1974, 1975, and 1977. The club also won the Scottish League Cup in five successive seasons, from 1965-66 through to 1969-70, and again in 1974-75. Stein's greatest triumph, however, came as the Celtic team beat Herrera's Internazionale to win the European Cup in 1967 – with the pupil out-witting the master just four years after Stein had met Herrera. Celtic reached the European Cup final again in 1970, but lost to Feyenoord, and also made the semi-finals in 1972 and 1974.

Much of the success of the Celtic team stemmed from the way in which Stein moulded the talents of young players, and encouraged them to play attacking football. As he put it, "The best place to defend is in the other side's penalty box". Allied to this, Stein was a master of coaching techniques, man *management, and attention to detail – he even oversaw the cutting of the grass on the Parkhead pitch. In 1975 he was seriously injured in a car crash, following which he had to recuperate for a year, before returning to the manager's role, and further success.*

In 1978 he became manager of Leeds United, being replaced as manager by Billy McNeil, a member of the team which had won the European Cup in 1967. Stein's reign at Leeds was brief – a mere 45 days (an echo of Brian Clough's stint at Leeds four years earlier) – before taking the role of Scotland manager. Stein replaced Ally McLeod, whose period as Scotland manager had ended with a flop at the 1978 World Cup finals. During this second spell as national manager, Stein led Scotland to the 1982 World Cup finals, where they performed creditably, but were eliminated in the first round. On September 10 1985, Scotland drew 1-1 away to Wales, thereby taking a big step towards qualification for the 1986 World Cup finals, but the tense encounter caused Stein to have a fatal heart attack at the end of the match. Jock Stein, a man who had given so much to Scottish football, had tragically died for the cause.

1967-68

Celtic's victory was followed a year later by another British triumph, as Manchester United became the first English club to win the European Cup, beating Benfica 4-1 in a dramatic final. Besides the emergence of an English club as continental champion, the 1967-68 competition brought a couple of organisational changes. The draw was seeded, in order to prevent the strongest clubs meeting, and eliminating each other, at the start of the competition. Alongside this came the introduction of the 'away goals rule', whereby aggregate draws are won, where possible, by the team which has scored more goals away from home. In 1967-68 this rule only applied in the first round and second round, but it was subsequently extended to the latter stages.

Celtic's hold on the trophy proved to be very brief, as they were eliminated by Dynamo Kiev in the first round. The Soviets tumbled out of the competition, against Gornik Zabrze, who had won the Polish championship for the fifth successive season a few months earlier.

Manchester United beat Gornik Zabrze 2-0 at Old Trafford in the quarter-finals – an own goal from Florenski being followed by a last minute strike from Brian Kidd – and then secured their place in the last four by limiting their opponents to a single goal victory on a frozen pitch in Poland. Gornik's goal was scored by Wlodzimierz Lubanski, the striker who would torment England when Poland beat them 2-0 in a World Cup qualifier at Katowice in 1973. Whereas the away goals rule had been used in the first round, when Eintracht Brunswick and Juventus drew their quarter-final 3-3 on aggregate, the established play-off method was used to settle the tie. Juventus won the decider 1-0.

Manchester United's semi-final opponents were Real Madrid, who had beaten them at the same stage in 1957. The first leg, in Manchester, was a close match, in which the home team scored the only goal; George Best driving a powerful shot high into the net late in the first half. Real controlled the first half of the return match, with some excellent football, and built up a 3-1 lead, as four goals were scored in the space of 12 minutes late in the half. Pirri and then Gento scored for the Spaniards, before an own goal from Zoco briefly restored the balance, following which Amancio found the net. At half time, Matt Busby roused the demoralised United players, telling them: "Go back out there with your heads up. We aren't losing 3-1, because George scored at Old Trafford. There's only a goal in it, so don't give up hope. Play your football. Let's attack".

United took the game to Real in the second half, and pulled a goal back with 18 minutes remaining, scored by David Sadler, who had been moved forward from the defence by Busby. Six minutes later Bill Foulkes, another defender, unexpectedly joined an attack, and scored a goal which secured United a 3-3 draw on the night, and a 4-3 aggregate victory. United had been eliminated at the semi-final stage in each of their previous European Cup campaigns, but now a dramatic comeback had secured them a place in the final. The other semi-final was tame in comparison, with Benfica beating Juventus both home and away.

The final was played on May 29, at Wembley Stadium. Manchester United therefore had the advantage of playing in their own country, with support from almost all of the 92,225 crowd. They were weakened by the absence of the injured Denis Law, but fielded both Bobby Charlton and George Best. While Charlton was a quiet man, Best had acquired the trappings of a superstar lifestyle. He was one of the greatest players ever to emerge in the British Isles but, playing for a mediocre Northern Ireland team, he never appeared in either the World Cup or European Championship finals. At club level, Best also failed to fulfil his true potential, as his career imploded amidst disciplinary disputes, a drink problem, and the pressure of fame. He made and lost a fortune, later recalling: "I spent a lot of money on booze, birds, and fast cars – the rest I just squandered".

Benfica had won the European Cup in both 1961 and 1962, and been runners-up in 1963 and 1965. They were managed by Otto Gloria, a Brazilian who had performed that role for Portugal in the 1966 World Cup finals. Benfica's team included six players who had appeared for Portugal in the 1966 tournament, namely Augusto, Coluna, Eusebio, Graca, Simoes, and Torres. The final was officiated by Concetto Lo Bello, an Italian referee who had been on duty when United beat Benfica 5-1 in the 1966 quarter-final second leg.

Manchester United began the match with promising attacking play, but were soon stifled by numerous fouls from the Benfica players, while Lo Bello failed to exert authority. Manchester United had most of the play, but did not create many goalscoring chances, and half time arrived with the match still goalless. Indeed it was Benfica who came closest to scoring before the interval, as Eusebio glided through United's defence, and struck a 20 yard shot which hit the crossbar.

At the start of the second half Manchester United's play improved markedly. Eight minutes after the restart Sadler crossed from the left to Bobby Charlton, who scored with a well-directed header. Within a minute George Best appeared to have increased the lead, but his effort was disallowed for offside. Having gone ahead, United created a series of chances, but were unable to score, due to some poor finishing. As the second half progressed, Benfica posed an increasing threat, and eventually equalised with ten minutes remaining. Augusto crossed from the right, and Torres headed the ball into the path of Graca, who in turn drove it into the goal from close range. Having been on course for victory, Manchester United now faced a struggle. With two minutes remaining Eusebio broke free and seemed set to score, but Alex Stepney denied him with a brilliant save. Eusebio sportingly congratulated the goalkeeper, whose save rescued United from the threat of a surprise defeat and took the match into extra time.

In the break before extra time, Matt Busby gave his players calm encouragement, similar to that which had worked at half time in Madrid: "You are not playing your football. Stop giving the ball away. Benfica are shattered. Look at them. We are in much better shape. We've got this far, now let's finish it". United responded with a tremendous spell of football. Three minutes into the added period, as a clearance from Stepney was headed on by Brian Kidd, Best took advantage of hesitancy in Benfica's defence to score a brilliant goal, eluding a defender and then taking the ball around the advancing goalkeeper, Henrique, before putting it into an empty net.

A couple of minutes later a corner from Charlton on the left was headed by Sadler towards Kidd, whose header was half-saved by Henrique, before Kidd headed home the rebound, to increase United's lead. It was a great way for Kidd to celebrate his 19th birthday. Moments later, a cross from Best on the right, seeking Kidd, deflected off a Benfica player, and hit the crossbar, following which the defence scrambled the ball away. United continued to press forward, with Charlton passing to Kidd, who ran down the right wing and sent over a cross, which Charlton met at the near post, scoring with a clever shot lofted into the top left-hand corner of the net. United had overwhelmed Benfica with three goals in the space of seven minutes, and built up a decisive 4-1 lead. During the second period of extra time, although the outcome of the match was no longer in doubt, both teams continued to make a fine effort. Manchester United created further chances, while Eusebio was twice denied by good saves from Stepney – being unable to add to the tally of six goals which made him the leading scorer in this season's European Cup. United's burst of three goals at the start of extra time had proved to be decisive.

After many years of disappointment, Manchester United's dream of winning the European Cup had finally come true. Matt Busby, who had been fortunate to survive the Munich air crash ten years earlier, had fulfilled an ambition that became an obsession. Charlton and Eusebio, a winner and a loser, held each other in a tearful embrace, before Charlton, one of two survivors from the Munich air crash to play in the 1968 final – the other was Bill Foulkes – collected the trophy. Charlton's two goals, and general contribution as captain, had been a vital part of United's victory. Equally important was the inspiration of Matt Busby, who declared: "I am the proudest man in England tonight".

1967-68

First round

		1st leg	2nd leg	agg
Manchester United	Hibernians	4-0	0-0	4-0
Olympiakos Nicosia	Sarajevo	2-2	1-3	3-5
Gornik Zabrze	Djurgardens	3-0	1-0	4-0
Celtic	Dynamo Kiev	1-2	1-1	2-3
Ajax	Real Madrid	1-1	1-2	2-3
FC Basle	Hvidovre	1-2	3-3	4-5
Skeid Oslo	Sparta Prague	0-1	1-1	1-2
FC Karl-Marx-Stadt	Anderlecht	1-3	1-2	2-5
Olympiakos	Juventus	0-0	0-2	0-2
Botev Plovdiv	Rapid Bucharest	2-0	0-3	2-3
Besiktas	Rapid Vienna	0-1	0-3	0-4
Dundalk	Vasas Budapest	0-1	1-8	1-9
Valur Reykjavik	Jeunesse D'Esch	1-1	3-3	4-4
Valur Reykjavik won on away goals				
Saint-Etienne	KuPS Kuopio	2-0	3-0	5-0
Glentoran	Benfica	1-1	0-0	1-1
Benfica won on away goals				
Eintracht Brunswick walked over, Dynamo Tirana withdrew				

Second round

		1st leg	2nd leg	agg
Sarajevo	Manchester United	0-0	1-2	1-2
Dynamo Kiev	Gornik Zabrze	1-2	1-1	2-3
Sparta Prague	Anderlecht	3-2	3-3	6-5
Hvidovre	Real Madrid	2-2	1-4	3-6
Juventus	Rapid Bucharest	1-0	0-0	1-0
Rapid Vienna	Eintracht Brunswick	1-0	0-2	1-2

| Vasas Budapest | Valur Reykjavik | 6-0 | 5-1 | 11-1 |
| Benfica | Saint-Etienne | 2-0 | 0-1 | 2-1 |

Quarter-finals

		1st leg	2nd leg	agg
Manchester United	Gornik Zabrze	2-0	0-1	2-1
Real Madrid	Sparta Prague	3-0	1-2	4-2
Eintracht Brunswick	Juventus	3-2	0-1	3-3

Play off

Juventus 1 Eintracht Brunswick 0 (Berne)

| Vasas Budapest | Benfica | 0-0 | 0-3 | 0-3 |

Semi-finals

		1st leg	2nd leg	agg
Manchester United	Real Madrid	1-0	3-3	4-3
Benfica	Juventus	2-0	1-0	3-0

Final

May 29 1968 Wembley

Manchester United 4	Benfica 1 (after extra time)
Charlton 2	Graca
Best	
Kidd	

Manchester United: Stepney, Brennan, Stiles, Foulkes, Dunne, Crerand, Charlton, Sadler, Best, Kidd, Aston
Benfica: Henrique, Adolfo, Humberto, Jacinto, Cruz, Graca, Coluna, Augusto, Eusebio, Torres, Simoes
HT: 0-0
FT: 1-1
Referee: Lo Bello (Italy)
Attendance: 92,225

Matt Busby

Matt Busby was born on May 26 1909, at Orbiston, near Glasgow, being the son of a miner. Busby's playing career – he was a right half – was spent with Manchester City and Liverpool, two clubs which have been great rivals of Manchester United. He joined Manchester City in 1928, and gained an FA Cup winners' medal as City beat Portsmouth 2-1 in the 1934 final, before moving to Liverpool in 1936. During the Second World War, Busby served with the armed forces, and played for Scotland in several unofficial internationals. Busby's sole appearance for Scotland in a full international had come several years earlier, in a 3-2 defeat against Wales in 1933. The Welsh team included Jimmy Murphy, who would later be Busby's assistant at Manchester United.

Busby became manager of Manchester United in 1945, accepting this post in preference to an opportunity to join the backroom staff at Liverpool. United rapidly flourished under Busby, and won the FA Cup in 1948, beating Blackpool 4-2 in the final. That same year Busby coached the British amateur team which took fourth place in the Olympic Games football tournament. Manchester United won the League in 1952, after being second four times in the previous five seasons. This title was regained in 1956, with a youthful team nicknamed the 'Busby Babes', in honour of the work the manager had done in developing a youth policy. Busby's enthusiasm for the new competition took Manchester United into the European Cup in 1956-57. Besides reaching the semi-finals at the first attempt, United retained the League title, and reached the FA Cup final that season. The following season brought the tragedy of the Munich air crash, in which eight members of the United team were killed. Busby narrowly escaped death, and lay in hospital in a critical condition for several weeks. Murphy managed the United team for the latter part of the season, during which they were beaten in both the European Cup semi-finals and the FA Cup final. Busby managed Scotland for a short period in 1958, but his injuries prevented him from leading them in that year's World Cup finals.

Over the next few years Busby rebuilt the United team. They were runners-up in the League in 1959, won the FA Cup in 1963, and then regained the League title in 1965 – a year in which they also reached the UEFA Cup semi-finals. In 1965-66 the club were defeated in the European Cup semi-finals for a third time. A further League title in 1967, clinched with a famous 6-1 win away to West Ham United, set up another European Cup campaign. This time Manchester United became the first English club to win the trophy, beating Benfica 4-1 in the 1968 final. Busby's determined efforts were now recognised with the award of a knighthood. United were beaten in the European Cup semi-finals in 1968-69, and at the end of that season Busby moved to a new role, as general manager of the club, while Wilf McGuinness, a former 'Busby Babe', became coach of the first team. McGuinness struggled, and was dismissed at the end of 1970, whereupon Busby resumed the full managerial position for the remainder of the 1970-71 season.

Busby's managerial role ended in the summer of 1971, upon the appointment of Frank O'Farrell – one of a series of United managers who failed to revive the glory days. After 26 years as manager of Manchester United, Busby was appointed to the board of directors. He subsequently also held positions with both the Football League and Football Association. In 1980 he was promoted from the United board of directors to become the first president of the club, a position he retained for the remainder of his life. During his final years, Busby acted as an inspirational father figure, and was able to enjoy the revival of its fortunes under Alex Ferguson, a fellow Scot.

Busby died on January 20 1994, at the age of 84, having dedicated almost half a century to Manchester United. Among the many tributes paid to Busby in the aftermath of his death, one of the most eloquent came from Eric Cantona, who wrote: "I am sad to hear the news of the death of the father of the Manchester United family, Matt Busby. Nobody can ever write or speak about Manchester United without mentioning his name. You sense and feel that his blood runs through every vein of the club's body. His name is engraved in the hearts of all those who love beautiful football. His kindness, courage, gentility and resilience serve as an inspiration and example to everybody. His legacy of playing with style – win, lose or draw – will be preserved. His ideals, principles and beliefs will not be forgotten. I am pleased that I played in front of him, and that he lived to see United champions once more".

Busby's influence did indeed continue to be felt after his death, as United maintained the tradition of attacking football that he advocated, while Ferguson's revival of the youth policy paid handsome dividends. It was fitting that United's win against Bayern Munich in the 1999 Champions League final should occur on the ninetieth anniversary of Busby's birth.

1968-69

On August 20 1968 the armies of several Warsaw Pact states invaded Czechoslovakia, and overthrew the government, led by Alexander Dubcek, as its reforming nature was seen by the Soviet Union as a threat to the stability of Communist rule in eastern Europe. The events in Czechoslovakia had a major influence upon the European Cup, which had until now been largely untouched by political concerns. Celtic announced their withdrawal from the tie they had been drawn to play against Ferencvaros, in protest at Hungary's participation in the invasion of Czechoslovakia. Other west European clubs also threatened to boycott matches against eastern opponents. Faced with this prospect, UEFA carried out a new draw, in which the eastern European clubs were kept apart from their western counterparts. This, however, only had the effect of prompting the withdrawal of most of the eastern teams, who argued they had been treated unfairly.

The first round eventually went ahead with matches in 13 of the planned 16 ties, plus a walkover for Red Star Belgrade. Spartak Trnava, the Czechoslovak champions, surprisingly competed, and beat Steaua Bucharest 5-3 on aggregate. England had double representation, in the form of both Manchester clubs. Manchester United featured as holders of the European Cup, while Manchester City were reigning English champions, having beaten their neighbours to the title by two points. Malcolm Allison, the flamboyant assistant to Joe Mercer, the manager of Manchester City, jingoistically claimed "we shall frighten the cowards of Europe". A bizarre irony saw City fall at the first hurdle, against Fenerbahce of Turkey, a country that straddles Europe and Asia.

Manchester United began with a 10-2 aggregate win over Waterford, from the Republic of Ireland. Denis Law, who scored three times in the first leg and four times in the second leg, was on his way to being the leading marksman for the season, with an eventual total of nine goals. Law, who had been European Footballer of the Year in 1964, scored 30 goals for Scotland in 55 international appearances – he remains Scotland's joint top scorer along with Kenny Dalglish.

Celtic, back after their withdrawal, recovered from a 2-0 defeat away to Saint-Etienne, winning the return 4-0. Saint-Etienne were managed by Albert Batteux, who had taken Reims to the final in both 1956 and 1959. Benfica were held to a surprise goalless draw by Valur Reykjavik, but, helped by a Jose Torres hat-trick, won the return 8-1, while Real Madrid enjoyed a pair of 6-0 wins against AEL Limassol, with Pirri scoring three in the first leg.

Besides starting their defence of the European Cup in the autumn of 1968, Manchester United faced Estudiantes de la Plata, from Argentina, in the World Club Championship. This tie saw a repeat of the violence that marred Celtic's clash with Racing Club a year earlier. United lost the away leg 1-0, and had Nobby Stiles sent off. The return match was a 1-1 draw, in which George Best and José Medina, of Estudiantes, were sent off for fighting. For the second successive season, an Argentinian club had won an unsatisfactory world title clash against British opposition.

The effects of the disrupted European Cup draw were felt in the second round, with 14 clubs having reached this stage. To even the numbers in time for the quarter finals, Benfica and Milan were allowed byes through the second round. Manchester United faced Anderlecht, who had eliminated Glentoran, from Northern Ireland, in their previous tie. United won 3-0 at home to Anderlecht, but only just scraped through after a 3-1 defeat in the second leg.

Celtic's charmed progress continued, with a 6-2 aggregate win against Red Star Belgrade. At half time in Glasgow, with the score 1-1, Jock Stein told Jimmy Johnstone, who had a phobia about flying, that his presence would not be required in Belgrade if Celtic could take a four goal lead there. Johnstone responded to the challenge in spectacular style, scoring twice, and setting up two other goals, as Celtic ran in four second half goals. The surprise of the round was the elimination of Real Madrid on away goals.

In the quarter finals Manchester United beat Rapid Vienna 3-0 at Old Trafford, with two goals coming from an inspired George Best, before holding on for a goalless draw in Austria. Celtic's progress was ended by Milan. Both teams played defensive games in their away legs, but Milan scored the only goal of the tie, through Pierino Prati, after 12 minutes in the second leg at Glasgow. Ajax looked to be on their way out when they lost 3-1 at home to Benfica – the latter's players wearing gloves and tights on a snowy night. In the first half hour of the second leg, in a performance reminiscent of Manchester United's destruction of Benfica at the Stadium of Light in 1966, Ajax built up a three goal lead, with Johan Cruyff scoring twice. Torres pulled a goal back for Benfica in the second half to level the tie. A play-off was staged in Paris, with Ajax winning 3-0, due to a burst of goalscoring in extra time.

In 1962-63 Milan had reached the European Cup final by beating both an English and a Scottish club, and now they repeated this feat. Having eliminated Celtic in the quarter finals, Milan disposed of Manchester United in the semi-finals. After Milan won 2-0 at the San Siro, while United's John Fitzpatrick was sent off, the return was a tussle between United's attack and Milan's defence. The latter held out until Charlton gave United the lead with 13 minutes remaining. A few minutes later Law appeared to have levelled the tie for United, but Marcel Machin, the French referee, ruled that the ball had not crossed the line before Milan's Dino Santin scrambled it away. Angry United supporters started to throw objects on to the pitch, and Fabio Cudicini, the Milan goalkeeper, had to be treated for an injury. It was a sad end to United's reign as European champions. They had been England's strongest representatives in the European Cup, and only winner of the trophy to date, but 24 years would pass before they re-appeared in the competition. United's failure to return to the European Cup immediately after the 1968-69 season was particularly disappointing for George Best, who felt the club rested upon its laurels after winning the trophy, rather than pressing for further success: "With a bit of foresight, 1968 could have been the start of three or four years domination of Europe. For me, personally, the later years when we were out of Europe were depressing. I hear people say the League championship is the most important thing to win. It was only important to me because it meant we were in the European Cup the following year. There was so much atmosphere at those games. For one thing they were usually night matches, which I loved. They were one-offs, and I missed them terribly. After we were out of Europe, there was just an empty feeling".

In the other semi-final, Ajax won 3-0 at home to Spartak Trnava, but required a great display from their goalkeeper Gert Bals to restrict the Czechs to a 2-0 victory in the return. Given the circumstances behind their participation, and this being the first time they had appeared in the European Cup, reaching the semi-finals was a great achievement by Spartak Trnava.

Milan and Ajax thus met in the final at Madrid's Bernabeu Stadium, before a crowd of only 31,782. The match was played on May 28, the anniversary of Milan's defeat against Real Madrid in the 1958 final. In one respect, Milan were fortunate to be in the 1969 final, having been on the verge of withdrawing from the competition when drawn against Levski Sofia for the first round, before the re-draw paired them with Malmo. On the other hand, they had proved their quality by beating both Celtic, winners of the trophy in 1967, and Manchester United, the reigning champions. Milan retained two players from their 1963 win, Gianni Rivera and Giovanni Trapattoni, while Nereo Rocco, who had managed the earlier team, was back in charge, having returned to the role in 1967-68. The Milan team for the final featured Kurt Hamrin, who had starred for Sweden in the World Cup finals as far back as 1958, and Karl-Heinz Schnellinger, who had played for West Germany in the 1966 finals. More recently, Lodetti, Prati, and Rosato had been part of the Italian team which won the 1968 European Championship as host nation, beating Yugoslavia 2-0 in a replayed final.

Milan's campaign had been based on their defensive strength, while Ajax, coached by Rinus Michels, had shown great attacking quality. In the final, Milan suddenly displayed their attacking ability, and thrashed Ajax 4-1. Cruyff played for Ajax, but he was not fully fit, and it was Milan's Pierino Prati who was the outstanding player in the match, scoring a hat-trick. He struck after only five minutes, heading in a pass from Angelo Sormani, Milan's Brazilian captain. Five minutes before half time Prati scored again, with a powerful shot, set up for him by Rivera. Ajax were given hope on the hour as Velibor Vasovic scored from a penalty. Vasovic, who had been on target for Partizan

Belgrade in 1966, thereby became the first player to score for two different clubs in European Cup finals. Milan soon restored the margin of their lead, Sormani scoring with a long-range shot at the mid-point of the second half. Prati completed his hat-trick with 16 minutes remaining, scoring his second headed goal of the match, with Rivera being the provider of the chance.

1968-69
First round

		1st leg	2nd leg	agg
Manchester City	Fenerbahce	0-0	1-2	1-2
Anderlecht	Glentoran	3-0	2-2	5-2
Waterford	Manchester United	1-3	1-7	2-10
Real Madrid	AEL Limassol	6-0	6-0	12-0
Floriana	Lahden Reipas	1-1	0-2	1-3
Saint-Etienne	Celtic	2-0	0-4	2-4
AEK Athens	Jeunesse D'Esch	3-0	2-3	5-3
Valur Reykjavik	Benfica	0-0	1-8	1-8
Rosenborg	Rapid Vienna	1-3	3-3	4-6
Nuremberg	Ajax	1-1	0-4	1-5
Steaua Bucharest	Spartak Trnava	3-1	0-4	3-5
Malmo	Milan	2-1	1-4	3-5
FC Zurich	Akademisk Copenhagen	1-3	2-1	3-4

Red Star Belgrade walked over, Carl Zeiss Jena withdrew.
Levski Sofia, Ferencvaros, Dynamo Kiev, and Ruch Chorzow withdrew

Second round

		1st leg	2nd leg	agg
Manchester United	Anderlecht	3-0	1-3	4-3
Rapid Vienna	Real Madrid	1-0	1-2	2-2

Rapid Vienna won on away goals

		1st leg	2nd leg	agg
Celtic	Red Star Belgrade	5-1	1-1	6-2
Lahden Reipas	Spartak Trnava	1-9	1-7	2-16
AEK Athens	Akademisk Copenhagen	0-0	2-0	2-0
Ajax	Fenerbahce	2-0	2-0	4-0

Quarter-finals

		1st leg	2nd leg	agg
Manchester United	Rapid Vienna	3-0	0-0	3-0
Milan	Celtic	0-0	1-0	1-0
Ajax	Benfica	1-3	3-1	4-4

Play off
Ajax 3 Benfica 0 (Paris)

Spartak Trnava	AEK Athens	2-1	1-1	3-2

Semi-finals

		1st leg	2nd leg	agg
Milan	Manchester United	2-0	0-1	2-1
Ajax	Spartak Trnava	3-0	0-2	3-2

Final
May 28 1969 Madrid
Milan 4   Ajax 1
Prati 3   Vasovic (penalty)
Sormani
Milan: Cudicini, Malatrasi, Anquilletti, Schnellinger, Rosato, Trapattoni, Lodetti, Rivera, Hamrin, Sormani, Prati
Ajax: Bals, Suurbier (Muller), Hulshoff, Vasovic, Van Duivenbode, Pronk, Groot (Nuninga), Swart, Cruyff, Danielsson, Keizer
HT: 2-0
Referee: De Mendibil (Spain)
Attendance: 31,782

Bobby Charlton

Bobby Charlton was one of England's greatest, and most popular, footballers. A prolific goalscorer for Manchester United and England, he gained winners' medals in both the European Cup and the World Cup. He was adept first as a winger and then an attacking midfielder. He had a powerful shot, was a great runner with the ball, and excelled at long-range passing. His determined work-rate contributed much to the performances of the teams he played for. Allied to this, Bobby Charlton was a great sportsman and enthusiast for the game, who was shy initially, but developed in confidence, while remaining modest about his considerable achievements. Bobby was booked only once in his career – a blot on his copybook that was subsequently judged an error, and rescinded. At the 1970 World Cup finals, he was one of two players presented with a medal by the Mexican authorities to honour "services to football and to sportsmanship". The other recipient of this award was no less a figure than Pele.

Born on October 11 1937, at Ashington, in Northumberland, his mother, Cissie, was a cousin of Jackie Milburn, the Newcastle United and England centre forward during the 1950s, while four of her brothers played professional football. After joining Manchester United in 1953, Charlton made his first team debut on October 6 1956, coincidentally against Charlton Athletic, scoring twice in a 4-2 win. He also scored on his European Cup debut, this being the 2-2 draw against Real Madrid towards the end of the 1956-57 season, in which United won the League. In 1957-58 Charlton scored in both legs of the European Cup tie against Red Star Belgrade, and was lucky to escape the Munich air crash with only minor injuries. Indeed he was fit enough to make his England debut a few weeks later, on April 19, and scored in a 4-0 win against Scotland. He met a cross from Tom Finney with a brilliant volley from the edge of the penalty area, which prompted Tommy Younger, the Scotland goalkeeper, to generously run up the pitch to congratulate him. Charlton held a regular place in the England team thereafter, and appeared in the 1962 World Cup finals. A major inspiration to the United team as Matt Busby rebuilt after the Munich disaster, he helped them to win the FA Cup in 1963, and the League in 1965.

In 1966, a few weeks after United's elimination by Partizan Belgrade in the European Cup, Bobby Charlton played for England in the World Cup finals. The team included his brother Jack, who was to play for Leeds United in the European Cup, and later manage the Republic of Ireland. Bobby gave a great display in the 4-2 win against West Germany in the final and that year he received two personal honours, winning both the English Footballer of the Year and the European Footballer of the Year awards.

Manchester United won the League in 1966-67, and went on to win the European Cup the following season. The 4-1 victory over Benfica in the European Cup final in May 1968 was especially sweet for Bobby Charlton, as he was one of the survivors from the Munich air crash, and scored two of United's goals. The following month he scored for England as they beat the Soviet Union 2-0, to take third place in the European Championship. In 1969 Bobby scored in his final European Cup match, this being the second leg of United's semi-final against Milan.

His England career ended at the 1970 World Cup finals, as he was substituted in the 3-2 defeat against West Germany. He remains England's leading international goalscorer, with 49 goals while his 106 appearances have been surpassed only by Peter Shilton (125) and by Bobby Moore (108).

Three years later Bobby left United, having helped them to narrowly avoid relegation at the end of the 1972-73 season – just five years after their European triumph. He had played 754 matches for United, and scored 247 goals – both remain club records. A few months before he left, Matt Busby *wrote an appreciation of the player to coincide with his testimonial. Part of this ran as follows: "He has broken all records and won everything possible that there is to win. Yet he has remained completely unspoiled, still prepared to do more than his fair share for the cause of Manchester United. The shy boy has blossomed now into a man with a great sense of assurance, confidence and responsibility".*

Bobby ended his professional career with a brief spell at Preston North End, as player and then player-manager. During the last 30 years he has remained active in football, in a variety of roles, with his enthusiasm continuing to shine. He has organised coaching schools for youngsters, been a BBC television pundit, and a figurehead for England's campaign to stage the 2006 World Cup finals. Having coined the phrase "Theatre of Dreams" to describe the Old Trafford stage on which he performed with such grace, Bobby Charlton has been a director of Manchester United since 1994.

1969-70

Normal service was resumed during 1969-70, after the upheavals in the previous season's competition. Indeed there was a new tidiness about the competition, with virtually all matches in each round being played on dates laid down by UEFA, rather than the previous practice of the clubs involved agreeing dates between themselves. The first round was notable for a series of very high aggregate scores. Leeds United ran up the biggest margin, beating SOFK Lyn Oslo 16-0. Leeds, appearing in the competition for the first time, were a tough and disciplined team, managed by Don Revie, who specialised in thorough preparation, including the production of dossiers on opponents. Leeds played in an all-white strip, chosen by Revie in homage to Real Madrid.

The Leeds team included Jack Charlton, who had played for England in the 1966 World Cup final. Jack Charlton would also appear for England in the 1970 finals, along with three of his Leeds' team-mates – Allan Clarke, Terry Cooper, and Norman Hunter. Clarke had been bought from Leicester City in the summer of 1969, for a British transfer record of £165,000. Four of Leeds' goals against SOFK Lyn Oslo were scored by Mick Jones, who went on to be the competition's leading scorer, with eight goals. Feyenoord beat KR Reykjavik 16-2, with their 12-2 win in the first leg being the highest scoring match in the history of the European Cup. Ruud Geels scored six times for Feyenoord in the tie, and Ove Kindvall four times. Real Madrid won 14-1 against Olympiakos Nicosia, Red Star Belgrade thrashed Linfield 12-2, and Legia Warsaw ran up a 10-1 scoreline against UT Arad. By comparison, Milan opening their defence of the title with an 8-0 win against Avenir Beggen was not particularly spectacular.

Leeds were again the biggest aggregate winners in the second round, beating Ferencvaros 6-0 with Jones scoring three. Celtic, who had beaten FC Basle in the previous round, eliminated Benfica on the toss of a coin, after each team had won its home leg 3-0, with UEFA having decided to end the use of play-offs as a tie-breaker. Meanwhile Galatasaray also advanced, at the expense of Spartak Trnava, on the toss of a coin. Milan's campaign was unexpectedly ended by a 2-1 aggregate defeat against Feyenoord, while Francisco Gento scored a penalty for Real Madrid in the second leg of their tie with Standard Liege, as he made his final European Cup appearance, at the age of 36.

In the quarter finals, Leeds beat Standard Liege by a single goal in both legs. Celtic won 3-0 at home to Fiorentina – appearing in the European Cup for the first time since they were runners-up in 1957 – before losing the return by a single goal. These results set up a semi-final between the English and Scottish champions, which was immediately dubbed 'The Battle of

Britain'. Leeds were a tired team, affected by fixture congestion as they chased the League, FA Cup, and European Cup. The first leg, at Elland Road, was Leeds' eighth game in a packed 14 days. Celtic scored through George Connelly in the second minute, and held that lead for the remainder of the match. The return was moved from Celtic's Parkhead ground to Hampden Park, to accommodate the masses of supporters who wished to be present. A crowd of 136,505 gathered at Hampden, with this being a record for the European Cup, exceeding that set when the 1960 final was played at the same venue. Leeds took the lead with a goal from Billy Bremner, their Scottish captain, but Celtic scored twice early in the second half, through John Hughes and Bobby Murdoch, to win both the match and the tie. Leeds' season ended in anti-climax, with the European Cup elimination being compounded by their finishing as runners-up to Everton in the League, and Chelsea in the FA Cup.

Celtic's opponents in the final staged at Milan's San Siro stadium, refereed by Concetto Lo Bello, the Italian who had taken charge of the 1968 final, were Feyenoord. Celtic were the favourites, as they were still managed by Jock Stein, and retained seven players from the team which had won the 1967 final – Auld, Gemmell, Johnstone, Lennox, McNeill, Murdoch, and Wallace. Feyenoord, appearing in their first European Cup final, were coached by Ernst Happel, who had played for Austria in the 1954 and 1958 World Cup finals, and for Rapid Vienna in the early years of the European Cup. The Feyenoord team included Theo Van Duivenbode, who had appeared for Ajax in the 1969 final, plus three players destined to play for the Netherlands in the 1974 World Cup finals – Rinus Israel, Wim Jansen, and Wim Van Hanegem,

Tommy Gemmell, who scored when Celtic took the trophy in 1967, opened the scoring, shooting through a crowd of players from 25 yards after 29 minutes. But they were punished for some poor defending, as Rinus Israel equalised for Feyenoord a couple of minutes later, heading in a free kick from Franz Hasil, an Austrian midfielder. Hasil hit a post at the start of the second half, and Feyenoord dominated the play thereafter, but the score remained level, and the match moved into extra time. Feyenoord continued to have the edge, but were denied by good goalkeeping from Evan Williams, until they deservedly scored three minutes from the end of the added period. A long ball from Israel was handled by Celtic's Billy McNeil, but the referee played the advantage, as the ball reached Ove Kindvall, a Swede, who chipped it over Williams, and into the net and Feyenoord had secured a 2-1 win.

Celtic had been undone by their own attitude. As Stein put it: "I think we believed we had done the hardest part, beating Leeds. We had watched Feyenoord and had not seen much to frighten us. I think we would have won the final with a wee bit more care, but we got even more complacent after scoring the first goal".

Celtic's defeat ended the chance of a clean sweep for British clubs in Europe this season, with Manchester City having won the Cup-Winners' Cup, while Arsenal took the Fairs Cup. A year after Ajax had been thrashed by Milan, Feyenoord – who had eliminated Milan on the way to the 1970 final – had become the first team from the Netherlands to win the European Cup. The 1970 instalment was the 15th European Cup final, but the first not to feature a team from either Italy, Portugal, or Spain – the traditional giants of the competition. A shift in power to the north of the continent, initiated by the victories of Celtic and Manchester United, had now seen clubs from the Netherlands join Europe's elite. On the other hand, the Netherlands and Scotland both failed to reach the 1970 World Cup finals, which were staged in Mexico. England's hold on their world title ended with a 3-2 defeat against West Germany in the quarter finals, following which Brazil regained the trophy, beating a negative Italy 4-1 in the final.

1969-70
Preliminary round

		1st leg	2nd leg	agg
TPS Turku	KB Copenhagen	0-1	0-4	0-5

First round

		1st leg	2nd leg	agg
Leeds United	SOFK Lyn Oslo	10-0	6-0	16-0
CSKA Sofia	Ferencvaros	2-1	1-4	3-5
Standard Liege	17 Nentori Tirana	3-0	1-1	4-1
Real Madrid	Olympiakos Nicosia	8-0	6-1	14-1
FC Basle	Celtic	0-0	0-2	0-2
Benfica	KB Copenhagen	2-0	3-2	5-2
FK Austria	Dynamo Kiev	1-2	1-3	2-5
Fiorentina	Osters Vaxjo	1-0	2-1	3-1
Galatasaray	Waterford	2-0	3-2	5-2
Hibernians	Spartak Trnava	2-2	0-4	2-6
UT Arad	Legia Warsaw	1-2	0-8	1-10
Bayern Munich	Saint-Etienne	2-0	0-3	2-3
Vorwarts Berlin	Panathinaikos	2-0	1-1	3-1
Red Star Belgrade	Linfield	8-0	4-2	12-2
Milan	Avenir Beggen	5-0	3-0	8-0
Feyenoord	KR Reykjavik	12-2	4-0	16-2

Second round

		1st leg	2nd leg	agg
Leeds United	Ferencvaros	3-0	3-0	6-0
Standard Liege	Real Madrid	1-0	3-2	4-2
Celtic	Benfica	3-0	0-3	3-3

Celtic won on the toss of a coin

		1st leg	2nd leg	agg
Dynamo Kiev	Fiorentina	1-2	0-0	1-2
Spartak Trnava	Galatasaray	1-0	0-1	1-1

Galatasaray won on the toss of a coin

		1st leg	2nd leg	agg
Legia Warsaw	Saint-Etienne	2-1	1-0	3-1
Vorwarts Berlin	Red Star Belgrade	2-1	2-3	4-4

Vorwarts Berlin won on away goals

		1st leg	2nd leg	agg
Milan	Feyenoord	1-0	0-2	1-2

Quarter-finals

		1st leg	2nd leg	agg
Standard Liege	Leeds United	0-1	0-1	0-2
Celtic	Fiorentina	3-0	0-1	3-1
Galatasaray	Legia Warsaw	1-1	0-2	1-3
Vorwarts Berlin	Feyenoord	1-0	0-2	1-2

Semi-finals

		1st leg	2nd leg	agg
Leeds United	Celtic	0-1	1-2	1-3
Legia Warsaw	Feyenoord	0-0	0-2	0-2

Final

May 6 1970 Milan
Feyenoord 2   Celtic 1 (after extra time)
Israel   Gemmell
Kindvall

Feyenoord: Pieters-Graafland, Romeijn (Haak), Laseroms, Israel, Van Duivenbode, Hasil, Jansen, Van Hanegem, Wery, Kindvall, Moulijn

Celtic: Williams, Hay, Brogan, McNeill, Gemmell, Murdoch, Auld (Connelly), Johnstone, Lennox, Wallace, Hughes

HT: 1-1, FT: 1-1

Referee: Lo Bello (Italy)

Attendance: 53,187

Chapter 4

Double Hat-trick – 1970-1976

1970-71

The early and mid-1970s was the era of 'Total Football', a tactical innovation developed by Rinus Michels, who managed both Ajax and the Netherlands. The theory was that static team formations should be replaced with a system where all of the outfield players were capable of inter-changing their roles. It was not totally flexible in practice, but it did produce some brilliant football. One of the immediate effects of 'Total Football' was that Ajax won the European Cup in 1971, eclipsing fellow-countrymen, Feyenoord, who had taken the title the previous season.

The 1970-71 season brought a couple of modifications to the competition. Penalty shoot-outs were introduced as a tie-breaker where teams were level on both aggregate score and away goals, to replace the toss of a coin. The other innovation was the use of yellow and red cards by referees, to signal bookings and sendings off.

These had been introduced at the 1970 World Cup finals. The idea came from Ken Aston, the head of the referees' committee at the 1966 finals, following the confusion at the match between England and Argentina over the referee's decisions. While waiting at a set of traffic lights, Aston realised that the use of coloured cards would greatly simplify matters.

Holders Feyenoord were surprisingly eliminated in the first round, losing to UT Arad, from Romania, on away goals while beaten finalists Celtic thrashed KPV Kokkola 14-0 on aggregate in their opening tie, with Harry Hood scoring a hat-trick in the first leg. Celtic then made further high-scoring progress, beating Waterford 10-2 on aggregate – this time it was Willie Wallace who netted a hat-trick in the opening match.

Waterford were the first club from the Republic of Ireland to appear in the second round, having previously beaten Glentoran, from Northern Ireland, home and away. A more significant first was the absence of Real Madrid from the European Cup, after 15 successive seasons in the competition.

The new Spanish champions were Real's neighbours, Atletico Madrid. In the second round, Atletico eliminated Cagliari, who had recently won their sole Italian title, with a team that included Luigi Riva, a star for Italy in the 1970 World Cup finals.

Everton, representing England for the second time, disposed of IBK Keflavik in the first round, winning 9-2 on aggregate, with Alan Ball scoring a hat-trick in the first leg. Everton then met Borussia Monchengladbach, who had previously beaten EPA Larnaca 16-0 on aggregate – Horst Koppel and Herbert Laumen both scoring twice in each leg. The clubs drew 1-1 in each match and with extra time failing to produce any goals, the winners were decided by a penalty shoot-out. The tension of the occasion was later recalled by Everton's Howard Kendall, one of the Everton players: "The atmosphere was unbearable. Half our lot did not want to look. Tommy Wright, our full back who had played in the World Cup for England in Mexico, was so scared of being asked to take one of the penalties that he kept looking at the bench, and pointing to his groin, making out he was injured".

Everton won the shoot-out 4-3, with Kendall among the scorers. Kendall would later have three spells as manager of Everton in the 1980s and 1990s, but the post-Heysel ban on English clubs prevented him from returning to the European Cup after they won the League in 1985. Everton's opponents in the quarter-finals were Panathinaikos.

The Greeks surprisingly won the tie, with a 1-1 draw at Goodison Park, followed by a goalless return, taking them through on the away goals rule, Antonis Antoniadis scoring the vital goal. Celtic's run was halted more convincingly, as they lost 3-0 away to Ajax – the goals came from Johan Cruyff, Barry Hulshoff, and Piet Keizer – and could only win the return 1-0.

In the semi-finals, Ajax recovered from a single goal defeat away to Atletico Madrid, winning their home leg 3-0, with Keizer scoring again. In the other tie, Red Star Belgrade looked set for success, as they won 4-1 at home to Panathinaikos in the first leg, with a hat-trick from Stefan Ostojic. Eventually the lone Greek goal in the first leg, scored by Aristidis Kamaras, proved very significant, as Panathinaikos pulled off a surprise in the second leg, winning 3-0 – Kamaras scoring again to add to two from Antoniadis – to take the tie on away goals.

The final , played at Wembley for the second time in the space of four seasons, attracted a crowd of 83,179 – many of whom had made the relatively short journey from the Netherlands. Ajax were the clear favourites to win, in view of their impressive run to the final – after the opening struggle against 17 Nentori Tirana. They also retained six members of the team which had played in the 1969 final – Cruyff, Hulshoff, Kiezer, Suurbier, Swart, and Vasovic. Panathinaikos, who were managed by Ferenc Puskas, had been fortunate to become the first Greek club to reach the final, having required penalties and away goals respectively to win their two preceding ties. Nevertheless, the manner of their eventual win over Red Star Belgrade suggested a team of great spirit.

The match proved a disappointment. Ajax took the lead after five minutes, as Dick Van Dijk headed in a cross from Keizer, and always looked likely to win. The Dutch controlled the play in the first half, but were held at bay by a good performance from goalkeeper Takis Oeconomopoulos. In the second half Ajax played cautiously. Panathinaikos had a lot of possession but their attack, led by Antoniadis, the leading scorer in this season's competition with ten goals, proved ineffective. With three minutes remaining Ajax scored again, to complete a 2-0 victory. A fine run by Cruyff set up an opportunity for Arie Haan, whose shot was deflected into the net by Anthimos Kapsis, for an own goal.

The trophy was collected by Velibor Vasovic, the Ajax captain, who had been on the losing side in both the 1966 and 1969 finals. The manner in which Ajax became the second successive Dutch club to win a European Cup final was rather muted, but during the course of the season they had displayed plenty of 'Total Football', and were worthy champions, while Johan Cruyff had laid claim to be one of the world's greatest footballers.

1970-71

Preliminary round

		1st leg	2nd leg	agg
Levski Spartak	FK Austria	3-1	0-3	3-4

64

First round

		1st leg	2nd leg	agg
Jeunesse D'Esch	Panathinaikos	1-2	0-5	1-7
Slovan Bratislava	B1903 Copenhagen	2-1	2-2	4-3
Everton	IBK Keflavik	6-2	3-0	9-2
EPA Larnaca	Borussia Monchengladbach	0-6	0-10	0-16
Fenerbahce	Carl Zeiss Jena	0-4	0-1	0-5
Sporting Lisbon	Floriana	5-0	4-0	9-0
Ujpest Dozsa	Red Star Belgrade	2-0	0-4	2-4
Feyenoord	UT Arad	1-1	0-0	1-1
UT Arad won on away goals				
Atletico Madrid	FK Austria	2-0	2-1	4-1
Cagliari	Saint-Etienne	3-0	0-1	3-1
IFK Gothenburg	Legia Warsaw	0-4	1-2	1-6
Rosenborg	Standard Liege	0-2	0-5	0-7
Celtic	KPV Kokkola	9-0	5-0	14-0
Glentoran	Waterford	1-3	0-1	1-4
Spartak Moscow	FC Basle	3-2	1-2	4-4
FC Basle won on away goals				
17 Nentori Tirana	Ajax	2-2	0-2	2-4

Second round

		1st leg	2nd leg	agg
Panathinaikos	Slovan Bratislava	3-0	1-2	4-2
Borussia Monchengladbach	Everton	1-1	1-1	2-2
Everton won 4-3 on penalties				
Carl Zeiss Jena	Sporting Lisbon	2-1	2-1	4-2
Red Star Belgrade	UT Arad	3-0	3-1	6-1
Cagliari	Atletico Madrid	2-1	0-3	2-4
Standard Liege	Legia Warsaw	1-0	0-2	1-2
Waterford	Celtic	0-7	2-3	2-10
Ajax	FC Basle	3-0	2-1	5-1

Quarter-finals

		1st leg	2nd leg	agg
Everton	Panathinaikos	1-1	0-0	1-1
Panathinaikos won on away goals				
Carl Zeiss Jena	Red Star Belgrade	3-2	0-4	3-6
Atletico Madrid	Legia Warsaw	1-0	1-2	2-2
Atletico Madrid won on away goals				
Ajax	Celtic	3-0	0-1	3-1

Semi-finals

		1st leg	2nd leg	agg
Red Star Belgrade	Panathinaikos	4-1	0-3	4-4
Panathinaikos won on away goals				
Atletico Madrid	Ajax	1-0	0-3	1-3

Final

June 2 1971 Wembley
Ajax 2   Panathinaikos 0
Van Dijk
Kapsis (own goal)
Ajax: Stuy, Neeskens, Hulshoff, Vasovic, Suurbier, Rijnders (Blankenburg), G Muhren, Swart (Haan), Cruyff, Van Dijk, Keizer
Panathinaikos: Oeconomopoulos, Tomaras, Kapsis, Sourpis, Vlahos, Kamaras, Elefterakis, Grammos, Antoniadis, Domazos, Filakouris
HT: 1-0
Referee: Taylor (England)
Attendance: 83,179

Rinus Michels

Rinus Michels was manager of the Ajax team that won the European Cup in 1971. Although he was only at the helm for one of Ajax's three successive European Cup triumphs, he stands as one of the most influential managers in the history of football. He is generally regarded as the inventor of 'Total Football', an idea that rejuvenated the game and he played a major role, as manager of both Ajax and the Dutch national team, in the emergence of the Netherlands as a world power in football during the 1970s. It is a position the Dutch have retained, with Michels being the link between their two greatest national teams. He managed them when they were runners-up in World Cup of 1974, and again when they were winners of the European Championship in 1988

Michels was born on February 9 1928 the year the Netherlands staged the Olympic Games, but were eliminated in the first round of the football tournament by Uruguay, the eventual gold medallists. A centre forward for Ajax, he played five times in the 1950s for a Dutch national team that was midway through a long period in the international wilderness. Football in the Netherlands was amateur until 1954, when it became semi-professional. Full professionalism was introduced ten years later, the year in which Michels became the coach of Ajax. He led the club to a series of domestic honours, imposing strong discipline and earning the nickname 'Iron Rinus', but encouraging the players to express themselves on the field. With the development of 'Total Football', Ajax also became a force in the European Cup, reaching the final in 1969, and then winning the trophy with a 2-0 win against Panathinaikos in the 1971 final.

Ajax had reached their peak, and were to retain the European Cup in 1972 and 1973, but Michels had abruptly departed in 1971. He replaced Vic Buckingham (who had preceded him at Ajax) as manager of Barcelona, with that club offering him more money than he could earn in Holland. In 1973, the prospect of massive earnings also persuaded Johan Cruyff to move from Ajax to Barcelona, with Michels commenting that "football is a business, and business is business". Under Michels, Barcelona won the Spanish League in 1974, for the first time since 1960. Meanwhile Michels was appointed manager of the Dutch national team especially for the 1974 World Cup finals – with Frantisek Fadrhonc, the previous coach, acting as his assistant. The Netherlands, with Cruyff in amazing form, dazzled opponents, until they lost in the final against West Germany, who had adapted the ideas of 'Total Football' from their neighbours and rivals.

In 1974-75 Michels guided Barcelona in the European Cup, but he was blamed for their defeat against Leeds United in the semi-finals, and left the club shortly afterwards. After a brief return to Ajax, and a second spell at Barcelona between 1976 and 1978, he moved to the USA, coaching Los Angeles Aztecs. Returning to Europe in 1980, he became coach of Cologne, the West German football authorities allowing him to work despite his lack of official coaching qualifications in deference to his great experience.

In July 1984, a decade after guiding the Dutch in the World Cup finals, Michels returned to the position of national manager. The Netherlands had been runners-up in the 1978 finals, but had failed to qualify for the 1982 tournament, and now hoped Michels would lead them to the 1986 finals. Unfortunately defeat in a play-off against their neighbours Belgium, on away goals, meant another absence from the World Cup finals. Health problems forced him to take a break from coaching the national team, and he was not actually in charge at the time of the play-off. On his return, Michels built a Netherlands team that echoed the glories of the 1970s. In 1988 the Dutch finally fulfilled their potential by winning the European Championship, beating the Soviet Union 2-0 in the final. Michels' second spell as Dutch manager ended with that tournament, and he returned to club management with Bayer Leverkusen.

In September 1990, a few months after the Netherlands had given an indifferent performance in the World Cup finals, Michels was appointed as national coach for a third time. During this swansong, Michels again motivated the team to play some great football, and they reached the semi-finals of the European Championship in 1992, only to lose against Denmark on penalties. That match marked the end of Michels' final spell as Dutch manager, but he continued to contribute his expertise, as a member of UEFA's Technical Committee, which he had joined in 1990. In 2002 Michels' legendary career was marked with the award of UEFA's Order of Merit. In the words of UEFA, this honour "thanks and rewards, by means of a decoration and official diploma, individuals who have devoted a large part of their life to football, and who have contributed to the game's development and history".

Rinus Michels died, aged 77, on March 3 2005.

1971-72

Ajax retained the European Cup in 1972, beating Internazionale 2-0 in the final, with virtually an unchanged team, but they did have a new manager, Michels having moved to Barcelona, to be replaced by Stefan Kovacs, a Romanian. Ajax produced several fine displays of 'Total Football' this season, but overall the 1971-72 European Cup was an undistinguished competition. One indicator was that Johan Cruyff only required five goals to emerge as joint leading scorer, along with Lou Macari of Celtic, and Sylvester Takac of Standard Liege. More significantly, Inter progressed by a dubious route, involving a heavy defeat that was removed from the record, an away goals win in the quarter-finals, and a non-scoring semi-final, before completely failing to deliver in the final.

Unfortunately the main drama prior to the final was provided by the controversial clash between Inter and Borussia Monchengladbach in the second round. The Germans won their home leg 7-1, but were helped by the departure of Internazionale's Roberto Boninsegna, who was hit on the head by a drink can, thrown by a spectator, after 29 minutes, with Borussia leading 2-1. Boninsegna had to be substituted, and Borussia went on to thrash their dispirited opponents. Internazionale requested that the match be awarded to them with a 3-0 scoreline, as UEFA had indicated it would take such a step for matches disrupted by the throwing of fireworks from the crowd. In the absence of any competition regulation covering the incident that had actually affected the match, UEFA annulled the result, and ordered a replay of the match at a different ground. Inter won their home match, which became the new first leg, 4-2. The return, at West Berlin, was a goalless draw, in which Borussia's Ludwig Muller ironically broke a leg in a tackle with Boninsegna. The outcome of all this was that Inter took the tie, and a place in the last eight.

In the quarter-finals Ajax beat Arsenal 2-1 in Amsterdam, with an outstanding display, in which Gerrie Muhren scored twice, and followed this with a 1-0 victory at Highbury where George Graham was unlucky to score an own goal. Celtic kept British hopes alive, with a 3-2 success against Ujpest Dozsa, Macari scoring twice.

The semi-finals were characterised by football that lacked adventure, and produced only one goal across the four matches. That was scored by Ajax's Sjaak Swart, as they won against Benfica. Two goalless draws between Internazionale and Celtic, the clubs that had contested the 1967 final, meant that penalties were required to settle a place in the 1972 final, with the Italians winning 5-4.

Inter's run to the final had been lucky but, once there, fortune seemed to favour Ajax, with the match being played in their home country, albeit in Rotterdam. Ajax featured nine players who had appeared in the previous season's final – Blankenburg, Cruyff, Haan, Hulshoff, Keizer, Muhren, Stuy, Suurbier, and Swart. The newcomers included Johan Neeskens, a midfield player who was in the process of building a brilliant partnership with Cruyff. Inter retained four players from the 1967 final – Bedin, Burgnich, Facchetti, and Mazzola.

Piet Keizer, who had replaced the departed Vasovic as captain, later recalled this match as the pinnacle of Ajax's achievements, saying: "We were a bit worried before the final about the reaction of the crowd, because Ajax were playing in the stadium of our biggest rivals, Feyenoord. But the fans were on our side from the start, and you could not find flaw in the way we played that night".

Ajax gave one of the ultimate displays of 'Total Football', and could easily have won by more than 2-0. They dominated the first half with attacking play, but were unable to score. Ruud Krol, a full back, went closest, with a powerful 25 yard shot, that hit a post. Inter simply concentrated on massed defence. A couple of minutes into the second half, Ajax's Wim Suurbier crossed from the right, and caused confusion in the Inter defence, with goalkeeper Ivano Bordon and Gabriele Oriali attempting to intercept, but colliding with each other, whereupon the ball fell to Cruyff, who scored a simple goal. Bordon's error was an unfortunate lapse in a fine personal performance, which kept the margin of Inter's defeat at a reasonable level. Ajax continued to control the play, and Cruyff scored again 12 minutes from time, meeting a free kick from Keizer on the left with a fine header. Ajax's positive play had deservedly defeated the negative approach of Internazionale.

1971-72

Preliminary round

		1st leg	2nd leg	agg
Valencia	Union Luxembourg	3-1	1-0	4-1

First round

		1st leg	2nd leg	agg
Galatasaray	CSKA Moscow	1-1	0-3	1-4
Standard Liege	Linfield	2-0	3-2	5-2
B1903 Copenhagen	Celtic	2-1	0-3	2-4
Feyenoord	Olympiakos Nicosia	8-0	9-0	17-0
Internazionale	AEK Athens	4-1	2-3	6-4
Ujpest Dozsa	Malmo	4-0	0-1	4-1
Valencia	Hajduk Split	0-0	1-1	1-1
Valencia won on away goals				
Cork Hibernians	Borussia Monchengladbach	0-5	1-2	1-7
Wacker Innsbruck	Benfica	0-4	1-3	1-7
Ajax	Dynamo Dresden	2-0	0-0	2-0
Stromsgodset	Arsenal	1-3	0-4	1-7
Dynamo Bucharest	Spartak Trnava	0-0	2-2	2-2
Dynamo Bucharest won on away goals				
Marseille	Gornik Zabrze	2-1	1-1	3-2
CSKA Sofia	Partizan Tirana	3-0	1-0	4-0
Lahden Reipas	Grasshoppers	1-1	0-8	1-9
IA Akranes	Sliema Wanderers	0-4	0-0	0-4

Second round

		1st leg	2nd leg	agg
CSKA Moscow	Standard Liege	1-0	0-2	1-2
Dynamo Bucharest	Feyenoord	0-3	0-2	0-5
Valencia	Ujpest Dozsa	0-1	1-2	1-3

Internazionale	Borussia Monchengladbach	4-2	0-0	4-2
Benfica	CSKA Sofia	2-1	0-0	2-1
Grasshoppers	Arsenal	0-2	0-3	0-5
Marseille	Ajax	1-2	1-4	2-6
Celtic	Sliema Wanderers	5-0	2-1	7-1

Quarter-finals

		1st leg	2nd leg	agg
Ajax	Arsenal	2-1	1-0	3-1
Feyenoord	Benfica	1-0	1-5	2-5
Ujpest Dozsa	Celtic	1-2	1-1	2-3
Internazionale	Standard Liege	1-0	1-2	2-2

Internazionale won on away goals

Semi-finals

		1st leg	2nd leg	agg
Ajax	Benfica	1-0	0-0	1-0
Internazionale	Celtic	0-0	0-0	0-0

Internazionale won 5-4 on penalties

Final

May 31 1972 Rotterdam
Ajax 2   Internazionale 0
Cruyff 2
Ajax: Stuy, Suurbier, Blankenburg, Hulshoff, Krol, Neeskens, Haan, G.Muhren, Swart, Cruyff, Keizer
Internazionale: Bordon, Burgnich, Facchetti, Bellugi, Oriali, Giubertoni (Bertini), Bedin, Frustalupi, Jair (Pellizarro), Mazzola, Boninsegna
HT: 0-0
Referee: Helles (France)
Attendance: 61,354

1972-73

Ajax completed their hat-trick of European Cup victories in 1972-73, with some brilliant football, culminating in a famous win against Juventus. Prior to this Juventus scored a dubious semi-final win against Derby County. Formed in 1884 as an offshoot of Derbyshire County Cricket Club, the idea being that a successful football team would raise revenue to support the cricketing activities, Derby County had been founder members of the Football League in 1888. They won the FA Cup in 1946, but did not take the League title until 1972. Derby's belated league success owed much to the influence of their manager, Brian Clough, and his assistant, Peter Taylor. A few years later Clough and Taylor would weave the same magic with Nottingham Forest, and twice win the European Cup. Derby opened with a pair of victories against Zeljeznicar Sarajevo. Celtic did likewise against Rosenborg. There was no entrant from Northern Ireland this season, with the troubles there preventing Glentoran, the national champions, from participating. Waterford, from the Republic of Ireland, lost to Omonia Nicosia.

The Cypriot champions were then beaten 13-0 on aggregate by Bayern Munich in the second round, with Gerd Muller scoring five goals in the first leg, and two in the second leg. Meanwhile Derby achieved a fine 3-0 win at home to Benfica – with goals from Roy McFarland, Kevin Hector and John McGovern – and secured their place in the next round with a goalless draw at the Stadium of Light. Prior to the second leg, Derby's laid-back approach, led by Clough, had included a training session on a Portuguese beach. Celtic won 2-1 at home to Ujpest Dozsa, with Kenny Dalglish scoring both of their goals, but exited with a 3-0 defeat in Hungary.

Ajax, given a bye through the first round, began their defence with a convincing 6-1 aggregate win against CSKA Sofia, Cruyff scoring twice in the second leg. During the season, Ajax competed in the World Club Championship for the first time, beating Independiente, and defeated Rangers in the inaugural European Super Cup.

In January 1973, during the winter break from the European Cup, an unusual representative match was staged at Wembley. To mark the accession of the United Kingdom, the Republic of Ireland, and Denmark to the EEC, a team drawn from those three countries met a line-up from the six existing members of the community. The Three, as they were known, beat the Six 2-0. Several of the members of the Six team were drawn from Ajax and Bayern Munich, two clubs who would meet a few weeks later in the European Cup quarter-finals.

Bayern featured several players from the West German team which had won the European Championship in 1972 but Ajax dominated the first leg, winning 4-0, although they had to wait until the last half hour to score the goals, Arie Haan getting two. Bayern won the return 2-1, both being scored by Gerd Muller. Muller had the consolation of finishing as the European Cup's leading scorer this season, with 11 goals. Derby County's progress continued, as they overcame a 1-0 first leg defeat to eliminate Spartak Trnava, with Kevin Hector scoring both second leg goals.

In the semi-finals, Derby met Juventus, who had required the away goals rule to beat Ujpest Dozsa at the previous stage. The simple story of the action on the field is that Juventus won 3-1 in Turin, before holding Derby to a goalless draw at the Baseball Ground, with Alan Hinton missing a penalty and Roger Davies being sent off. Off the pitch, the tie was surrounded by accusations of corruption. Derby were convinced that Gerhard Schulenberg, the West German referee for the first leg, was bribed by Juventus to favour them, with Helmut Haller, a Juventus substitute and fellow-countryman of Schulenberg, acting as an intermediary.

Francisco Lobo, the Portuguese referee of the return match, reported to UEFA that an attempt to bribe him had been made by Dezso Solti, a Hungarian-born holder of Argentinian nationality, who lived in Italy, and had a reputation for shady connections with Inter, in the 1960s, and then Juventus. UEFA investigated the bribery claims, but took no action against Juventus, despite evidence from Brian Glanville and Keith Botsford of *The Sunday Times* that there was a case to answer. There was no question about the manner of Ajax's semi-final victory, as they beat Real Madrid twice with assured performances.

For the second year in a row Ajax met an Italian team in the final. The match was played in Belgrade before a crowd of 89,484. Ajax retained ten of the players who had appeared in the 1972 final, with Johnny Rep being the only newcomer, in place of Swart. Four of the Ajax team were appearing in their fourth final for the club in the space of five seasons – namely Cruyff, Hulshoff, Keizer, and Suurbier. Juventus were appearing in their first final. Their team included Jose Altafini, who had won the trophy with Milan ten years earlier, and Pietro Anastasi, for whom they had paid a world record transfer fee of £500,000 to Varese in 1968. Juventus fielded several Italian internationals, including the goalkeeper Dino Zoff, who was in the early stage of keeping a lengthy series of clean sheets for his country.

Ajax scored quickly. After four minutes a cross from Horst Blankenburg on the left wing found Johnny Rep at the far post, and he headed the ball into the net. For the first half hour Ajax played some brilliant football, sending the Juventus players round in circles, with Cruyff being the orchestrator, but failed to take the further goalscoring chances that they created. The brilliance tailed off towards the interval, but half time arrived with Ajax still ahead, and in control. They continued to dominate the play in the second half and although they could not score again their victory was rarely in doubt.

Ajax had deservedly won the European Cup for the third successive season, with this being the best run of victories since Real Madrid in the opening five seasons of the competition.

1972-73

First round

		1st leg	2nd leg	agg
Real Madrid	IBK Keflavik	3-0	1-0	4-0
Anderlecht	Vejle	4-2	3-0	7-2
Ujpest Dozsa	FC Basle	2-0	2-3	4-3
Celtic	Rosenborg	2-1	3-1	5-2
Galatasaray	Bayern Munich	1-1	0-6	1-7
Marseille	Juventus	1-0	0-3	1-3
Malmo	Benfica	1-0	1-4	2-4
Wacker Innsbruck	Dynamo Kiev	0-1	0-2	0-3
CSKA Sofia	Panathinaikos	2-1	2-0	4-1
Sliema Wanderers	Gornik Zabrze	0-5	0-5	0-10
Magdeburg	TPS Turku	6-0	3-1	9-1
Aris Bonnevoie	Arges Pitesti	0-2	0-4	0-6
Derby County	Zeljeznicar Sarajevo	2-0	2-1	4-1
Waterford	Omonia Nicosia	2-1	0-2	2-3

Second round

		1st leg	2nd leg	agg
Bayern Munich	Omonia Nicosia	9-0	4-0	13-0
Spartak Trnava	Anderlecht	1-0	1-0	2-0
Derby County	Benfica	3-0	0-0	3-0
Celtic	Ujpest Dozsa	2-1	0-3	2-4
Dynamo Kiev	Gornik Zabrze	2-0	1-2	3-2
Juventus	Magdeburg	1-0	1-0	2-0
Arges Pitesti	Real Madrid	2-1	1-3	3-4
CSKA Sofia	Ajax	1-3	0-3	1-6

Quarter-finals

		1st leg	2nd leg	agg
Juventus	Ujpest Dozsa	0-0	2-2	2-2
Juventus won on away goals				
Spartak Trnava	Derby County	1-0	0-2	1-2
Dynamo Kiev	Real Madrid	0-0	0-3	0-3
Ajax	Bayern Munich	4-0	1-2	5-2

Semi-finals

		1st leg	2nd leg	agg
Juventus	Derby County	3-1	0-0	3-1
Ajax	Real Madrid	2-1	1-0	3-1

Final

May 30 1973 Belgrade
Ajax 1   Juventus 0
Rep
Ajax: Stuy, Suurbier, Hulshoff, Blankenburg, Krol, Neeskens, G. Muhren, Haan, Rep, Cruyff, Keizer
Juventus: Zoff, Salvadore, Marchetti, Morini, Longobucco, Causio (Cuccureddu), Furino, Capello, Altafini, Anastasi, Bettega
(Haller)
HT: 1-0
Referee: Gugulovic (Yugoslavia)
Attendance: 89,484

Johan Cruyff

Johan Cruyff was the star of the Ajax team that won the European Cup in 1971, 1972 and 1973. On a personal level, Cruyff won the European Footballer of the Year award three times, and established himself as arguably the greatest player in the world, in succession to Pele, who retired from international football in 1971. With both Ajax and the Netherlands, Cruyff played a leading role in the development of 'Total Football', an exciting, if short-lived, phenomenon. In a break with traditional categorisation, Cruyff – who wore a number 14 shirt for both club and country – was nominally a centre forward, but enjoyed a roving role, which would also take him out to the wings, or back to a deep-lying position. In this respect, Cruyff emulated his hero, and role model Alfredo Di Stefano. Besides having great vision, pace, and goalscoring ability, Cruyff introduced a legendary drag back, which often wrong-footed defenders. Cruyff's only fault appeared to be a volatile temperament, which often led him into controversy.

Born on April 25 1947, in Amsterdam, Cruyff was 12 when he joined the youth programme at Ajax, with help from his mother, who was employed by the club as a cleaner. He made rapid progress, being put into the first team as a 17-year-old in 1964 by Vic Buckingham, the English manager. Buckingham would later describe Cruyff as "God's gift to mankind, in the football sense".

Buckingham departed in 1964, being replaced by Rinus Michels, under whose guidance Ajax won the Dutch championship in 1965-66. In September 1966 Cruyff made his debut for the national team, and scored a last-minute equaliser in the 2-2 draw with Hungary in a European Championship qualifier. Cruyff's second international was not a success, as he was sent off in a 2-1 defeat against Czechoslovakia. This led to a lengthy exclusion from the national team although once he returned in 1967, he was to be a regular member for a decade.

The 1966 title was the first of a hat-trick for Ajax, with Cruyff emerging as the star of the team. In 1967 they also won the Dutch cup and became serious contenders in the European Cup, reaching the final in 1969, only to lose 4-1 to Milan. In 1970 Ajax also won the Dutch league and cup double, and the following year the team fulfilled its potential, by winning the European Cup, beating Panathinaikos 2-0 in the final. They also retained the Dutch cup that year. In a personal triumph, Cruyff won the European Footballer of the Year title in 1971, becoming the first Dutchman to achieve this honour. Ajax moved on to even greater heights in the 1971-72 season, winning the European Cup – Internazionale were beaten 2-0 in the final, in which Cruyff excelled, and scored both goals – plus the Dutch league and cup. This was the third successive season in which Ajax had won the cup. Meanwhile Cruyff was the top scorer in the Dutch championship, with 25 goals. In September 1972 Ajax won the World Club Championship, beating Independiente. This was followed by victory over Rangers in the inaugural European Super Cup, in January 1973. At the end of the 1972-73 season Ajax retained the Dutch title, and also won the European Cup for the third time, beating Juventus 1-0 in the final – with Cruyff inspiring a brilliant spell of football at the start of the match. His fame had now reached such heights that a documentary film, "Number 14 – Johan Cruyff", was a major success in cinemas across the Netherlands during the Spring of 1973.

In the summer of 1973 Cruyff moved from Ajax to Barcelona, for a world record fee of £922,000 – following in the footsteps of Michels, who had made the same transition at managerial level a couple of years earlier. In Cruyff's first season with the club, Barcelona won the Spanish league of 1973-74. The birth of Jordi Cruyff, the son of Johan and his wife Danny, at Amsterdam in February 1974, also helped build what was to become an enduring bond between the player and his new club. The birth was induced, to enable Johan to share the event with his wife, before rushing back to Spain for a vital league fixture, in which he helped Barcelona thrash Real Madrid 5-0.

The name Jordi was chosen simply because Danny liked it, but it also happened to be the name of the patron saint of Catalonia. Use of the name for Spanish children had actually been prohibited by Franco's government, but with Jordi having been born in the Netherlands, the Spanish dictatorship was unable to prevent its use in this case. Johan and Jordi thereby became unintentional symbols of Catalan defiance of Madrid. While at Barcelona, Cruyff won the European Footballer of the Year award for both 1973 and 1974. He also participated in Barcelona's run to the European Cup semi-finals in 1974-75. After the league success in 1974, Barcelona surprisingly gained only one further trophy during Cruyff's spell with the club, this being the Spanish Cup in 1978.

The highlight of Cruyff's international career was the 1974 World Cup finals, held in West Germany. He gave a series of brilliant displays, scoring twice in the 4-0 win against Argentina, and once in the 2-0 win against Brazil that booked a place in the final. In the first minute of the final, a run by Cruyff through West Germany's defence won a penalty, from which Johan Neeskens scored. West Germany, however, recovered to win the match 2-1.

Two years later Cruyff was part of the Dutch team which took third place in the 1976 European Championship. In February 1977 Cruyff gave what he later described as his best ever performance, as he inspired a 2-0 victory for the Netherlands against England at Wembley. That year, however, brought the end of his international career. He made a good contribution to his team's campaign in the World Cup qualifiers, but said he would not play in the following year's finals, due to security fears in Argentina. Cruyff bowed out with a total of 33 goals in 48 international appearances.

Cruyff's contribution to the 1978 World Cup finals was limited to the role of a studio pundit for ITV, where he worked alongside Brian Clough. Shortly before his death in 2004, Clough voted for Cruyff as the latter took first place in a UEFA poll of players and coaches, aimed at establishing who were Europe's most brilliant footballers. Clough explained his vote as follows: "Johan Cruyff was so talented he made opponents look like chumps for a pastime. He had pace, great dribbling skills, never faded from a game, and dominated matches with his massive ego. On top of that, he was a great captain and orchestrator, who hated giving the ball away".

Clough's point about the importance of the player's ego mirrors the view of Cruyff, who has said: "Football is a game you play with your brain. The game consists of different elements; technique, tactics, and stamina. But the main thing is tactics: insight, trust, and daring".

In 1979 Cruyff, having planned to retire at this point, joined the growing exodus of European stars to the North American Soccer League, where he played for Los Angeles Aztecs and then Washington Diplomats. Disliking the artificial pitches in the USA, Cruyff returned to Spain in 1981, joining Levante. He soon moved back to his homeland, and Ajax, with whom he won the Dutch league in 1982, followed by the league and cup double in 1983. Cruyff also won the league and cup double in 1984, but as part of a Feyenoord team, as his playing career ended with a short spell at the arch-rivals of Ajax.

Cruyff rapidly moved into management, enjoying successful spells in charge of both Ajax and Barcelona, the two clubs at the centre of his playing career. Besides the winning of trophies, Cruyff's success as a manager was reflected in the continuation of the tactical innovation that had been a vital part of his brilliance as a player. He led Ajax to the European Cup-Winners' Cup in 1987, beating Locomotive Leipzig 1-0 in the final. Two years later he won the same trophy with Barcelona, as they beat Sampdoria 2-0 in the final. In 1991, shortly after Cruyff had recovered from a heart attack, Barcelona appeared in the European Cup-Winners' Cup final again, but were beaten 2-1 by Manchester United, in Rotterdam. In the following year, Cruyff led Barcelona to win the European Cup for the first time, with Sampdoria being the beaten finalists – Ronald Koeman, a fellow-Dutchman, scored the only goal with a brilliant strike in extra time.

On the domestic front, Cruyff's Barcelona broke the dominance of Real Madrid, and won the Spanish league in four successive years from 1991 through to 1994. In the last of those years Barcelona also reached the European Cup final, but were crushed 4-0 by Milan. Thereafter a dip in Barcelona's form threatened Cruyff's position. There were also suggestions within the club that the manager was unduly favouring Jordi – his son having now become part of the squad – and also Jesus Angoy, a player who was married to Johan's daughter, Chantal. Cruyff was dismissed in 1996, being replaced by Bobby Robson, the former England manager. Cruyff was bitter at the way in which his association with the club ended, and has not returned to football management since the sacking. Despite his current absence from active participation in the game, Cruyff deservedly retains a legendary status as one of the greatest figures in the history of football.

1973-74

This season saw Ajax's dominance of the European Cup give way to the supremacy of Bayern Munich, the club they had eliminated in the previous season's quarter-finals. Ajax were given a bye through the first round in 1973-74, but then lost 2-1 on aggregate to CSKA Sofia, a club they had thrashed the previous season. The 'Total Football' invented by Ajax was now being developed by both Bayern and West Germany. Franz Beckenbauer, one of several Bayern players in the national team, was key to this, having effectively introduced the new role of attacking sweeper. Beckenbauer, nicknamed 'The Kaiser', was to win the World Cup with West Germany as both a player, in 1974, and a manager, in 1990, achievements which cemented his reputation as the greatest figure in the history of German football.

Bayern Munich's run in the 1973-74 European Cup almost ended before it began, as they struggled to beat Atvidabergs in the first round. After winning 3-1 at home, Bayern collapsed to a three goal deficit in Sweden, and required a late goal from Uli Hoeness to force extra time, following which they won the tie on penalties.

Liverpool had won both the English league and the UEFA Cup the previous season. Appearing in the European Cup for the first time since 1966-67, Liverpool made heavy weather of beating Jeunesse D'Esch, perennial representatives of Luxembourg, before their campaign was ended by a couple of 2-1 defeats against Red Star Belgrade, who played some great attacking football. The legendary Liverpool manager Bill Shankly grumbled about Red Star being "a bunch of fancy men". But the Kop applauded the Yugoslavs from the field.

Celtic continued their impressive European Cup record. A 9-1 aggregate win against TPS Turku, in the opening stage, was followed by a single goal victory for Celtic against Vejle in the second round. Bobby Lennox was the scorer.

In the first leg of their semi-final, Celtic were held to a goalless draw at home by Atletico Madrid. The Spanish champions stifled Celtic with brutality, and managed to avoid conceding a goal despite having three players sent off. Those dismissed included Ruben Ayala, an Argentinian striker who was to be one of the most recognisable players at the 1974 World Cup finals, due to hair that nearly reached his waist. UEFA admonished and fined Atletico, but failed to take real action. By contrast, when Partizan Tirana had four players sent off in a single match in 1987-88 they were disqualified from the competition, and banned for a further four years. In the return match, back at their own ground, Atletico Madrid played some football, and won 2-0. For the second time in three seasons, Celtic were beaten semi-finalists. In the other tie, Bayern Munich drew 1-1 away to Ujpest Dozsa, and then won the second leg 3-0 – Gerd Muller and Conny Torstensson each scoring twice .

Their appearance at the Heysel Stadium meant Bayern were the first club from West Germany to appear in the final since Eintracht Frankfurt faced Real Madrid in 1960. They included six players who had appeared for West Germany when they beat the Soviet Union 3-0, at the Heysel, in the 1972 European Championship final – Franz Beckenbauer, Paul Breitner, Uli Hoeness, Sepp Maier, Gerd Muller, and Georg Schwarzenbeck. Atletico Madrid had finally emerged from the shadow of their neighbours, Real Madrid. Atletico were managed by Juan Carlos Lorenzo, an Argentinian who had taken charge of his country's team in the 1966 World Cup finals, where their performance against England had provoked Alf Ramsey to call them "animals".

For 90 minutes the two teams were evenly matched, but did not manage to produce a goal. The deadlock continued through most of extra time, until Luis Aragones gave Atletico the lead from a free kick, with seven minutes remaining. Bayern dramatically saved the match in the final minute of extra time, as Schwarzenbeck scored with a shot from 30 yards. With the score level at 1-1, the teams moved to a replay, at the same venue, two days later. Bayern Munich's manager Udo Lattek fielded the same team for the replay, but Atletico made two changes, one of them enforced by the suspension of Javier Irureta. While the first match had attracted a crowd of 48,722, only 23,325 turned up for the replay, the smallest ever crowd for a European Cup final in the only final replay in the history of the competition. It was very different from the first match, as Bayern Munich dominated to win 4-0. Uli Hoeness opened the scoring after 27 minutes and Muller increased the lead 11 minutes into the second half, following a cross from Jupp Kapellmann. During his retirement, Muller picked this out as the best goal of his career, recalling that "I brought the ball down, turned, and thrashed it into the roof of the net from a really tight angle". He scored again 20 minutes from time, to take his tally for the season to nine, which made him the European Cup's leading scorer. On 82 minutes Hoeness scored his second goal of the match, running half the length of the pitch, taking the ball around goalkeeper Miguel Reina and clipping it into the net. Bayern Munich had became the first German club to win the European Cup, their victory owing a great deal to Beckenbauer's outstanding performance.

A few weeks later, the six Bayern players who had played in the 1972 European Championship final achieved their greatest success, appearing for West Germany as they beat the Netherlands 2-1 in the 1974 World Cup final.

1973-74

First round

		1st leg	2nd leg	agg
Waterford	Ujpest Dozsa	2-3	0-3	2-6
Bayern Munich	Atvidabergs	3-1	1-3	4-4
Bayern Munich won 4-3 on penalties				
Benfica	Olympiakos	1-0	1-0	2-0
TPS Turku	Celtic	1-6	0-3	1-9
Dynamo Dresden	Juventus	2-0	2-3	4-3
Zarja Voroshilovgrad	Apoel Nicosia	2-0	1-0	3-0
Red Star Belgrade	Stal Mielec	2-1	1-0	3-1

		1st leg	2nd leg	agg
Brugge	Floriana	8-0	2-0	10-0
Jeunesse D'Esch	Liverpool	1-1	0-2	1-3
Atletico Madrid	Galatasaray	0-0	1-0	1-0
Viking Stavanger	Spartak Trnava	1-2	0-1	1-3
Vejle	Nantes	2-2	1-0	3-2
CSKA Sofia	Wacker Innsbruck	3-0	1-0	4-0
FC Basle	Fram Reykjavik	5-0	6-2	11-2
Crusaders	Dynamo Bucharest	0-1	0-11	0-12

Second round

		1st leg	2nd leg	agg
Benfica	Ujpest Dozsa	1-1	0-2	1-3
Celtic	Vejle	0-0	1-0	1-0
Spartak Trnava	Zarja Voroshilovgrad	0-0	1-0	1-0
Red Star Belgrade	Liverpool	2-1	2-1	4-2
Brugge	FC Basle	2-1	4-6	6-7
Dynamo Bucharest	Atletico Madrid	0-2	2-2	2-4
Ajax	CSKA Sofia	1-0	0-2	1-2
Bayern Munich	Dynamo Dresden	4-3	3-3	7-6

Quarter-finals

		1st leg	2nd leg	agg
Spartak Trnava	Ujpest Dozsa	1-1	1-1	2-2

Ujpest Dozsa won 4-3 on penalties

		1st leg	2nd leg	agg
Bayern Munich	CSKA Sofia	4-1	1-2	5-3
Red Star Belgrade	Atletico Madrid	0-2	0-0	0-2
FC Basle	Celtic	3-2	2-4	5-6

Semi-finals

		1st leg	2nd leg	agg
Ujpest Dozsa	Bayern Munich	1-1	0-3	1-4
Celtic	Atletico Madrid	0-0	0-2	0-2

Final

May 15 1974 Brussels
Bayern Munich 1   Atletico Madrid 1 (after extra time)
Schwarzenbeck   Luis Aragones
Bayern Munich: Maier, Hansen, Breitner, Schwarzenbeck, Beckenbauer, Roth, Zobel, Hoeness, Torstensson (Durnberger), Muller, Kapellmann
Atletico Madrid: Reina, Melo, Capon, Adelardo, Heredia, Luis Aragones, Eusebio, Irureta, Ufarte (Becerra), Garate, Salcedo (Alberto)
HT: 0-0
FT: 0-0
Referee: Loraux (Belgium)
Attendance: 48,722

Replay

May 17 1974 Brussels
Bayern Munich 4   Atletico Madrid 0
Hoeness 2
Muller 2
Bayern Munich: Maier, Hansen, Breitner, Schwarzenbeck, Beckenbauer; Roth, Zobel, Hoeness, Torstensson, Muller, Kapellmann
Atletico Madrid: Reina, Melo, Capon, Adelardo (Benegas), Heredia, Luis Aragones, Eusebio, Alberto (Ufarte), Garate, Salcedo, Becerra
HT: 1-0
Referee: Delcourt (Belgium)
Attendance: 23,325

1974-75

Leeds United won the English championship in the spring of 1974, under the managership of Don Revie, who had led them to the European Cup semi-finals in 1970 but during the summer of 1974 he replaced the sacked Alf Ramsey as England manager. Brian Clough, who had led Derby County to the European Cup semi-finals the previous year, took the reins at Leeds. After an unsteady ride, featuring personality clashes with players, Clough was sacked by the club after just 44 days.

So Leeds began their European Cup campaign in the autumn without a first team manager, but they beat FC Zurich 5-3 on aggregate, with their goal poacher Allan Clarke, nicknamed 'Sniffer', netting three times.

Jimmy Armfield, who had played for England in the 1962 World Cup finals, was appointed manager in time for their next tie, which was against Ujpest Dozsa. Leeds won 2-1 in Hungary, despite the sending off of Duncan McKenzie, and 3-0 at Elland Road. Scottish international central defender Gordon McQueen scored in each leg. The remainder of the challenge from the British Isles was rapidly dispatched. Celtic were unexpectedly eliminated by Olympiakos in the first round. This season marked the end of a run of nine successive appearances by Celtic in the European Cup. Coleraine, making their only appearance to date, were thrashed 11-1 on aggregate by Feyenoord, with Krenz and Schoenmaker each scoring four times. Cork Celtic were given a walkover as Omonia Nicosia withdrew, before losing 7-1 to Ararat Erevan.

After a bye through the first round, Bayern Munich started their bid to retain the cup against Magdeburg, from East Germany. Magdeburg had also received a bye, benefiting from the reduction of the field for this season's competition to only 30 clubs. Part of the reason for the smaller than normal entry was that Lazio, the Italian champions, had been banned from Europe, due to hooliganism by their supporters when they lost to Ipswich Town in the 1973-74 UEFA Cup. Bayern beat Magdeburg 5-3 on aggregate although Magdeburg took a two goal lead in the first half at Munich. A second half hat-trick from Gerd Muller gave Bayern a 3-2 victory. He then scored twice as Bayern won the second leg 2-1. Jurgen Sparwasser, who had scored the only goal when East Germany unexpectedly beat West Germany in the 1974 World Cup finals, scored once in each leg for Magdeburg.

In the quarter-finals, Leeds beat Anderlecht 3-0 at home, with goals from a trio of Scottish internationals – Joe Jordan, Gordon McQueen, and Peter Lorimer – and then 1-0 away, the scorer being Billy Bremner, another Scottish international. In between the second round and the quarter-finals, internal strife at Bayern Munich had led to the resignation of Udo Lattek, who was replaced by Dettmar Cramer. Bayern now struggled to eliminate Ararat Erevan, scoring twice late in the first leg, before losing the second leg by a single goal. Barcelona, who were in the competition for the first time since losing the 1961 final, won 5-0 on aggregate against Atvidabergs, the first Swedish club to reach the last eight since Malmo in 1961. Barcelona's new strength owed much to the influence of Johan Cruyff and Johan Neeskens, both of whom had followed Rinus Michels, the manager, from Ajax.

Barcelona's opponents in the semi-finals were Leeds, who won the first leg 2-1, with an excellent display, featuring goals from Bremner and Clarke. An early goal from Lorimer, followed by some stout defending by Leeds, restricted Barcelona to a 1-1 draw at the Nou Camp, despite Leeds having McQueen sent off. Leeds thereby became the first British team to reach the final since Celtic in 1970. In the other semi-final Bayern Munich ended Saint-Etienne's run, drawing 0-0 in France, and winning 2-0 in West Germany.

A crowd of 48,374 watched the final at the Parc des Princes. The Paris stadium, used in 1956, was chosen in honour of this being the twentieth European Cup final. A reunion was held in Paris by some of the leading personalities of the early European Cup, and a plaque was unveiled at the Ambassador Hotel to mark the meeting there in April 1955, which had set the scene for the inaugural competition.

Nine players in Bayern Munich's team had featured when they won the final a year earlier – Beckenbauer, Hoeness, Kapellmann, Maier, Muller, Roth, Schwarzenbeck, Torstensson, and Zobel. Despite the absence of the suspended McQueen, the Leeds team included nine players who were current internationals for either England, Scotland, Wales, or the Republic of Ireland – the two exceptions were Frank Gray and David Stewart, both of whom later played for Scotland. Terry Yorath, a Welsh international, is often recalled nowadays as the father of Gabby, a woman who presents Champions League coverage on British television.

Bayern Munich were the pre-match favourites, but it was Leeds who controlled the play in the first half. They created a series of goalscoring opportunities, and were twice unlucky to have penalty appeals turned down by Michel Kitabdjian, the French referee, who had a poor game. Both appeals stemmed from infringements by Franz Beckenbauer, who handled on the first occasion, and subsequently tripped Clarke. Leeds continued to take the game to the Germans after the break, and appeared to have taken the lead on 66 minutes, as Lorimer struck a powerful volley, but the referee disallowed the attempt, as Bremner had been in an offside position when his team-mate hit the shot – but it was questionable whether he was interfering with play. Five minutes later Bayern unexpectedly took the lead, as Roth completed a swift counter-attack. Leeds fought back with further attacking football, but Bayern Munich resisted, and then doubled their lead eight minutes from time. Gerd Muller scored in another breakaway attack, to make himself the leading scorer in the European Cup for the third successive season – this time his total was six goals. Muller, nicknamed 'The Bomber', scored a total of 37 goals in the European Cup. He was also West Germany's leading international goalscorer, with a phenomenal 68 goals in 62 games.

Jimmy Armfield later recalled the bitterness felt by Leeds due to the defeat: "The scene in the dressing room afterwards was awful. The lads came in and just tossed their losers' medals to one side. I told them to put them on the table, because they would want them later. Then, as they sat down, I suddenly realised that I did not know what to say to them. For the first time in my life I was lost for words. I started to tell them how well they had done after the terrible beginning to the season. Then I saw Billy Bremner just staring at me, and I knew I should have kept my mouth shut".

Unfortunately a hooligan minority among the Leeds' followers reacted aggressively to their misfortune, vandalising the seats in which they were sat, throwing debris on to the field, and fighting with the French police. The closing stages of the match were played out against this ugly and dangerous backdrop, and Leeds' hooligans rioted in Paris for several hours after the match. A year earlier supporters of Tottenham Hotspur had rioted as their club lost to Feyenoord in the UEFA Cup final. UEFA had fined Tottenham a mere £500, and ordered them to play their next three home European matches away from their own ground. A few weeks after the 1975 European Cup final, UEFA took decisive action, banning Leeds United from the European competitions for four years. Leeds, who felt they had been severely punished for the actions of a minority among their supporters, appealed against the ban, and UEFA reduced it to a single year. The rioting of Tottenham and Leeds supporters began a series of hooligan outbreaks by Englishmen following club and country on the continent, which was to descend into the Heysel tragedy in 1985.

78

1974-75

First round

		1st leg	2nd leg	agg
Leeds United	FC Zurich	4-1	1-2	5-3
Celtic	Olympiakos	1-1	0-2	1-3
Universitatea Craiova	Atvidabergs	2-1	1-3	3-4
Valletta	HJK Helsinki	1-0	1-4	2-4
Levski Spartak	Ujpest Dozsa	0-3	1-4	1-7
Jeunesse D'Esch	Fenerbahce	2-3	0-2	2-5
Viking Stavanger	Ararat Erevan	0-2	2-4	2-6
Hvidovre	Ruch Chorzow	0-0	1-2	1-2
Slovan Bratislava	Anderlecht	4-2	1-3	5-5
Anderlecht won on away goals				
Feyenoord	Coleraine	7-0	4-1	11-1
Saint-Etienne	Sporting Lisbon	2-0	1-1	3-1
Voest Linz	Barcelona	0-0	0-5	0-5
Hajduk Split	IBK Keflavik	7-1	2-0	9-1
Cork Celtic walked over, Omonia Nicosia withdrew				

Second round

		1st leg	2nd leg	agg
Ujpest Dozsa	Leeds United	1-2	0-3	1-5
Bayern Munich	Magdeburg	3-2	2-1	5-3
Hajduk Split	Saint-Etienne	4-1	1-5	5-6
Feyenoord	Barcelona	0-0	0-3	0-3
Cork Celtic	Ararat Erevan	1-2	0-5	1-7
Ruch Chorzow	Fenerbahce	2-1	2-0	4-1
HJK Helsinki	Atvidabergs	0-3	0-1	0-4
Anderlecht	Olympiakos	5-1	0-3	5-4

Quarter-finals

		1st leg	2nd leg	agg
Bayern Munich	Ararat Erevan	2-0	0-1	2-1
Leeds United	Anderlecht	3-0	1-0	4-0
Ruch Chorzow	Saint-Etienne	3-2	0-2	3-4
Barcelona	Atvidabergs	2-0	3-0	5-0

Semi-finals

		1st leg	2nd leg	agg
Saint-Etienne	Bayern Munich	0-0	0-2	0-2
Leeds United	Barcelona	2-1	1-1	3-2

Final

May 28 1975 Paris
Bayern Munich 2   Leeds United 0
Roth
Muller
Bayern Munich: Maier, Beckenbauer, Schwarzenbeck, Durnberger, Andersson (Weiss), Zobel, Roth, Kapellmann, Hoeness (Wunder), Muller, Torstensson
Leeds United: Stewart, Reaney, F Gray, Madeley, Hunter, Bremner, Giles, Yorath, (E Gray), Lorimer, Clarke, Jordan
HT: 0-0
Referee: Kitabdjian (France)
Attendance: 48,374

1975-76

Following Derby's appearance in the 1973 semi-finals, Brian Clough had left the club, and been replaced by Dave Mackay. Prior to this Mackay had been in charge at Nottingham Forest, the club to which Clough moved after managing Derby and Leeds. Mackay led Derby to their second League title in four seasons in 1974-75. Derby started by losing by a single goal away to Slovan Bratislava in the first round of the European Cup, but won the return 3-0, with Francis Lee scoring twice. In the next round Derby achieved a great 4-1 victory at home to Real Madrid, in which Charlie George scored a hat-trick. Real in turn won their home leg 5-1, after extra time, to seal a dramatic 6-5 aggregate win. Derby have yet to return to the European Cup, but Clough was destined for further glory.

Rangers, who had ended Celtic's run of nine successive Scottish titles, were in the European Cup for the first time since 1964-65. They began with a straightforward win against Bohemians, who were representing the Republic of Ireland for the first time, but lost twice to Saint-Etienne at the next stage.

Bayern Munich had finished only 10th in the Bundesliga but were in the competition as defending champions and started with an 8-1 aggregate win against Jeunesse D'Esch, in which Schuster scored five times. The West German champions were Borussia Monchengladbach who beat Wacker Innsbruck 7-2, with Jupp Heynckes scoring four times in the second leg. Ujpest Dozsa's run of six consecutive appearances was ended by Benfica.

The Portuguese faced Bayern in the quarter-finals, drawing 0-0 at home, before being thrashed 5-1, with Bernd Durnberger and Gerd Muller each scoring twice. By contrast Borussia Monchengladbach's run ended, as they lost to Real Madrid on away goals. Real's Carlos Santillana and Borussia's Jupp Heynckes, who were the joint leading scorers this season, with six goals each, both scored in the tie. PSV Eindhoven recovered from a 2-0 defeat away to Hajduk Split, by winning the second leg 3-0, after extra time. Exactly the same pattern saw Saint-Etienne fight back to beat Dynamo Kiev, with Dominique Rocheteau scoring the decisive goal in extra time.

The semi-finals brought the first European Cup meeting between Real Madrid and Bayern Munich, which set the scene for an intense rivalry. The first leg, at the Bernabeu, was a rather drab 1-1 draw, the flashpoint coming when the players and officials were leaving the pitch at the end. A Real Madrid supporter ran on to the field, threatened Erich Linemayr, the Austrian referee, before hitting Gerd Muller. He was restrained by other Bayern players and arrested by the police. Muller scored Bayern's goal, and he was to strike twice more as Bayern won the second leg 2-0. Paul Breitner, who had moved from Bayern to Real in 1974, played for the Spanish club in the second leg. Breitner was a controversial personality, with pronounced left-wing opinions, who scored for West Germany in the final of both the 1974 and 1982 World Cups. In the other semi-final, Saint-Etienne beat PSV Eindhoven by a single goal.

Bayern were the favourites to win the final in Glasgow. The team selected by Dettmar Cramer included nine players who had played for them in either or both of the 1974 and 1975 finals, namely Beckenbauer, Durnberger, Hansen, Hoeness, Kappellmann, Maier, Muller, Roth, and Schwarzenbeck. Sepp Maier, the goalkeeper, caused some amusement with his large gloves and shorts, but his consistent performances were a major strength of the Bayern team, for whom he made an amazing 442 consecutive appearances. Saint-Etienne were managed by Robert Herbin, who had played for France in the 1966 World Cup finals. They were weakened by the absence from the starting line-up of Rocheteau, an exciting 21-year-old forward, who had been injured against PSV, and had to be put on the substitutes' bench. Saint-Etienne were the first French club to reach the European Cup final since Reims in 1959. They had knocked Bayern out of the competition back in 1969-70, but Bayern had won the more recent meeting, in the 1974-75 semi-finals.

The 1960 final had been a wonderful match, with ten goals, played before a crowd of 134,000 at Hampden Park. Sixteen years later the 1976 final was unlikely to match this, but a smaller crowd of 54,864 were still treated to an enthralling contest, albeit one settled by a single goal. Bayern appeared to have taken the lead within two minutes, through Gerd Muller, but Karoly Palotai, the Hungarian referee, ruled it out for offside. The decision stemmed from an error by a linesman, as Muller had timed correctly his run on to a pass from Bernd Durnberger.

During the first half, Saint-Etienne had most of the play, putting together some fine attacks, while Bayern concentrated on defensive strength, and occasional counter-attack. The French were unlucky not to score, as they twice hit the woodwork towards the interval, through a shot from Dominique Bathenay, and then a header by Jacques Santini (who was later to manage the French national team and briefly Tottenham Hotspur). Bayern broke the deadlock 12 minutes after half time, as Beckenbauer tapped a free kick to Franz Roth, who scored with a powerful shot. For the second year in succession Roth had given Bayern the lead in the final, and both times it was against the run of play. Saint-Etienne pushed for an equaliser during the remainder of the match, and went close several times as their play was improved by the introduction of Rocheteau, as a substitute, eight minutes from time.

Bayern Munich had now matched Ajax, by winning a hat-trick of European Cups. Bayern's football did not quite reach the heights achieved by Ajax a few years earlier, but it did keep alive the ideals of 'Total Football'.

1975-76

First round

		1st leg	2nd leg	agg
Benfica	Fenerbahce	7-0	0-1	7-1
Borussia Monchengladbach	Wacker Innsbruck	1-1	6-1	7-2
KB Copenhagen	Saint-Etienne	0-2	1-3	1-5
CSKA Sofia	Juventus	2-1	0-2	2-3
Floriana	Hajduk Split	0-5	0-3	0-8
Jeunesse D'Esch	Bayern Munich	0-5	1-3	1-8
Linfield	PSV Eindhoven	1-2	0-8	1-10
Malmo	Magdeburg	2-1	1-2	3-3
Malmo won 2-1 on penalties				
Olympiakos	Dynamo Kiev	2-2	0-1	2-3
Rangers	Bohemians	4-1	1-1	5-2
Real Madrid	Dynamo Bucharest	4-1	0-1	4-2
Ruch Chorzow	KuPS Kuopio	5-0	2-2	7-2
Slovan Bratislava	Derby County	1-0	0-3	1-3
Ujpest Dozsa	FC Zurich	4-0	1-5	5-5
Ujpest Dozsa won on away goals				
RWD Molenbeek	Viking Stavanger	3-2	1-0	4-2
Omonia Nicosia	IA Akranes	2-1	0-4	2-5

Second round

		1st leg	2nd leg	agg
Benfica	Ujpest Dozsa	5-2	1-3	6-5
Borussia Monchengladbach	Juventus	2-0	2-2	4-2
Derby County	Real Madrid	4-1	1-5	5-6

Dynamo Kiev	IA Akranes	3-0	2-0	5-0
Hajduk Split	RWD Molenbeek	4-0	3-2	7-2
Malmo	Bayern Munich	1-0	0-2	1-2
Ruch Chorzow	PSV Eindhoven	1-3	0-4	1-7
Saint-Etienne	Rangers	2-0	2-1	4-1

Quarter-finals

		1st leg	2nd leg	agg
Benfica	Bayern Munich	0-0	1-5	1-5
Borussia Monchengladbach	Real Madrid	2-2	1-1	3-3
Real Madrid won on away goals				
Dynamo Kiev	Saint-Etienne	2-0	0-3	2-3
Hajduk Split	PSV Eindhoven	2-0	0-3	2-3

Semi-finals

		1st leg	2nd leg	agg
Real Madrid	Bayern Munich	1-1	0-2	1-3
Saint-Etienne	PSV Eindhoven	1-0	0-0	1-0

Final

May 12 1976 Glasgow
Bayern Munich 1   Saint-Etienne 0
Roth
Bayern Munich: Maier, Hansen, Schwarzenbeck, Beckenbauer, Horsmann, Roth, Durnberger, Kapellmann, Rummenigge, Muller, Hoeness
Saint-Etienne: Curkovic, Repellini, Piazza, Lopez, Janvion, Bathenay, Santini, Larque, P Revelli, H Revelli, Sarramagna (Rocheteau)
HT: 0-0
Referee: Palotai (Hungary)
Attendance: 54,864

Franz Beckenbauer

Franz Beckenbauer won virtually every major honour he competed for as player and manager, before becoming an influential football administrator. His enormous reputation has been cemented by the manner of his success, with the authority that led to him being nicknamed the 'Kaiser' being mixed with elegance, tactical innovation, determination, and sportsmanship. When UEFA ran dual polls in 2004 to rank Europe's greatest footballers, Beckenbauer took second place among the supporters, and third place from the players and coaches.

He was born in Munich on September 11 1945, four months after the surrender of Germany in the Second World War. As a youth he combined football with work as an insurance salesman, as his club, Bayern Munich, were left as a regional league team when the national Bundesliga was formed in 1963. Beckenbauer made his debut for Bayern in 1964, as an outside left, but soon moved to a midfield role. His club were promoted to the Bundesliga in 1965, won the cup in both 1966 and 1967, and followed this with a league and cup double in 1969. Bayern also tasted continental success for the first time, beating Rangers 1-0 in the 1967 European Cup-Winners' Cup final.

Beckenbauer first played for West Germany in September 1965, when Sweden were beaten 2-1 in a vital World Cup qualifier. At the age of only 20, Beckenbauer emerged as one of the stars of the 1966 World Cup finals, and scored four times. He was nearly suspended from the final, as it appeared that he had been booked twice in the tournament, but on the morning of the match the Germans persuaded FIFA that there had been a case of mistaken identity. Beckenbauer's role in the match, under the direction of Helmut Schoen, the German manager, was to shadow Bobby Charlton. Beckenbauer restricted Charlton's influence, but at the cost of being unable to add his own strength to the German attack, as England won 4-2.

At the start of the 1970s, Beckenbauer invented a new position, that of the libero, a sweeper who broke with the defensive conventions of catenaccio, and frequently advanced upfield to instigate attacks. With Beckenbauer playing this new role, Bayern Munich and West Germany developed the concept of 'Total Football', which originated with Ajax and the Netherlands. West Germany took third place at the 1970 World Cup finals, Beckenbauer scoring the team's first goal against England in the quarter-finals, as a 2-0 deficit was turned into a 3-2 victory, after extra time. In the semi-finals, the Germans lost 4-3 to Italy, in an amazing contest, as Beckenbauer bravely played through extra time with an arm strapped to his chest, having been injured by a cynical challenge. In 1972 West Germany, with Beckenbauer as captain, won the European Championship. England were defeated in the quarter-finals, and in the final the Soviet Union were beaten 3-0.

After Bayern won the West German cup in 1971, they followed it with the Bundesliga a year later, and Beckenbauer was voted European Footballer of the Year. Bayern retained the West German title in 1973, and completed a hat trick of titles the following year. 1974 also saw the club win the European Cup for the first time, with Beckenbauer orchestrating a 4-0 win against Atletico Madrid in a replayed final.

A few weeks later West Germany won the World Cup. Their 2-1 win against the Netherlands in the final, at Munich, was a marvellous exhibition of 'Total Football', in which Beckenbauer's team outwitted Johan Cruyff and the Dutch masters. A rivalry between Beckenbauer and Cruyff, based on mutual respect, led to a lasting friendship. Cruyff has said of his relationship with Beckenbauer: "We both think about what is best for the game, and how you can improve things. On the field our quality was football – controlling the ball, trying to win, guiding the team. That is why we were both exceptional in that sense. If you are like that, you can never be enemies in football. Before, during, and after, we are friends".

Bayern retained the European Cup in 1975, with a fortunate 2-0 win against Leeds United, who had two strong appeals for penalties, due to apparent infringements by Beckenbauer, turned down. The following year, they were continental champions for a third successive season, beating Saint Etienne 1-0 in the final, and competed in the World Club Championship for the first time, beating Cruzeiro of Brazil 2-0 on aggregate. Beckenbauer featured in both of these victories, and also regained the European Footballer of the Year award. West Germany reached a second successive European Championship final in 1976, only to lose on penalties to Czechoslovakia, following a brilliant match that was drawn 2-2 after extra time. This was the last of the five major international tournaments in which Beckenbauer played.

In 1977 he retired from the national team, having played 103 games, scoring 14 goals. He also left Bayern, moving to the USA, where he joined New York Cosmos, and played alongside Pele. Beckenbauer helped them win the North American Soccer League title in 1977, 1978, and 1980. Following the last of these victories, he returned to West Germany, spending a couple of seasons with Hamburg and helping them to win the Bundesliga in 1982. During his spells with Bayern Munich and Hamburg, Beckenbauer played a total of 424 games in the Bundesliga, and scored 44 goals. His playing career ended in 1983, with a season back at New York Cosmos.

Beckenbauer was controversially appointed coach of the West German national team in 1984, despite being only thirty eight years old and lacking any previous coaching experience. When the team arrived in Mexico for the 1986 World Cup finals, Beckenbauer alienated the players by publicly saying that they lacked the experience required to win the trophy. The team battled through to the final, where they lost 3-2 against Argentina. Two years later, as hosts to the European Championship finals, West Germany lost 2-1 to the Netherlands in a semi-final.

Beckenbauer's reign as national manager ended in triumph, at the 1990 World Cup finals. After beating England on penalties in the semi-finals, West Germany reversed their defeat of four years earlier with a 1-0 victory over Argentina. Beckenbauer had emulated Brazil's Mario Zagalo, by winning the World Cup as both a player and manager. Fifteen years later, when requested to nominate his most unforgettable moment, Beckenbauer replied: "I have been asked this many times. Spontaneously, the moment that always comes to mind is when I was walking alone across the pitch of the Olympic Stadium in Rome after the 1990 final. Why? Even today, I cannot explain. It was simple intuition, like waking up from a dream that you cannot remember. But it was very definitely a wonderful dream".

A spell at Marseille in 1990-91, as coach and then general manager, was unsatisfactory for Beckenbauer in personal terms, although the club won the French league at the end of the season, and reached the European Cup final – losing to Red Star Belgrade. Beckenbauer followed this with a welcome return to Bayern Munich. He coached them to the Bundesliga title in 1994, followed by the UEFA Cup in 1996 – with Bordeaux being beaten 5-1 on aggregate in the final – and was promoted to become president of the club.

In 1998 Beckenbauer was appointed vice-president of the German football federation, and spearheaded their bid to stage the 2006 World Cup finals – while Bobby Charlton played a similar role for the rival English bid. When FIFA made the decision in July 2000, Germany were successful, being narrowly selected ahead of South Africa amidst disputes over the process, with England trailing far behind. Beckenbauer continued to steer the project, as head of the World Cup organising committee, and in June 2005 spoke about the prospects for the tournament: "Abroad, a perfect World Cup in Germany is taken as read because the Germans are regarded as perfectionists. We can and want to reinforce this reputation, by succeeding in turning the biggest global sporting event to take place in this country since reunification into one huge celebratory get-together – in a colourful, cheerful, easy-going, and peaceful country. First and foremost, the World Cup should be a festival of football. That is the focus of all our plans and activities". After more than forty years in the spotlight as player, coach, and administrator, Franz Beckenbauer continues to contribute his massive ability, and belief, to the game of football.

Chapter 5

English Triumph 1976-1982

1976-77

The 1976-77 competition marked the beginning of a new stage in the history of the European Cup, in which English clubs were dominant. Liverpool – appearing in the competition for the first time since 1973-74 – led the way. The club were enjoying the early stage of a mastery of English domestic football that eventually stretched across 18 seasons, from 1972-73 to 1989-90. During that period they won the Football League title 11 times, and finished as runners-up six times. Meanwhile they took the FA Cup three times, and were beaten finalists twice. The club also won the League Cup four times, and were runners-up twice. This amazing run of success was inspired by four managers – Bill Shankly, Bob Paisley, Joe Fagan, and Kenny Dalglish – each of whom enjoyed long associations with the club, and built a series of outstanding teams.

In the autumn of 1976 it appeared to be a case of business as usual, in the form of German domination of the European Cup. Bayern Munich opened their defence of the title they had won for the previous three seasons with a 7-1 aggregate win against Koge. Borussia Monchengladbach, West Germany's second representative in this season's competition, beat FK Austria 3-1. Saint-Etienne, the previous season's beaten finalists, also progressed, but only by scoring the single goal in their two meetings with CSKA Sofia.

Liverpool beat Crusaders, from Northern Ireland, 7-0 on aggregate, but the margin of victory was deceptive – four of the goals were scored in the last nine minutes of the second leg. The remainder of the challenge from the British Isles evaporated immediately. Rangers lost 2-1 on aggregate to FC Zurich, while Dundalk, from the Republic of Ireland, gained a creditable 1-1 draw at home to PSV Eindhoven, but lost the return 6-0, Rene van der Kerkhof scoring four in the latter match.

The shift in power only became apparent in the closing stages of the competition, during the spring of 1977. In the quarter-finals, Liverpool lost their away leg by a single goal against Saint-Etienne, for whom Dominique Bathenay scored late in the game. The return match was full of drama, and ranks among the most famous ever played by Liverpool. Kevin Keegan unintentionally opened the scoring in the second minute, with a mis-hit cross. Early in the second half Bathenay restored the French champions' aggregate lead, with a long-range shot. Ray Kennedy put Liverpool back ahead on the night a few minutes later. As time ticked away, Liverpool faced elimination on the away goals rule until David Fairclough scored a brilliant goal six minutes from time – weaving through the St Etienne defence before unleashing a powerful shot. Liverpool had won 3-1 on the night, and 3-2 on aggregate. The decisive strike was one of a series of vital goals scored by Fairclough as a substitute, earning him the nickname 'Supersub'.

Bayern Munich's dominance of the European Cup was unexpectedly ended by Dynamo Kiev, who won 2-1 on aggregate – both of the Kiev goals being scored in the last seven minutes of the second leg, after they had lost the first match. Borussia Monchengladbach continued to fly the flag for West Germany, with a 3-2 win against Brugge, but Dynamo Dresden, from East Germany, lost to FC Zurich on away goals.

In the semi-finals, Liverpool were paired with FC Zurich, the team who had disposed of Rangers. The Swiss took an early lead in their home leg, as Peter Risi put away a penalty, but Liverpool took control of the tie with a 3-1 victory, as Phil Neal scored twice – one from the penalty spot. The second leg was a formality, which Liverpool won 3-0, with Jimmy Case scoring twice. Liverpool's 6-1 aggregate win was the largest margin in a European Cup semi-final since 1965, when Benfica beat Vasas Gyor 5-0.

A year earlier, in 1964, FC Zurich had been on the wrong end of an 8-1 semi-final scoreline against Real Madrid. The margin of Zurich's defeat against Liverpool belied the contribution they had made to the competition that season, which included five goals from Franco Cucinotta, who emerged as the joint leading scorer, along with Bayern Munich's Gerd Muller. In the other semi, Borussia Monchengladbach avoided a repeat of the slip up experienced by Bayern Munich, as they beat Dynamo Kiev (who were becoming the first team from the Soviet Union to appear in the semi-finals) 2-1 on aggregate.

During the latter part of the season a great deal of attention was focused on the attempt by Liverpool to achieve a unique treble, by winning the Football League, FA Cup, and European Cup. The League title was duly won, but Liverpool's attempt to complete the domestic double failed, as they were beaten 2-1 by Manchester United in the FA Cup final. Hopes of the treble had therefore been ended when Liverpool travelled to Rome to meet Borussia Monchengladbach on May 25, just four days after the FA Cup final. Liverpool sought to lift themselves again, and become the first British club to win the European title since Manchester United had done so nine years earlier.

One good omen was that the 1977 final was being played on the tenth anniversary of Celtic becoming the first British club to win the European Cup. Liverpool fielded seven past or present England internationals – Ian Callaghan, Ray Clemence, Emlyn Hughes, Kevin Keegan, Ray Kennedy, Phil Neal, and Tommy Smith. Emlyn Hughes, the captain of the team, eventually played 657 senior matches for Liverpool. An enthusiastic defender, who had picked up the nickname 'Crazy Horse', Hughes appeared 62 times for England between 1969 and 1980. Following his retirement from football, he worked in television, but tragically died from a brain tumour at the age of 57, in 2004.

Although Liverpool had beaten Borussia Monchengladbach in the UEFA Cup final of 1973, the Germans were formidable opponents. They had won West Germany's Bundesliga for the third successive year in 1977 – they had also won the UEFA Cup in 1975. Borussia fielded four players from the West Germany team which won the World Cup in 1974, namely Rainer Bonhof, Jupp Heynckes, Berti Vogts, and Herbert Wimmer. They also had the advantage of being managed by Udo Lattek, who led Bayern Munich to victory in the 1974 European Cup final.

Liverpool had the better of the early play, but without creating many clear goalscoring opportunities. Borussia went close to scoring after 20 minutes, as Bonhof beat Clemence with a powerful shot from outside the penalty area, only to see his effort hit a post. A couple of minutes later fortune was again unkind to Borussia, as they lost Wimmer due to an injury.

On 27 minutes Liverpool's Callaghan intercepted the ball from Bonhof, and fed Steve Heighway on the right wing, whereupon the latter player directed a fine pass into the path of Terry McDermott, who drove a first-time shot past Wolfgang Kneib, the Borussia goalkeeper, and into the left-hand corner of the net.

This cleverly-worked goal gave Liverpool a lead which they held until half time, with methodical football. One of the main reasons for Liverpool's control of the match was the performance of Keegan, whose consistently inventive attacking play gave Vogts, his ever-attendant marker, a torrid time. As the players walked into the tunnel at half time, Keegan asked Vogts: "Are you going into our dressing room or yours?"

Borussia Monchengladbach roused themselves to put pressure on Liverpool at the start of the second half, and equalised just five minutes after the restart, with a goal from Allan Simonsen – the man who led the revival of Danish football from the late 1970s. A pass from Liverpool's Case to Neal was seized upon by Simonsen, who cut in from the left wing, and drove a long-range shot into the top right-hand corner of the goal.

Twelve minutes later Borussia almost took the lead, as Simonsen fed Uli Stielike, but the latter's shot was blocked by Clemence's knees. The save proved to be the turning point. Liverpool regained the lead a couple of minutes later, when Heighway's corner from the left was met at the near post with a powerful header from Tommy Smith. It was a rare goal for Smith, a rugged defender who was making his 600th senior appearance for Liverpool.

Now that they were back in the lead, Liverpool made no mistake, dominating the remainder of the match. Keegan's torment of Vogts culminated with a powerful run into the Borussia area seven minutes from time, which caused the German to concede a penalty. Neal scored from the spot, his fourth goal of the European campaign – three of which were pentalties – and completed Liverpool's historic 3-1 victory.

The Liverpool players and club officials held a celebratory banquet at their hotel, and Vogts sportingly dropped in to buy Keegan a drink. It was the beginning of a lasting friendship between Keegan, who was about to move to Hamburg, and Vogts, who would later manage Germany and Scotland. Bob Paisley told the party: "This is the second time I have beaten the Germans here. The first time was in 1944. I drove into Rome on a tank when the city was liberated. If anyone had told me I would be back here to see us win the European Cup 33 years later I would have told them they were mad".

It was not the most diplomatic comment, but understandable in the excitement. Liverpool had emulated Manchester United's European triumph, but in contrast to United's swift decline – they were relegated from the First Division just six years after winning the European Cup – this was just the start of European dominance for Liverpool.

1976-77

First round

		1st leg	2nd leg	agg
IA Akranes	Trabzonspor	1-3	2-3	3-6
FK Austria	Borussia Monchengladbach	1-0	0-3	1-3
Brugge	Steaua Bucharest	2-1	1-1	3-2
CSKA Sofia	Saint-Etienne	0-0	0-1	0-1
Dynamo Dresden	Benfica	2-0	0-0	2-0
Dundalk	PSV Eindhoven	1-1	0-6	1-7

Ferencvaros	Jeunesse D'Esch	5-1	6-2	11-3
Dynamo Kiev	Partizan Belgrade	3-0	2-0	5-0
Omonia Nicosia	PAOK Salonika	0-2	1-1	1-3
Rangers	FC Zurich	1-1	0-1	1-2
Stal Mielec	Real Madrid	1-2	0-1	1-3
Viking Stavanger	Banik Ostrava	2-1	0-2	2-3
Torino	Malmo	2-1	1-1	3-2
Liverpool	Crusaders	2-0	5-0	7-0
Koge	Bayern Munich	0-5	1-2	1-7
Sliema Wanderers	TPS Turku	2-1	0-1	2-2

TPS Turku won on away goals

Second round

		1st leg	2nd leg	agg
Dynamo Kiev	PAOK Salonika	4-0	2-0	6-0
Ferencvaros	Dynamo Dresden	1-0	0-4	1-4
Real Madrid	Brugge	0-0	0-2	0-2
Saint-Etienne	PSV Eindhoven	1-0	0-0	1-0
Torino	Borussia Monchengladbach	1-2	0-0	1-2
Trabzonspor	Liverpool	1-0	0-3	1-3
FC Zurich	TPS Turku	2-0	1-0	3-0
Banik Ostrava	Bayern Munich	2-1	0-5	2-6

Quarter-finals

		1st leg	2nd leg	agg
Bayern Munich	Dynamo Kiev	1-0	0-2	1-2
Borussia Monchengladbach	Brugge	2-2	1-0	3-2
Saint-Etienne	Liverpool	1-0	1-3	2-3
FC Zurich	Dynamo Dresden	2-1	2-3	4-4

FC Zurich won on away goals

Semi-finals

		1st leg	2nd leg	agg
Dynamo Kiev	Borussia Monchengladbach	1-0	0-2	1-2
FC Zurich	Liverpool	1-3	0-3	1-6

Final

May 25 1977 Rome

Liverpool 3   Borussia Monchengladbach 1

McDermott   Simonsen

Smith

Neal (penalty)

Liverpool: Clemence, Neal, Jones, Smith, Hughes, Case, R Kennedy, Callaghan, McDermott, Keegan, Heighway

Borussia Monchengladbach: Kneib, Vogts, Klinkhammer, Wittkamp, Schaffer, Wohlers (Hannes), Wimmer (Kulik), Stielike, Bonhof, Simonsen, Heynckes

HT: 1-0

Referee: Wurtz (France)

Attendance: 52,078

Kevin Keegan

Although not the most gifted Kevin Keegan was among the outstanding players of his generation. He won the European Cup with Liverpool, reached the final with Hamburg, and was twice winner of the European Footballer of the Year award. He also played 63 times for England, scoring 21 goals. His playing career has been followed by a variety of managerial roles, including a spell as England coach. All of this sprang from modest beginnings. Keegan lacked either great height or physical stature, and was not blessed with natural footballing talent, but he more than compensated for this with work-rate, and determination to succeed. It was a combination that led to Keegan being nicknamed 'Mighty Mouse' by the fans of Hamburg.

He was born on February 1 1951, at Armthorpe in Yorkshire. After leaving school, he was employed at a brass factory in Doncaster, and played in the works' football team. This led to Keegan being signed in 1968 by Scunthorpe United, who were relegated to the Fourth Division that year. In 1971 Keegan moved to Liverpool, who paid Scunthorpe a fee of £35,000. Although most Liverpool recruits had to spend time in the reserves learning the Liverpool way Keegan gained a regular place during the 1971-72 season, helping them to third place in the League, just a point behind the champions, Derby County. In November 1972 he made his debut for England, appearing in a 1-0 World Cup qualifying victory over Wales.

At the end of the 1972-73 season Liverpool won the League, and Keegan scored twice in the 3-2 aggregate win against Borussia Monchengladbach in the UEFA Cup final. A year later Keegan also netted twice, as Liverpool beat Newcastle United 3-0 in the 1974 FA Cup final. In between those two finals, he appeared in Liverpool's short campaign in the 1973-74 European Cup. The summer of 1974 brought a low point for Keegan, as he and Billy Bremner, of Leeds United, were sent off for fighting in the Charity Shield, following which each player received a lengthy suspension. In 1976 Liverpool repeated the dual League and UEFA Cup victory of 1973, beating Brugge 4-3 on aggregate in the final of the latter competition, with Keegan accounting for two of the goals. Keegan's Liverpool career climaxed in 1977, a year in which they retained the League title, reached the FA Cup final, and then beat Borussia Monchengladbach 3-1 in the European Cup final. After starring in the European Cup win, Keegan, seeking a new challenge, moved to Hamburg for £500,000.

Initially he found it hard to settle at Hamburg, and within a few months received the second lengthy suspension of his career, having been sent off for hitting an opponent. Gradually, however, Keegan won over his new team-mates, and emerged as a star of the Hamburg team, helping them to win the Bundesliga in 1979. Keegan's growing ability as a player led to him winning the European Footballer of the Year award in both 1978 and 1979. In 1980 he appeared for Hamburg in the European Cup final, as they lost to Nottingham Forest.

During the summer of 1980 Keegan played for England in the European Championship finals. He also left Hamburg, to surprisingly join Southampton. In 1982 England appeared in the World Cup finals for the first time since 1970, but Keegan was left on the sidelines, due to an injury. He managed only 27 minutes play, as a substitute, on football's highest stage, and headed wide when presented with an easy chance in England's 0-0 draw with Spain. Unfortunately that was the end of his England playing career. His club career, however, ended on a high note, at Newcastle United, when he helped them win promotion from the Second Division in 1984.

After several years living in Spain, Keegan returned to centre-stage in 1992, as manager of

Newcastle. Keegan remained at St James's Park for five years, moulding an attacking team that finished as runners-up in the Premiership in both 1995-96 and 1996-97. But the pressures of the job led him to resign before the end of the latter season. Keegan therefore missed out on leading Newcastle's first European Cup campaign in 1997-98. He returned to club management in 1998 at Fulham, and then took the national manager's role in 1999, following the departure of Glenn Hoddle. He led England to the Euro 2000 finals, where they beat Germany 1-0 – this being their first competitive win against either West Germany or Germany since the 1966 World Cup final – but lost 3-2 against both Portugal and Romania. Later that year, a 1-0 defeat against Germany, in a World Cup qualifier – the last match played at Wembley Stadium, before it was demolished and rebuilt – prompted Keegan's immediate resignation. Keegan admitted, with refreshing honesty, that he lacked the tactical understanding required to bring success as an international manager, and departed saying "I have no complaints. I have not been quite good enough. I blame no one but myself".

Keegan soon bounced back, becoming manager of Manchester City, a club where he oversaw the same type of adventurous football as Newcastle United had played under his leadership. Manchester City won the First Division in 2001-02, which was Keegan's first season in charge, scoring 108 goals in 46 matches. City subsequently struggled in the Premiership, and Keegan left in March 2005. Throughout the many changes of fortune in his career as player and manager, Kevin Keegan has retained an enthusiastic and positive outlook. They are qualities that have led the football community to hold Keegan in high regard.

1977-78

Liverpool retained the European Cup in 1978, but in rather mixed fashion, as a series of excellent performances on the way to the final were followed by a scrappy victory against an unimpressive Brugge. After a bye through the first round, Liverpool opened with a 5-1 win at home to Dynamo Dresden, which was more than enough to render their 2-1 defeat in the return match academic. Following this Liverpool met Hamburg, whose team included Kevin Keegan, in the European Super Cup. After a 1-1 draw in the away leg, Liverpool thrashed Hamburg 6-0 at Anfield, with Terry McDermott scoring a hat-trick, to become the first British club to take the Super Cup. On the other hand, Liverpool declined the opportunity to compete in the World Club Championship.

This was Jock Stein's final season as manager of Celtic. They thrashed Jeunesse D'Esch in their first tie, but fell against their next opponents, Wacker Innsbruck. Glentoran chalked up a rare success for a club from Northern Ireland by beating Valur Reykjavik in the first round, but then lost 6-0 on aggregate to Juventus at the next stage. Borussia Monchengladbach, the previous season's runners-up, demonstrated that they remained a threat with an 8-1 aggregate win against Red Star Belgrade in the second round. Three of Borussia's goals against Red Star were scored by Allan Simonsen, who finished as the competition's leading scorer this season, with five goals.

In the quarter-finals, Liverpool achieved an outstanding pair of victories against Benfica, winning 2-1 in a rainy Lisbon, and 4-1 at home. Borussia Monchengladbach required a second leg fight-back, and the away goals rule, to beat Wacker Innsbruck. Meanwhile Ajax, appearing in the European Cup for the first time since 1973-74, lost to Juventus on penalties – a reverse of their win in the 1973 final. The semi-finals brought together Liverpool and Borussia Monchengladbach, the teams that had contested the 1977 final. Liverpool were beaten 2-1 by Borussia Monchengladbach in the first leg, but a magnificent 3-0 win at Anfield, with goals from Ray Kennedy, Kenny Dalglish, and Jimmy Case, took Liverpool into the final.

Brugge made steady progress through the competition. A 9-2 aggregate defeat of KuPS Kuopio in their opening tie was followed by a narrow win against Panathinaikos. In the quarter-finals, Brugge beat Atletico Madrid by the odd goal in seven. They then met Juventus in the semi-finals, and lost by a single goal in Turin.

The Belgians recovered by winning the return 2-0, with the decisive goal from René Vandereycken being scored five minutes from the end of extra time. Brugge were surprise finalists, as they had only appeared in the European Cup twice before, being eliminated in the second round in 1973-74, and the quarter-finals in 1976-77. Meanwhile only one Belgian club had previously reached the semi-finals, namely Standard Liege, back in 1961-62.

As in 1977, Liverpool's opponents in the final were a club they had previously beaten in a UEFA Cup final. Bob Paisley selected six of the players who had appeared for Liverpool in the previous season's European Cup final – Jimmy Case, Ray Clemence, Emlyn Hughes, Ray Kennedy, Terry McDermott, and Phil Neal. The newcomers included Kenny Dalglish, Alan Hansen, and Graeme Souness, a trio of outstanding Scots. Dalglish, who had previously appeared in the European Cup for Celtic, would later manage Liverpool and then Celtic. The Brugge team was weakened by the absence of two key players, Raoul Lambert and Paul Courant, who were both injured.

Brugge were coached by Ernst Happel, the Austrian who had managed the Feyenoord team which won in 1970. A few weeks after the 1978 European Cup final, Happel coached the Netherlands team in the World Cup finals, taking them to the final, where they were beaten by Argentina, the host nation.

The Wembley final was refereed by Charles Corver, from the Netherlands, who had conspicuously failed to control a rough Brazilian team which drew 1-1 against England at the same venue the previous month. He was not troubled by Liverpool and Brugge. Unfortunately neither team managed to play with the expected quality. As in 1968 Wembley saw an English team victorious, but the drama of Manchester United's 4-1 win against Benfica was not repeated as Liverpool won 1-0. The goal was scored on 65 minutes, in a rare moment of inspiration.

Souness threaded the ball, from just outside the penalty area, through a line of Brugge defenders, into the path of Dalglish, on the right-hand side of the area, and he calmly chipped the ball over advancing goalkeeper Birger Jensen. Up to this point the match had been a contest between a lack-lustre Liverpool attack and massed-defence from Brugge.

During the remainder of the game Brugge put together a few attacks, but the only time they looked like scoring was when a misplaced back-pass from Hansen to Clemence allowed Daniel De Cubber a chance, but Phil Thompson rescued his fellow defender by clearing the ball off the line. Although the final had been drab, Liverpool could justifiably take satisfaction from retaining the trophy, and becoming the first British club to win the European Cup twice. Liverpool's growing reputation was reinforcing their success. Emlyn Hughes, captain in both the 1977 and 1978 finals, recalled: "Continental teams were frightened to death of us. They were scared of our record, and the fact we played 70 games a season. They expected us to be super-fit, every one of us a man-mountain. They did not dare go forward in case we crushed them".

1977-78

First round

		1st leg	2nd leg	agg
FC Basle	Wacker Innsbruck	1-3	1-0	2-3
Celtic	Jeunesse D'Esch	5-0	6-1	11-1

		1st leg	2nd leg	agg
Benfica	Torpedo Moscow	0-0	0-0	0-0
Benfica won 4-1 on penalties				
Dynamo Dresden	Halmstad	2-0	1-2	3-2
Dukla Prague	Nantes	1-1	0-0	1-1
Nantes won on away goals				
Floriana	Panathinaikos	1-1	0-4	1-5
KuPS Kuopio	Brugge	0-4	2-5	2-9
Levski Spartak	Slask Wroclaw	3-0	2-2	5-2
Lillestrom	Ajax	2-0	0-4	2-4
Omonia Nicosia	Juventus	0-3	0-2	0-5
Red Star Belgrade	Sligo Rovers	3-0	3-0	6-0
Trabzonspor	B1903 Copenhagen	1-0	0-2	1-2
Vasas Budapest	Borussia Monchengladbach	0-3	1-1	1-4
Valur Reykjavik	Glentoran	1-0	0-2	1-2
Dynamo Bucharest	Atletico Madrid	2-1	0-2	2-3

Second round

		1st leg	2nd leg	agg
Benfica	B1903 Copenhagen	1-0	1-0	2-0
Brugge	Panathinaikos	2-0	0-1	2-1
Celtic	Wacker Innsbruck	2-1	0-3	2-4
Glentoran	Juventus	0-1	0-5	0-6
Levski Spartak	Ajax	1-2	1-2	2-4
Liverpool	Dynamo Dresden	5-1	1-2	6-3
Nantes	Atletico Madrid	1-1	1-2	2-3
Red Star Belgrade	Borussia Monchengladbach	0-3	1-5	1-8

Quarter-finals

		1st leg	2nd leg	agg
Benfica	Liverpool	1-2	1-4	2-6
Ajax	Juventus	1-1	1-1	2-2
Juventus won 3-0 on penalties				
Brugge	Atletico Madrid	2-0	2-3	4-3
Wacker Innsbruck	Borussia Monchengladbach	3-1	0-2	3-3
Borussia Monchengladbach won on away goals				

Semi-finals

		1st leg	2nd leg	agg
Borussia Monchengladbach	Liverpool	2-1	0-3	2-4
Juventus	Brugge	1-0	0-2	1-2

Final

May 10 1978 Wembley
Liverpool 1   Brugge 0
Dalglish
Liverpool: Clemence, Neal, Thompson, Hansen, Hughes, McDermott, R Kennedy, Souness, Case (Heighway), Fairclough, Dalglish
Brugge: Jensen, Bastijns, Krieger, Leekens, Maes (Volders), Cools, De Cubber, Vandereycken, Ku (Sanders), Simoen, Sorensen
HT: 0-0
Referee: Corver (Netherlands)
Attendance: 92,500

Bob Paisley

Bob Paisley's football career began at Bishop Auckland, with whom he won the FA Amateur Cup in 1939. His ability as a left half led to him being bought that year by Liverpool, where Matt Busby, another man who would win the European Cup as a manager, was already on the playing staff. Paisley, born on January 23 1919, at Hetton-le-Hole, in Durham, received a signing fee of £10 from Liverpool, plus £5 per week in wages, but the outbreak of the Second World War, a few months after his arrival, prevented him from making an immediate breakthrough as a professional. He spent most of the war in the army, fighting in north Africa and Italy.

When the Football League resumed in 1946-47, Liverpool won the title, with Paisley a regular. Three years later Liverpool were beaten 2-0 by Arsenal in the FA Cup final, but Paisley was not selected, despite having scored against Everton in the semi-finals. At the request of Liverpool, the FA provided a runners-up medal for him, but his disappointment caused him to think about leaving the club. He decided, however, to remain loyal, and was soon given the role of team captain.

His playing career ended in 1953-54, with an anti-climax, as Liverpool were relegated. He remained at the club, fulfilling a dual role, coach of the reserve team and a physiotherapist. Later he was promoted to assistant manager under Bill Shankly, who had arrived in 1959. Shankly oversaw Liverpool's revival in the 1960s and the start of their domination of the English game in the 1970s. Shankly retired in 1974 and Liverpool, seeking continuity, chose Paisley as his successor.

It was initially felt by many, including himself, that Paisley would not be able to emulate the achievements of the extrovert Shankly. Paisley was a quiet and modest man, but he had a great deal of experience at Liverpool, and was able to motivate the team to even greater successes. The crowning achievement of his spell as manager was the triple success in the European Cup, won in 1977, 1978, and 1981. During the course of this success, he threw light on the experience of regular participation in the competition with the following thoughts: "You moan about the European Cup. You curse the hotels, raise hell about the training pitches, lug your own food about, worry about the referees, about the injuries, about the air strikes, the heating in the players' rooms, the travel weariness. Then the moment you are out of it, you are empty inside. The icing is off the cake. God you do miss it".

Besides the European Cup, Paisley's Liverpool won the UEFA Cup in 1976, and the European Super Cup in 1977. On the domestic front, they took the League title six times – 1976, 1977, 1979, 1980, 1982, and 1983 – and won the League Cup three times – in 1981, 1982, and 1983. The one competition that eluded him was the FA Cup, as Liverpool were beaten by Manchester United in the 1977 final. On a personal level, Paisley's skill was recognised with the Manager of the Year award on six occasions – 1975-76, 1976-77, 1978-79, 1979-80, 1981-82, and 1982-83.

After retiring in 1983, Paisley remained part of the Anfield set-up for several more years. He was a director, and also acted as advisor to Kenny Dalglish, after the latter's appointment as player-manager in 1985. Paisley's association with Liverpool, which lasted more than half a century, was only ended by the terrible onset of Alzheimer's disease, from which he was to die on February 14 1996, aged 77. Among the many tributes one of the most illuminating was paid by Kenny Dalglish, who said: "There was only one Bob Paisley, and he was the greatest of them all. He went through the card in football. He played for Liverpool, he treated the players, he coached them, he managed them, and then he became a director. He could tell if someone was injured, and what the problem was, just by watching them walk a few paces. He was never boastful, but had great football knowledge. I owe Bob more than I owe anybody else in the game".

1978-79

Liverpool were joined in this season's European Cup by Nottingham Forest, a club which, under the managership of Brian Clough, had won the English League in 1977-78 only a year after gaining promotion from the Second Division. Clough had led Derby to the European Cup semi-finals in 1973, with a team that included Archie Gemmill, John McGovern, and John O'Hare, who had all joined him at Forest. The two English clubs were paired with each other in the first round. Forest won their home leg 2-0, with goals from Garry Birtles and Colin Barrett. Liverpool's European experience was expected to lead them to a decisive victory in the second leg, but Forest held them to a 0-0 draw. Liverpool, the champions of Europe in both 1977 and 1978, were suddenly out of the competition at the first hurdle. To add to their disappointment, Liverpool lost 4-3 on aggregate to Anderlecht in this season's European Super Cup, played in December. Meanwhile Liverpool decided against meeting Boca Juniors, of Argentina, for the World Club Championship, which went uncontested.

Brugge, the runners-up to Liverpool the previous season, also fell in the first round, losing to Wisla Krakow. Rangers achieved an excellent pair of aggregate victories in the early part of the competition. After losing 1-0 away to Juventus, Rangers won 2-0 in the return. They followed this with a goalless draw against PSV Eindhoven at Ibrox, and a dramatic 3-2 win in the second leg – with goals from Alex MacDonald, Derek Johnstone, and Bobby Russell – after they had trailed 1-0 in the first minute, and 2-1 during the second half.

The elimination of Brugge, Juventus, and Liverpool left Real Madrid as the only club that had previously appeared in a European Cup final to reach the second round but Real were quickly eliminated, surprisingly beaten by Grasshoppers, on away goals, with Claudio Sulser scoring all three of the Swiss team's goals in the tie. Prior to this Sulser had scored six times – five in the first leg – as Grasshoppers beat Valletta 13-3. Vllaznia Shkoder, the first Albanian entrants since 1971-72, were beaten by FK Austria in the first round. Bohemians, from the Republic of Ireland, defeated Omonia Nicosia, and held Dynamo Dresden to a goalless draw, but lost the return 6-0.

Nottingham Forest went on to prove that their elimination of Liverpool was not a fluke, with a series of impressive displays, characterised by neat passing, and frequent goalscoring. In the second round, they thrashed AEK Athens, who were managed by Ferenc Puskas, 7-2 on aggregate, with Birtles accounting for three of their goals. Forest then beat Grasshoppers 5-2 in the quarter-finals.

Both of Grasshoppers' goals were scored by Sulser, who was this season's leading scorer with 11. In the semi-finals, Forest met Cologne, who had eliminated Rangers with a 2-1 aggregate win in the quarter-finals. Forest drew 3-3 at home to Cologne, after trailing 2-0 after only eight minutes. Forest then pulled off an excellent away win, with Ian Bowyer scoring the only goal, and Peter Shilton making a brilliant save in the last minute from Harald Konopka, to book a place in the final.

Nottingham Forest's opponents in the final would be Malmo, whose path had featured solid, but dour, football. They began with a single goal aggregate victory against Monaco, followed by a 2-0 win against Dynamo Kiev. The quarter-final, in which Malmo beat Wisla Krakow 4-1 in the second leg, to overturn a 2-1 defeat in the opener, broke with their steady, low-scoring, progress. In the semi-final, Malmo reverted to type, drawing 0-0 away to FK Austria, and winning 1-0 at home.

The 57,500 crowd at Munich's Olympic Stadium was significantly short of the ground's capacity, when Malmo became the first Swedish finalists. The Swedish club was managed by Bob Houghton, an Englishman who had led them to their domestic title three times. The Nottingham Forest team selected by Brian Clough included Trevor Francis, a player making his European

Cup debut, having been bought from Birmingham City in February 1979, in a transfer a pound short of £1,000,000. Clough did not want to burden Francis with the tag of first million pound player!

A striker with pace and flair, who made his first appearance for Birmingham at the age of 16, Francis played 52 times for England between 1977 and 1986. Having recently become eligible for the European Cup, Francis nearly missed the final, only making the team due to the absence of the injured Archie Gemmill and Martin O'Neill.

The match was reminiscent of the 1978 final, as an English team achieved an unconvincing victory, by a single goal, against defensive opponents. Indeed Peter Taylor, Clough's assistant, admitted after the match that: "As a final, it was a non-event. We won, and that was that". Forest controlled the first half, while Malmo sat back and comfortably absorbed the pressure, until the stroke of half time. Forest then produced a fine goal, as John Robertson ran down the left wing, and hit a powerful cross which Francis met at the far post with a flying header high into the net. On the hour, Forest nearly scored a second goal, which would have been the inverse of their first, but when a cross from Francis found Robertson the latter's effort hit a post. Forest produced few other clear-cut chances, while Malmo's efforts to come out of defence in the second half, and find an equaliser, led nowhere. The manner of their victory in the final was forgettable, but Nottingham Forest's achievement in becoming only the third English club to win the European Cup, with an assured campaign, just two years after gaining promotion from the Second Division, was the stuff of legends.

1978-79

Preliminary round

		1st leg	2nd leg	agg
Monaco	Steaua Bucharest	3-0	0-2	3-2

First round

		1st leg	2nd leg	agg
Nottingham Forest	Liverpool	2-0	0-0	2-0
Juventus	Rangers	1-0	0-2	1-2
Linfield	Lillestrom	0-0	0-1	0-1
Real Madrid	Progres Niedercorn	5-0	7-0	12-0
AEK Athens	Porto	6-1	1-4	7-5
Fenerbahce	PSV Eindhoven	2-1	1-6	3-7
Vllaznia Shkoder	FK Austria	2-0	1-4	3-4
Malmo	Monaco	0-0	1-0	1-0
Cologne	IA Akranes	4-1	1-1	5-2
Zbrojovka Brno	Ujpest Dozsa	2-2	2-0	4-2
Partizan Belgrade	Dynamo Dresden	2-0	0-2	2-2
Dynamo Dresden won 5-4 on penalties				
Grasshoppers	Valletta	8-0	5-3	13-3
Brugge	Wisla Krakow	2-1	1-3	3-4
OB Odense	Lokomotiv Sofia	2-2	1-2	3-4
Valkeakoski Haka	Dynamo Kiev	0-1	1-3	1-4
Omonia Nicosia	Bohemians	2-1	0-1	2-2
Bohemians won on away goals				

Second round

		1st leg	2nd leg	agg
AEK Athens	Nottingham Forest	1-2	1-5	2-7
Rangers	PSV Eindhoven	0-0	3-2	3-2
Real Madrid	Grasshoppers	3-1	0-2	3-3

Grasshoppers won on away goals

Dynamo Kiev	Malmo	0-0	0-2	0-2
Lokomotiv Sofia	Cologne	0-1	0-4	0-5
Bohemians	Dynamo Dresden	0-0	0-6	0-6
FK Austria	Lillestrom	4-1	0-0	4-1
Zbrojovka Brno	Wisla Krakow	2-2	1-1	3-3

Wisla Krakow won on away goals

Quarter-finals

		1st leg	2nd leg	agg
Nottingham Forest	Grasshoppers	4-1	1-1	5-2
Cologne	Rangers	1-0	1-1	2-1
Wisla Krakow	Malmo	2-1	1-4	3-5
FK Austria	Dynamo Dresden	3-1	0-1	3-2

Semi-finals

		1st leg	2nd leg	agg
Nottingham Forest	Cologne	3-3	1-0	4-3
FK Austria	Malmo	0-0	0-1	0-1

Final

May 30 1979 Munich
Nottingham Forest 1   Malmo 0
Francis
Nottingham Forest: Shilton, Anderson, Lloyd, Burns, Clark, Francis, McGovern, Bowyer, Robertson, Woodcock, Birtles
Malmo: Moller, R Andersson, Jonsson, M. Andersson, Erlandsson, Tapper (Malmberg), Ljungberg, Prytz, Kinnvall, Hansson
(T Andersson), Cervin
HT: 1-0
Referee: Linemayr (Austria)
Attendance: 57,500

1979-80

This season's competition opened with a preliminary round tie, between Dundalk, from the Republic of Ireland, and Linfield, from Northern Ireland, a match which was sure to be highly charged given that Northern Ireland was in the middle of the 'troubles'. Dundalk's home leg, was drawn 1-1, and accompanied by crowd trouble, provoked by the murder, in the Republic, two days earlier of Lord Mountbatten, a member of the British royal family, by the Irish Republican Army. UEFA decided that the second leg should not be played in Northern Ireland and the match was switched to Haarlem, in the Netherlands, where Dundalk won 2-0. In the first round Dundalk eliminated Hibernians, from Malta, following which they lost 3-2 on aggregate against Celtic. Prior to this, Celtic had opened their campaign with a surprise 1-0 defeat away to Partizan Tirana, but won the return 4-1 with two goals from Roy Aitken.

For the second successive season, England were represented by both Liverpool and Nottingham Forest, but now Forest were the reigning European champions, while Liverpool were the English champions. As in 1978-79, Liverpool departed in the first round. They lost 3-0 away to Dynamo Tbilisi, after a 2-1 win at Anfield. Having beaten Malmo in the 1979 final, Forest opened the defence of their title against another Swedish team, beating Osters Vaxjo 3-1 on aggregate.

Elsewhere in the early rounds, Ajax were involved in a couple of high scoring ties. Ajax twice beat HJK Helsinki 8-1, and then won 10-0 against Omonia Nicosia, before losing the return 4-0. Sören Lerby scored five times in the victory over Omonia Nicosia, while Ton Blanker scored a hat-trick. Blanker had previously scored four times in the latter of the victories over HJK. When the goalscoring abruptly stopped with the defeat in Cyprus, the Ajax players were fined by the club for their poor performance. Dynamo Tbilisi's run was ended by a couple of defeats against Hamburg, for whom Kevin Keegan scored in both legs.

In the early weeks of 1980, Nottingham Forest won the European Super Cup, beating Barcelona 2-1 on aggregate. Following this, they came back from a 1-0 defeat at home to Dynamo Berlin in the European Cup quarter-finals, with a fine 3-1 win in the return, in which Trevor Francis scored twice. Celtic won 2-0 against Real Madrid at Parkhead, but lost the second leg 3-0 to go out of the competition, as Real staged a recovery similar to that which had seen off Derby County in 1975-76.

Forest won 2-0 at home to Ajax in the semi-finals, with goals from Francis and John Robertson, the latter scoring from a penalty. A solid defensive display in the Netherlands restricted Ajax to a single goal victory. The goal was scored by Lerby, a Danish striker who was the leading scorer this season, with ten goals, but it was Forest who advanced to the final. Real Madrid beat Hamburg 2-0 at the Bernabeu, and looked set to appear in the final, but Hamburg won their home leg 5-1, with Horst Hrubesch and Manni Kaltz both scoring twice, to take the tie 5-3 on aggregate.

In the absence of Real Madrid, the crowd at the Bernabeu stadium for the final was a relatively small 51,000 – only half of the capacity. The match was played on May 28, the anniversary of a previous final between teams from England and West Germany, with Bayern Munich having beaten Leeds United on that date in 1975.

The Nottingham Forest team featured eight players who had appeared in the previous season's final – Viv Anderson, Garry Birtles, Ian Bowyer, Kenny Burns, Larry Lloyd, John McGovern, John Robertson, and Peter Shilton.

They were, however, without Francis, who had scored the only goal of the 1979 final, but was now injured. Hamburg's main goalscorer, Hrubesch, was not fully fit, but he was available as a substitute. Keegan, who had won the competition with Liverpool three years earlier, was in the Hamburg starting line-up. Hamburg were managed by Branco Zebec, a Yugoslav who had played for Partizan Belgrade in the first ever European Cup match, 25 years earlier.

Hamburg dominated the early play, with Forest limited to counter-attacks. In one of these attacks, Forest took the lead after 20 minutes, as Robertson exchanged passes with Birtles, and then struck a low shot from just outside the penalty area, that fizzed into the net via a post. Hamburg thought they had equalised a minute later, but the effort from Willi Reimann was ruled out by Antonio Garrido, the Portuguese referee, as a linesman flagged for offside against Keegan.

Hamburg, for whom Hrubesch played the second half, continued to have most of the play for the remainder of the match, but Forest held on to win 1-0. Forest's victory was largely attributable to determined defending, and an outstanding display of goalkeeping from Shilton, who had required pain-killing injections before the match, due to a calf strain.

This was one of many peaks in Shilton's lengthy career. He played an English record of 1,390 senior matches between 1966 and 1997 – and remains England's most capped player, with 125 appearances between 1970 and 1990. Forest had emulated Liverpool's two successive European Cup triumphs and in contrast to the dour final of 1979, this had been an absorbing contest with Forest distinguishing themselves with tenacious resistance.

Whereas Peter Taylor had been downbeat about the 1979 final, Brian Clough said of the 1980 equivalent: "It was one of the best 90 minutes we have ever had. Absolutely marvellous".

1979-80

Preliminary round

		1st leg	2nd leg	agg
Dundalk	Linfield	1-1	2-0	3-1

First round

		1st leg	2nd leg	agg
Liverpool	Dynamo Tbilisi	2-1	0-3	2-4
Nottingham Forest	Osters Vaxjo	2-0	1-1	3-1
Partizan Tirana	Celtic	1-0	1-4	2-4
Dundalk	Hibernians	2-0	0-1	2-1
Levski Spartak	Real Madrid	0-1	0-2	0-3
Arges Pitesti	AEK Athens	3-0	0-2	3-2
Start Kristiansand	Strasbourg	1-2	0-4	1-6
Dynamo Berlin	Ruch Chorzow	4-1	0-0	4-1
Ujpest Dozsa	Dukla Prague	3-2	0-2	3-4
Red Boys Differdange	Omonia Nicosia	2-1	1-6	3-7
HJK Helsinki	Ajax	1-8	1-8	2-16
Valur Reykjavik	Hamburg	0-3	1-2	1-5
Hajduk Split	Trabzonspor	1-0	1-0	2-0
Vejle	FK Austria	3-2	1-1	4-3
Porto	Milan	0-0	1-0	1-0
Servette	Beveren	3-1	1-1	4-2

Second round

		1st leg	2nd leg	agg
Nottingham Forest	Arges Pitesti	2-0	2-1	4-1
Celtic	Dundalk	3-2	0-0	3-2
Dynamo Berlin	Servette	2-1	2-2	4-3
Dukla Prague	Strasbourg	1-0	0-2	1-2
Hamburg	Dynamo Tbilisi	3-1	3-2	6-3
Vejle BK	Hajduk Split	0-3	2-1	2-4
Ajax	Omonia Nicosia	10-0	0-4	10-4
Porto	Real Madrid	2-1	0-1	2-2

Real Madrid won on away goals

Quarter-finals

		1st leg	2nd leg	agg
Nottingham Forest	Dynamo Berlin	0-1	3-1	3-2
Celtic	Real Madrid	2-0	0-3	2-3
Hamburg	Hajduk Split	1-0	2-3	3-3

Hamburg won on away goals

		1st leg	2nd leg	agg
Strasbourg	Ajax	0-0	0-4	0-4

Semi-finals

		1st leg	2nd leg	agg
Nottingham Forest	Ajax	2-0	0-1	2-1
Real Madrid	Hamburg	2-0	1-5	3-5

Final

May 28 1980 Madrid
Nottingham Forest 1   Hamburg 0
Robertson
Nottingham Forest: Shilton, Anderson, Gray (Gunn), Lloyd, Burns, O'Neill, McGovern, Bowyer, Mills (O'Hare), Robertson, Birtles
Hamburg: Kargus, Kaltz, Nogly, Buljan, Jakobs, Hieronymus (Hrubesch), Magath, Memering, Keegan, Reimann, Milewski
HT: 1-0
Referee: Garrido (Portugal)
Attendance: 51,000

Brian Clough

"I would not say I was the best manager in the business, but I was in the top one". This was Brian Clough's typically bold, and humorous, assessment of his ability. At both Derby County and Nottingham Forest, he made the most of limited resources, creating and inspiring teams that were to give great performances in both English domestic football and the European Cup. Much of this was achieved in partnership with Peter Taylor, who acted as his assistant at a series of clubs. Taylor, a goalkeeper, had been a team-mate of Clough, a centre forward, at Middlesbrough. But whereas Taylor was quiet, Clough was a controversial and outspoken personality, who earned the nickname 'Old Big 'Ead' – this being his alternative suggestion when he was awarded the Order of the British Empire in 1991. He was also a strong disciplinarian, who insisted upon impeccable behaviour, and good sportsmanship, from the players he managed. When asked, during his time as manager of Derby, how he dealt with players who disagreed with his guidance, Clough replied: "I ask him which way he thinks it should be done. We get down to it, and then talk about it for 20 minutes. Then we decide I was right".

Clough began his playing career at Middlesbrough, the club from the city in which he was born on March 21 1935. He was signed at the end of 1951, but did not make his League debut until 1955. Once in the first team, Clough established his position as a prolific goalscorer, an attribute which resulted in two caps for England in 1959 although Middlesbrough were in the Second Division at the time. He left in 1961, being bought by Sunderland, another Second Division club, for £45,000 but a knee injury suffered on an icy pitch on Boxing Day 1962 curtailed, and ultimately ended, his playing career. After a long battle to regain fitness, Clough made a short comeback in 1964, but was soon forced to accept the inevitable. At the age of 29, he retired from playing, having scored 251 goals in 274 League games – a remarkable average of 0.92 goals per game.

After a short spell on the coaching staff at Sunderland, Clough became manager of Hartlepools United, a Fourth Division club, in 1965, with Taylor as his assistant. Two years later they moved to Derby County, winning the Second Division in 1968-69. Three years later they were First Division champions, for the first time in the club's history. This was followed by a run to the European Cup semi-finals in 1972-73. Clough and Taylor left Derby in October 1973, following a row with Sam Longson, the club chairman, and soon moved to Brighton and Hove Albion. The winning touch temporarily deserted Clough, and Brighton ended the season in the lower part of the Third Division. Despite this, Clough was appointed as manager of Leeds United in the summer of 1974, as Don Revie became the England manager. Clough clashed with the players at Leeds, and left the post after only 44 days. At the start of 1975, Clough moved to Nottingham Forest, a club where he would repeat, and then improve upon, his record with Derby County. Clough was joined at Forest in 1976 by Taylor, who had stepped up to the manager's role at Brighton when Clough departed for Leeds. Forest's rise began with them winning promotion from the Second Division in 1977.

Clough worked regularly as a TV pundit during the 1970s and 1980s and in this role famously described Jan Tomaszewski as a "clown", only to see the Polish goalkeeper perform brilliantly in the 1-1 draw with England in 1973 which brought England's elimination from the World Cup. Clough was often spoken of as a possible England manager and after the departure of Revie in 1977, he was interviewed for the role. The Football Association selected the less charismatic, but more solid, Ron Greenwood. Clough and Taylor were now given coaching posts with the England youth team, but did not hold them for long, as they preferred to concentrate on their club responsibilities.

Forest won the First Division in 1977-78 – the season after their promotion – finishing seven points clear of a Liverpool team that was about to retain the European Cup. In 1978 Forest also beat Liverpool in the League Cup final, while Clough picked up the manager of the year award. In 1978-79 Nottingham Forest won the European Cup, beating Malmo 1-0 in the final, and also the League Cup. Clough and the Forest team reached their peak in 1980, as they retained the European Cup by beating Hamburg 1-0 in the final, a few months after defeating Barcelona in the European Super Cup. By contrast 1980-81 was a disappointing season, as Forest experienced an early exit from the European Cup – which was to be regained by Liverpool – plus defeat in both the World Club Championship and European Super Cup.

Taylor retired from Forest in 1982, but soon re-emerged as the manager of Derby County. Taylor's purchase for Derby of John Robertson from Forest, while Clough was away on holiday, ended the friendship between them and they were never reconciled. It was a rift which Clough lamented after Taylor's death in 1990. Forest were now a club in decline, although Clough remained a focus of attention. After the European Cup success in 1980, the club did not win another trophy until the League Cup was regained in 1989, and then retained in 1990. Two of Forest's goals in the 3-1 win against Luton Town in the 1989 League Cup final were scored by Nigel Clough, the son of Brian. Forest reached the FA Cup final in 1991, but were beaten by 3-1 by Tottenham Hotspur. This was the only time that Clough reached the FA Cup final as either player or manager. In 1993 Nottingham Forest were relegated at the end of the inaugural Premier League season, and Clough retired. It was a sad end to Clough's remarkable career in professional football, which had stretched across nearly 40 years.

Clough's retirement was plagued by ill health. He admitted to a long-standing drink problem, and required a liver transplant at the start of 2003 to save his life. Shortly afterwards he was diagnosed to be suffering from stomach cancer, but he remained in the public eye, as the most famous supporter of non-league Burton Albion, a club managed by son Nigel.

It was cancer which caused the death of Brian Clough, at the age of 69, on September 20 2004. Tributes paid to Clough that day included the following from Alex Ferguson: "Brian Clough was a fantastic manager. All of his teams were difficult to beat. There was a determination about them that mirrored the man himself. Clough achieved something unique – he won two Leagues with provincial clubs, not big guns. He also won the European Cup twice in a row, with a provincial team, and that was very, very difficult to do. He was eccentric at times. I quite enjoyed some of it – even though I was on the end of it sometimes. The game needs characters like Brian Clough".

Martin O'Neill, who played for Forest in the 1980 European Cup final, but did not enjoy easy relations with his manager, recalled Clough by saying: "He would be the first to say he was the greatest of all time. He was like England's version of Muhammed Ali. He was just so charismatic. He had a great opinion on football, and an opinion on everything that he didn't have a clue about".

1980-81

For the third season in succession, England were represented by Liverpool and Nottingham Forest, and for the third time in a row one of these clubs fell in the first round. This time it was Forest. They had won the European Cup in 1979 and 1980, but they flopped at the start of the 1980-81 competition, losing both legs against CSKA Sofia by a single goal. Following this Forest lost to Valencia in the European Super Cup, and Nacional in the World Club Championship.

Liverpool were held to a 1-1 draw by OPS Oulo in Finland, but won the return of this first round tie 10-1, with both Graeme Souness and Terry McDermott scoring hat-tricks. Aberdeen became the first club other than Celtic or Rangers to represent Scotland in the European Cup since Kilmarnock had done so in 1965-66. Aberdeen had won the Scottish League for the first time since 1954-55. Back in 1955, Aberdeen had been denied the chance to appear in the first European Cup, as Hibernian represented Scotland by invitation.

Twenty five years later Aberdeen, managed by Alex Ferguson, who would later win the trophy with Manchester United, eliminated FK Austria in their first European Cup tie. In the next round Aberdeen were drawn against Liverpool, and the English champions comprehensively beat their Scottish counterparts, winning 5-0 on aggregate. Back in the first round Linfield, of Northern Ireland, had lost to Nantes, while Limerick United, from the Republic of Ireland, at least had the distinction of losing a prestige tie, going down to Real Madrid 7-2 on aggregate, after taking the lead in the first leg.

The competition had opened with a blast from the past, as the legendary Honved, appearing in the European Cup for the first time since 1956-57, beat Valletta 11-0 on aggregate in the preliminary round. Honved then beat Sporting Lisbon 3-0 on aggregate, before falling to Real Madrid by the same scoreline in the second round. Brugge, finalists as recently as 1978, were thrashed 5-1 by Basle in the first round. The biggest tie of the second round brought together two of the giants of the previous decade, with Bayern Munich beating Ajax 6-3, with the help of three goals from Karl-Heinz Rummenigge.

In the quarter finals, Liverpool succeeded where Forest had failed, beating CSKA Sofia 6-1 on aggregate, with Souness scoring his second hat-trick of the competition in the first leg. Bayern Munich continued to make impressive progress, with a 6-2 win against Banik Ostrava. The other ties at this stage brought narrow victories for Internazionale and Real Madrid over Red Star Belgrade and Spartak Moscow respectively. This meant that each of the four quarter finals had seen a west European club beat opposition from the eastern half of the continent.

In the semi-finals Liverpool were held to a goalless draw at home to Bayern Munich. The second leg looked set to end in the same way, until Ray Kennedy broke the deadlock for Liverpool seven minutes from time. Karl-Heinz Rummenigge equalised with three minutes to play, but the 1-1 draw saw Liverpool through on the away goals rule.

In 1975 the Parc des Princes in Paris had been the scene of rioting, as Leeds United lost the final to Bayern Munich, but six years later it was a better story for the English. Liverpool, making their third appearance in the final in five seasons, were pitted against Real Madrid, who had been absent from the final since 1966. Liverpool, still managed by Bob Paisley, fielded eight players who had appeared in either, or both, of the 1977 and 1978 finals, namely Ray Clemence, Kenny Dalglish, Alan Hansen, Ray Kennedy, Terry McDermott, Phil Neal, Graeme Souness, and Phil Thompson.

The team was captained by Thompson, who shared a strong central defensive partnership with Hansen. Being very confident on the ball, Hansen often advanced to set up Liverpool attacks. Following his retirement, the Scot became one of Britain's most respected TV pundits. Souness and McDermott were destined to finish the season as the European Cup's joint leading scorers, along with Rummenigge of Bayern Munich, with six goals each.

On the domestic front this had been a relatively poor season for Liverpool, as they finished fifth in the League – this being the only season between 1972-73 and 1990-91 in which they were not winners or runners-up. On the other hand, they won the League Cup in 1981 – indeed they took that trophy in four successive seasons from 1980-81 to 1983-84. This Real Madrid team had the potential to echo the club's golden era of the 1950s and 1960s, having completed a hat-trick of Spanish league titles in 1980, and also won the Spanish Cup that year, thrashing Castilla 6-1 in the final. Real were now managed by Vujadin Boskov, who had played for Yugoslavia in the 1954 and 1958 World Cup finals. Besides several Spanish internationals, the team included Laurie Cunningham, an England international, who was to tragically die in a car crash in 1989, at the age of 32. Real also fielded Uli Stielike, a member of the West Germany team which had won the 1980 European Championship. Prior to that Stielike had played for Borussia Monchengladbach against Liverpool, in the 1977 European Cup final.

The match did not equal its potential, with both teams below their best. The first half was cagey, with few chances created. Liverpool gained the initiative after the interval, but were unable to achieve a decisive breakthrough for most of the second half. With the match seemingly heading for extra time, Liverpool scored with eight minutes remaining. Ray Kennedy took a throw-in on the left wing, finding Alan Kennedy, who skipped past Garcia Cortes, and then drove the ball past the goalkeeper, Augustin, from a narrow angle. This proved to be the only goal of the final. It had not been a great performance on the day from Liverpool, but Phil Thompson, their captain, was justified in saying "We have joined the immortals. We are one of the greats, and we have beaten two more of them on the way, Bayern and Real". Liverpool had now won the European Cup three times in five seasons, and Bob Paisley had become the first manager to take the trophy for a third time.

1980-81

Preliminary round

		1st leg	2nd leg	agg
Honved	Valletta	8-0	3-0	11-0

First round

		1st leg	2nd leg	agg
Linfield	Nantes	0-1	0-2	0-3
Aberdeen	FK Austria	1-0	0-0	1-0
Brugge	Basle	0-1	1-4	1-5
CSKA Sofia	Nottingham Forest	1-0	1-0	2-0
Dynamo Berlin	Apoel Nicosia	3-0	1-2	4-2
Dynamo Tirana	Ajax	0-2	0-1	0-3
Internazionale	Universitatea Craiova	2-0	1-1	3-1
Jeunesse D'Esch	Spartak Moscow	0-5	0-4	0-9
Limerick United	Real Madrid	1-2	1-5	2-7
Olympiakos	Bayern Munich	2-4	0-3	2-7
OPS Oulu	Liverpool	1-1	1-10	2-11
Sporting Lisbon	Honved	0-2	0-1	0-3
Trabzonspor	Szombierski Bytom	2-1	0-3	2-4
Viking Stavanger	Red Star Belgrade	2-3	1-4	3-7
IBV Vestmannaeyjar	Banik Ostrava	1-1	0-1	1-2
Halmstads	Esbjerg	0-0	2-3	2-3

Second round

		1st leg	2nd leg	agg
Nantes	Internazionale	1-2	1-1	2-3
Real Madrid	Honved	1-0	2-0	3-0
Bayern Munich	Ajax	5-1	1-2	6-3
Aberdeen	Liverpool	0-1	0-4	0-5
CSKA Sofia	Szombierski Bytom	4-0	1-0	5-0
Banik Ostrava	Dynamo Berlin	0-0	1-1	1-1
Banik Ostrava won on away goals				
Spartak Moscow	Esbjerg	3-0	0-2	3-2
Basle	Red Star Belgrade	1-0	0-2	1-2

Quarter-finals

		1st leg	2nd leg	agg
Liverpool	CSKA Sofia	5-1	1-0	6-1
Bayern Munich	Banik Ostrava	2-0	4-2	6-2
Internazionale	Red Star Belgrade	1-1	1-0	2-1
Spartak Moscow	Real Madrid	0-0	0-2	0-2

Semi-finals

		1st leg	2nd leg	agg
Liverpool	Bayern Munich	0-0	1-1	1-1
Liverpool won on away goals				
Real Madrid	Internazionale	2-0	0-1	2-1

Final

May 27 1981 Paris
Liverpool 1   Real Madrid 0
A Kennedy
Liverpool: Clemence, Neal, Thompson, Hansen, A Kennedy, Lee, McDermott, Souness, R Kennedy, Dalglish (Case), Johnson
Real Madrid: Agustin, Cortes (Pineda), Navajas, Sabido, Del Bosque, Angel, Camacho, Stielike, Juanito, Santillana, Cunningham
HT: 0-0
Referee: Palotai (Hungary)
Attendance: 48,360

1981-82

The double representation from England continued, with Liverpool, the reigning champions, being joined by Aston Villa, who had won the English title for the first time since 1910. Villa had a smooth introduction to the European Cup, beating Valur Reykjavik 7-0 on aggregate, as Terry Donovan, Peter Withe, and Gary Shaw each scored twice. For the second successive season Liverpool began with a tie against OPS Oulo. They won 8-0 – with Kenny Dalglish and Terry McDermott scoring two each. The English cubs had a narrow passage in the second round. Liverpool beat AZ67 Alkmaar 5-4 on aggregate – Alan Hansen scoring a late winner in the second leg – while Aston Villa overcame Dynamo Berlin on away goals – Tony Morley having struck twice in Berlin. Bayern Munich emerged as one of the strongest teams in the early rounds. They began with a 6-0 aggregate win against Osters Vaxjo, in which Karl-Heinz Rummenigge scored three times, and Dieter Hoeness twice. Bayern then held Benfica to a goalless draw, before winning 4-1 at home, with Hoeness scoring a hat-trick.

Liverpool took part in the World Club Championship for the first time in December 1981, but lost 3-0 to Flamengo. When the European Cup resumed in March, Liverpool's run was ended by CSKA Sofia – the club which had eliminated Nottingham Forest, but then lost to Liverpool, the previous season. Liverpool won by a single goal at Anfield, following which CSKA beat them 2-0, after extra time, in Bulgaria. Aston Villa's chances in the competition appeared to have been harmed by the surprise resignation of Ron Saunders, their experienced manager, in February 1982, following a disagreement with the club's directors. Saunders was replaced, initially on a caretaker basis, by Tony Barton, who had been the assistant manager. A few weeks after the changeover, Villa's progress continued, as they eliminated Dynamo Kiev, drawing 0-0 away, and winning 2-0 at home. In the other quarter-finals Anderlecht and Bayern Munich beat Red Star Belgrade and Universitatea Craiova respectively. As in 1980-81, each of the four ties had matched west with east, but this time CSKA had prevented a western whitewash.

In the semi-finals, Aston Villa won by a single goal against Anderlecht, at Villa Park, as a shot from Tony Morley went in off a post. In Brussels, Villa held Anderlecht to a goalless draw, and therefore took a place in the final, but the match was marred by the hooliganism of some Villa fans. This caused the referee to stop play for several minutes at one point, and led to UEFA fining Aston Villa nearly £15,000. The other tie produced 11 goals, which was the highest aggregate score for a semi-final since Eintracht Frankfurt beat Rangers 12-4 back in 1960. CSKA Sofia, becoming the first Bulgarian club to appear in the semi-finals since they had done so in 1967, ran up a 3-0 lead at home to Bayern Munich in the first 18 minutes. CSKA were 4-1 ahead for most of the second half, but late goals from Dieter Hoeness and Paul Breitner reduced the margin of the Bulgarians' victory to 4-3. Bayern completed their recovery back in Munich, winning 4-0, with two goals each from Breitner and Rummenigge, to take the tie 7-4 on aggregate.

When Aston Villa and Bayern Munich met at Rotterdam for the final Bayern were the favourites, their team featuring three players from the hat-trick of European Cup victories in the 1970s – Breitner, Bernd Durnberger, and Udo Horsmann – plus Rummenigge, who had won the European Footballer of the Year award in both 1980 and 1981. Dieter Hoeness, the brother of Uli from the 1970s team, was the leading scorer in the 1981-82 European Cup, with seven goals, one ahead of Rummenigge, while Breitner (who returned to Bayern in 1978, after spells with Real Madrid and Eintracht Brunswick) had netted five times in Bayern's high-scoring run to the final. Man-for-man, Aston Villa had a less impressive line-up. Four of their team had played international football, but not to any great extent. Peter Withe had appeared five times for England, Tony Morley had played twice, and Jimmy Rimmer had won a single cap back in 1976, while Allan Evans had played a couple of games for Scotland. Tony Barton had been made permanent manager by Villa after the quarter-final victory, but his profile was still rather low. His name did not even appear in the official programme for the final. Although they lacked Bayern's experience, Aston Villa's rapid attacking play, combined with solid defence, made them a team to be reckoned with.

Aston Villa suffered a setback when Jimmy Rimmer, their goalkeeper, had to be replaced after only eight minutes, due to a neck injury. Rimmer had waited a long time to play in a European Cup final, having been an unused substitute for Manchester United when they had beaten Benfica 4-1, 14 years earlier. His replacement, Nigel Spink, had only made one full appearance for Aston Villa. Despite being thrown in at the deep end, Spink played confidently, making a series of fine saves as Bayern dominated the play throughout the match. An excellent save that denied Rummenigge in the first half seemed to bemuse the German. Spink said "Rummenigge just kept looking at me after that – he kept looking back up the pitch at me". The Villa defence also performed well, in the face of concerted pressure. Villa rarely attacked, but midway through the second half they scored the only goal of the match, as Morley ran down the left wing, and crossed to Withe, who was fortunate to find the target with a miss-hit shot from close range, via the inside of a post. The goal increased Villa's confidence, and they continued to hold Bayern at bay for the remainder of the match, the only real fright coming when Hoeness put the ball into the net, only to have his effort ruled out for offside.

Aston Villa had matched Nottingham Forest's achievement, by winning the European Cup in their first campaign in the competition. They had also continued the English run of success, with this being the sixth successive season in which an English club had won, the longest such run for any country, eclipsing the five Spanish victories that Real Madrid had achieved single-handedly between 1955-56 and 1959-60. In contrast to West Germany's superiority to England at international level, Liverpool, Forest, and Villa had each beaten a club from West Germany in a European Cup final.

1981-82
Preliminary round

		1st leg	2nd leg	agg
Saint-Etienne	Dynamo Berlin	1-1	0-2	1-3

First round

		1st leg	2nd leg	agg
Aston Villa	Valur Reykjavik	5-0	2-0	7-0
Dynamo Berlin	FC Zurich	2-0	1-3	3-3
Dynamo Berlin won on away goals				
FK Austria Vienna	Partizan Tirana	3-1	0-1	3-2
Dynamo Kiev	Trabzonspor	1-0	1-1	2-1
Hibernians	Red Star Belgrade	1-2	1-8	2-10
Ferencvaros	Banik Ostrava	3-2	0-3	3-5
Celtic	Juventus	1-0	0-2	1-2
Widzew Lodz	Anderlecht	1-4	1-2	2-6
CSKA Sofia	Real Sociedad	1-0	0-0	1-0
Progres Niedercorn	Glentoran	1-1	0-4	1-5
Start Kristiansand	AZ 67 Alkmaar	1-3	0-1	1-4
OPS Oulu	Liverpool	0-1	0-7	0-8
Universitatea Craiova	Olympiakos	3-0	0-2	3-2
KB Copenhagen	Athlone Town	1-1	2-2	3-3
KB Copenhagen won on away goals				
Benfica	Omonia Nicosia	3-0	1-0	4-0
Osters Vaxjo	Bayern Munich	0-1	0-5	0-6

Second round

		1st leg	2nd leg	agg
Dynamo Berlin	Aston Villa	1-2	1-0	2-2
Aston Villa won on away goals				
FK Austria Vienna	Dynamo Kiev	0-1	1-1	1-2
Banik Ostrava	Red Star Belgrade	3-1	0-3	3-4
Anderlecht	Juventus	3-1	1-1	4-2
CSKA Sofia	Glentoran	2-0	1-2	3-2
AZ 67 Alkmaar	Liverpool	2-2	2-3	4-5
KB Copenhagen	Universitatea Craiova	1-0	1-4	2-4
Benfica	Bayern Munich	0-0	1-4	1-4

Quarter-finals

		1st leg	2nd leg	agg
Dynamo Kiev	Aston Villa	0-0	0-2	0-2
Anderlecht	Red Star Belgrade	2-1	2-1	4-2
Liverpool	CSKA Sofia	1-0	0-2	1-2
Universitatea Craiova	Bayern Munich	0-2	1-1	1-3

Semi-finals

		1st leg	2nd leg	agg
Aston Villa	Anderlecht	1-0	0-0	1-0
CSKA Sofia	Bayern Munich	4-3	0-4	4-7

Final

May 26 1982 Rotterdam
Aston Villa 1   Bayern Munich 0
Withe
Aston Villa: Rimmer (Spink), Swain, Evans, McNaught, Williams, Bremner, Cowans, Mortimer, Shaw, Withe, Morley
Bayern Munich: Muller, Dremmler, Weiner, Augenthaler, Horsmann, Mathy (Guttler), Breitner, Kraus (Niedermayer), Durnberger, Rummenigge, Hoeness
HT: 0-0
Referee: Konrath (France)
Attendance: 46,000

Chapter 6

English Epilogue – The Heysel Disaster 1982-1985

1982-83

The run of six successive English victories from 1977 to 1982 was followed by a twilight period over the next three seasons. English clubs remained a major force in the European Cup, and Liverpool won the trophy in 1984, but there were signs of decline, which were rapidly overshadowed, off the pitch, by the Heysel tragedy. English teams appeared in nine of the 11 European Cup finals between 1975 and 1985, winning seven of them, but the sequence started with a riot in 1975, and ended with a disaster ten years later.

The tide turned against English clubs in the 1982-83 European Cup, and the competition was won by Hamburg, the club Nottingham Forest had beaten in the 1980 final. Aston Villa, the reigning European champions, were joined by Liverpool, the perennial English champions. In the first round Aston Villa had to play their home leg against Besiktas behind closed doors, as part of the UEFA punishment for the trouble caused by their supporters in the tie against Anderlecht the previous season. Liverpool accounted for Dundalk, from the Republic of Ireland, while Northern Ireland's Linfield lost to 17 Nentori Tirana, on away goals.

This rare success for an Albanian club was followed by their withdrawal against Dynamo Kiev in the next round. Celtic began with an impressive 4-3 aggregate win against an Ajax team that featured Johan Cruyff, who had returned to his original club a decade after the peak of his career there. In a first round clash between West and East Germany, Hamburg beat Dynamo Berlin. In the second round Aston Villa impressively beat Dynamo Bucharest 2-0 away and 4-2 at home – with Gary Shaw scoring a hat-trick in the latter match.

During the winter break Aston Villa lost 2-0 against Penarol in the World Club Championship, but beat Barcelona in the European Super Cup. After losing by a single goal in the Nou Camp, Villa won the return 3-0, after extra time, with an outstanding display at Villa Park. A few weeks later, the English advance in the European Cup was suddenly halted, with a dual elimination in the quarter finals. Aston Villa were outclassed by Juventus, who won 2-1 in Birmingham, and 3-1 in Turin, with Michel Platini scoring twice in the second leg. Liverpool surprisingly lost 2-0 away to Widzew Lodz, with their goalkeeper, Bruce Grobbelaar, at fault for both goals. Liverpool won the return 3-2, but the Poles took the tie 4-3 on aggregate. This match marked the end of the association between Bob Paisley and the European Cup, as the manager was to retire at the end of the season. The anti-climax in Europe was offset by Paisley leading Liverpool to victory in both the League and the League Cup this season.

In the semi-finals Widzew Lodz fell to Juventus. The Italians won their home leg 2-0, with goals from Marco Tardelli and Roberto Bettega, before drawing 2-2 in the return. The other semi-final was a close contest between Hamburg and Real Sociedad, which the Germans clinched 3-2 on aggregate, with the decisive goal from Thomas Von Heesen being scored six minutes from the end of the second leg.

Juventus were the first Italian club to appear in the European Cup final since 1973, when they had been beaten by Ajax but they were favourites to win in Athens, as their team featured six players who had appeared for Italy in the World Cup victory against West Germany the previous year – Antonio Cabrini, Claudio Gentile, Gaetano Scirea, Marco Tardelli, Paolo Rossi, and Dino Zoff. Rossi and Tardelli had both scored in the final, with the latter's goal – and his ecstatic celebration – being the most memorable moment of the match. Juventus fielded two other stars from the 1982 World Cup, Michel Platini of France, and Zbigniew Boniek of Poland. Roberto Bettega, who had played for Juventus in the European Cup final ten years earlier, along with Zoff, was again in their team. The Italians were coached by Giovanni Trapattoni, who had played for the Milan teams which won the 1963 and 1969 finals.

Hamburg's manager was the vastly-experienced Ernst Happel, who had led Feyenoord to victory in 1970, and Brugge to runners-up spot in 1978. In contrast to Juventus, the Hamburg line-up only included two players from the 1982 World Cup final, Horst Hrubesch and Manni Kaltz. On the other hand, these two players, plus Holger Hieronymus, Ditmar Jakobs, Felix Magath, and Jürgen Milewski, survived from Hamburg's appearance in the 1980 European Cup final.

Hamburg surprised Juventus with a goal after only eight minutes, as Magath's shot from just outside the penalty area, on the left, flew into the top right-hand corner. After this bright start, the match deteriorated, with few goalscoring opportunities, and no more goals. This was the sixth year in a row in which the European Cup final ended with a 1-0 scoreline – a poor contrast with the seven goals that had been scored in the first final back in 1956.

Juventus failed to show the form which had taken them to the final, with Rossi being particularly disappointing. He had been the leading scorer in the 1982 World Cup finals, and repeated that feat in the 1982-83 European Cup, with six goals each time, but in this match he was substituted shortly after half time.

Hamburg lacked players with flair, but their cohesion and work-rate enabled them to win. Hamburg's run in the competition already meant that a team from West Germany had appeared in the last four of the European Cup in ten successive seasons, from 1973-74 to 1982-83. Now Hamburg had become the first club from West Germany to win the trophy since Bayern Munich completed their hat-trick of victories in 1976.

1982-83

Preliminary round

		1st leg	2nd leg	agg
Dynamo Bucharest	Valerenga	3-1	1-2	4-3

First round

		1st leg	2nd leg	agg
Dynamo Berlin	Hamburg	1-1	0-2	1-3
Olympiakos	Osters Vaxjo	2-0	0-1	2-1

		1st leg	2nd leg	agg
17 Nentori Tirana	Linfield	1-0	1-2	2-2

17 Nentori Tirana won on away goals

		1st leg	2nd leg	agg
Grasshoppers	Dynamo Kiev	0-1	0-3	0-4
Dynamo Zagreb	Sporting Lisbon	1-0	0-3	1-3
AS Monaco	CSKA Sofia	0-0	0-2	0-2
Celtic	Ajax	2-2	2-1	4-3
Viking Reykjavik	Real Sociedad	0-1	2-3	2-4
Hibernians	Widzew Lodz	1-4	1-3	2-7
Avenir Beggen	Rapid Vienna	0-5	0-8	0-13
Omonia Nicosia	HJK Helsinki	2-0	0-3	2-3
Dundalk	Liverpool	1-4	0-1	1-5
Aston Villa	Besiktas	3-1	0-0	3-1
Dynamo Bucharest	Dukla Prague	2-0	1-2	3-2
Standard Liege	Vasas Gyor	5-0	0-3	5-3
Hvidovre	Juventus	1-4	3-3	4-7

Second round

		1st leg	2nd leg	agg
Hamburg	Olympiakos	1-0	4-0	5-0
CSKA Sofia	Sporting Lisbon	2-2	0-0	2-2

Sporting Lisbon won on away goals

		1st leg	2nd leg	agg
Real Sociedad	Celtic	2-0	1-2	3-2
Rapid Vienna	Widzew Lodz	2-1	3-5	5-6
HJK Helsinki	Liverpool	1-0	0-5	1-5
Dynamo Bucharest	Aston Villa	0-2	2-4	2-6
Standard Liege	Juventus	1-1	0-2	1-3

Dynamo Kiev walked over, 17 Nentori Tirana withdrew

Quarter-finals

		1st leg	2nd leg	agg
Dynamo Kiev	Hamburg	0-3	2-1	2-4
Sporting Lisbon	Real Sociedad	1-0	0-2	1-2
Widzew Lodz	Liverpool	2-0	2-3	4-3
Aston Villa	Juventus	1-2	1-3	2-5

Semi-finals

		1st leg	2nd leg	agg
Real Sociedad	Hamburg	1-1	1-2	2-3
Juventus	Widzew Lodz	2-0	2-2	4-2

Final

May 25 1983 Athens
Hamburg 1   Juventus 0
Magath
Hamburg: Stein, Kaltz, Hieronymus, Jakobs, Wehmeyer, Groh, Rolff, Magath, Milewski, Bastrup (Von Heesen), Hrubesch
Juventus: Zoff, Gentile, Brio, Scirea, Cabrini, Bonini, Tardelli, Bettega, Platini, Rossi, (Marocchino), Boniek
HT: 1-0
Referee: Rainea (Romania)
Attendance: 73,500

Michel Platini

Michel Platini is one of France's greatest ever footballers – only Zinedine Zidane compares with him in that respect – and a major international ambassador for the game. He won the European Championship with France, and both the European Cup and World Club Championship with Juventus. He also appeared for France in three World Cup final tournaments, and was capped 72 times. The only player ever to win the European Footballer of the Year award three successive times, Platini was an inspirational midfield general, renowned for the high quality of his vision and passing, besides being a free kick and penalty expert.

Platini was born on June 21 1955, at Joeuf, a village in north east France. After playing as a youth for AS Joeuf, Platini moved to Nancy in 1973. At the age of 20, he made his debut for France, scoring in a 2-2 draw against Czechoslovakia in March 1976. Later that year he was a member of the French team which reached the quarter finals of the football tournament in the Olympic Games, at Montreal. In 1978 Nancy won the Cup, and Platini played in the World Cup finals. The following year he moved to Saint-Etienne, who were to win the league in 1980-81, only to be eliminated by Dynamo Berlin in the preliminary round of the next season's European Cup.

In 1982 Platini was one of the stars of the French team which reached the semi-finals of the World Cup, only to lose a brilliant, and controversial, struggle against West Germany. Platini scored from the penalty spot in both the match, which was a 3-3 draw, and the shoot-out which cruelly decided a place in the World Cup final. The match turned on the incident where Toni Schumacher, the German goalkeeper, went unpunished by Charles Corver, the Dutch referee, for a brutal challenge on France's Patrick Battiston. Years later, a philosophic Platini recalled: "That was my most beautiful game. What happened in those two hours encapsulated all the sentiments of life itself. Regarding the incident, had the referee seen Schumacher hurtling out of his goal and colliding with Patrick Battiston, as he bore down on goal, the red card would have come out, and we would have gone on to the World Cup final, and maybe even won the trophy. But he did not see the penalty offence, and did not flourish his red card to Schumacher as a result. What can you do?"

Following the World Cup finals, Platini moved to Juventus. At the end of the 1982-83 season, he played in the European Cup final defeat by Hamburg. Juventus won the Italian Cup in 1983, followed by both the Italian league and the European Cup-Winners' Cup the next year. In 1985 this Juventus team reached its peak, beating Liverpool in both the European Super Cup and the European Cup final, and then defeating Argentinos Juniors in the World Club Championship. Platini scored the only goal in the European Cup final from a penalty, but the success was overshadowed by the Heysel disaster. Another penalty from Platini contributed to the 2-2 draw against Argentinos Juniors, following which Juventus won the match 4-2 on penalties.

The pinnacle of Platini's international career came when he captained the French team that won the 1984 European Championship, as the host nation. Platini was the tournament's leading scorer with nine goals, finding the net in each of France's five matches. He scored hat-tricks against both Belgium and Yugoslavia, and opened the scoring in the 2-0 win against Spain in the final. The combination of Platini's success with Juventus and France led to him being voted European Footballer of the Year in 1983, 1984, and 1985. He was the first Frenchman to take the accolade since Raymond Kopa in 1958.

In 1986, shortly after helping Juventus to regain the Italian title, Platini played in his third World Cup finals. He scored the last of his 41 goals for France in the brilliant 1-1 draw against Brazil, in the quarter finals, on his 31st birthday. He surprisingly shot over the bar in the penalty contest that settled the match, but France still won 4-3 on penalties. Defeat against West Germany in the semi-finals was a bitter blow for Platini, and he did not feature in the weakened French team which beat Belgium to take third place.

In 1987 Platini ended his playing days, at the age of just 32. He later explained his reasoning as follows: "I had no more fuel left. I had been a professional for 15 seasons, during one of which I had been injured. I loved to score goals, but with age came the reality that what I could do with great frequency as a younger man would not always be possible, given that I was now playing alongside and against younger players. Thus it became my ambition to retire while I was still at my peak, and it is something about which I have no regrets".

Platini's final game was played for a Rest of the World team, managed by Terry Venables, against the Football League, at Wembley Stadium in August 1987. The Football League won 3-0, but the highlight of the match was the midfield brilliance of Platini and Diego Maradona. Platini was substituted midway through the second half, and left the field to thunderous applause from the Wembley crowd.

Platini returned to the international stage in 1988, as manager of France. His team failed to reach the 1990 World Cup finals, but won all eight of their qualifying matches for the 1992 European Championship, and were unbeaten in 19 matches between April 1989 and November 1991. A poor display by France at the Euro '92 finals prompted Platini to resign. He was soon back in the limelight, taking the role of co-president of the organising committee for the World Cup finals, held in France in 1998. Fernand Sastre, the other co-president, with whom Platini worked for several years, died just three days after the opening of the tournament. A shocked Platini continued his duties with dignity and dedication, attending as many matches around France as was physically possible. When France beat Brazil 3-0 in the final, to win the World Cup for the first time, Platini was watching in the stands, proudly wearing a French shirt. Platini has remained an active football official in recent years, and currently combines roles with the French Football Federation, UEFA, and FIFA.

1983-84

The 1983-84 season brought a strong British challenge, with Liverpool surprisingly being accompanied through to the latter stages of the competition by Dundee United. Liverpool were managed by Joe Fagan, who had replaced Bob Paisley on the latter's retirement at the end of the previous season. It had been a smooth transition, as Fagan was a member of the famous Liverpool 'boot room', the workplace of the backroom assistants to the manager, from which Paisley himself had graduated.

Fagan was Liverpool's trainer when Bill Shankly was manager, and then assistant manager to Paisley. Dundee United were an attractive team, who joined Aberdeen during the 1980s in challenging the dominance of Celtic and Rangers in Scottish domestic football. Dundee United had won the Scottish title for the only time in their history the previous season. Their team included Eamonn Bannon, Richard Gough, Maurice Malpas, and David Narey – each of whom played for Scotland in the World Cup finals in either 1982, 1986, or 1990.

In the first round reigning champions Hamburg benefited from one of the frequent Albanian withdrawals, the club in this case being Vllaznia Shkoder. Hamburg promptly lost 5-3 to Dynamo Bucharest when they took the field in the second round. Liverpool squeezed past Athletic Bilbao, appearing in the European Cup for the first time since 1956-57, by a single goal scored by Ian Rush in Bilbao, but Dundee United progressed in more impressive fashion, drawing 0-0 away to Standard Liege, before beating them 4-0 in the return leg, Ralph Milne scoring twice.

The draw for the quarter-finals paired Liverpool with Benfica, who had previously eliminated

Linfield. Liverpool repeated their impressive defeat of the Portuguese at the same stage of the competition six years earlier, winning 1-0 at home, before crushing the Portuguese team 4-1 in the second leg – with two goals from Ronnie Whelan, and one apiece from Craig Johnston and Ian Rush being added to that scored by Rush at Anfield. Dundee United continued their run by getting the better of Rapid Vienna on away goals with Davie Dodds scoring in each leg. Meanwhile Dynamo Bucharest beat Dynamo Minsk, and Dynamo Berlin lost to Roma. Viktor Sokol of Dynamo Minsk was the leading scorer this season, with a total of six goals – one more than Rush accumulated.

In the semi-finals, Liverpool accounted for Dynamo Bucharest, the first Romanian club to reach that stage, winning 1-0 at home, and then 2-1 away. Rush scored both of the Liverpool goals in a bruising encounter in Bucharest, played in heavy rain. At one point an all-British final looked a real possibility. Dundee United, becoming the first Scottish team to play in the semi-finals since Celtic in 1974, won 2-0 at home to Roma, with goals from Davie Dodds and Derek Stark. The dream ended, however, as Roma won the second leg 3-0, with Roberto Pruzzo scoring twice. Alongside the advance of Dundee United, there was further Scottish success this season, as Aberdeen, winners of the previous season's European Cup-Winners' Cup, beat Hamburg in the European Super Cup.

Liverpool might have imagined that as Rome was the venue for the final the omens favoured them. They had won in 1977 at the Olympic Stadium, but it was also the home of their opponents, Roma. This meant that Liverpool had to play before a crowd of 69,693 mostly composed of Roma fans. The Roma team included Francesco Graziani and Bruno Conti, both of whom had been World Cup winners with Italy in 1982, plus Falcao and Cerezo from the exciting Brazilian team that had looked likely to win that tournament, until they were beaten 3-2 by Italy in an unforgettable match. The disappointment of that defeat was felt so painfully by Falcao, who had scored a wonderful goal, that he considered retirement, only to be persuaded to continue his career by his mother. Roma were coached by Nils Liedholm, who had appeared in the European Cup final for Milan in 1958, a few weeks before playing for the Sweden team that finished as runners-up to Brazil in the World Cup. Joe Fagan's selection included six players who had appeared for Liverpool in a previous European Cup final, namely Kenny Dalglish, Alan Hansen, Alan Kennedy, Sammy Lee, Phil Neal, and Graeme Souness.

Liverpool began well, and took the lead after a quarter of an hour. Whelan challenged Franco Tancredi, the Roma goalkeeper, and the latter dropped the ball into the path of Phil Neal, who duly scored, with Erik Fredriksson, the Swedish referee, unmoved by Roma's claims that Tancredi had been fouled. A minute later Graeme Souness put the ball in the net, but this time the goal was disallowed for offside. As the half progressed, Roma gained strength, and they equalised three minutes before the interval, as a cross from Conti was headed in by Roberto Pruzzo. Roma had the better of the second half, but were thwarted by Liverpool's defence, and good goalkeeping from Bruce Grobbelaar. Liverpool were now mostly limited to counter-attacks. With the score still level at 1-1 when the end of normal time arrived, the match went into extra time. With both teams tiring, the extra 30 minutes did not break the deadlock. For the first time, a European Cup final would be decided by a penalty contest.

Fagan's advice ahead of the shoot-out included the suggestion that Grobbelaar "try to put them off" when Roma were taking their kicks. Liverpool went first, but Steve Nicol sent his kick over the crossbar, following which Agostino Di Bartolomei put Roma ahead. Neal, who had scored a penalty during normal play in the 1977 final, did likewise in the shoot-out. Conti stepped up next for Roma, while Grobbelaar tried some antics, pretending to be afflicted with wobbly legs. Grobbelaar succeeded in unnerving Conti, who put his shot over the crossbar. Each team scored from its third kick, Souness being on target for Liverpool, while Ubaldo Righetti replied for Roma. Rush restored Liverpool's lead, following which Graziani hit the crossbar. This meant that if Liverpool converted their next penalty, they would take the trophy. Alan Kennedy, whose goal from open play had secured victory in the 1981 final, calmly scored to give Liverpool a 4-2 win in the penalty contest. Afterwards there were some complaints from the Roma players about Grobbelaar, but Liedholm praised Liverpool's technical ability, saying "They knew how to keep the ball, which we usually do".

Liverpool's fourth European title in the space of eight seasons was an amazing achievement. The club had eclipsed the record of the Ajax and Bayern Munich teams of the 1970s, and could justifiably claim to be one of the strongest in the history of the competition, not far behind the Real Madrid team that had dominated the early tournaments. On the other hand, UEFA's decision to settle the match by a penalty contest, as opposed to the replay option taken in 1974, devalued the final. Unfortunately several more penalty contests would decide European Cup finals in the years ahead. More importantly, attacks by Roma hooligans on Liverpool fans, after the 1984 final, sowed the seeds of a resentment that would have tragic repercussions a year later.

1983-84
First round

		1st leg	2nd leg	agg
OB Odense	Liverpool	0-1	0-5	0-6
Lech Poznan	Athletic Bilbao	2-0	0-4	2-4
Ajax	Olympiakos	0-0	0-2	0-2
Benfica	Linfield	3-0	3-2	6-2
Dynamo Minsk	Grasshoppers	1-0	2-2	3-2
Vasas Gyor	Viking Reykjavik	2-1	2-0	4-1
Kuusysi Lahti	Dynamo Bucharest	0-1	0-3	0-4
Hamrun Spartans	Dundee United	0-3	0-3	0-6
Athlone Town	Standard Liege	2-3	2-8	4-11
Fenerbahce	Bohemians	0-1	0-4	0-5
Rapid Vienna	Nantes	3-0	1-3	4-3
Dynamo Berlin	Jeunesse D'Esch	4-1	2-0	6-1
Partizan Belgrade	Viking Stavanger	5-1	0-0	5-1
CSKA Sofia	Omonia Nicosia	3-0	1-4	4-4
CSKA Sofia won on away goals				
Roma	IFK Gothenburg	3-0	1-2	4-2
Hamburg walked over, Vllaznia Shkoder withdrew				

Second round

		1st leg	2nd leg	agg
Liverpool	Athletic Bilbao	0-0	1-0	1-0
Olympiakos	Benfica	1-0	0-3	1-3
Raba Vasas Gyor	Dynamo Minsk	3-6	1-3	4-9
Dynamo Bucharest	Hamburg	3-0	2-3	5-3
Standard Liege	Dundee United	0-0	0-4	0-4
Bohemians	Rapid Vienna	2-1	0-1	2-2
Rapid Vienna won on away goals				
Dynamo Berlin	Partizan Belgrade	2-0	0-1	2-1
CSKA Sofia	Roma	0-1	0-1	0-2

Quarter-finals

		1st leg	2nd leg	agg
Liverpool	Benfica	1-0	4-1	5-1
Dynamo Minsk	Dynamo Bucharest	1-1	0-1	1-2

Ian Bowyer (left) and Kenny Burns celebrate Nottingham Forest's 1979 victory over Malmo.

Getting used to it. Nottingham Forest manager, the late Brian Clough, happy after the 1980 win against Hamburg.

Aston Villa can hardly believe it. A 1-0 win against Bayern Munich. (back) Ken McNaught and injured goalkeeper Jimmy Rimmer. (front) Allan Evans, Dennis Mortimer and Kenny Swain.

Liverpool captain Phil Neal (left) and teammate Alan Kennedy wearing Juventus shirts after the tragic 1985 final.

Nadal (left) of Barcelona moves in to tackle Dejan Savicevic of AC Milan in the Italian club's 4-0 victory in 1994.

Ole Gunnar Solskjaer pounces to score what must be the most famous goal in Manchester United's illustrious history – the one that won the 1999 final in added time against Bayern Munich in Barcelona.

Real Madrid win the cup again at Hampden Park. This time against Bayer Leverkusen in 2002.

Jerzy Dudek saves Andrei Shevchenko's penalty and Liverpool have come back from a 3-0 half time deficit to win the competition for a fifth time.

		1st leg	2nd leg	agg
Rapid Vienna	Dundee United	2-1	0-1	2-2
Dundee United won on away goals				
Roma	Dynamo Berlin	3-0	1-2	4-2

Semi-finals

		1st leg	2nd leg	agg
Liverpool	Dynamo Bucharest	1-0	2-1	3-1
Dundee United	Roma	2-0	0-3	2-3

Final

May 30 1984 Rome
Liverpool 1 Roma 1 (after extra time)
Neal Pruzzo
Liverpool won 4-2 on penalties
Liverpool: Grobbelaar, Neal, Lawrenson, Hansen, A Kennedy, Johnston (Nicol), Lee, Souness, Whelan, Dalglish (Robinson), Rush
Roma: Tancredi, Nappi, Bonetti, Righetti, Nela, Di Bartolomei, Falcao, Cerezo (Strukelj), Conti, Pruzzo (Chierico), Graziani
HT: 1-1
FT: 1-1
Referee: Fredriksson (Sweden)
Attendance: 69,693

1984-85

The 1984-85 European Cup will always be remembered for the Heysel disaster. The riot before the final caused the deaths of 39 spectators, plunging the competition to the lowest point in its history. Events off the pitch overshadowed the football, and rendered the result of the match insignificant compared to the enormity of the tragedy.

Liverpool opened their ninth successive campaign with a 5-0 aggregate victory against Lech Poznan, with John Wark scoring once in the first leg, and three times in the return. Aberdeen lost to Dynamo Berlin on penalties, and an all-Irish tie saw Linfield eliminate Shamrock Rovers on away goals. IFK Gothenburg enjoyed a scoring spree, with a 17-0 aggregate win against Avenir Beggen – five of the goals being scored by Torbjorn Nilsson. In the second round, Liverpool edged past Benfica – who they were meeting for the third time in eight seasons – winning 3-2 on aggregate, thanks to a first leg hat-trick from Ian Rush. Linfield lost 2-1 away to Panathinaikos, but built up a 3-0 lead in the first half hour of the return. The Greeks then recovered, to draw 3-3 on the night, and win the tie 5-4 on aggregate.

During the winter break Liverpool lost 1-0 to Independiente in the World Club Championship, and 2-0 to Juventus in the European Super Cup. Fixture congestion caused the Super Cup to be played as a single match at Juventus' stadium, rather than the normal two-legged tie. This match was nearly postponed due to the stadium being enveloped in heavy snow, but went ahead before a reduced-capacity crowd. On a frozen pitch, Zbigniew Boniek scored both of the goals. The European Cup quarter-finals saw a return to form for Liverpool, as they beat FK Austria 5-2 on aggregate. Elsewhere Juventus beat Sparta Prague, Panathinaikos squeezed past Gothenburg, and Bordeaux beat Dnepr Dnepropetrovsk on penalties. Dnepr's defeat meant that clubs from the Soviet Union had now been eliminated in the quarter-finals for a fifth successive season.

Liverpool comfortably beat Panathinaikos in the semi-finals, with a 4-0 win at Anfield, in which Rush scored twice, virtually deciding the tie. Panathinaikos had most of the play in the second leg, but Liverpool won again, this time by a single goal from Mark Lawrenson. In the other tie, Juventus beat Bordeaux 3-0 in Turin. The return was very different, as Bordeaux controlled the play, and won 2-0, being unlucky not to square the tie. Bordeaux, who had won the French league in 1984 for the first time since 1950, featured Patrick Battiston, Alain Giresse, Bernard Lacombe, and Jean Tigana, each of whom had played for France when they beat Spain 2-0 in the 1984 European Championship final. The star of that victorious French team had been Michel Platini, whose outstanding performance for Juventus in the first leg of this semi-final was ironically a major cause of the defeat of Bordeaux.

The Liverpool and Juventus teams arrived at the Heysel stadium, in Brussels, on May 29 1985 anticipating a European Cup final that was expected to be a greater occasion than their recent meeting in the Super Cup. Instead of this the safety issues caused by snow in Turin were followed by a riot, and 39 deaths. The disaster unfolding in the Heysel stadium forced UEFA to delay the kick off. A degree of order was eventually restored, with help from appeals to the spectators over the public address system by the captains of the two teams, Phil Neal and Gaetano Scirea. UEFA officials wanted to go ahead with the match, seeing this as the best chance to avoid a possible resumption of rioting, and further loss of life. The two teams reluctantly accepted this reasoning, although it is not clear how much they were told about what had happened. Recalling the events during an interview in 1999, Michel Platini said: "It may seem strange to a spectator who watched the game on television, but it was not a difficult game for the players to play. Why? Because we did not know there had been a tragedy in the stadium. The teams were in their respective dressing rooms when we received warning that the kick-off would be delayed. It was only when we picked up the papers the following day that just what had actually happened hit home".

Liverpool's players appeared to be better informed. Mark Lawrenson said: "We had heard some people had died and we knew there was trouble because a few of us had been out to look at what was going on, but we did not know the scale".

The Liverpool team selected by Joe Fagan included eight who had featured in the previous season's final – Lawrenson, Kenny Dalglish, Bruce Grobbelaar, Alan Hansen, Phil Neal, Steve Nicol, Ian Rush, and Ronnie Whelan. Fagan, who was about to retire, has the distinction of taking Liverpool to the European Cup final in each of the two seasons that he managed them. Fagan was to be replaced by Dalglish, who would lead Liverpool to the English League and FA Cup double the following season, as a player-manager. Juventus were managed by Giovanni Trapattoni, who was also able to call upon eight of the players he had fielded in the 1983 final – Zbigniew Boniek, Massimo Bonini, Sergio Brio, Antonio Cabrini, Michel Platini, Paolo Rossi, Gaetano Scirea, and Marco Tardelli.

Liverpool were stronger in the early stages, but Juventus created the better chances during the latter part of the first half. Ten minutes after half time, a long-range pass from Platini found Boniek, who outran two defenders, Gary Gillespie and Alan Hansen, and appeared set to score before being brought down. The challenge occurred just outside the penalty area, but Andre Daina, the Swiss referee, gave a penalty, from which Platini scored – a sort of justice. Platini thereby joined Gothenburg's Nilsson as joint leading scorer for the season, with seven goals each. Liverpool attacked steadily during the remainder of the match but Juventus held on to win 1-0. This was the first time that Juventus had won the trophy, while Trapattoni had emulated Miguel Munoz, by winning the trophy as both player and manager. The circumstances made it a hollow success for Juventus.

1984-85
First round

		1st leg	2nd leg	agg
Ilves Tampere	Juventus	0-4	1-2	1-6
Grasshoppers	Honved	3-1	1-2	4-3
Labinoti Elbasan	Lyngby	0-3	0-3	0-6
Valerenga	Sparta Prague	3-3	0-2	3-5
Trabzonspor	Dnepr Dnepropetrovsk	1-0	0-3	1-3
Levski Spartak	VFB Stuttgart	1-1	2-2	3-3
Levski Spartak won on away goals				
Dynamo Bucharest	Omonia Nicosia	4-1	1-2	5-3
Bordeaux	Athletic Bilbao	3-2	0-0	3-2
Feyenoord	Panathinaikos	0-0	1-2	1-2
Linfield	Shamrock Rovers	0-0	1-1	1-1
Linfield won on away goals				
IA Akranes	Beveren	2-2	0-5	2-7
Avenir Beggen	IFK Gothenburg	0-8	0-9	0-17
FK Austria	Valletta	4-0	4-0	8-0
Aberdeen	Dynamo Berlin	2-1	1-2	3-3
Dynamo Berlin won 5-4 on penalties				
Red Star Belgrade	Benfica	3-2	0-2	3-4
Lech Poznan	Liverpool	0-1	0-4	0-5

Second Round

		1st leg	2nd leg	agg
Juventus	Grasshoppers	2-0	4-2	6-2
Sparta Prague	Lyngby	0-0	2-1	2-1
Levski Spartak	Dnepr Dnepropetrovsk	3-1	0-2	3-3
Dnepr Dnepropetrovsk won on away goals				
Bordeaux	Dynamo Bucharest	1-0	1-1	2-1
Panathinaikos	Linfield	2-1	3-3	5-4
IFK Gothenburg	Beveren	1-0	1-2	2-2
IFK Gothenburg won on away goals				
Dynamo Berlin	FK Austria	3-3	1-2	4-5
Liverpool	Benfica	3-1	0-1	3-2

Quarter-finals

		1st leg	2nd leg	agg
Juventus	Sparta Prague	3-0	0-1	3-1
Bordeaux	Dnepr Dnepropetrovsk	1-1	1-1	2-2
Bordeaux won 5-3 on penalties				
IFK Gothenburg	Panathinaikos	0-1	2-2	2-3
FK Austria	Liverpool	1-1	1-4	2-5

Semi-finals

		1st leg	2nd leg	agg
Juventus	Bordeaux	3-0	0-2	3-2
Liverpool	Panathinaikos	4-0	1-0	5-0

Final
May 29 1985 Brussels
Juventus 1   Liverpool 0
Platini (penalty)
Juventus: Tacconi, Favero, Cabrini, Brio, Scirea, Bonini, Platini, Tardelli, Briaschi (Prandelli), Rossi (Vignola), Boniek
Liverpool: Grobbelaar, Neal, Beglin, Lawrenson (Gillespie), Hansen, Nicol, Dalglish, Whelan, Wark, Rush, Walsh (Johnston)
HT: 0-0
Referee: Daina (Switzerland)
Attendance: 58,000

The Heysel Disaster

The Heysel disaster stands alongside the Munich air crash as one of the most tragic events in the history of the European Cup. The 1985 final was played after 39 people were killed on the terraces of the Heysel stadium, while around 400 people were injured. The tragedy had its roots in many things; the reaction by Liverpool supporters to being attacked by Roma fans the year before; lack of adequate policing and stewarding; an old and crumbling stadium but the main cause was a charge by Liverpool hooligans on a section of Italians after tickets for the 'Liverpool' end had found their way into the hands of Italian travel agents. The tragedy was the culmination of a series of hooligan outbreaks, which had affected the European Cup, and the other European competitions, with the problem escalating from the early 1970s onwards.

In 1971-72 a European Cup match between Borussia Monchengladbach and Internazionale had to be replayed after Roberto Boninsegna was injured by a drink can thrown onto the pitch.

In 1972 Glasgow Rangers fans fought with Barcelona riot police after their team beat Dynamo Moscow in the European Cup-Winners Cup. But it was the followers of English clubs who were most culpable. Supporters of Tottenham Hotspur had rioted at the away leg of the 1974 UEFA Cup final against Feyenoord. In 1975 the closing stages of the European Cup final were played out against a backdrop of Leeds United fans damaging the stadium in which their team was beaten 2-0 by Bayern Munich. Two years later Manchester United were expelled from the European Cup-Winners' Cup, as some of their supporters rioted at a match against Saint-Etienne, in France. United were re-admitted to the competition on appeal, but had to play the return leg of the tie at least 125 miles from Manchester – they selected the ground of Plymouth Argyle. In 1982 rioting Aston Villa supporters caused a delay in their European Cup semi-final against Anderlecht, with the result that the club had to play its first home European Cup match the following season behind closed doors.

A fortnight before the 1985 European Cup final, Everton (Liverpool's close neighbours) had beaten Rapid Vienna 3-1 in the European Cup-Winners' Cup final, staged in Rotterdam. The large travelling contingent of Everton fans had behaved excellently. With little previous record of hooliganism from the Liverpool supporters, who had been regulars in Europe for two decades, a similar outcome was expected in Brussels. Nevertheless a series of scuffles broke out between Liverpool and Juventus supporters in the city on the day of the match, apparently due to lingering rivalries between the English and Italians. English hooliganism had been much in evidence during the 1980 European Championship finals in Italy. More recently, Roma supporters had attacked Liverpool's travelling supporters after the 1984 European Cup final.

The clashes intensified as the supporters made their way into the stadium during the early evening. Later investigations concluded that inadequate ticketing and segregation arrangements, the ready availability of alcohol, and the poor state of repair in the ageing stadium – which had previously staged European Cup Finals in 1958, 1966, and 1974 – contributed to the mayhem. The eventual flashpoint was the terrace behind one of the goals when a charge by a group from Liverpool resulted in the suffocation and the crushing of Juventus supporters. Almost all of those killed in the incident were Italian. As dead bodies were retrieved from the terraces by police and medical staff, fights between hooligans continued. Amidst the violence, there was a great deal of confusion, with most of the spectators being unaware of the full extent of the horror that had unfolded. The match eventually kicked off an hour-and-a-quarter late, with Juventus beating Liverpool 1-0, in what was now an academic exercise.

The disaster was swiftly followed by action from the football authorities. Bert Millichip and Ted Croker, respectively chairman and secretary of the Football Association, were flying across the Atlantic at the time of the carnage in Brussels, to join the England team for a mini-tournament in Mexico. Upon learning about the disaster, they immediately returned, in order to meet with British Prime Minister Margaret Thatcher. They informed her that the FA would withdraw English clubs from European competition the following season. On June 2 UEFA banned English clubs from European competitions for an indefinite period – there were indications that the ban could be expected to last for several years. An immediate issue was the match between England and Italy in the Mexican tournament, scheduled for June 6. After discussions between the respective football authorities, the match went ahead, in a spirit of reconciliation, with Italy winning 2-1. On June 20 UEFA gave a further judgement on the disaster. Liverpool were handed a ban to cover the first three seasons in which they qualified for the European competitions, to run after the expiry of the general ban on English clubs. UEFA also punished Juventus and the Belgian federation. FIFA in turn announced a ban on English clubs playing anywhere else in the world, which proved to be short-lived. Four of the English clubs that would have competed in Europe the following season started a legal challenge against the FA over the ban, which soon failed, to the relief of the authorities.

The English clubs were destined to spend several years in the wilderness. Hopes of an early return to European competition were undermined by continued hooliganism, most notably by followers of the national team at the 1988 European Championship finals, in West Germany. Isolation led to a decline of English interest in the European Cup and the final ceased to be shown live on British television from 1987. The Hillsborough disaster of 1989 was another tragic blow for Liverpool, as 95 of their supporters were crushed to death ahead of the FA Cup semi-final against Nottingham Forest. This time the conclusion was that outdated stadium design, and poor crowd management, were the main causes of the tragedy, rather than hooliganism.

During the 1989-90 season UEFA indicated that good behaviour by England supporters at the 1990 World Cup finals, in Italy, could pave the way back to the European club competitions. The England fans and football authorities responded positively, and the re-admittance took place at the start of the 1990-91 season. Manchester United competed in the 1990-91 European Cup-Winners' Cup, and went on to win the trophy that season, while Aston Villa represented England in the UEFA Cup. There was not, however, any English club in the 1990-91 European Cup, as Liverpool had won the League the previous season. In April 1991 UEFA ended the additional ban on Liverpool. Their dominance of English domestic football was, however, coming to an end, and Liverpool were not to return to the continent's leading competition until 2001-02, when they competed in the expanded UEFA Champions League by virtue of finishing third in the Premiership the previous season. While Liverpool played in the UEFA Cup in 1991-92, the privilege of the English return to the European Cup fell to Arsenal. Meanwhile UEFA awarded the staging of the 1992 European Cup final to Wembley Stadium, thereby setting the seal on England's rehabilitation seven years after the Heysel disaster.

Chapter 7

Eastern Challenge –
Penalty Deciders 1985-1991

1985-86

For English football the 1985-86 competition marked the beginning of the wilderness years of the post-Heysel ban. The ban was most keenly felt at the outset by Everton, who had won both the English title and the European Cup-Winners' Cup the previous season, but were prevented from taking their place in the 1985-86 European Cup, while the European Super Cup was not staged this season. There was still interesting football for English fans to follow in the European Cup, albeit from the outside. The British challenge in 1985-86 came from Aberdeen, who were still managed by Alex Ferguson, the man who had led their two previous excursions in the European Cup. They opened with a 7-2 aggregate win against IA Akranes and then faced Servette Geneva, who had only beaten a battling Linfield 4-3 in their previous tie. Aberdeen beat the Swiss champions by a single goal, but in the quarter finals they succumbed to IFK Gothenburg, on away goals.

The 1985-86 season was the first since 1963-64 in which no British club reached the final of any of the European competitions. Nevertheless one Englishman was very involved in the European Cup this season, as Terry Venables (nicknamed 'El Tel' by the English when he went to Spain) was manager of Barcelona, who were appearing for the first time since 1974-75. Barcelona reached the final, but their passage was far from convincing. In the opening two rounds, they required the away goals rule to dispose of Sparta Prague and then Porto – for whom Juary scored a second leg hat-trick.

The quarter finals saw Barcelona eliminate the reigning champions, Juventus, by a 2-1 margin – prior to this Juventus had beaten Verona in an all-Italian tie. In the semi-finals, Barcelona lost 3-0 away to IFK Gothenburg, for whom Torbjorn Nilsson scored twice. Nilsson, who had been joint-leading scorer the previous season, was sole leading scorer in 1985-86, with seven goals. Barcelona won the return match 3-0, thanks to a hat-trick from Pichi Alonso, and then took the tie on penalties.

Barcelona's opponents in the final were Steaua Bucharest. After a 5-2 aggregate win against Vejle, Steaua had disposed of Honved with a 4-2 scoreline. In the quarter finals, Steaua struggled to beat Kuusysi Lahti, the first Finnish team to reach this stage, by a single goal, scored by Piturca five minutes from the end of the second leg. Steaua lost 1-0 away to Anderlecht in the first leg of their semi-final, but won the home leg 3-0, with two of the goals being scored by Piturca. Steaua's progress to the final was unexpected, as they had failed to win a tie in their six previous seasons in the European Cup – three of them under their old name, CCA Bucharest.

Steaua Bucharest were the team of the Romanian army, and drew a lot of their strength from the backing of the dictatorship of Nicolae Ceaucescu, whose son Nicu exercised a personal involvement in the running of the club. Political influence was also apparent in the participation in this season's European Cup of Trakia Plovdiv. Trakia had finished third in the Bulgarian league in 1984-85, but were then awarded the title by the country's government, which temporarily disbanded CSKA Sofia and Levski Spartak, the two clubs that finished ahead of them. The reason for this was a riot between the players when CSKA beat Levski 2-1 in the 1985 cup final. Trakia Plovdiv's outing in Europe was very short, as they lost to IFK Gothenburg in the first round. Meanwhile Dynamo Berlin, who lost to FK Austria in the first round, were making one of ten successive appearances in the European Cup, which stretched from 1979-80 to 1988-89. Dynamo Berlin had the backing of East Germany's secret police, the Stasi – with Erich Mielke the head of the Stasi being president of the club – and regularly won the domestic league with government help.

The final was earlier than usual, on May 7, to make way for the World Cup finals, which opened at the end of May. Barcelona were the favourites to win in Seville, as they were playing in their home country, and had the support of the vast majority of the 70,000 crowd. By contrast the Steaua Bucharest supporters able to make the trip from behind the Iron Curtain could be counted in hundreds. Steaua had become only the second team from eastern Europe to reach the European Cup final, their predecessor being Partizan Belgrade in 1966. Barcelona had made one previous appearance in the final, losing to Benfica in 1961.

The match is mainly remembered as the first final in the history of the European Cup to finish goalless. This was the logical extension of a recent trend, with seven of the eight finals between 1978 and 1985 having been settled by a 1-0 scoreline – the exception being the 1-1 draw between Liverpool and Roma in 1984, which was decided by penalties. European Cup finals were too often becoming cautious games, in which fear of defeat outweighed positive attempts to win. There was a shortage of goalmouth action throughout the 1986 final, although both teams played football of a good technical quality, with Steaua having the edge. The inability of the two teams to score continued into the penalty contest, with each of the first four shots being saved. Marius Lacatus then put Steaua ahead, before Pichi Alonso's kick was saved. Gavril Balint extended the Romanians' lead, which meant that Marcos had to score to keep the Spaniards in the contest. Remarkably Marcos' shot became the fourth consecutive Barcelona penalty to be saved by Helmut Ducadam, the Steaua goalkeeper, leaving the Romanian team as 2-0 winners of a notably low-scoring penalty contest. Emerich Jenei, Steaua Bucharest's manager, said after the game "Barcelona are a fine team, but we knew what we had to do, and we did it". Steaua Bucharest had become the first team from eastern Europe to take the continental title, and remain one of the great surprises among European Cup winners.

1985-86

First round

		1st leg	2nd leg	agg
Vejle	Steaua Bucharest	1-1	1-4	2-5
Honved	Shamrock Rovers	2-0	3-1	5-1
Zenit Leningrad	Valerenga	2-0	2-0	4-0
Kuusysi Lahti	Sarajevo	2-1	2-1	4-2
Gornik Zabrze	Bayern Munich	1-2	1-4	2-6
Dynamo Berlin	FK Austria	0-2	1-2	1-4
Rabat Ajax	Omonia Nicosia	0-5	0-5	0-10

		1st leg	2nd leg	agg
IFK Gothenburg	Trakia Plovdiv	3-2	2-1	5-3
Bordeaux	Fenerbahce	2-3	0-0	2-3
Linfield	Servette Geneva	2-2	1-2	3-4
IA Akranes	Aberdeen	1-3	1-4	2-7
Jeunesse D'Esch	Juventus	0-5	1-4	1-9
Verona	PAOK Salonika	3-1	2-1	5-2
Porto	Ajax	2-0	0-0	2-0
Sparta Prague	Barcelona	1-2	1-0	2-2

Barcelona won on away goals

Second round

		1st leg	2nd leg	agg
Honved	Steaua Bucharest	1-0	1-4	2-4
Zenit Leningrad	Kuusysi Lahti	2-1	1-3	3-4
Bayern Munich	FK Austria	4-2	3-3	7-5
Anderlecht	Omonia Nicosia	1-0	3-1	4-1
IFK Gothenburg	Fenerbahce	4-0	1-2	5-2
Servette Geneva	Aberdeen	0-0	0-1	0-1
Verona	Juventus	0-0	0-2	0-2
Barcelona	Porto	2-0	1-3	3-3

Barcelona won on away goals

Quarter-finals

		1st leg	2nd leg	agg
Steaua Bucharest	Kuusysi Lahti	0-0	1-0	1-0
Bayern Munich	Anderlecht	2-1	0-2	2-3
Aberdeen	IFK Gothenburg	2-2	0-0	2-2

IFK Gothenburg won on away goals

		1st leg	2nd leg	agg
Barcelona	Juventus	1-0	1-1	2-1

Semi-finals

		1st leg	2nd leg	agg
Anderlecht	Steaua Bucharest	1-0	0-3	1-3
IFK Gothenburg	Barcelona	3-0	0-3	3-3

Barcelona on 5-4 on penalties

Final

May 7 1986 Seville

Steaua Bucharest 0   Barcelona 0 (after extra time)

Steaua Bucharest won 2-0 on penalties

Steaua Bucharest: Ducadem, Iovan, Belodedic, Bumbescu, Barbulescu, Balint, Balan (Iordanescu), Boloni, Majaru, Lacatus, Piturca (Radu)

Barcelona: Urruti, Gerardo, Migueli, Alesanco, Julio Alberto, Victor, Marcos, Schuster (Moratalla), Pedraza, Archibald (Pichi Alonso), Carrasco

Referee: Vautrot (France)

Attendance: 70,000

1986-87

Steaua Bucharest's defence of their European title was brief. After being given a bye through the first round, they were unexpectedly eliminated at the next stage by Anderlecht, the team they had beaten in the 1985-86 semi-finals. Steaua lost 3-0 away before winning by a single goal at home. On the other hand, Steaua beat Dynamo Kiev in the European Super Cup, in a rare example of a European title being decided by a match between two clubs from the eastern part of the continent. In place of the usual two-legged contest, this season's European Super Cup was a one-off match, played in Monaco, in which Steaua's Gheorghe Hagi scored the only goal. Although Steaua Bucharest failed in the European Cup, there was a strong eastern challenge this season, with Dynamo Kiev reaching the semi-finals, and Red Star Belgrade progressing to the quarter finals.

Celtic, who had previously eliminated Shamrock Rovers from the Republic of Ireland, fell to Dynamo Kiev in the second round, losing 4-2 on aggregate. Northern Ireland's Linfield predictably lost to Rosenberg in the first round. In the second round Red Star Belgrade beat Rosenborg 7-1 on aggregate, with Borislav Cvetkovic scoring twice in each leg. He was to be the leading scorer this season, with seven goals. One surprise advance from the first round was that of Apoel Nicosia, who gained a rare Cypriot win, beating HJK Helsinki on away goals. Apoel went no further, as they failed to appear for their next match, against Besiktas, due to the hostility between the Greek Cypriots and the Turks, stemming from the Turkish invasion of Cyprus in 1974, and the resulting partition of the island. The strongest tie in the early part of the competition brought together Real Madrid and Juventus, in the second round. After a pair of 1-1 draws, the Spanish champions took the tie on penalties. In the previous round Juventus had beaten Valur Reykjavik 11-0 on aggregate, with Michael Laudrup scoring a hat-trick in the first leg, following which he and Michel Platini each scored twice in the return match. Porto had also run up a large win in the first round, but after beating Rabat Ajax 9-0 in their home leg, with Gomes scoring four times, they could only win 1-0 in Malta.

In the quarter finals Real Madrid produced a great comeback to eliminate Red Star Belgrade. After trailing 3-0 at half time in Belgrade, Real pulled the score back to 4-2, with Hugo Sanchez, their Mexican striker, scoring twice. Real then won 2-0 at home, to clinch the tie on away goals. Dynamo Kiev's run continued with a 7-0 aggregate win against Besiktas, in which Oleg Blokhin and Vadim Yevtushenko each scored three goals. Blokhin, who won the European Footballer of the Year award in 1975, was the Soviet Union's leading player for a decade. With Blokhin now approaching the end of his career, he was in the process of being eclipsed by Igor Belanov, another Dynamo Kiev player, who had won the European Footballer of the Year award at the end of 1986. Bayern Munich, who reached this stage with steady wins against PSV Eindhoven and FK Austria, also ran up a large victory, winning 7-2 against Anderlecht, the club which had beaten them in the previous season's quarter finals.

The semi-final between Bayern Munich and Real Madrid, becoming bitter European Cup rivals, brought unpleasant incidents on and off the pitch. Bayern won their home leg 4-1, with Lothar Matthaus scoring two penalties, while Real had two players sent off. Crowd trouble delayed the start in Madrid, and continued for much of the match. Bayern had Klaus Augenthaler sent off, but Real could only reduce the margin of their overall defeat with a single goal win.

Bayern Munich were playing in their fifth European Cup final, but for Porto the match in Vienna was their first. Bayern were managed by Udo Lattek, who had led them to victory in the 1974 final. Only Dieter Hoeness remained from Bayern's defeat by Aston Villa in 1982. Besides Hoeness, Bayern's team for the 1987 final included three others players who had featured for West Germany when they lost 3-2 to Argentina in the 1986 World Cup final, in Mexico, namely Andreas Brehme, Norbert Eder, and Lothar Matthaus. Bayern were without their captain, Augenthaler, who was suspended, but Porto, coached by Artur Jorge, were missing Fernando Gomes and Lima Pereira, both of whom had suffered broken legs.

This final was the best for several years, ending the long run of low-scoring, and unadventurous, contests. Both teams created several chances as the early part of the match saw open football, and a goal only looked to be a matter of time. It duly arrived on 24 minutes, but in a questionable manner. Alexis Ponnet, the Belgian referee, ordered Porto's Jaime Magalhaes to retreat when he made a legitimate attempt to block the flight of a throw-in to be taken by Bayern on their left wing. When the throw-in was taken, the ball deflected off of Magalhaes into the path of Bayern's Ludwig Kogl, who scored with a header. Fast, attacking, football continued through until half time, but without further goals.

The pattern of the second half was imaginative Porto attack, and the defensive attempt by Bayern to hold on to their lead. Juary, who arrived as a substitute for Quim, at the start of the second half, played a major role in galvanising Porto. After several near misses, Porto deservedly equalised 13 minutes from time, as Juary ran through the right-hand side of the penalty area, before centring to Madjer, the latter of whom made a nonsense of the supposedly awkward position in which he received the ball, facing away from the goal, by rapidly backheeling the ball out of the reach of Jean-Marie Pfaff, the Bayern goalkeeper. Madjer was injured in Porto's energetic celebration of the goal, but soon recovered to combine again with Juary. Just two minutes after Juary set up the equaliser for Madjer, the compliment was returned, with Madjer crossing form the left to Juary, who volleyed a goal that completed Porto's revival, and gave them a 2-1 victory.

Five years earlier Madjer had tormented the Germans at international level, scoring for Algeria in their shock 2-1 win against West Germany in the 1982 World Cup finals. Now he contributed to Porto beating Bayern Munich by the same score. Udo Lattek, about to become technical director at Cologne, was rather bitter, and contradictory, in his post-match summary, saying: "I was disappointed with several of our players, including Matthaus, but I do not wish to make criticisms of individual players. I am pleased to be leaving the club now. It saves me the problem of what to do about players who do not obey their orders, and refuse to play their normal attacking game".

Bayern's performance had dipped in the second half, but the flair displayed by Porto meant they had deservedly become the first Portuguese winners of the European Cup since Benfica in 1962. A quarter of a century after Eusebio, from Mozambique, had inspired Benfica's triumph against Real Madrid, Porto had Juary, a Brazilian, and Madjer, an Algerian, to thank for their victory.

1986-87

First round

		1st leg	2nd leg	agg
PSV Eindhoven	Bayern Munich	0-2	0-0	0-2
Porto	Rabat Ajax	9-0	1-0	10-0
Avenir Beggen	FK Austria	0-3	0-3	0-6
Juventus	Valur Reykjavik	7-0	4-0	11-0
Red Star Belgrade	Panathinaikos	3-0	1-2	4-2
Beroe Stara Zagora	Dynamo Kiev	1-1	0-2	1-3
Young Boys Berne	Real Madrid	1-0	0-5	1-5
Anderlecht	Gornik Zabrze	2-0	1-1	3-1
Brondby	Honved	4-1	2-2	6-3
Besiktas	Dynamo Tirana	2-0	1-0	3-0
Apoel Nicosia	HJK Helsinki	1-0	2-3	3-3
Apoel Nicosia won on away goals				
Rosenborg	Linfield	1-0	1-1	2-1
Orgryte	Dynamo Berlin	2-3	1-4	3-7
Shamrock Rovers	Celtic	0-1	0-2	0-3
Paris Saint-Germain	Vitkovice	2-2	0-1	2-3

Second round

		1st leg	2nd leg	agg
Bayern Munich	FK Austria	2-0	1-1	3-1
Real Madrid	Juventus	1-0	0-1	1-1
Real Madrid won 3-1 on penalties				
Vitkovice	Porto	1-0	0-3	1-3

Rosenborg	Red Star Belgrade	0-3	1-4	1-7
Anderlecht	Steaua Bucharest	3-0	0-1	3-1
Celtic	Dynamo Kiev	1-1	1-3	2-4
Brondby	Dynamo Berlin	2-1	1-1	3-2

Besiktas walked over, Apoel Nicosia failed to appear

Quarter-finals

		1st leg	2nd leg	agg
Bayern Munich	Anderlecht	5-0	2-2	7-2
Besiktas	Dynamo Kiev	0-5	0-2	0-7
Red Star Belgrade	Real Madrid	4-2	0-2	4-4

Real Madrid won on away goals

Porto	Brondby	1-0	1-1	2-1

Semi-finals

		1st leg	2nd leg	agg
Bayern Munich	Real Madrid	4-1	0-1	4-2
Porto	Dynamo Kiev	2-1	2-1	4-2

Final

May 27 1987 Vienna

Porto 2	Bayern Munich 1
Madjer	Kogl
Juary	

Porto: Mlynarczyk, Joao Pinto, Eduardo Luis, Celso, Inacio (Frasco), Quim (Juary), Magalhaes, Madjer, Sousa, Andre, Futre
Bayern Munich: Pfaff, Winklhofer, Nachtweih, Eder, Pflugler, Flick (Lunde), Brehme, Matthaus, M Rummenigge, Hoeness, Kogl
HT: 0-1
Referee: Ponnet (Belgium)
Attendance: 57,500

1987-88

Porto were joined in the 1987-88 European Cup by Benfica, who had beaten them to the Portuguese championship the previous season, but while Porto progressed comfortably with a pair of 3-0 wins against Vardar Skopje, Benfica were embroiled in a brutal match with Partizan Tirana. In the first leg Benfica won 4-0 but the Albanians had four players sent off. This led UEFA to disqualify Partizan from the competition, with the tie being awarded to Benfica. While the Portuguese teams faced weak opposition, the representatives of two other Latin nations met each other in a sterner test, as Real Madrid faced a Napoli team that had won the Italian league for the first time in the club's history, largely due to the inspiration of Diego Maradona. Real won 2-0 in the first leg, which was played behind closed doors at the Bernabeu stadium, due to the hooligan problems there in the previous season's match against Bayern Munich. The return match was a 1-1 draw. In the second round, Porto lost both home and away against Real Madrid, while Benfica struggled to beat Aarhus by a single goal.

Glasgow Rangers were led by player-manager Graeme Souness, who had won the European Cup as a player with Liverpool. His team featured several Englishmen, including Trevor Francis, who had won the trophy with Nottingham Forest in 1979. Rangers did well to eliminate Dynamo Kiev, but appeared to benefit from some sharp practice. Having lost the first leg 1-0, Rangers recovered to win 2-0 in Glasgow, on a pitch Souness had narrowed to the legal minimum in an attempt to stifle the wing play of the Kiev team, after the latter had trained on the full size pitch. Dynamo Kiev's secretary, Mikhail Oshenkov, grumbled "There used to be gentlemen in British football".

Bayern Munich met Real Madrid, in a quarter-final that saw good quality football replace the animosity of the previous season's encounter. Bayern led by three goals early in the second half of their home leg, but Real scored twice late in the match to reduce the margin of defeat to 3-2, and then won their home leg 2-0. Benfica edged past Anderlecht, while PSV Eindhoven beat Bordeaux on away goals. A goal from Edward Linskens at the Bernabeau gave PSV an away goals semi-final victory over Real Madrid, while in the other tie Benfica ended Steaua Bucharest's hopes of reaching a second final in three seasons by winning 2-0 in Portugal, with a pair of goals from Rui Aguas, following a goalless match in Romania.

PSV, appearing in the final for the first time, were managed by Guus Hiddinck, a man whose long and successful career was to include spells as the national manager of both the Netherlands and South Korea (he took the latter to fourth place in the 2002 World Cup). Benfica, their opponents in Stuttgart, had reached the final five times, but each occasion had been back in the 1960s, and this was their first final for 20 years. Their team included Rui Aguas, whose father had played, and scored, for the club in both the 1961 and 1962 finals. In another echo from the past, Eusebio was now assistant to the Benfica manager, Toni.

In contrast to the thrilling final of 1987, this match echoed the dull outcome of the 1986 contest, with two hours of goalless football giving way to a penalty decider. PSV were slightly the better team, but neither they or Benfica showed the quality expected in such a prestigious match. But while in 1986 even the penalty contest had been short of goals, the 1988 decider brought a high strike rate. Each team scored from their first five penalties to take the tie-breaker into sudden death. Substitute Anton Janssen now scored for PSV Eindhoven, but the effort from Benfica's Veloso was saved by Hans Van Breukelen. PSV therefore emerged as 6-5 winners on penalties, with Benfica failing to emulate their past successes in winning the trophy, or that of their fellow-countrymen, Porto, in 1987.

PSV's European Cup victory was unexpected, given that the teams representing the Netherlands had been eliminated in the first round in each of the preceding five seasons, and far from convincing. After an aggregate success against Galatasaray, featuring a win and a defeat, followed by two wins against Rapid Vienna in the second round, PSV drew all five of their matches in the quarter finals, semi-finals, and final, stumbling to victory via away goals and penalties. The drab final, and PSV's route to the trophy, reflected the generally unimpressive nature of this season's European Cup. Another measure of this was the absence of any prolific goalscorer. Six players tied as leading scorer, with just four goals each – namely Jean-Marc Ferreri (Bordeaux), Gheorghe Hagi (Steaua Bucharest), Rabah Madjer (Porto), Ally McCoist (Rangers), Michel (Real Madrid), and Rui Aguas (Benfica).

1987-88
First round

		1st leg	2nd leg	agg
Rapid Vienna	Hamrun Spartans	6-0	1-0	7-0
Aarhus	Jeunesse D'Esch	4-1	0-1	4-2
Shamrock Rovers	Omonia Nicosia	0-1	0-0	0-1
Real Madrid	Napoli	2-0	1-1	3-1
Bordeaux	Dynamo Berlin	2-0	2-0	4-0
Olympiakos	Gornik Zabrze	1-1	1-2	2-3
Fram Reykjavik	Sparta Prague	0-2	0-8	0-10
Lillestrom	Linfield	1-1	4-2	5-3
PSV Eindhoven	Galatasaray	3-0	0-2	3-2
Benfica	Partizan Tirana	4-0		
Tie awarded to Benfica, Partizan Tirana disqualified				
Porto	Vardar Skopje	3-0	3-0	6-0
Bayern Munich	CSKA Sofia	4-0	1-0	5-0

		1st leg	2nd leg	agg
Steaua Bucharest	MTK Budapest	4-0	0-2	4-2
Malmo	Anderlecht	0-1	1-1	1-2
Neuchatel Xamax	Kuusysi Lahti	5-0	1-2	6-2
Dynamo Kiev	Rangers	1-0	0-2	1-2

Second round

		1st leg	2nd leg	agg
Rapid Vienna	PSV Eindhoven	1-2	0-2	1-4
Aarhus	Benfica	0-0	0-1	0-1
Rangers	Gornik Zabrze	3-1	1-1	4-2
Real Madrid	Porto	2-1	2-1	4-2
Lillestrom	Bordeaux	0-0	0-1	0-1
Steaua Bucharest	Omonia Nicosia	3-1	2-0	5-1
Neuchatel Xamax	Bayern Munich	2-1	0-2	2-3
Sparta Prague	Anderlecht	1-2	0-1	1-3

Quarter-finals

		1st leg	2nd leg	agg
Bordeaux	PSV Eindhoven	1-1	0-0	1-1

PSV Eindhoven won on away goals

		1st leg	2nd leg	agg
Benfica	Anderlecht	2-0	0-1	2-1
Bayern Munich	Real Madrid	3-2	0-2	3-4
Steaua Bucharest	Rangers	2-0	1-2	3-2

Semi-finals

		1st leg	2nd leg	agg
Real Madrid	PSV Eindhoven	1-1	0-0	1-1

PSV Eindhoven won on away goals

		1st leg	2nd leg	agg
Steaua Bucharest	Benfica	0-0	0-2	0-2

Final

May 25 1988 Stuttgart

PSV Eindhoven 0   Benfica 0 (after extra time)

PSV Eindhoven won 6-5 on penalties

PSV Eindhoven: Van Breukelen, Gerets, Van Aerle, Koeman, Nielsen, Heintze, Vanenburg, Linskens, Lerby, Kieft, Gillhaus (Janssen)

Benfica: Silvino, Veloso, Dito, Mozer, Alvaro, Elzo, Sheu, Chiquinho, Pacheco, Aguas (Vando), Magnusson (Hajiri)

Referee: Agnolin (Italy)

Attendance: 68,000

1988-89

The 1988-89 competition was most notable for the re-emergence of Milan, who were to win the European Cup for the first time in 20 years, with some outstanding football. After thrashing Real Madrid in the semi-finals, Milan secured the trophy with a brilliant 4-0 win in the final against Steaua Bucharest, who continued to rank among the best teams in the continent. A major factor in Milan's success was their use of a new tactic called "pressing", the idea being that a team in possession of the ball should push men forward, seeking to attack in numbers, while also stifling the development of counter-attacks by the opposition. Milan's talented players, and their tactics, were blended by the coach Arrigo Sacchi, who had built a successful career in management despite his not playing professional football. As Sacchi explained to doubters, "I did not know that a jockey had to be born a horse to ride one".

PSV Eindhoven, the reigning champions, were given a bye through the first round. Benfica, the defeated finalists in 1988, had not retained their domestic title, and Portugal were represented by Porto, who opened with a 3-0 win against HJK Helsinki, before losing the second leg 2-0. Celtic overcame a single goal defeat away to Honved – before a paltry crowd of 8,000 – with an impressive 4-0 win in the return match. By contrast Glentoran, from Northern Ireland, lost 3-1 on aggregate to Spartak Moscow, and Dundalk, from the Republic of Ireland, were thrashed 8-0 by Red Star Belgrade. An all-German tie brought drama, as Dynamo Berlin, representing East Germany for a tenth successive season, beat Werder Bremen, from West Germany, 3-0 in the first leg, but lost the second leg 5-0. Milan's 7-2 aggregate win over Vitosha Sofia owed a great deal to Marco Van Basten, scorer of four goals in the second leg. Meanwhile Gheorghe Hagi and Marius Lacatus both scored three times as Steaua Bucharest beat Sparta Prague 7-3 on aggregate. 17 Nentori Tirana achieved a rare Albanian European success, beating Hamrun Spartans 3-2 on aggregate.

PSV Eindhoven opened their defence with an emphatic 5-0 win against Porto, which rendered their 2-0 defeat in the return match academic. Milan had a much closer victory, beating Red Star Belgrade on penalties but only after coming within 29 minutes of being eliminated. After drawing 1-1 in Milan a goal from Dejan Savicevic put Red Star ahead only for the game to be abandoned because of fog. The replayed game ended 1-1. Monaco thrashed Brugge 6-2 on aggregate, with Youssouf Fofana scoring a hat-trick in the second leg, while Steaua Bucharest also chalked up an impressive success, beating Spartak Moscow 5-1, with Gheorge Hagi scoring twice.

In the quarter finals, PSV lost 3-2 on aggregate to Real Madrid, who clinched victory in extra time thanks to a goal from Martin Vasquez. Steaua Bucharest ran up a large victory for the third successive round, disposing of IFK Gothenburg 5-2 on aggregate – Lacatus scoring a hat-trick in the second leg. Galatasaray beat Monaco 2-1 by winning away and drawing at home. Milan's victory against Werder Bremen came courtesy of a single goal, Van Basten scoring from a penalty in the second leg.

Milan drew 1-1 away to Real Madrid in the first leg of their semi-final – Van Basten again scoring – and produced a stunning performance to thrash their opponents 5-0 with goals from Carlo Ancelotti, Frank Rijkaard, Ruud Gullit, Van Basten, and Roberto Donadoni. Real had now been eliminated in the semi-finals for a third successive season. In the other tie Steaua Bucharest beat Galatasaray 4-0, before drawing the return 1-1. The semi-final second legs were preceded by a minute's silence in memory of the victims of the Hillsborough tragedy, which had occurred four days earlier on April 15. In a terrible echo of the Heysel disaster of 1985, over-crowding at a FA Cup semi-final between Liverpool and Nottingham Forest had caused the death of 95 Liverpool supporters. In a spontaneous tribute to the Liverpool fans, Milan supporters also sang "You'll Never Walk Alone" ahead of their team's match at the Giuseppe Meazza Stadium.

So Milan and Steaua Bucharest lined up at Barcelona's Nou Camp stadium. This was Milan's fourth appearance in a European Cup final – they had been winners in 1963 and 1969, after losing the 1958 final. Steaua had been winners in their only previous appearance in the final, as recently as 1986. Steaua fielded four members of the team which had won the 1986 final, namely Adrian Bumbescu, Stefan Iovan, Marius Lacatus, and Victor Piturca. Since then the Steaua team had been strengthened by the acquisition of Gheorghe Hagi, Romania's greatest ever player – an addition insisted upon by Nicu Ceauscescu. Steaua were coached by Anghel Iordanescu, who had played for them in the 1986 final. Milan's team was built around three outstanding Dutchmen, Gullit, Van Basten, and Rijkaard, who had been instrumental in the Netherlands winning the European Championship the previous year. Gullit played despite not being fully fit. After being carried off in the 5-0 win against Real Madrid five weeks earlier, he had needed surgery on his right knee two days later, followed by intense physiotherapy. Although the match was played in Spain, it seemed to be a home fixture for Milan, with an amazing 80,000 out of the 97,000 crowd being their fans. The match was televised in around 80 nations, but not in Spain, due to an industrial dispute involving television engineers.

After many years during which the European Cup final was routinely broadcast live in Britain, only highlights were shown each year from 1987 to 1991, with the BBC and ITV reflecting reduced English interest in the competition during the post-Heysel ban.

Milan dominated from the start. After 12 minutes a possible goal for Van Basten was ruled out, as Gullit had been caught offside. Four minutes later a pass from Franco Baresi found Gullit, whose shot hit the post, following which Angelo Colombo's effort from the rebound went into the side netting. The expected goal for Milan arrived on 17 minutes, as Gullit scored following a goalmouth scramble which also involved Colombo and Van Basten. A couple of minutes later Steaua threatened for the first time, with a shot from Hagi being deflected away from goal by Milan defender Alessandro Costacurta. After 26 minutes, as the Steaua defence only half-cleared a corner, a cross from Mauro Tassoti was met by a header from Van Basten, which put Milan further ahead – with a decoy run from Gullit contributing to the breaching of the Steaua defence. Milan added a third goal on 38 minutes, as Donadoni crossed from the left, and Gullit brilliantly controlled the ball and shot past Silviu Lung, the Steaua goalkeeper. Four minutes before the interval a rare mix-up in the Milan defence presented a chance to Piturca, but he miscued his shot so badly that it ended up near the corner flag.

With little more than a minute of the second half played, Rijkaard set up a chance for Van Basten, who scored with a powerful shot. Milan now led 4-0, with both Gullit and Van Basten having scored twice. Van Basten's goals took his total for this European Cup campaign to ten, a figure which made him the leading scorer, ahead of Lacatus, with seven goals, and Hagi, with six. All three played in the final, but the two Steaua players looked unlikely to add to their personal tallies. With victory almost certain, it was surprising that Arrigo Sacchi had not replaced Gullit, giving the player a chance to rest his injured knee. Gullit's continued efforts unfortunately led him to aggravate the injury, with the result that he had to be substituted on 59 minutes. Gullit left the field to a standing ovation, as his performance had been a major factor in Milan's control of the match. Besides scoring two goals, and hitting a post, Gullit had been dominant in the air, and formed a great striking partnership with Van Basten. Milan freewheeled during the remaining half hour of the match, and wasted the opportunity to add further goals with some erratic finishing. Pietro Virdis, who had replaced Gullit, was particularly culpable, most notably when he shot high over the bar from close range eight minutes from time. Steaua made gallant efforts but were simply outplayed.

Milan had won the European Cup for the first time since 1969, when the final had also been staged in Spain. The trophy was collected by their captain Baresi. Meanwhile Paolo Maldini, another member of Milan's defence, emulated his father Cesare, who had won the European Cup with Milan in 1963, the first father and son pairing to win the competition. In the post-match interviews Arrigo Sacchi said: "We deserved to win. The Champions Cup deserves a high standard of football, and I think that is what we provided. I am lucky in being able to work with such superb players, and a superb president. I would like to thank them all publicly for that". The Milan president, Silvio Berlusconi, was the owner of a broadcasting empire.

Anghel Iordanescu pointed out that Steaua's relative failure was largely caused by the tiredness of the players. Some of them had played 11 matches in the space of 32 days, as they sought the European Cup plus their domestic league and cup titles, combining this with international duty for Romania. Steaua won the Romanian league title for the fifth successive year in 1989, and the Romanian Cup for the third successive year. Steaua did not do themselves justice in the European Cup final, but the lasting impression of that match, and the season, was the wonderful football produced by Milan.

1988-89

First round

		1st leg	2nd leg	agg
Dynamo Berlin	Werder Bremen	3-0	0-5	3-5
Sparta Prague	Steaua Bucharest	1-5	2-2	3-7
Real Madrid	Moss	3-0	1-0	4-0
Pezoporikos Larnaca	IFK Gothenburg	1-2	1-5	2-7
Brugge	Brondby	1-0	1-2	2-2
Porto	HJK Helsinki	3-0	0-2	3-2
Rapid Vienna	Galatasaray	2-1	0-2	2-3
Spartak Moscow	Glentoran	2-0	1-1	3-1
Vitosha	Milan	0-2	2-5	2-7
Hamrun Spartans	17 Nentori Tirana	2-1	0-2	2-3
Gornik Zabrze	Jeunesse D'Esch	3-0	4-1	7-1
Larissa	Neuchatel Xamax	2-1	1-2	3-3
Neuchatel Xamax won 3-0 on penalties				
Honved	Celtic	1-0	0-4	1-4
Dundalk	Red Star Belgrade	0-5	0-3	0-8
Valur Reykjavik	Monaco	1-0	0-2	1-2

Second round

		1st leg	2nd leg	agg
Celtic	Werder Bremen	0-1	0-0	0-1
Milan	Red Star Belgrade	1-1	1-1	2-2
Milan won 4-2 on penalties				
Neuchatel Xamax	Galatasaray	3-0	0-5	3-5
PSV Eindhoven	Porto	5-0	0-2	5-2
Steaua Bucharest	Spartak Moscow	3-0	2-1	5-1
17 Nentori Tirana	IFK Gothenburg	0-3	0-1	0-4
Brugge	Monaco	1-0	1-6	2-6
Gornik Zabrze	Real Madrid	0-1	2-3	2-4

Quarter-finals

		1st leg	2nd leg	agg
IFK Gothenburg	Steaua Bucharest	1-0	1-5	2-5
PSV Eindhoven	Real Madrid	1-1	1-2	2-3
Monaco	Galatasaray	0-1	1-1	1-2
Werder Bremen	Milan	0-0	0-1	0-1

Semi-finals

		1st leg	2nd leg	agg
Steaua Bucharest	Galatasaray	4-0	1-1	5-1
Real Madrid	Milan	1-1	0-5	1-6

Final

May 24 1989 Barcelona
Milan 4   Steaua Bucharest 0
Gullit 2
Van Basten 2
Milan: G Galli, Tassotti, Costacurta (F Galli), Baresi, Maldini, Colombo, Rijkaard, Ancelotti, Donadoni, Gullit (Virdis), Van Basten
Steaua Bucharest: Lung, Iovan, Petrescu, Bumbescu, Ungureanu, Hagi, Stoica, Minea, Rotariu (Balaci), Lacatus, Piturca
HT: 3-0
Referee: Tritschler (West Germany)
Attendance: 97,000

Ruud Gullit

The re-emergence of Milan as one of the leading forces in Europe during the late 1980s, and early 1990s, owed a great deal to the brilliance of Ruud Gullit. This was the high point in the remarkable career of a player who could have rivalled Johan Cruyff as the greatest ever Dutch footballer, had his progress not been blighted by injuries. Gullit, like Cruyff, possessed a brilliant footballing brain. He began his career as a sweeper, but soon converted to a player who was nominally a striker, but had the ability to drift between attack and midfield to devastating effect. His timing and control were outstanding, his shooting was powerful, and he was a fine header of the ball. In 1990, Gullit's brilliance was summed up by George Best: "Ruud Gullit is a great player by any standards. He has all the skills. He's not afraid to do things with the ball. And he looks as if he is enjoying every second of it. By my reckoning that's what makes him an even better player than Maradona. Both have the key quality you will find in all the best players: balance. You just can't knock them off the ball. It was the same with Pele, Beckenbauer and Cruyff".

Ruud Gullit was born in Amsterdam on September 1 1962. He began his professional career with Haarlem, joining the club in 1978. Three years later, on his 19th birthday, he made his debut for the Netherlands, in a 2-1 defeat against Switzerland. In 1982 Gullit moved to Feyenoord, with whom he won the Dutch league and cup in 1984, playing alongside Cruyff. Gullit was on the move again in 1985, joining PSV Eindhoven, a club he would help to win the Dutch league in both 1986 and 1987. At the end of 1987 Gullit won the European Footballer of the Year award. He was now playing for Milan, having moved there in the summer on a £5,500,000 transfer. Milan won the Italian league in 1987-88, Gullit's first season with the club. In June 1988 he captained the Netherlands as they won the European Championship, and scored in their 2-0 win against the Soviet Union in the final. The following year Milan won the European Cup, with Gullit scoring twice in the 4-0 win against Steaua Bucharest in the final, a victory he shared with his Dutch international team-mates, Marco Van Basten and Frank Rijkaard.

Recurring knee injuries prevented Gullit from reaching new heights. He missed most of the 1989-90 season, including Milan's victories in the World Club Championship and European Super Cup, but did appear in the 1-0 victory against Benfica, by which they retained the European Cup. Gullit led the Netherlands at the 1990 World Cup finals, and scored in their 1-1 draw against the Republic of Ireland, but looked unfit when they were eliminated by a 2-1 defeat against West Germany.

Milan retained the World Club Championship and European Super Cup in 1990-91, with Gullit appearing in both contests, and scoring against Sampdoria in the Super Cup. In 1992 Milan regained the Italian league title. Gullit played for the Netherlands in that year's European Championship finals, but defeat against Denmark, on penalties, in the semi-finals, ended their hopes of retaining the title. The following year, after winning another Italian championship with Milan, Gullit moved to Sampdoria, this being the start of a yo-yo process. Gullit won the Italian Cup with Sampdoria in 1994, moved back to Milan, and then re-joined Sampdoria later in the year.

Ruud Gullit has always been a justifiably confident man, but has a tendency to lapse into an arrogance that undermines his dealings with others. He had a series of rows with Dick Advocaat, during the latter's first spell as Dutch national coach, between 1992 and 1994. These saw Gullit move in and out of the national squad, and walk out on a chance of playing in the 1994 World Cup finals. He played his final match for the Netherlands in 1995, ending an international career that had lasted 14 years, during which he had scored 16 goals in 66 matches.

Gullit's second spell with Sampdoria only lasted a few months. In 1995 he moved to Chelsea. In the following year Gullit became a player-manager, as Glenn Hoddle moved from Chelsea to replace Terry Venables as England coach. Chelsea won the FA Cup in 1997, beating Middlesbrough 2-0 in the final, and Gullit, at the age of 34, became the youngest manager to win that trophy. He did not, however, play in the final, due to a long-term ankle injury. In February 1998 Gullit was unexpectedly sacked by Chelsea – with team-mate Gianluca Vialli replacing him as player-manager.

The sacking by Chelsea ended Gullit's playing career, but he was soon active on the managerial merry-go-round, replacing Kenny Dalglish at Newcastle United in August 1998. Newcastle reached the FA Cup final at the end of the 1998-99 season, but lost 2-0 against Manchester United. Gullit quit at the start of the following season, being unhappy with developments at Newcastle, and suffering from the supporters' anger at seeing him sideline Alan Shearer, the club's talismanic striker. Gullit spent a period away from direct participation in football, preferring to concentrate on a new career in television – he hosted a Dutch programme that reported on the lives of celebrities. He had previously been an articulate pundit for the BBC, and his views on the game were still courted by the media. Gullit's complex personal life has often been the subject of media interest. He has been married three times – his third wife being Estelle Cruyff, the niece of Johan – and has six children. After a hiatus of four years, Gullit returned to management in 2003, as coach of the Dutch under-20 team. He joined Feyenoord as coach in 2004, but this intriguing new stage in his career was halted by dismissal in May 2005.

1989-90

This season's European Cup was played against a backdrop of immense political changes in eastern Europe. The dismantling of the Berlin Wall, and the overthrow of the Ceaucescu regime – backers of Steaua Bucharest – in Romania, two events that happened within a few weeks of each other late in 1989, were the most potent symbols of the fall of communist dictatorship. These changes in turn led to the end of the Cold War between west and east.

Milan retained the European Cup in 1990, but their 1-0 win over Benfica in the final, in contrast to the 4-0 thrashing of Steaua Bucharest in 1989, reflected a dip in the quality of their performance. After easily disposing of HJK Helsinki in the first round, Milan beat Real Madrid 2-1 on aggregate, in a bad-tempered encounter. In the quarter-finals Milan drew 0-0 away to Mechelen, and required extra time to win the return 2-0 with goals from Marco Van Basten and Marco Simone. Both teams had a player sent off in the latter match. Milan also required extra time against Bayern Munich in the semi-finals, eventually winning the tie because of Stefano Borgonovo's away goal, having drawn 2-2 on aggregate.

Benfica's road to the final began with a straightforward victory against Derry City. In 1965-66 Derry City had represented Northern Ireland in the European Cup, but now they flew the flag of the Republic of Ireland, having moved leagues during the intervening years. In the second round Benfica thrashed Honved 9-0 on aggregate, with César Brito, Vata Garcia, and Mats Magnusson each scoring twice in the second leg. An impressive pair of wins against Dnepr Dnepropetrovsk, from the Soviet Union, took Benfica through the quarter-finals. They nearly came unstuck against Marseille, as they lost the away leg 2-1, and only won the return by a single goal eight minutes from time from Vata Garcia, which looked to have been the result of his handling the ball. Benfica therefore drew the tie 2-2, and booked their place in the final on away goals – matching Milan in this respect.

Internazionale, who entered the competition as reigning Italian champions – Milan had finished third the previous season – departed in the first round, losing to Malmo. Meanwhile Rangers lost 3-1 at home to Bayern Munich, who were content to play out a dull 0-0 draw in the return, to the derision of their fans. A battle of the minnows saw Albania's 17 Nentori Tirana achieve a surprisingly large 5-0 home win against Malta's Sliema Wanderers, after losing the first leg 1-0. 17 Nentori Tirana were predictably thrashed by Bayern Munich in the next round.

Steaua Bucharest were unable to repeat their success of the previous season, as they lost 5-1 away to PSV Eindhoven – for whom Romario scored a hat-trick – after winning the first leg of this second round tie 1-0. Romario was joint leading scorer this season, along with Jean-Pierre Papin of Marseille, each of them netting six times. In contrast to the failure of Steaua, two clubs from eastern Europe reached the quarter-finals this season, namely CSKA Sofia and Dnepr. CSKA Sofia were rapidly re-formed as CFKA Sredets after being disbanded in 1985, and had now reverted to their original name. In the first couple of rounds CSKA eliminated a couple of their east European neighbours, Ruch Chorzow and Sparta Prague, with their star player, Hristo Stoichkov, scoring three time in the 5-2 aggregate win against the Czechoslovakians.

Milan and Benfica met for the final at the Prater Stadium in Vienna – where the two clubs' great rivals, Internazionale and Porto, had won the European Cup in 1964 and 1987 respectively. Milan and Benfica had contested the 1963 final, with Milan's victorious team having included Cesare Maldini. His son Paolo played in the 1990 final, as Arrigo Sacchi made only one change from the team he had selected a year earlier – Alberigo Evani replacing Roberto Donadoni. As in 1989, Sacchi was taking a risk in fielding Ruud Gullit, whose persistent injury problems had caused him to miss almost the entire season. Benfica were managed by Sven-Goran Eriksson, a Swede who had led Gothenburg to the Swedish title in 1981, and Benfica to the Portuguese title in 1983 and 1984. After a spell in Italy, managing Roma and then Fiorentina, Eriksson had returned to Benfica in 1989. He would subsequently take Benfica to another Portuguese title in 1991, and win the Italian league with Lazio in 2000, before becoming England coach in 2001.

In 1963 Milan had come from behind to beat Benfica 2-1, in a rather disappointing final. The 1990 final brought an even less impressive win for Milan, achieved with a single goal. Benfica had the majority of the possession in the first half, but were thwarted by Milan's defence. In contrast to the attacking play that had destroyed Steaua Bucharest the previous year, Milan now played a cautious game, based on their defensive strength. At the start of the second half Van Basten set up a great chance for Gullit, but the latter's hurried shot was saved by Silvino Louro, the Benfica goalkeeper. Milan now became more of an attacking force, and they scored in the 68th minute, as a pass from Van Basten carved open the Benfica defence, and picked out Frank Rijkaard, who found the net with a powerful shot. This was a well-deserved moment of glory for Rijkaard, who did not equal the brilliance of his compatriots, Gullit and Van Basten, but was still one of the finest players in Europe, and able to switch effortlessly between midfield and defence. Once they fell behind, Benfica lacked the inspiration necessary to get back into the match, and Milan became the first club to win the European Cup in successive seasons since Nottingham Forest a decade earlier, by strolling to a rather anti-climactic victory.

1989-90

First round

		1st leg	2nd leg	agg
Tirol	Omonia Nicosia	6-0	3-2	9-2
Rangers	Bayern Munich	1-3	0-0	1-3

Derry City	Benfica	1-2	0-4	1-6
Marseille	Brondby	3-0	1-1	4-1
Honved	Vojvodina Novi Sad	1-0	1-2	2-2
Honved won on away goals				
Linfield	Dnepr Dnepropetrovsk	1-2	0-1	1-3
Milan	HJK Helsinki	4-0	1-0	5-0
Spora Luxembourg	Real Madrid	0-3	0-6	0-9
Sliema Wanderers	17 Nentori Tirana	1-0	0-5	1-5
Rosenborg	Mechelen	0-0	0-5	0-5
PSV Eindhoven	Lucerne	3-0	2-0	5-0
Ruch Chorzow	CSKA Sofia	1-1	1-5	2-6
Steaua Bucharest	Fram Reykjavik	4-0	1-0	5-0
Malmo	Internazionale	1-0	1-1	2-1
Sparta Prague	Fenerbahce	3-1	2-1	5-2
Dynamo Dresden	AEK Athens	1-0	3-5	4-5

Second round

		1st leg	2nd leg	agg
Marseille	AEK Athens	2-0	1-1	3-1
Honved	Benfica	0-2	0-7	0-9
Milan	Real Madrid	2-0	0-1	2-1
Bayern Munich	17 Nentori Tirana	3-1	3-0	6-1
Steaua Bucharest	PSV Eindhoven	1-0	1-5	2-5
Malmo	Mechelen	0-0	1-4	1-4
Sparta Prague	CSKA Sofia	2-2	0-3	2-5
Dnepr Dnepropetrovsk	Tirol	2-0	2-2	4-2

Quarter-finals

		1st leg	2nd leg	agg
Mechelen	Milan	0-0	0-2	0-2
CSKA Sofia	Marseille	0-1	1-3	1-4
Benfica	Dnepr Dnepropetrovsk	1-0	3-0	4-0
Bayern Munich	PSV Eindhoven	2-1	1-0	3-1

Semi-finals

		1st leg	2nd leg	agg
Marseille	Benfica	2-1	0-1	2-2
Benfica won on away goals				
Milan	Bayern Munich	1-0	1-2	2-2
Milan won on away goals				

Final

May 23 1990 Vienna
Milan 1   Benfica 0
Rijkaard
Milan: G.Galli, Tassotti, Costacurta, Baresi, Maldini, Colombo (F Galli), Rijkaard, Ancelotti (Massaro), Evani, Gullit, Van Basten
Benfica: Silvino, Jose Carlos, Aldair, Ricardo, Samuel, Vitor Paneira (Vata Garcia), Valdo, Thern, Hernani, Magnusson, Pacheco (Brito)
HT: 0-0
Referee: Kohl (Austria)
Attendance: 57,500

1990-91

As holders, Milan received a bye through the first round because the field was reduced to 31 by the absence of a representative from the Netherlands. Ajax, the Dutch champions, were suspended from Europe, due to crowd trouble when they played FK Austria in the previous season's UEFA Cup. In the next round Milan scraped through against Brugge thanks to a goal from Angelo Carbone.

Rangers opened with a 10-0 aggregate win against Valletta. Mo Johnston, a Catholic playing for the staunchly-Protestant team, scored five times. Rangers' run was promptly ended by Red Star Belgrade. Portadown were thrashed 13-1 on aggregate by Porto – Rabah Madjer and Stéphane Paille each scoring four. Real Madrid, winners of the Spanish league for a fifth successive time, also opened with some high goal-scoring, beating OB Odense 10-1 and Tirol 11-3. Hugo Sanchez scored four times in the first leg against Tirol. Bayern Munich beat Apoel Nicosia 7-2 and CSKA Sofia 7-0. Napoli's love affair with Diego Maradona was now going sour, partly because he had led Argentina to victory, on penalties, against Italy in a 1990 World Cup semi-final, played at the club's stadium in Naples. Maradona scored twice as they beat Ujpest Dozsa, but in the next round they went out on penalties against Spartak Moscow, following two goalless draws.

The strong eastern challenge of recent years continued. Six teams from that part of the continent reached the second round, and three reached the quarter finals. Spartak Moscow sprang a surprise in the last eight, beating Real Madrid 3-1 in Madrid, with Dimitri Radchenko scoring twice, after a goalless draw in Moscow. Real's collapse brought the end of Alfredo Di Stefano's second spell as caretaker-manager. An all-eastern tie between Red Star Belgrade and Dynamo Dresden was afflicted by crowd trouble. Red Star had won 3-0 at home, and were leading 2-1 in Dresden when a riot forced the abandonment of the match, which was then awarded to Red Star with a 3-0 margin. Another match at this stage was abandoned, but this time it was petulant players, rather than hooligans, who were the cause. Milan had been held to a 1-1 draw at home to Marseille, and were trailing 1-0 in the return, Chris Waddle having scored for the French club, when the floodlights failed late in the match. The Milan players left the field, and refused to return when the lights were put back in working order. Milan's hopes of a replay were ended by UEFA awarding the match to Marseille, again 3-0. It was a tawdry end to Milan's attempt to win the trophy for a third successive season. In the remaining quarter-final, Bayern Munich beat Porto, to reverse their defeat in the 1987 final.

Both of the semi-finals paired a team from the west with one from the east. Red Star Belgrade came from behind to win 2-1 away to Bayern Munich, and led 1-0 at half time in the return, but the Germans scored twice in four minutes midway through the second half, to level the aggregate score. Extra time beckoned, until Bayern's Klaus Augenthaler, who had scored their first goal, had the misfortune to chalk up an own goal a minute from time, leaving Red Star as 4-3 aggregate winners. In the other tie, Marseille played consistently excellent football to overcome Spartak Moscow, winning 3-1 away, and 2-1 at home.

Marseille and Red Star Belgrade were both through to the final for the first time. Red Star had been regular participants in the competition since the 1950s, and had reached the semi-finals in 1957 and 1971. Marseille had been eliminated in the early rounds in both 1971-72 and 1972-73, and then reached the semi-finals in 1989-90. The final was played at Bari, in an attractive stadium that had been built for the 1990 World Cup finals but the match did not live up to its setting. For the third time in six seasons, the final was dull and goalless, through both normal time and extra time. Indeed this match was arguably the poorest ever European Cup final.

The drama was concentrated in the penalty contest that settled the match. Red Star Belgrade went first, with Robert Prosinecki scoring. Manuel Amoros then stepped up for Marseille, but his kick was saved by Stevan Stojanovic. Both teams then scored each of their next three kicks, before Darko Pancev put away Red Star's final penalty, to take the contest 5-3. The Red Star team included such excellent players as Miodrag Belodedic, Sinisa Mihajlovic, Darko Pancev, Robert Prosinecki, and Dejan Savicevic, but the negative approach laid down by their manager, Ljubko

Petrovic, meant they did not distinguish themselves. Afterwards Petrovic was quoted as saying: "Put simply, we won on penalties after an extraordinary match. Tactics dominated the night. All my players worked to their utmost to produce victory".

Extraordinary was a strange adjective to describe the match. Perhaps Petrovic was describing the game he imagined rather than the one that everybody else saw, or it may be that something was lost in translation. While Red Star concentrated on their tactics, Marseille lacked the ability to create more than a few half-chances, despite having an attack led by Jean-Pierre Papin (later to be voted European Footballer of the Year), Chris Waddle (the first Englishman to appear in the European Cup final since the Heysel ban), and Abedi Pele (a Ghanian who won the 1991 African Footballer of the Year award). Papin was the competition's joint leading scorer for a second successive season, with six goals, a tally he shared with Peter Pacult of Tirol, but rarely looked like adding to the total in the final.

Red Star Belgrade had improved upon the record of their closest rivals, Partizan Belgrade, who were beaten finalists in 1966, and emulated the Steaua Bucharest team of 1986, becoming the second club from eastern Europe to win the European Cup. Coincidentally, Belodedic played in both the 1986 and 1991 finals, thereby becoming the first player to win the European Cup with two clubs. With the 1991 final having been settled on penalties after a goalless draw, a repeat of the drab outcomes in 1986 and 1988, football followers were looking for an alternative way to settle drawn matches at this level. The case for sudden death extra time, in which a single goal would settle a match, and the lottery of the penalty contest could be dispensed with, was looking attractive, but the challenge was not taken up by the football authorities. Instead of this, UEFA were looking towards a re-modelling of the format of the competition, which was destined to have a major impact over the next few years.

1990-91

First round

		1st leg	2nd leg	agg
Tirol	Kuusysi Lahti	5-0	2-1	7-1
Apoel Nicosia	Bayern Munich	2-3	0-4	2-7
OB Odense	Real Madrid	1-4	0-6	1-10
Marseille	Dynamo Tirana	5-1	0-0	5-1
Akureyri	CSKA Sofia	1-0	0-3	1-3
Napoli	Ujpest Dozsa	3-0	2-0	5-0
Union Luxembourg	Dynamo Dresden	1-3	0-3	1-6
Valletta	Rangers	0-4	0-6	0-10
Lillestrom	Brugge	1-1	0-2	1-3
Lech Poznan	Panathinaikos	3-0	2-1	5-1
Porto	Portadown	5-0	8-1	13-1
Dynamo Bucharest	St. Patrick's Athletic	4-0	1-1	5-1
Malmo	Besiktas	3-2	2-2	5-4
Sparta Prague	Spartak Moscow	0-2	0-2	0-4
Red Star Belgrade	Grasshoppers	1-1	4-1	5-2

Second round

		1st leg	2nd leg	agg
Real Madrid	Tirol	9-1	2-2	11-3
Milan	Brugge	0-0	1-0	1-0
Napoli	Spartak Moscow	0-0	0-0	0-0
Spartak Moscow won 5-3 on penalties				
Lech Poznan	Marseille	3-2	1-6	4-8
Bayern Munich	CSKA Sofia	4-0	3-0	7-0

		1st leg	2nd leg	agg
Dynamo Bucharest	Porto	0-0	0-4	0-4
Red Star Belgrade	Rangers	3-0	1-1	4-1
Dynamo Dresden	Malmo	1-1	1-1	2-2

Dynamo Dresden won 5-4 on penalties

Quarter-finals

		1st leg	2nd leg	agg
Milan	Marseille	1-1	0-3	1-4

Second leg abandoned with Marseille leading 1-0. Awarded to Marseille 3-0.

		1st leg	2nd leg	agg
Bayern Munich	Porto	1-1	2-0	3-1
Spartak Moscow	Real Madrid	0-0	3-1	3-1
Red Star Belgrade	Dynamo Dresden	3-0	3-0	6-0

Second leg abandoned with Red Star Belgrade leading 2-1. Awarded to Red Star Belgrade 3-0.

Semi-finals

		1st leg	2nd leg	agg
Bayern Munich	Red Star Belgrade	1-2	2-2	3-4
Spartak Moscow	Marseille	1-3	1-2	2-5

Final

May 29 1991 Bari

Red Star Belgrade 0   Marseille 0 (after extra time)

Red Star Belgrade won 5-3 on penalties

Red Star Belgrade: Stojanovic, Belodedic, Najdoski, Sabanadzovic, Jugovic, Marovic, Mihajlovic, Binic, Savicevic (Stosic), Prosinecki, Pancev

Marseille: Olmeta, Amoros, Boli, Mozer, Di Meco (Stojkovic), Fournier (Vercruysse), Germain, Casoni, Pele, Papin, Waddle

Referee: Lanese (Italy)

Attendance: 56,000

Chapter 8

Advent of the Champions League
1991-1997

1991-92

This season brought a modification to the format of the European Cup by UEFA, which opened the way for major changes in its structure over the following decade, and even the re-naming of the competition. The initial change was the replacement of the knock-out quarter-finals and semi-finals with two mini-leagues. The main aim of the league stage, which several of Europe's leading clubs had been pressing for in recent years, was to increase the number of matches played by the elite, and therefore add to revenue.

English clubs had returned to the European Cup-Winners' Cup and the UEFA Cup the previous season, but not the European Cup, as Liverpool, the reigning champions, were still banned. In the autumn of 1991 Arsenal became the first English team to play in the European Cup since the Heysel disaster. Managed by George Graham, who had played for them in the 1971-72 competition, Arsenal began with a 6-1 win against FK Austria, with Alan Smith scoring four times, before losing the return by a single goal. In the second round Arsenal faced a much tougher test, in the form of Benfica, who had just beaten Hamrun Spartans 10-0 on aggregate, with Sergei Yuran scoring five times. A 1-1 draw at the Stadium of Light gave Arsenal hope, but they were outplayed at Highbury, where Benfica won 3-1, after extra time.

Rangers went out on away goals in the first round, against Sparta Prague, who were appearing in the competition for the fifth successive season. Sparta were managed by Zdenek Nehoda, who had been a member of the Czechoslovakia team which won the European Championship in 1976. Sparta also won their next tie on away goals, overcoming Marseille, the previous season's runners-up. Marseille ran up a 3-0 lead by the hour mark in their home leg, but Sparta Prague pulled back two goals that night, and then won 2-1 in the return. Prior to this Marseille had twice beaten Union Luxembourg 5-0. Jean-Pierre Papin scored seven goals in Marseille's two ties, a total that was to leave him as leading scorer at the end of the season.

Holders Red Star Belgrade made their way through the knock-out stage with big wins against Portadown and Apollon Limassol. Prior to meeting Red Star, Apollon had surprisingly come back from a 2-0 defeat against Universitatea Craiova in Romania with a 3-0 win in Cyprus. Germany managed to field two teams, with UEFA accepting both Kaiserslautern, winners of the Bundesliga, and Hansa Rostock, who had won the final East German championship in 1990-91. Neither of them had appeared in the European Cup before. Hansa Rostock were eliminated by Barcelona in the first round, and the Spaniards also accounted for Kaiserslautern at the next stage, scrambling through on away goals as Bakero scored in the last minute. Another newcomer was Sampdoria, who had won the Italian title for the first time. They thrashed Rosenborg 7-1 on aggregate, and then beat Kispest-Honved 4-3.

The two knock-out rounds took place between mid-September and early November while the league stage started with matches in November and December, followed by the usual winter break, and was completed in March and April. In the week before the league stage began Manchester United, who had won the previous season's European Cup-Winners' Cup, beat Red Star Belgrade 1-0, to become the first English winners of the European Super Cup since Aston Villa in 1982-83. The Super Cup was decided by a single match at Old Trafford, rather than a two-legged tie, as UEFA had ordered that Red Star Belgrade could not play European matches in Yugoslavia, due to that country's descent into civil war.

The ban on Red Star playing at home hampered their efforts in the league stage of the European Cup, as they tussled with Sampdoria for the top spot in Group A. Sampdoria beat Red Star 2-0 in Genoa on the opening day, with their strikers, Roberto Mancini and Gianluca Vialli both scoring, and had the edge for most of the time thereafter. Sampdoria's 3-2 defeat against Anderlecht at the midway point allowed Red Star, who beat Panathinaikos 2-0 on the same day, to pull ahead. Sampdoria subsequently came from behind to win 3-1 against Red Star, in a match played at Sofia in Bulgaria, and eventually finished two points clear of them. Anderlecht recovered from a slow start to draw level with Red Star on points, by beating them on the final match day.

Barcelona dominated Group B, and won it with a three point margin, ahead of Sparta Prague. Hristo Stoichkov, a Bulgarian striker known as much for his moody personality as his goals, was in great form for Barcelona, scoring twice in each of their victories against Dynamo Kiev. A defeat against Sparta Prague in their penultimate game was the only setback for Barcelona. This meant that their passage to the final was not secured until the last set of group matches, when they won 2-1 against Benfica, with goals from Stoichkov and Jose Maria Bakero, while Sparta Prague lost to Dynamo Kiev.

UEFA had given a further vote of confidence to the return of English football by allocating the final to Wembley Stadium, which staged the contest on May 20 1992 – for the first time since 1978. Barcelona had beaten Sampdoria 2-0 in the 1989 European Cup-Winners' Cup final, and were expected to repeat that success. They were coached by Johan Cruyff, three times winner of the trophy with Ajax, and besides several Spanish internationals, Barcelona fielded three outstanding foreigners, namely Stoichkov, Michael Laudrup, who was a Danish midfielder, and Ronald Koeman, the Dutch sweeper, who had won the trophy with PSV Eindhoven in 1988. Sampdoria were managed by Vujadin Boskov, the Yugoslav who had taken Real Madrid to the 1981 final, and featured several of Italy's leading players, including Attilio Lombardo, Mancini, Gianluca Pagliuca, Vialli, and Pietro Vierchowod.

Barcelona held the initiative during the first half, while Sampdoria were mostly intent on soaking up pressure. Barcelona's Stoichkov came closest to scoring, with a header that pulled a fine save from Pagliuca midway through the half. The second half was more open, as Sampdoria started to attack more frequently, but Vialli failed to take a couple of good chances, missing the target on both occasions. Stoichkov again went close, but saw an excellent shot hit a post. As in 1991, a goalless final went into extra time, but this was proving to be a much better match than the previous year's equivalent. Stoichkov was again frustrated, as Pagliuca made a good save from one of his shots. With ten minutes left in extra time, the deadlock was finally broken. Barcelona were awarded a free kick 25 yards from goal by Aron Schmidhuber, the German referee, although it was not clear that Giovanni Invernizzi's challenge on Eusebio was a foul. Bakero tapped the free kick to Ronald Koeman, who hit a brilliant diagonal drive into the left hand corner of the net, giving Pagliuca no chance to make a save. Besides winning the match for Barcelona, Koeman's strike was notable as the only goal to be scored in the added 30 minutes in any of the nine European Cup finals between 1984 and 2005 that went to extra time.

This was the first time Barcelona had won the European Cup, and the players, who had worn a change strip of orange during the match, put on their normal maroon and blue shirts to receive the trophy. An ecstatic Cruyff remarked "It's been a great night because it's been such a long time coming". That was an understatement. Barcelona had first appeared in the European Cup in 1959-60, when they lost to Real Madrid in the semi-finals. Barcelona eliminated Real the following season, but lost to Benfica in the final. Their next appearance, in 1974-75, with Cruyff in the team, ended in defeat against Leeds United in the semi-finals. In 1986 they lost to Steaua Bucharest in the final, on penalties. Barcelona had been beaten in the final or semi-finals in each of their four previous campaigns in the European Cup, but now they had finally won the competition. A few weeks after this European Cup victory, the city of Barcelona staged a successful Olympic Games, which included Spain winning the gold medal in the football tournament. These two events gave a great boost to Catalan pride.

1991-92

First round

		1st leg	2nd leg	agg
Barcelona	Hansa Rostock	3-0	0-1	3-1
Kaiserslautern	Etar Veliko Tarnovo	2-0	1-1	3-1
Union Luxembourg	Marseille	0-5	0-5	0-10
Sparta Prague	Rangers	1-0	1-2	2-2
Sparta Prague won on away goals				
Hamrun Spartans	Benfica	0-6	0-4	0-10
Arsenal	FK Austria	6-1	0-1	6-2
Brondby	Zaglebie Lubin	3-0	1-2	4-2
HJK Helsinki	Dynamo Kiev	0-1	0-3	0-4
Fram Reykjavik	Panathinaikos	2-2	0-0	2-2
Panathinaikos won on away goals				
IFK Gothenburg	Flamurtari	0-0	1-1	1-1
IFK Gothenburg won on away goals				
Besiktas	PSV Eindhoven	1-1	1-2	2-3
Anderlecht	Grasshoppers	1-1	3-0	4-1
Red Star Belgrade	Portadown	4-0	4-0	8-0
Universitatea Craiova	Apollon Limassol	2-0	0-3	2-3
Kispest Honved	Dundalk	1-1	2-0	3-1
Sampdoria	Rosenborg	5-0	2-1	7-1

Second round

		1st leg	2nd leg	agg
Barcelona	Kaiserslautern	2-0	1-3	3-3
Barcelona won on away goals				
Marseille	Sparta Prague	3-2	1-2	4-4
Sparta Prague won on away goals				
Benfica	Arsenal	1-1	3-1	4-2
Dynamo Kiev	Brondby	1-1	1-0	2-1

Panathinaikos	IFK Gothenburg	2-0	2-2	4-2
PSV Eindhoven	Anderlecht	0-0	0-2	0-2
Red Star Belgrade	Apollon Limassol	3-1	2-0	5-1
Kispest Honved	Sampdoria	2-1	1-3	3-4

Group A

Sampdoria 2 Red Star Belgrade 0
Anderlecht 0 Panathinaikos 0
Panathinaikos 0 Sampdoria 0
Red Star Belgrade 3 Anderlecht 2
Panathinaikos 0 Red Star Belgrade 2
Anderlecht 3 Sampdoria 2
Sampdoria 2 Anderlecht 0
Red Star Belgrade 1 Panathinaikos 0
Panathinaikos 0 Anderlecht 0
Red Star Belgrade 1 Sampdoria 3
Anderlecht 3 Red Star Belgrade 2
Sampdoria 1 Panathinaikos 1

	P	W	D	L	F	A	Pts
Sampdoria	6	3	2	1	10	5	8
Red Star Belgrade	6	3	0	3	9	10	6
Anderlecht	6	2	2	2	8	9	6
Panathinaikos	6	0	4	2	1	4	4

Group B

Barcelona 3 Sparta Prague 2
Dynamo Kiev 1 Benfica 0
Sparta Prague 2 Dynamo Kiev 1
Benfica 0 Barcelona 0
Dynamo Kiev 0 Barcelona 2
Benfica 1 Sparta Prague 1
Sparta Prague 1 Benfica 1
Barcelona 3 Dynamo Kiev 0
Sparta Prague 1 Barcelona 0
Benfica 5 Dynamo Kiev 0
Dynamo Kiev 1 Sparta Prague 0
Barcelona 2 Benfica 1

	P	W	D	L	F	A	Pts
Barcelona	6	4	1	1	10	4	9
Sparta Prague	6	2	2	2	7	7	6
Benfica	6	1	3	2	8	5	5
Dynamo Kiev	6	2	0	4	3	12	4

Final

May 20 1992 Wembley
Barcelona 1   Sampdoria 0 (after extra time)
Koeman
Barcelona: Zubizarreta, Ferrer, Koeman, Nando, Juan Carlos, Bakero, Guardiola (Alexanco), Eusebio, Laudrup, Salinas (Goicoechea), Stoichkov
Sampdoria: Pagliuca, Mannini, Lanna, Vierchowod, Katanec, Lombardo, Pari, Cerezo, Bonetti (Invernizzi), Vialli (Buso), Mancini
HT: 0-0
FT: 0-0
Referee: Schmidhuber (Germany)
Attendance: 70,827

1992-93

The 1992-93 competition drew an increased entry of 36 clubs, as seven countries were represented for the first time – Estonia, the Faroe Islands, Israel, Latvia, Lithuania, Slovenia, and Ukraine. Israel had recently been accepted as a member by UEFA, despite not being part of Europe, in order to end the football isolation caused by their disputes with Arab neighbours. Most of the other new entrants stemmed from the creation of new states, upon the disintegration of both the Soviet Union and Yugoslavia. The descent of Yugoslavia into civil war left the national champions Red Star Belgrade, winners of the European Cup as recently as 1991, ineligible for this season's competition. United Nations' sanctions against Yugoslavia had forced UEFA to disqualify the national team from the 1992 European Championship finals, in Sweden. Yugoslavia's place was taken by Denmark, who unexpectedly won the trophy, beating Germany 2-0 in the final. As the map of Europe changed so did the continent's political complexion. The Warsaw pact had been dissolved in the summer of 1991, with the collapse of the old Soviet bloc. In the west, plans were being made for an expansion of the EEC, and its conversion into a European Union, with more integration between member states.

England's representatives were Leeds United, who had pipped Manchester United to the English title in 1991-92. A major factor in Leeds' success had been the mid-season acquisition of Eric Cantona, a fiery Frenchman, who had appeared for Marseille in the European Cup during the 1990-91 season. Participating in the European Cup for the first time since their defeat against Bayern Munich in the 1975 final, Leeds were plunged, after a 17 year gap, into another controversial meeting with a German club. Leeds appeared to have thrown away their tie against Stuttgart by losing 3-0 in the away leg. A 4-1 win by Leeds in the return levelled the aggregate score, but they appeared to have been defeated on away goals. Stuttgart, however, had fielded four foreign players, exceeding the current competition limit of three such players per match. In the surprising absence of any provision in the European Cup's rules to deal with such an infringement, UEFA considered the matter for a few days, before awarding the second leg to Leeds 3-0, and ordering that the tie be settled by a play-off at a neutral venue. Leeds completed their great escape by beating Stuttgart 2-1 at Barcelona's Nou Camp stadium, before only 7,000 spectators.

This meant Stuttgart were the first club from West Germany or Germany to be eliminated in the first round since this had happened to them in 1984-85. In the next round Leeds met Rangers, in a clash of Britain's two best clubs. Leeds took the lead in the first minute at Ibrox, with a 20 yard volley from Gary McAllister, himself a Scot, but Rangers bounced back to win 2-1. Rangers also won the return match 2-1, with Mark Hateley, an Englishman, being one of their scorers, while Eric Cantona scored for Leeds. Northern Ireland's Glentoran lost 8-0 on aggregate to Marseille in the first round. Barcelona, the reigning champions, struggled to beat Viking Stavanger by a single goal, and then surprisingly lost to CSKA Moscow. Having drawn 1-1 away from home, and built up a two goal lead at the Nou Camp, Barcelona looked to have the tie secure, but CSKA Moscow hit back to win the second leg 3-2, and therefore took the tie 4-3 on aggregate.

After the initial knock-out phase, the group stage was retained, but there was a slight change in the regulations. Whereas in the previous season goal difference was the tie-breaker between teams level on points, from 1992-93 onwards the head-to-head record between teams with the same points was the determining factor. If the new factor failed to separate teams, then goal difference across all of their matches in the group was used as a secondary tie-breaker. UEFA now gave the name Champions League to the group stage, and took over its financial administration. By attracting corporate sponsors, UEFA were able to offer the participating clubs large prize money. Initially the name Champions League only applied to the group stage, with the overall competition still being known as the European Champion Clubs' Cup, but the two names became interchangeable over the next few years. In 1995-96 the final was officially designated the UEFA Champions League final for the first time. UEFA's official statistics now retrospectively use the name Champions League for the entire competition from the 1992-93 season onwards.

Group A opened with Rangers drawing 2-2 at home to Marseille, after trailing 2-0. The group developed into a close struggle between these two, who also drew in Marseille, and were both unbeaten through six games. In their final match Marseille beat Brugge 1-0, while Rangers were held to a 0-0 draw by CSKA Moscow, which meant that Marseille took the group by a single point. Rangers had narrowly failed to emulate the appearance of their Glasgow rivals, Celtic, in the 1967 final.

Milan dominated Group B from start to finish, winning all six of their matches, and only conceding a single goal in the process. Milan began with a 4-0 win against Gothenburg, who were to finish as runners-up, fully six points adrift. Marco Van Basten scored all four goals for Milan against Gothenburg. PSV Eindhoven finished bottom of the group, with a single point, but Romario, their Brazilian striker, was to finish the season as the European Cup's leading scorer, with seven goals – which included a hat-trick in a 3-0 win against AEK Athens during the knock-out phase.

Milan were the favourites to win at Munich's Olympic Stadium, as their team featured eight players who had appeared in either, or both, of their wins in the 1989 and 1990 finals – Franco Baresi, Alessandro Costacurta, Roberto Donadoni, Paolo Maldini, Daniele Massaro, Frank Rijkaard, Mauro Tassotti and Marco Van Basten. The newcomers included Gianluigi Lentini, a player bought from Torino for a world record fee of £13,000,000. On the other hand, the team selected by the Milan coach Fabio Capello (who had played for Juventus in the 1973 final) omitted Ruud Gullit. The decision to field Van Basten was a risk, as he had only recently recovered from an ankle injury, which had forced him to miss much of the season. Milan's run to the 1993 final had seen them win all ten of their matches, scoring 23 goals, and conceding just one. Marseille had also been unbeaten in the competition this season, but with six wins and four draws. As in the 1991 final, Marseille were coached by Raymond Goethals. He retained just three players from the team that had been beaten by Red Star Belgrade two years earlier – Basile Boli, Eric Di Meco, and Abedi Pele. The newcomers included Fabien Barthez, Marcel Desailly, and Didier Deschamps – each of whom would win the World Cup with France in 1998 – plus Alen Boksic, a Croatian, and Rudi Voller, from Germany.

Milan controlled the opening half hour of the match, creating a series of excellent goalscoring opportunities, but failed to take any of them, with Daniele Massaro being particularly wasteful. With Milan unable to the take a decisive grip on the match, Marseille started to gain in confidence, and created their own chances in the latter part of the first half. A couple of minutes before the interval, a corner from Abedi Pele on the right was met by a fine header from Basile Boli, and the ball flashed into the net. Marseille were suddenly ahead, and Milan had a real fight on their hands. The second half began with a new period of Milan pressure, and a glaring miss by Van Basten. Milan continued to have most of the play, but the Marseille defence limited them to a small number of chances in the remainder of the match. Jean-Pierre Papin, who had played for Marseille in the 1991 final, now played against them, appearing as a Milan substitute, in place of Roberto Donadoni. Papin looked lively, and beat Fabien Barthez, the Marseille goalkeeper, with a shot 13 minutes from time, only for the ball to go just wide of a post. Shortly afterwards, a struggling Van Basten was substituted. Marseille held on for an unexpected 1-0 victory, to become the first French club to win the European Cup, 38 years after the inauguration of a competition which had been a French idea.

Marseille's moment of triumph soon turned sour. It emerged that the 1-0 win against Valenciennes by which Marseille secured the French league title, for a fifth successive year, three days before beating Milan, had been helped by the bribery of several Valenciennes players. The bribery scandal led to Marseille being stripped of the French title, and relegated to the Second Division, by the French Football Federation, while the club President, Bernard Tapie, was eventually jailed for his role in the affair. UEFA banned Marseille from the 1993-94 European Cup, with their place being taken by Monaco, while Milan were to compete in place of Marseille in both the World Club Championship and European Super Cup.

1992-93

Preliminary round

		1st leg	2nd leg	agg
Shelbourne	Tavria Simferopol	0-0	1-2	1-2
Valletta	Maccabi Tel-Aviv	1-2	0-1	1-3
KI Klaksvik	Skonto Riga	1-3	0-3	1-6
Olimpia Ljubljana	Norma Tallinn	3-0	2-0	5-0

First round

		1st leg	2nd leg	agg
Milan	Olimpia Ljubljana	4-0	3-0	7-0
Lech Poznan	Skonto Riga	2-0	0-0	2-0
PSV Eindhoven	Zalgiris Vilnius	6-0	2-0	8-0
Barcelona	Viking Stavanger	1-0	0-0	1-0
Kuusysi Lahti	Dynamo Bucharest	1-0	0-2	1-2
Rangers	Lyngby	2-0	1-0	3-0
Slovan Bratislava	Ferencvaros	4-1	0-0	4-1
FK Austria	CSKA Sofia	3-1	2-3	5-4
Sion	Tavria Simferopol	4-1	3-1	7-2
Union Luxembourg	Porto	1-4	0-5	1-9
Víkingur Reykjavik	CSKA Moscow	0-1	2-4	2-5
Maccabi Tel-Aviv	Brugge	0-1	0-3	0-4
AEK Athens	Apoel Nicosia	1-1	2-2	3-3
AEK Athens won on away goals				
IFK Gothenburg	Besiktas	2-0	1-2	3-2
Glentoran	Marseille	0-5	0-3	0-8
Stuttgart	Leeds United	3-0	0-3	3-3

Leeds United had won the second leg 4-1, giving a 4-4 aggregate, with Stuttgart winning on on away goals. Leeds United appealed as Stuttgart had fielded an ineligible player in the second leg. UEFA awarded the second leg to Leeds United 3-0, giving a 3-3 aggregate, and the tie was settled by a play-off.

Play off
Leeds United 2 Stuttgart 1 (Barcelona)

Second round

		1st leg	2nd leg	agg
IFK Gothenburg	Lech Poznan	1-0	3-0	4-0
Rangers	Leeds United	2-1	2-1	4-2
Slovan Bratislava	Milan	0-1	0-4	0-5
Dynamo Bucharest	Marseille	0-0	0-2	0-2
Brugge	FK Austria	2-0	1-3	3-3

Brugge won on away goals

Sion	Porto	2-2	0-4	2-6
AEK Athens	PSV Eindhoven	1-0	0-3	1-3
CSKA Moscow	Barcelona	1-1	3-2	4-3

Group A

Brugge 1 CSKA Moscow 0
Rangers 2 Marseille 2
CSKA Moscow 0 Rangers 1
Marseille 3 Brugge 0
Brugge 1 Rangers 1
CSKA Moscow 1 Marseille 1
Marseille 6 CSKA Moscow 0
Rangers 2 Brugge 1
Marseille 1 Rangers 1
CSKA Moscow 1 Brugge 2
Brugge 0 Marseille 1
Rangers 0 CSKA Moscow 0

	P	W	D	L	F	A	Pts
Marseille	6	3	3	0	14	4	9
Rangers	6	2	4	0	7	5	8
Brugge	6	2	1	3	5	8	5
CSKA Moscow	6	0	2	4	2	11	2

Group B

Porto 2 PSV Eindhoven 2
Milan 4 IFK Gothenburg 0
PSV Eindhoven 1 Milan 2
IFK Gothenburg 1 Porto 0
Porto 0 Milan 1
PSV Eindhoven 1 IFK Gothenburg 3
Milan 1 Porto 0
IFK Gothenburg 3 PSV Eindhoven 0
IFK Gothenburg 0 Milan 1
PSV Eindhoven 0 Porto 1
Milan 2 PSV Eindhoven 0
Porto 2 IFK Gothenburg 0

	P	W	D	L	F	A	Pts
Milan	6	6	0	0	11	1	12
IFK Gothenburg	6	3	0	3	7	8	6
Porto	6	2	1	3	5	5	5
PSV Eindhoven	6	0	1	5	4	13	1

Final

May 26 1993 Munich

Marseille 1	Milan 0

Boli

Marseille: Barthez, Angloma (Durand), Boli, Sauzee, Desailly, Eydelie, Di Meco, Boksic, Voller (Thomas), Pele, Deschamps
Milan: Rossi, Tassotti, Maldini, Albertini, Costacurta, Baresi, Lentini, Rijkaard, Van Basten (Eranio), Donadoni (Papin), Massaro
HT: 1-0
Referee: Rothlisberger (Switzerland)
Attendance: 64,400

Marco Van Basten

Marco Van Basten was one of the greatest strikers ever to play in the European Cup. A prolific goalscorer, able to find the target with either foot, or his head, he combined the traditional height and physical strength of a striker with great close control, and the ability to make fools of defenders. He emulated his fellow-countryman Johan Cruyff by winning the European Footballer of the Year award three times. Many of Van Basten's achievements were shared with Ruud Gullit, alongside whom he played for both Milan and the Netherlands. Injuries plagued the careers of both players, but Van Basten suffered more than Gullit, as a persistent ankle injury forced his premature retirement from the game.

Born at Utrecht on October 31 1964, Marco Van Basten began his professional career with Ajax, who signed him in 1981. He scored in his single league appearance in 1981-82, as an Ajax team that also featured Cruyff, recently returned after several years abroad, won the Dutch league. Ajax won both the Dutch league and cup in 1983, following which Van Basten's performances for the Netherlands in the World Youth Cup attracted international attention. In September of that year he made his debut for the full international team, as they beat Iceland 3-0 in a European Championship qualifier. Later that month Van Basten scored for the Netherlands in a 1-1 draw against Belgium, this being the first of his 24 goals in 58 full internationals.

With Ajax, Van Basten won a third Dutch championship in 1985, and a second Dutch cup the following year. His 37 goals in 1985-86 also won him the European Golden Boot, as the continent's leading scorer. Ajax retained the Dutch cup in 1987, and also won the European Cup-Winners' Cup, with Van Basten scoring the only goal of the final, against Lokomotiv Leipzig. Van Basten then moved to Milan, who paid Ajax £1,500,000 for him – a bargain compared with the £5,500,000 they had to spend to acquire Gullit from PSV Eindhoven that same year. Van Basten and Gullit spearheaded the Milan team which won Italy's Serie A in 1988, for the first time since 1979.

The attentions of tough-tackling defenders were starting to affect Van Basten, and injury made him doubtful for the 1988 European Championship finals. Restricted to half an hour as a substitute as the Netherlands lost 1-0 to the Soviet Union in their first match, Van Basten made up for lost time by scoring a hat-trick in the 3-1 win against England. A last minute goal from Van Basten secured a 2-1 win against West Germany in the semi-final. The Netherlands beat the Soviet Union 2-0 in the final. Gullit provided the first goal, but the real glory went to Van Basten, who produced what is frequently lauded as one of the greatest goals ever scored, with a stunning volley from an acute angle. His five goals in the tournament made him the leading scorer, and led to his winning the European Footballer of the Year award at the end of 1988.

Each of the three Dutch championship wins by Ajax during Van Basten's time with the club had been followed by elimination in the first round of the European Cup the next season. With Milan it was a different story, as they won the trophy in both 1989 and 1990. Van Basten played in the successive European Cup finals, and scored twice as Milan beat Steaua Bucharest 4-0 in the first of them. Milan won the World Club Championship, and also the European Super Cup, in both 1989-90 and 1990-91. Van Basten played in both of the world title contests, and scored in the 2-1 aggregate win against Barcelona in the first of the Super Cups, but missed the other Super Cup. During this great run of club honours, there were further personal successes for Van Basten, who was the leading scorer in the 1988-89 European Cup, and retained the European Footballer of the Year award in 1989.

Van Basten played in each of the Netherlands' four matches at the 1990 World Cup finals, but the team lacked the cohesion of 1988, and he failed to score. At the end of 1990 Van Basten found the net five times as the Dutch beat Malta 8-0 in a European Championship qualifier, but when the finals were played in 1992 he was unable to score any goals. The Netherlands lost to Denmark in the semi-finals, with Peter Schmeichel's save from Van Basten being the decisive moment of the penalty contest that settled the match. On a brighter note, Van Basten helped Milan to win the Italian league in 1991-92, and enjoyed a purple patch of goalscoring during the latter part of 1992, following which he won the European Footballer of the Year award, for the third time in five calendar years.

Milan retained the Italian title in 1992-93, but Van Basten missed the second half of the season, due to an ankle injury. Fabio Capello, the coach, gambled by selecting Van Basten for the European Cup final, but he was unable to deliver, and Milan lost 1-0 to Marseille. This proved to be the last match Van Basten ever played, at the age of just 28. He battled for a couple of years in an attempt to regain fitness, but in August 1995 Van Basten announced that injury had ended his career.

Following his retirement, Van Basten spent several years away from football, but played a lot of golf. In 2003 he returned to football, joining the coaching staff at Ajax. Following the departure of Dick Advocaat, whose second spell as coach of the Netherlands ended with the Euro 2004 finals, the national federation sought the view of Johan Cruyff on the appointment of a successor. Cruyff recommended that Van Basten be approached, and this in turn led to his surprise appointment as national coach. Van Basten's contract with the Dutch federation included a stipulation that the national team would play attractive football. It was a theme Van Basten expanded upon during his first press conference as coach, saying: "Our goal is to play attractive and attacking football. We should take the initiative, starting from the back. Football should be fun again. The players should have fun on the pitch, while the fans should return home in a satisfied mood".

1993-94

The 1993-94 competition brought an increase to 42 entrants, which meant an expanded preliminary round was required, ahead of the two knock-out rounds that preceded the group stage. This season also saw the resurrection of the semi-finals, but a wish to avoid fixture congestion limited these to an unsatisfactory single match on the home ground of one of the teams, rather than the usual two-legged contest – or a possible switch to a game on neutral territory. At least home advantage was earned, being given to the winners of the two groups, as they each faced the runners-up from the other group.

In the preliminary round, Cwmbran Town, the first club from Wales to appear in the European Cup, lost on away goals to Cork City, from the Republic of Ireland. Linfield, from Northern Ireland, only lost 3-2 on aggregate against Dynamo Tbilisi. The Georgians were then disqualified by UEFA, for allegedly attempting to bribe the match officials for their home leg, and the tie was awarded to Linfield. A reprieved Linfield won 3-0 at home to FC Copenhagen, but lost the return 4-0, after extra time. FC Copenhagen were in turn to lose 7-0 on aggregate against Milan, for whom Jean-Pierre Papin scored three times. Milan had opened their campaign with an unimpressive win against Aarau, from Switzerland, as Papin scored the only goal of the tie.

Manchester United had won the inaugural English Premier League, thereby becoming national champions for the first time since 1967. They were managed by Alex Ferguson, who previously led Aberdeen in the European Cup, while his assistant was Brian Kidd, who had scored for United in the 1968 final. United began with a 5-3 aggregate win against Kispest Honved. Their next opponents were Galatasaray, who had previously eliminated Cork City. United built up a two goal lead in the first quarter of an hour at Old Trafford, before Galatasaray came back strongly, and the home side needed a late goal from Eric Cantona to escape with a 3-3 draw. A bruising goalless draw in the second leg took the Turks through on away goals. After the final whistle, Cantona made a sarcastic gesture to Kurt Rothlisberger, the Swiss referee, which earned him a red card. Both Cantona and Bryan Robson were attacked by Turkish policemen during a skirmish in the players' tunnel.

Rangers also lost on away goals, in their case against Levski Sofia, in the first round. The highest ever score in a European Cup penalty contest saw Skonto Riga beat Olimpia Ljubljana 11-10 in the preliminary round. The Latvians promptly lost their next tie 9-0 on aggregate, the victors being Spartak Moscow, another team from the former Soviet Union. Monaco, arriving as a late replacement for the disgraced Marseille, overcame AEK Athens and then Steaua Bucharest. Barcelona recovered from a 3-1 defeat away to Dynamo Kiev in their first match, winning the return 4-1, and then booked their place in the group phase by removing FK Austria.

Barcelona led the way in Group A, winning four of their games, and drawing the other two. A victory over Monaco on the final match day ensured that the Spaniards emerged with a three point lead over Monaco, who also progressed to the semi-finals. Spartak Moscow, who experienced heavy defeats away to both Monaco and Barcelona, finished third. Galatasaray opened with two 0-0 draws, and lost their other four games, only scoring once.

Milan won Group B in rather unconvincing fashion, scoring only six goals in six games, spreading these across two wins and four draws. Half of Milan's goals came in a 3-0 win against Porto, who took second place in the group. Most of the entertainment centred around Werder Bremen, whose attacking football, and defensive frailty, led to 26 goals being scored in the six matches they played. They were managed by Otto Rehhagel, who would lead Greece to a surprise victory at Euro 2004, with a more cautious approach. Werder Bremen lost 3-2 and 5-0 against Porto, but recovered from a 3-0 half time deficit at home to Anderlecht to win 5-3. All five of Werder Bremen's goals in the latter match were scored in the last 25 minutes, including a brace from Wynton Rufer, a striker from New Zealand. Rufer would end the season as the competition's joint leading scorer, alongside Barcelona's Ronald Koeman, with eight goals each. Three of Koeman's total came from penalties, while Rufer struck twice from the spot.

Both of the semi-finals were decisively won by the team with home advantage. Milan beat Monaco 3-0 at the Giuseppe Meazza Stadium, despite having Alessandro Costacurta sent off shortly before half time. At the Nou Camp, Barcelona also ran up a 3-0 victory, in their case against Porto. Hristo Stoichkov scored twice, while Porto captain Joao Pinto was sent off.

For the second successive season, the final was played at an Olympic Stadium, this one being in Athens. Of the crowd of 70,000 about 30,000 were Milan supporters, hoping to see the team reverse their defeat in the 1993 final, and regain the trophy they had won in 1989 and 1990. Milan fielded seven players who had featured for them in one or more of those three finals, namely Demetrio Albertini, Roberto Donadoni, Filippo Galli, Paolo Maldini, Daniele Massaro, Sebastiano Rossi, and Mauro Tassotti. Barcelona's coach, Johan Cruyff, selected six players from the team which had won the 1992 final, these being Jose-Maria Bakero, Albert Ferrer, Josep Guardiola, Ronald Koeman, Hristo Stoichkov, and Andoni Zubizarreta.

Milan controlled the play throughout the match, with fluid football, featuring excellent passing, control, and movement. They had the ball in the net after eight minutes, but Christian Panucci's header was ruled out for offside by Philip Don, the English referee. After 21 minutes Milan's excellence was rewarded by a goal. Dejan Savicevic beat Nadal on the right, and then produced a cross which eluded goalkeeper Zubizarreta, whereupon Massaro directed the ball into the net at the far post. Following this tempers were briefly raised on both teams, and Don booked Stoichkov of Barcelona, and then Tassotti of Milan, for rash challenges. With Barcelona being outplayed, Stoichkov and his strike partner, Romario, had little influence upon this match. Milan doubled the lead on the stroke of half time, as a fine passing movement concluded with Zvonimir Boban feeding Donadoni on the left, whereupon the latter pulled the ball back from near the bye-line to Massaro, who scored with a powerful shot.

A couple of minutes into the second half Savicevic extended Milan's lead, with a 20 yard chip over Zubizarreta. There was an element of doubt over the goal, as it appeared that Savicevic had pushed Sergi immediately before shooting. Savicevic subsequently shot against a post, immediately before a move in which Albertini released Marcel Desailly, who rushed forward and scored with a fine shot to put Milan 4-0 ahead, 13 minutes into the second half. As in the 1989 final against Steaua Bucharest, Milan were unable to extend their lead during the latter part of the match. Milan continued to dominate the game, and Savicevic, who was Milan's best player on the night, saw another of his efforts hit the post, but there were no more goals. It was appropriate that Savicevic and Desailly were among the scorers, as they both now joined the small group of players who had won the European Cup with two clubs. Savicevic had played for Red Star Belgrade in 1991, while Desailly had been a member of the Marseille team which beat Milan in 1993.

Milan could have won by a larger scoreline than 4-0, but the four goal margin equalled the previous largest wins in a European Cup final, those of Real Madrid in 1960 (the 1994 final was played on the anniversary of Real's 7-3 win against Eintracht Frankfurt), Bayern Munich in the 1974 replay, and Milan's own performance in 1989. Amidst the celebrations after Milan's victory, their coach Fabio Capello said "My team played an extraordinary match, which demonstrated an enormous will to win". Milan had bounced back from their defeat in the 1993 final, to regain the trophy with a performance that reached new heights.

1993-94

Preliminary round

		1st leg	2nd leg	agg
HJK Helsinki	Norma Tallinn	1-1	1-0	2-1
Ekranas Panevezys	Floriana	0-1	0-1	0-2
B68 Toftir	Croatia Zagreb	0-5	0-6	0-11
Skonto Riga	Olimpia Ljubljana	0-1	1-0	1-1
Skonto Riga won 11-10 on penalties				
Cwmbran Town	Cork City	3-2	1-2	4-4
Cork City won on away goals				
Dynamo Tbilisi	Linfield	2-1	1-1	3-2
Dynamo Tbilisi disqualified, tie awarded to Linfield				
Avenir Beggen	Rosenborg	0-2	0-1	0-3
Partizan Tirana	IA Akranes	0-0	0-3	0-3
Omonia Nicosia	Aarau	2-1	0-2	2-3
Zimbru Chisinau	Beitar Jerusalem	1-1	0-2	1-3

First round

		1st leg	2nd leg	agg
Galatasaray	Cork City	2-1	1-0	3-1
Werder Bremen	Dynamo Minsk	5-2	1-1	6-3
Dynamo Kiev	Barcelona	3-1	1-4	4-5
Monaco	AEK Athens	1-0	1-1	2-1
Kispest Honved	Manchester United	2-3	1-2	3-5
Rangers	Levski Sofia	3-2	1-2	4-4
Levski Sofia won on away goals				

AIK Stockholm	Sparta Prague	1-0	0-2	1-2
Linfield	FC Copenhagen	3-0	0-4	3-4
HJK Helsinki	Anderlecht	0-3	0-3	0-6
IA Akranes	Feyenoord	1-0	0-3	1-3
Steaua Bucharest	Croatia Zagreb	1-2	3-2	4-4

Steaua Bucharest won on away goals

Rosenborg	FK Austria	3-1	1-4	4-5
Porto	Floriana	2-0	0-0	2-0
Skonto Riga	Spartak Moscow	0-5	0-4	0-9
Aarau	Milan	0-1	0-0	0-1
Lech Poznan	Beitar Jerusalem	3-0	4-2	7-2

Second round

		1st leg	*2nd leg*	*agg*
Porto	Feyenoord	1-0	0-0	1-0
Monaco	Steaua Bucharest	4-1	0-1	4-2
Levski Sofia	Werder Bremen	2-2	0-1	2-3
FC Copenhagen	Milan	0-6	0-1	0-7
Sparta Prague	Anderlecht	0-1	2-4	2-5
Manchester United	Galatasaray	3-3	0-0	3-3

Galatasaray won on away goals

Lech Poznan	Spartak Moscow	1-5	1-2	2-7
Barcelona	FK Austria	3-0	2-1	5-1

Group A

Monaco 4 Spartak Moscow 1
Galatasaray 0 Barcelona 0
Barcelona 2 Monaco 0
Spartak Moscow 0 Galatasaray 0
Monaco 3 Galatasaray 0
Spartak Moscow 2 Barcelona 2
Barcelona 5 Spartak Moscow 1
Galatasaray 0 Monaco 2
FC Barcelona 3 Galatasaray 0
Spartak Moscow 0 Monaco 0
Monaco 0 Barcelona 1
Galatasaray 1 Spartak Moscow 2

	P	W	D	L	F	A	Pts
Barcelona	6	4	2	0	13	3	10
Monaco	6	3	1	2	9	4	7
Spartak Moscow	6	1	3	2	6	12	5
Galatasaray	6	0	2	4	1	10	2

Group B

Anderlecht 0 Milan 0
Porto 3 Werder Bremen 2
Milan 3 Porto 0
Werder Bremen 5 Anderlecht 3
Anderlecht 1 Porto 0
Milan 2 Werder Bremen 1
Porto 2 Anderlecht 0
Werder Bremen 1 Milan 1
Milan 0 Anderlecht 0
Werder Bremen 0 Porto 5
Porto 0 Milan 0
Anderlecht 1 Werder Bremen 2

	P	W	D	L	F	A	Pts
Milan	6	2	4	0	6	2	8
Porto	6	3	1	2	10	6	7

Werder Bremen	6	2	1	3	11	15	5
Anderlecht	6	1	2	3	5	9	4

Semi-finals
Barcelona 3 Porto 0
Milan 3 Monaco 0

Final
May 18 1994 Athens

Milan 4   Barcelona 0
Massaro 2
Savicevic
Desailly
Milan: Rossi, Tassotti, Panucci, Albertini, F Galli, Maldini (Nova), Donadoni, Desailly, Boban, Savicevic, Massaro
Barcelona: Zubizarreta, Ferrer, Guardiola, Koeman, Nadal, Bakero, Sergi (Quique), Stoichkov, Amor, Romario, Beguiristain (Eusebio)
HT: 2-0
Referee: Don (England)
Attendance: 70,000

1994-95

For this season UEFA, in a move announced in December 1993, restricted the competition to 24 teams – the smallest field for a European Cup since 1957-58. Entry was limited to the strongest countries in the coefficient ranking of performances in the European competitions, with the champions of the weaker countries being relegated to the UEFA Cup. For nearly 40 years the European Cup had been open to the champions of each European nation, but now this all-inclusive approach was abandoned. The new focus was upon the league stage, which was doubled from two to four groups, with the top eight seeded teams being given automatic qualification to the league. The consolation for the traditionalists was that the group stage would be followed by home and away ties in both the newly-restored quarter-finals, and the semi-finals. The 16 teams who did not automatically advance to the league stage competed in the qualifying round. Rangers' hopes of a repeat of their 1992-93 campaign were ended by defeat against AEK Athens, but Steaua Bucharest, the only former champions appearing at this stage, beat Servette Geneva.

Manchester United, who had won the English Premier League and FA Cup double in 1993-94, became the first English club to feature in the group stage of the Champions League, having been given automatic qualification as one of the top seeds. United found themselves in Group A, which was won by Gothenburg. United finished level on points with Barcelona, but were eliminated due to the head-to-head record. Having drawn 2-2 in a thrilling match at Old Trafford, United were thrashed 4-0 in the Nou Camp, undone by defensive frailty, and the protracted absence of Eric Cantona, who was suspended from four matches, as a result of his sending off against Galatasaray the previous season. The effects of the three foreigners rule also caused selection problems for Alex Ferguson, as Scottish, Welsh and Irish players with English clubs were counted as foreigners.

Holders Milan struggled to emerge from Group D, ahead of Salzburg on a better head-to-head record, and five points behind Ajax. Part of the problem for Milan was that they had two points deducted by UEFA, due to a spectator throwing a bottle on to the field in their 3-0 home win over Salzburg, causing an injury to Otto Konrad, the Salzburg goalkeeper. Paris Saint-Germain – inspired by George Weah, a Liberian striker who was to be the leading scorer in this season's competition, with seven goals – won all six of their matches in Group B, to finish six points clear of runners-up Bayern Munich. The remaining group was won by Benfica, with Hajduk Split surprisingly pipping Steaua Bucharest to second spot.

In the quarter-finals, Milan eliminated Benfica, with Marco Simone scoring both of the goals in their 2-0 home win. Barcelona, the previous season's runners-up, fell to Paris Saint-Germain, who drew 1-1 at the Nou Camp, and came from behind to win 2-1 in Paris. Bayern Munich required the away goals rule to win their tie against Gothenburg. Ajax efficiently disposed of Hajduk Split, drawing 0-0 away, before winning 3-0 at home, with Frank de Boer scoring twice. Ajax gave further evidence of their quality in the semi-finals. After drawing 0-0 away to Bayern Munich, the Dutch champions produced a superb 5-2 win in the second leg, with Jari Litmanen, their Finnish striker, scoring twice. The other tie saw Milan twice beat Paris Saint-Germain, with a single goal in the first leg from Zvonimir Boban, a Croatian, and a brace in the return from Dejan Savicevic, a Yugoslav.

The final was staged at Vienna's Ernst Happel Stadium, named after the Austrian who enjoyed a lengthy career in the European Cup as both player and manager. This was the re-named Prater Stadium, the venue at which Milan had won the European Cup final in 1990. There were two other lucky omens for Milan. They had previously met Ajax in the 1969 final, and won 4-1, while the 1995 final was played on the anniversary of their 4-0 win against Steaua Bucharest in the 1989 final. Ajax had beaten Milan twice in the group stage this season, but Milan had not conceded a goal in their five European Cup matches since then. The Milan line-up selected by Fabio Capello included eight players from the 4-0 win against Barcelona a year earlier – Demetrio Albertini, Zvonimir Boban, Marcel Desailly, Roberto Donadoni, Paolo Maldini, Daniele Massaro, Christian Panucci, and Sebastiano Rossi. Milan were playing in their fifth European Cup final in the space of seven seasons, and Maldini had appeared in each of those matches, while Franco Baresi, Alessandro Costacurta, Donadoni, and Massaro were all playing in their fourth final. Ajax, coached by Luis Van Gaal, featured several Dutch internationals, including Frank Rijkaard, who was now playing against the club with whom he had won the European Cup, plus twins Frank and Ronald De Boer.

The match opened with a close contest between Ajax's attack and Milan's defence, with the latter coming out on top. As the first half progressed, Milan gradually became more positive, and created several chances. The second half saw Ajax enjoying most of the possession, while Milan concentrated on counter-attacks. Both teams made chances, but it began to look as though the 90 minutes would end with a goalless stalemate, to be followed by extra time. The deadlock was decisively broken with five minutes left to play. A neat passing move between Patrick Kluivert, Edgar Davids, and Frank Rijkaard set up a chance for Kluivert, who met the ball in the centre of the penalty area, with a prodded shot that ran along the ground, and just out of the reach of Rossi, the Milan goalkeeper. Kluivert had become the youngest player ever to score in a European Cup final, at the age of 18 years and 327 days. He later said: "My mum had a dream I was going to score. She told me before the match. I was not thinking about what she had said during the game, but I did score, and it was like a dream for me. She is not really a clairvoyant, but her dream came true".

The 1995 final was the eighth in succession where the losing team failed to score. Indeed in two of those matches the winning team also failed to score, with goalless draws being followed by penalty contests in both 1988 and 1991. By winning the 1995 final, Ajax (who were appearing in the European Cup this season for the first time since 1985-86) regained the trophy which they had last won in 1973 – with a reverse of their defeat against Milan in 1969. The new Ajax lacked the brilliance of the 'Total Football' team, led by Johan Cruyff, which had dazzled in winning a hat-trick of European titles, but their fine, attacking, play had deservedly undone a Milan team that had dominated the European

Cup for several years. Milan's run was now set to end, as they only finished fourth in the Italian league in 1994-95, and would not be back in the Champions League the following season.

1994-95

Qualifying round

		1st leg	2nd leg	agg
AEK Athens	Rangers	2-0	1-0	3-0
Avenir Beggen	Galatasaray	1-5	0-4	1-9
Legia Warsaw	Hajduk Split	0-1	0-4	0-5
Maccabi Haifa	Austria Salzburg	1-2	1-3	2-5
Paris Saint-Germain	Vac	3-0	2-1	5-1
Silkeborg	Dynamo Kiev	0-0	1-3	1-3
Sparta Prague	IFK Gothenburg	1-0	0-2	1-2
Steaua Bucharest	Servette Geneva	4-1	1-1	5-2

Group A

Barcelona 2 Galatasaray 1
Manchester United 4 IFK Gothenburg 2
Galatasaray 0 Manchester United 0
IFK Gothenburg 2 Barcelona 1
IFK Gothenburg 1 Galatasaray 0
Manchester United 2 Barcelona 2
Barcelona 4 Manchester United 0
Galatasaray 0 IFK Gothenburg 1
Galatasaray 2 Barcelona 1
IFK Gothenburg 3 Manchester United 1
Barcelona 1 IFK Gothenburg 1
Manchester United 4 Galatasaray 0

	P	W	D	L	F	A	Pts
IFK Gothenburg	6	4	1	1	10	7	9
Barcelona	6	2	2	2	11	8	6
Manchester United	6	2	2	2	11	11	6
Galatasaray	6	1	1	4	3	9	3

Group B

Dynamo Kiev 3 Spartak Moscow 2
Paris Saint-Germain 2 Bayern Munich 0
Bayern Munich 1 Dynamo Kiev 0
Spartak Moscow 1 Paris Saint-Germain 2
Dynamo Kiev 1 Paris Saint-Germain 2
Spartak Moscow 1 Bayern Munich 1
Bayern Munich 2 Spartak Moscow 2
Paris Saint-Germain 1 Dynamo Kiev 0
Bayern Munich 0 Paris Saint-Germain 1
Spartak Moscow 1 Dynamo Kiev 0
Dynamo Kiev 1 Bayern Munich 4
Paris Saint-Germain 4 Spartak Moscow 1

	P	W	D	L	F	A	Pts
Paris Saint-Germain	6	6	0	0	12	3	12
Bayern Munich	6	2	2	2	8	7	6
Moscow Spartak	6	1	2	3	8	12	4
Dynamo Kiev	6	1	0	5	5	11	2

Group C

Anderlecht 0 Steaua Bucharest 0
Hajduk Split 0 Benfica 0
Benfica 3 Anderlecht 1
Steaua Bucharest 0 Hajduk Split 1

Benfica 2 Steaua Bucharest 1
Hajduk Split 2 Anderlecht 1
Steaua Bucharest 1 Benfica 1
Anderlecht 0 Hajduk Split 0
Benfica 2 Hajduk Split 1
Steaua Bucharest 1 Anderlecht 1
Anderlecht 1 Benfica 1
Hajduk Split 1 Steaua Bucharest 4

	P	W	D	L	F	A	Pts
Benfica	6	3	3	0	9	5	9
Hajduk Split	6	2	2	2	5	7	6
Steaua Bucharest	6	1	3	2	7	6	5
Anderlecht	6	0	4	2	4	7	4

Group D

Ajax 2 Milan 0
Austria Salzburg 0 AEK Athens 0
AEK Athens 1 Ajax 2
Milan 3 Austria Salzburg 0
AEK Athens 0 Milan 0
Austria Salzburg 0 Ajax 0
Ajax 1 Austria Salzburg 1
Milan 2 AEK Athens 1
AEK Athens 1 Austria Salzburg 3
Milan 0 Ajax 2
Ajax 2 AEK Athens 0
Austria Salzburg 0 Milan 1

	P	W	D	L	F	A	Pts
Ajax	6	4	2	0	9	2	10
Milan	6	3	1	2	6	5	5
Austria Salzburg	6	1	3	2	4	6	5
AEK Athens	6	0	2	4	3	9	2

Milan had 2 points deducted

Quarter-finals

		1st leg	2nd leg	agg
Barcelona	Paris Saint-Germain	1-1	1-2	2-3
Bayern Munich	IFK Gothenburg	0-0	2-2	2-2

Bayern Munich won on away goals

		1st leg	2nd leg	agg
Hajduk Split	Ajax	0-0	0-3	0-3
Milan	Benfica	2-0	0-0	2-0

Semi-finals

		1st leg	2nd leg	agg
Bayern Munich	Ajax	0-0	2-5	2-5
Paris Saint-Germain	Milan	0-1	0-2	0-3

Final

May 24 1995 Vienna
Ajax 1   Milan 0
Kluivert
Ajax: Van Der Sar, Reiziger, Blind, Rijkaard, F De Boer, Seedorf (Kanu), Davids, Litmanen (Kluivert), George, R De Boer, Overmars
Milan: Rossi, Panucci, Baresi, Costacurta, Maldini, Desailly, Donadoni, Boban (Lentini), Albertini, Massaro (Eranio), Simone
HT: 0-0
Referee: Craciunescu (Romania)
Attendance: 49,730

European Footballer of the Year Award

The increasingly cosmopolitan nature of European football was reflected in 1995 by the decision of France Football, the magazine that has organised the European Footballer of the Year award since its inception in 1956, to make this honour open to non-European nationals who play in Europe. George Weah, a Liberian who played for Paris Saint Germain in the 1994-95 European Cup, before moving to Milan, was an immediate beneficiary, winning in 1995.

Success in the European Cup has often been a major factor in a player winning the award, which is decided by a poll among football writers, who vote on the basis of players' performances in the calendar year. The inaugural award was won by Stanley Matthews, in the year that the first European Cup final was played. Matthews, aged 41 at the time, is one of only two winners of the award not to have appeared in the European Cup, the other one being Lev Yashin. After Matthews' win, the awards for the next three years reflected the significance of Real Madrid's run of European triumphs, as Alfredo Di Stefano took the title twice, either side of a success by Raymond Kopa. The next time that a current Real Madrid player won the award was the year 2000, with Luis Figo being the winner.

Matthews has been followed by five other players from the British Isles – Denis Law, Bobby Charlton, George Best, Kevin Keegan, and Michael Owen. Ironically both of Keegan's successes came while he was playing for Hamburg in West Germany, rather than Liverpool, the club with whom he made his name, and won the European Cup. Keegan is one of five players to have won the award twice, the others being Di Stefano, Franz Beckenbauer, Karl-Heinz Rummenigge, and Ronaldo. An even more select group, of just three players, have won on three occasions. They are Johan Cruyff, Michel Platini, and Marco Van Basten – with Platini the only player to win in three successive years.

In contrast to the rare occasions on which clubs from eastern Europe have won the European Cup, a series of players from that part of the continent have taken the individual award. Josef Masopust led the way in 1962, being followed by Lev Yashin, Florian Albert, Oleg Blokhin, Igor Belanov, Hristo Stoichkov, Pavel Nedved and Andrei Shevchenko.

Weah's award was followed by success for Ronaldo and Rivaldo, both Brazilians. In a way, non-European winners of the award are nothing new. After all, Di Stefano was an Argentinian who became a naturalised Spaniard. Similarly Omar Sivori, who won as an Italian in 1961, was also born in Argentina. Thirty years before Weah won as an African, the award went to Eusebio, a Portuguese national who was born in Africa.

Sivori's club side when he won the award was Juventus, which holds the distinction of providing the winner on eight occasions, which is more than any other club has managed. Besides Sivori, the Juventus-based winners have been Paolo Rossi, Platini (three times), Roberto Baggio, Zinedine Zidane, and Nedved. The highest number of awards for a country is seven, a figure shared by the Netherlands with the combined total for West Germany and Germany. Three of the first five awards went to players from Spain, but that country has not provided the European Footballer of the Year since Luis Suarez won in 1960.

Winners

1956	Stanley Matthews (Blackpool and England)
1957	Alfredo Di Stefano (Real Madrid and Spain)
1958	Raymond Kopa (Real Madrid and France)
1959	Alfredo Di Stefano (Real Madrid and Spain)

1960	Luis Suarez (Barcelona and Spain)
1961	Omar Sivori (Juventus and Italy)
1962	Josef Masopust (Dukla Prague and Czechoslovakia)
1963	Lev Yashin (Dynamo Moscow and Soviet Union)
1964	Denis Law (Manchester United and Scotland)
1965	Eusebio (Benfica and Portugal)
1966	Bobby Charlton (Manchester United and England)
1967	Florian Albert (Ferencvaros and Hungary)
1968	George Best (Manchester United and Northern Ireland)
1969	Gianni Rivera (Milan and Italy)
1970	Gerd Muller (Bayern Munich and West Germany)
1971	Johan Cruyff (Ajax and Netherlands)
1972	Franz Beckenbauer (Bayern Munich and West Germany)
1973	Johan Cruyff (Barcelona and Netherlands)
1974	Johan Cruyff (Barcelona and Netherlands)
1975	Oleg Blokhin (Dynamo Kiev and Soviet Union)
1976	Franz Beckenbauer (Bayern Munich and West Germany)
1977	Alan Simonsen (Borussia Monchengladbach and Denmark)
1978	Kevin Keegan (Hamburg and England)
1979	Kevin Keegan (Hamburg and England)
1980	Karl-Heinz Rummenigge (Bayern Munich and West Germany)
1981	Karl-Heinz Rummenigge (Bayern Munich and West Germany)
1982	Paolo Rossi (Juventus and Italy)
1983	Michel Platini (Juventus and France)
1984	Michel Platini (Juventus and France)
1985	Michel Platini (Juventus and France)
1986	Igor Belanov (Dynamo Kiev and Soviet Union)
1987	Ruud Gullit (Milan and Netherlands)
1988	Marco Van Basten (Milan and Netherlands)
1989	Marco Van Basten (Milan and Netherlands)
1990	Lothar Matthaus (Internazionale and Germany)
1991	Jean-Pierre Papin (Marseille and France)
1992	Marco Van Basten (Milan and Netherlands)
1993	Roberto Baggio (Juventus and Italy)
1994	Hristo Stoichkov (Barcelona and Bulgaria)
1995	George Weah (Milan and Liberia)
1996	Matthias Sammer (Borussia Dortmund and Germany)
1997	Ronaldo (Internazionale and Brazil)
1998	Zinedine Zidane (Juventus and France)
1999	Rivaldo (Barcelona and Brazil)
2000	Luis Figo (Real Madrid and Portugal)
2001	Michael Owen (Liverpool and England)
2002	Ronaldo (Real Madrid and Brazil)
2003	Pavel Nedved (Juventus and Czech Republic)
2004	Andrei Shevchenko (Milan and Ukraine)

1995-96

The format that had been introduced the previous season was retained for the 1995-96 competition. There was, however, one modification, with three points being awarded for a win in the league stage instead of the previous two, as an incentive for positive football. Rangers struggled in their qualifying round tie against Anorthosis, winning 1-0 at home, and then drawing 0-0 away. Aalborg, from Denmark, lost twice against Dynamo Kiev, and appeared to be out of the competition, but received a lucky second chance. Dynamo Kiev were accused of bribing Lopez Nieto, the Spanish referee, in their 1-0 win at home to Panathinaikos at the start of the group stage. UEFA disqualified Dynamo Kiev, and banned them from Europe for the next two seasons. In order to retain four teams in Group A, UEFA allowed Aalborg back into the competition. Dynamo Kiev denied the accusation of bribery, and felt that their innocence had been tacitly accepted when UEFA announced, in April 1996, that the ban was being lifted, to avoid hindering the development of football in Ukraine.

After the false start, Panathinaikos won Group A. Having seen their defeat away to Dynamo Kiev removed from the records, Panathinaikos subsequently lost 2-1 away to Aalborg, but were unbeaten in their other five matches. Nantes joined Panathinaikos in advancing to the quarter-finals. The British challenge proved ineffective, with both Blackburn Rovers and Rangers finishing bottom of their groups. Blackburn, managed by Kenny Dalglish – who won the European Cup as a Liverpool player – had narrowly edged out Manchester United to win the English title for the first time since 1914. Blackburn experienced a torrid time in Group B, losing four of their six matches. The 3-0 defeat away to Spartak Moscow saw their players reduced to an ill-disciplined shambles, as Graeme Le Saux and David Batty exchanged punches, while Colin Hendry was sent off in a separate incident. Oleg Romantsev, the Spartak coach, commented "Before the match I told my players they will be playing against 11 guys ready to fight for each other for 90 minutes, but I did not expect it to be with each other".

Spartak Moscow stayed focused throughout the group stage, and won all six of their matches. Legia Warsaw, trailing by 11 points, joined them in the quarter-finals. Rangers drew three and lost three of their games in Group C. Juventus, who won Group C, beat Rangers 4-1 and 4-0. Paul Gascoigne, the most talented English player of his generation, and soon to be a star of the Euro 96 finals – alongside Blackburn's Alan Shearer – was sent off in Rangers' last match, as they drew 2-2 against Borussia Dortmund, who took the runners-up spot in the group. Ajax, the reigning champions, won Group D, finishing six points clear of the runners-up, Real Madrid, who they beat twice.

In December 1995, shortly after the completion of the group stage of this season's competition, the European Court of Justice issued a ruling that ended a long-running legal case, brought by Belgian player Jean-Marc Bosman. In 1990, Bosman had fallen into disagreement with his club, Liege, following which his attempts to secure a transfer to another club were blocked. The European Union now accepted Bosman's arguments, and ruled that current practices on player transfers, and the restriction of the number of foreign players in club teams, were illegal. An immediate effect of the ruling was the abandonment of UEFA's rule limiting clubs to three foreign players per match in European competitions. In the longer term, the Bosman ruling stimulated the rapid movement of players between clubs and countries, and salary inflation. These played a part in the growing commercial strength of football.

When the European Cup resumed the following spring, with the quarter-finals, Ajax beat Borussia Dortmund 3-0 on aggregate, and Panathinaikos accounted for Legia Warsaw by the same scoreline. Real Madrid won their home leg against Juventus by a single goal, but were eliminated, as the Italians won a bad-tempered return match 2-0 – with each team having a player sent off. Nantes won 2-0 at home to Spartak Moscow, who in turn built up a two goal lead in the first half of the second leg. In the second half Nantes recovered to draw 2-2 on the night, and take the tie.

Ajax lost 1-0 at home at Panathinaikos in the semi-final first leg, a defeat that ended Ajax's run of 20 unbeaten matches in the European Cup, stretching across the 1985-86, 1994-95, and 1995-96 seasons. Ajax returned to form in the second leg, winning 3-0, with Jari Litmanen scoring twice. In the other semi-final Juventus won 2-0 at home to Nantes, following which Nantes won their home leg 3-2, leaving Juventus as 4-3 aggregate winners.

Ajax and Juventus met in the final on May 22. With the match being played at Rome, Juventus had the advantage of playing in their own country. The pairing was a repeat of the 1973 final, in which Ajax had beaten Juventus 1-0. Ajax, who were still coached by Luis Van Gaal, fielded a starting line-up that contained eight members of the team which had beaten Milan in the 1995 final – Frank de Boer, Ronald de Boer, Danny Blind, Edgar Davids, Finidi George, Nwankwo Kanu, Jari Litmanen, and Edwin Van Der Sar. The scorer of the winning goal in 1995, Patrick Kluivert, would again feature as a substitute in the 1996 final. Juventus, managed by Marcello Lippi, had a team built around Italian internationals, plus Didier Deschamps from France, Paulo Sousa of Portugal, and Vladimir Jugovic of Yugoslavia.

In 1973 Ajax had won with a goal scored in the opening minutes. This time Juventus began with bright football, and took the lead after 11 minutes, with a moment of inspiration from Fabrizio Ravenelli. Ajax's goalkeeper, Van Der Sar, had a misunderstanding with one of the defenders, Frank De Boer, and Ravenelli took advantage by guiding a loose ball out of their reach, and then turning it into the net from a narrow angle. Ajax equalised four minutes before the interval, as a free kick from Frank De Boer was only parried by Angelo Peruzzi, and Jari Litmanen drove the loose ball into the net. Litmanen was the leading scorer in this season's Champions League, this being his ninth goal. The entertaining play continued in the second half, with Juventus having slightly the better of the exchanges, and nearly regaining their lead in the closing stages, as a shot from Gianluca Vialli hit the crossbar. With the score still level , the match went into extra time, during which Juventus were again the better team, but Ajax also created chances. With both goalkeepers being in good form, there was no addition to the scoring, and the match had to be settled by a penalty contest.

Davids of Ajax took the first penalty, and Peruzzi saved his kick, following which Ciro Ferrara scored for Juventus. Both teams put away each of their next two penalties, Litmanen and Anrold Scholten for Ajax, Gianluca Pessotto and Michele Padovano for Juventus. Ajax's next penalty, from Sonny Silooy, was saved by Peruzzi. Jugovic in turn scored for Juventus, who thereby won the penalty contest 4-2. Jugovic had previously won the European Cup with Red Star Belgrade in 1991, while Didier Deschamps had also now won the trophy with two different clubs, as he had been part of the victorious Marseille team in 1993. Ajax had failed to repeat their victory against Juventus in the 1973 final, and had not retained the trophy they had won by beating Milan in 1995. Instead it was Juventus who became European champions, for the first time since 1985. The settling of the match by penalties was unsatisfactory, but their performance over the 120 minutes of football made Juventus worthy winners. After the match, Gianluca Vialli, the Juventus captain, said: "I am very happy because this is the perfect climax to so many years of hard work. I have been very close to this cup before, four years ago, when I was with Sampdoria, and Barcelona beat us. We have all worked hard, and we have had some fun along the way".

1995-96

Qualifying round

		1st leg	2nd leg	agg
Austria Salzburg	Steaua Bucharest	0-0	0-1	0-1
Grasshoppers	Maccabi Tel-Aviv	1-1	1-0	2-1
Rangers	Anorthosis	1-0	0-0	1-0
Legia Warsaw	IFK Gothenburg	1-0	2-1	3-1
Dynamo Kiev	Aalborg	1-0	3-1	4-1
Rosenborg	Besiktas	3-0	1-3	4-3
Anderlecht	Ferencvaros	0-1	1-1	1-2
Panathinaikos	Hajduk Split	0-0	1-1	1-1

Panathinaikos won on away goals

Group A

Nantes 0 Porto 0
Panathinaikos 3 Nantes 1
Porto 2 Aalborg 0
Porto 0 Panathinaikos 1
Nantes 3 Aalborg 1
Aalborg 2 Panathinaikos 1
Panathinaikos 0 Porto 0
Aalborg 0 Nantes 2
Porto 2 Nantes 2
Panathinaikos 2 Aalborg 0
Nantes 0 Panathinaikos 0
Aalborg 2 Porto 2

	P	W	D	L	F	A	Pts
Panathinaikos	6	3	2	1	7	3	11
Nantes	6	2	3	1	8	6	9
Porto	6	1	4	1	6	5	7
Aalborg	6	1	1	4	5	12	4

Dynamo Kiev were disqualified for an alleged attempt to bribe the referee in their 1-0 win at home to Panathinaikos. Result of that match removed from records, and Aalborg, who had been beaten by Dynamo Kiev in the Qualifying round, allowed back into the competition.

Group B

Legia Warsaw 3 Rosenborg 1
Blackburn Rovers 0 Spartak Moscow 1
Spartak Moscow 2 Legia Warsaw 1
Rosenborg 2 Blackburn Rovers 1
Legia Warsaw 1 Blackburn Rovers 0
Rosenborg 2 Spartak Moscow 4
Blackburn Rovers 0 Legia Warsaw 0
Spartak Moscow 4 Rosenborg 1
Rosenborg 4 Legia Warsaw 0
Spartak Moscow 3 Blackburn Rovers 0
Legia Warsaw 0 Spartak Moscow 1
Blackburn Rovers 4 Rosenborg 1

	P	W	D	L	F	A	Pts
Spartak Moscow	6	6	0	0	15	4	18
Legia Warsaw	6	2	1	3	5	8	7
Rosenborg	6	2	0	4	11	16	6
Blackburn Rovers	6	1	1	4	5	8	4

Group C

Steaua Bucharest 1 Rangers 0
Borussia Dortmund 1 Juventus 3
Juventus 3 Steaua Bucharest 0

Rangers 2 Borussia Dortmund 2
Borussia Dortmund 1 Steaua Bucharest 0
Juventus 4 Rangers 1
Steaua Bucharest 0 Borussia Dortmund 0
Rangers 0 Juventus 4
Rangers 1 Steaua Bucharest 1
Juventus 1 Borussia Dortmund 2
Steaua Bucharest 0 Juventus 0
Borussia Dortmund 2 Rangers 2

	P	W	D	L	F	A	Pts
Juventus	6	4	1	1	15	4	13
Borussia Dortmund	6	2	3	1	8	8	9
Steaua Bucharest	6	1	3	2	2	5	6
Rangers	6	0	3	3	6	14	3

Group D

Ajax 1 Real Madrid 0
Grasshoppers 0 Ferencvaros 3
Ferencvaros 1 Ajax 5
Real Madrid 2 Grasshoppers 0
Ajax 3 Grasshoppers 0
Real Madrid 6 Ferencvaros 1
Grasshoppers 0 Ajax 0
Ferencvaros 1 Real Madrid 1
Real Madrid 0 Ajax 2
Ferencvaros 3 Grasshoppers 3
Ajax 4 Ferencvaros 0
Grasshoppers 0 Real Madrid 2

	P	W	D	L	F	A	Pts
Ajax	6	5	1	0	15	1	16
Real Madrid	6	3	1	2	11	5	10
Ferencvaros	6	1	2	3	9	19	5
Grasshoppers	6	0	2	4	3	13	2

Quarter-finals

		1st leg	2nd leg	agg
Legia Warsaw	Panathinaikos	0-0	0-3	0-3
Borussia Dortmund	Ajax	0-2	0-1	0-3
Nantes	Spartak Moscow	2-0	2-2	4-2
Real Madrid	Juventus	1-0	0-2	1-2

Semi-finals

		1st leg	2nd leg	agg
Ajax	Panathinaikos	0-1	3-0	3-1
Juventus	Nantes	2-0	2-3	4-3

Final

May 22 1996 Rome
Juventus 1   Ajax 1 (after extra time)
Ravanelli   Litmanen
Juventus won 4-2 on penalties
Juventus: Peruzzi, Ferrara, Torricelli, Vierchowod, Pessotto, Conte (Jugovic), Paulo Sousa (Di Livio), Deschamps, Del Piero, Vialli, Ravanelli (Padovano)
Ajax: Van Der Sar, Silooy, Blind, F De Boer (Scholten), R De Boer (Wooter), Davids, Litmanen, Musampa (Kluivert), George, Kanu, Bogarde
HT: 1-1
FT: 1-1
Referee: Vega (Spain)
Attendance: 70,000

158

1996-97

The 1996-97 competition began a few weeks after the successful Euro 96 finals, staged in England. The progress of the England team – managed by Terry Venables, who had led Barcelona to the 1986 European Cup final – to the semi-finals boosted national football pride, following the failure to qualify for the 1994 World Cup finals. An epic 1-1 draw against Germany in the semi-finals was followed by England's defeat on penalties. The Germans went on to beat the Czech Republic 2-1 in the final. The Czech Republic were one of the revelations of Euro 96, but their club champions, Slavia Prague, were thrashed 6-0 on aggregate by Grasshoppers in the qualifying round of the new Champions League. Rangers beat Alania Vladikavkaz 10-3, with Ally McCoist grabbing a hat-trick in the first 18 minutes of the second leg – he was to emerge as the leading scorer in the competition this season, with six goals. Steaua Bucharest, the only former European champions to feature at this stage, eliminated Brugge, beaten finalists back in 1978. The teams defeated in the qualifying round had the compensation of a second bite at the European cherry this season, with a rule change allowing them entry to the UEFA Cup. This link between the UEFA Champions League and the UEFA Cup was to be extended in the following seasons.

England were represented by Manchester United, who had won the Premiership and FA Cup double the previous season. United's surprise 1-0 defeat against Fenerbahce ended a proud record. Prior to this United had been unbeaten in the 58 matches they had played in England in all of the European competitions, stretching back to 1956. United promptly lost their next home match, against Juventus, but a tally of three wins, and three defeats, in Group C was enough to make them the first English team to advance from the league stage of the competition, as runners-up to Juventus. Manchester United's team this season included Jordi Cruyff, who had been bought from Barcelona in the summer of 1996, following the dismissal of Johan, his father, as manager of the latter club. Back in the 1994-95 season, Jordi had played for Barcelona against United in the European Cup. Rangers finished bottom of Group A, with only a single victory, while Auxerre – French champions for the first time – and Ajax progressed. Atletico Madrid and Borussia Dortmund advanced from Group B, both finishing nine points clear of Widzew Lodz and Steaua Bucharest. Porto romped to victory in the remaining group, seven points ahead of Rosenborg, while Milan finished third – their elimination being sealed by a 2-1 defeat at home to Rosenborg in their final match. Milan's team this season featured Roberto Baggio, who was European Footballer of the Year in 1993, and played for Italy in the World Cup finals of 1990, 1994, and 1998. Despite being one of Europe's greatest players at this time, Baggio made few appearances in the European Cup/Champions League. He was twice in the right place at the wrong time. Baggio played for Juventus at a time when Milan were the dominant Italian club, and then moved to Milan at the point when Juventus replaced them as a leading force in the Champions League.

In the quarter-finals, an inspired Manchester United beat Porto 4-0 at Old Trafford, producing one of their best-ever European performances, with goals from David May, Eric Cantona, Ryan Giggs, and Andy Cole. The return was leg was a goalless draw. The closest tie of the round saw Ajax beat Atletico Madrid by the odd goal in seven – three of the goals being scored during extra time in the second leg. Juventus disposed of Rosenborg, while Borussia Dortmund comfortably beat Auxerre home and away.

Manchester United's run came to an end in the semi-finals, as they lost both legs 1-0 to Borussia Dortmund. Rene Tretschok scored a quarter of an hour from time in Germany, with a long-range shot that deflected off United's Gary Pallister. Earlier in the second half United had been unlucky not to take the lead, as a shot from Nicky Butt hit a post. At Old Trafford Lars Ricken extended Borussia Dortmund's aggregate lead, seven minutes into the match, following which United created enough chances to win the tie, only to let themselves down with poor finishing. This proved to be Eric Cantona's final European match, as the wayward genius, who saw himself as the football equivalent of Arthur Rimbaud, the French poet, unexpectedly retired at the end of the season, aged only 30. Cantona was brilliant for both Leeds United and Manchester United in the Premiership, but curiously ineffective in the Champions League. The other semi-final brought a repeat of the previous season's final, but with a much more decisive result, as Juventus beat Ajax 6-2 on aggregate.

The final was played at Munich's Olympic Stadium before a crowd of 59,000. Borussia Dortmund were playing in their home country, but Juventus were the clear favourites to win the match. They were the reigning champions, and the more experienced team. Marcello Lippi's starting line-up featured five players who had appeared in the 1996 final, namely Didier Deschamps, Angelo Di Livio, Ciro Ferrara, Vladimir Jugovic, and Angelo Peruzzi. This was Borussia Dortmund's first European Cup final. After three campaigns between the 1950s and mid-1960s, they had been absent from the competition until the 1995-96 season. Their team featured Jurgen Kohler, Andy Moller, Stefan Reuter, Karl-Heinz Riedle, and Matthias Sammer, each of whom were German internationals, plus Paulo Sousa, from Portugal, who had won the trophy with Juventus the previous season. Sammer had won the European Footballer of the Year award at the end of 1996. The Borussia Dortmund coach, Ottmar Hitzfeld, was starting to prove himself as one of the best in Europe.

Juventus had the better of the early play, but Borussia Dortmund took the lead after 28 minutes. Following a corner taken by Moller on the left, Paul Lambert set up a chance for Karl-Heinz Riedle, who controlled the ball on his chest, and volleyed home from close range. Five minutes later Riedle struck again, to double the Germans' lead, heading in another corner taken by Moller on the left. In the closing stage of the first half Juventus twice went close to scoring, as a shot from Zinedine Zidane hit a post, following which Christian Vieri got the ball into the net, only for the effort to be disallowed by Sándor Puhl, the Hungarian referee, for handball. The Juventus revival continued at the start of the second half. Ten minutes after the re-start Alen Boksic hit the crossbar. Alessandro Del Piero, a half-time substitute, finally pulled a goal back on 64 minutes, turning in a cross from Boksic. Hopes of a Juventus comeback were dashed, however, 18 minutes from time, as Moller passed to Lars Ricken, who had just arrived as a substitute, and the latter beat goalkeeper Peruzzi with a brilliant chipped shot from 30 yards. Thereafter Borussia Dortmund smoothly completed a 3-1 victory, and became one of the surprise winners of the European Cup. This was the first time a German club had won the competition since Hamburg fourteen years earlier, in contrast to the continuing success of the Germans at international level.

1996-97

Qualifying round

		1st leg	2nd leg	agg
Maccabi Tel-Aviv	Fenerbahce	0-1	1-1	1-2
Rangers	Alania Vladikavkaz	3-1	7-2	10-3
Panathinaikos	Rosenborg	1-0	0-3	1-3
IFK Gothenburg	Ferencvaros	3-0	1-1	4-1
Widzew Lodz	Brondby	2-1	2-3	4-4
Widzew Lodz won on away goals				
Grasshoppers	Slavia Prague	5-0	1-0	6-0

| Brugge | Steaua Bucharest | 2-2 | 0-3 | 2-5 |
| Rapid Vienna | Dynamo Kiev | 2-0 | 4-2 | 6-2 |

Group A

Auxerre 0 Ajax 1
Grasshoppers 3 Rangers 0
Rangers 1 Auxerre 2
Ajax 0 Grasshoppers 1
Auxerre 1 Grasshoppers 0
Ajax 4 Rangers 1
Rangers 0 Ajax 1
Grasshoppers 3 Auxerre 1
Rangers 2 Grasshoppers 1
Ajax 1 Auxerre 2
Auxerre 2 Rangers 1
Grasshoppers 0 Ajax 1

	P	W	D	L	F	A	Pts
Auxerre	6	4	0	2	8	7	12
Ajax	6	4	0	2	8	4	12
Grasshoppers	6	3	0	3	8	5	9
Rangers	6	1	0	5	5	13	3

Group B

Atletico Madrid 4 Steaua Bucharest 0
Borussia Dortmund 2 Widzew Lodz 1
Widzew Lodz 1 Atletico Madrid 4
Steaua Bucharest 0 Borussia Dortmund 3
Atlético Madrid 0 Borussia Dortmund 1
Steaua Bucharest 1 Widzew Lodz 0
Widzew Lodz 2 Steaua Bucharest 0
Borussia Dortmund 1 Atletico Madrid 2
Widzew Lodz 2 Borussia Dortmund 2
Steaua Bucharest 1 Atletico Madrid 1
Atletico Madrid 1 Widzew Lodz 0
Borussia Dortmund 5 Steaua Bucharest 3

	P	W	D	L	F	A	Pts
Atletico Madrid	6	4	1	1	12	4	13
Borussia Dortmund	6	4	1	1	14	8	13
Widzew Lodz	6	1	1	4	6	10	4
Steaua Bucharest	6	1	1	4	5	15	4

Group C

Rapid Vienna 1 Fenerbahce 1
Juventus 1 Manchester United 0
Manchester United 2 Rapid Vienna 0
Fenerbahce 0 Juventus 1
Rapid Vienna 1 Juventus 1
Fenerbahce 0 Manchester United 2
Manchester United 0 Fenerbahce 1
Juventus 5 Rapid Vienna 0
Manchester United 0 Juventus 1
Fenerbahce 1 Rapid Vienna 0
Rapid Vienna 0 Manchester United 2
Juventus 2 Fenerbahce 0

	P	W	D	L	F	A	Pts
Juventus	6	5	1	0	11	1	16
Manchester United	6	3	0	3	6	3	9
Fenerbahce	6	2	1	3	3	6	7
Rapid Vienna	6	0	2	4	2	12	2

Group D

IFK Gothenburg 2 Rosenborg 3
Milan 2 Porto 3
Porto 2 IFK Gothenburg 1
Rosenborg 1 Milan 4
IFK Gothenburg 2 Milan 1
Rosenborg 0 Porto 1
Porto 3 Rosenborg 0
Milan 4 IFK Gothenburg 2
Porto 1 Milan 1
Rosenborg 1 IFK Gothenburg 0
IFK Gothenburg 0 Porto 2
Milan 1 Rosenborg 2

	P	W	D	L	F	A	Pts
Porto	6	5	1	0	12	4	16
Rosenborg	6	3	0	3	7	11	9
Milan	6	2	1	3	13	11	7
IFK Gothenburg	6	1	0	5	7	13	3

Quarter-finals

		1st leg	2nd leg	agg
Borussia Dortmund	Auxerre	3-1	1-0	4-1
Ajax	Atletico Madrid	1-1	3-2	4-3
Rosenborg	Juventus	1-1	0-2	1-3
Manchester United	Porto	4-0	0-0	4-0

Semi-finals

		1st leg	2nd leg	agg
Borussia Dortmund	Manchester United	1-0	1-0	2-0
Ajax	Juventus	1-2	1-4	2-6

Final

May 28 1997 Munich
Borussia Dortmund 3   Juventus 1
Riedle 2   Del Piero
Ricken

Borussia Dortmund: Klos, Kohler, Sammer, Kree, Reuter, Lambert, Paulo Sousa, Heinrich, Moller (Zorc), Riedle (Herrlich), Chapuisat (Ricken)
Juventus: Peruzzi, Porrini (Del Piero), Ferrara, Montero, Iuliano, Di Livio, Jugovic, Deschamps, Zidane, Boksic (Tacchinardi), Vieri (Amoruso)
HT: 2-0
Referee: Puhl (Hungary)
Attendance: 59,000

Chapter 9

Expansion and Revival 1997-2005

1997-98

UEFA now ended the restriction to 24 teams, and again made the Champions League open to the champions of each country in Europe. This pleased the weaker nations, who felt they had unfairly been denied access. On the other hand, a new move sparked further controversy, as UEFA diluted the competition's distinct nature as the preserve of national champions, by allowing the runners-up in the leagues of the eight strongest countries to also participate. This was a further attempt by UEFA to head off continuing ambitions for a rival European super league, which had not been halted by the introduction of the group stage in 1991-92, or its extension in 1994-95. The expanded 1997-98 competition brought together 55 teams from 46 countries – including four newcomers, Armenia, Azerbaijan, Macedonia, and Slovakia. For the first time ever, one country had three entrants in a single season, with Bayern Munich, the German champions, being joined by the runners-up, Bayer Leverkusen, while Borussia Dortmund took their place as reigning European champions. Thirty clubs participated in the first qualifying round, following which the 15 winners of those ties joined 17 other clubs – including the eight runners-up allowed into the competition – for the second qualifying round. The 16 teams to emerge from the qualifying stage plus the eight seeds met in a league stage that was now increased from four groups to six. The six group winners, plus the two runners-up with the best records, would then progress into the concluding knock-out stage.

Rangers had won the Scottish title for a ninth successive season in 1996-97, equalling the run of the great Celtic team from the mid-1960s to mid-1970s. They thrashed GI Gotu, from the Faroes, 5-0 and 6-0 in the first qualifying round – with Gordon Durie, Ally McCoist, and Marco Negri each scoring three times in the tie – but lost to Gothenburg at the next hurdle. Rangers, along with the other clubs eliminated in the second qualifying round, then moved to the UEFA Cup. Newcastle United – making their first appearance in the European Cup, having been runners-up in the Premiership the previous season – won a stirring tie against Croatia Zagreb 4-3 on aggregate, with Temuri Ketsbaia, a Georgian playing for the Geordies, scoring the decisive goal in the final minute of extra time. Steaua Bucharest were pleased that their 3-2 win against Paris Saint-Germain was improved to a 3-0 scoreline by UEFA, as the French club had fielded a suspended player, but this was followed by Paris Saint-Germain winning the second leg 5-0, with Rai scoring a hat-trick, to take the tie.

Manchester United, the English champions, won Group B convincingly with victories in their first five matches, before a 1-0 defeat away to Juventus, which enabled the Italian champions to reach the quarter-finals as one of the two best runners-up. Prior to this United had beaten Juventus 3-2 in an outstanding match at Old Trafford, despite going behind to a goal from Alessandro Del Piero after just 24 seconds. United's 3-1 win away to Feyenoord came courtesy of a hat-trick from Andy Cole, a player bought from Newcastle United in 1995 for a British record transfer fee of £7,000,000. Newcastle, who were managed by Kenny Dalglish, finished third in Group C. Newcastle opened with a 3-2 win against Barcelona at St James' Park, as Faustino Asprilla, their Colombian striker, netted a hat-trick, but failed to effectively build upon this. Dynamo Kiev won the group, while Barcelona finished bottom. Borussia Dortmund opened the defence of their title by winning Group A, six points clear of Parma. The other two German clubs also advanced to the quarter-finals. Bayern Munich won Group E, due to their better head-to-head record in the matches against Paris Saint-Germain, with whom they tied on points. Bayer Leverkusen finished behind Monaco in Group F, on the head-to-head decider, but joined them in the next stage as one of strongest second-placed teams. The remaining group was won by Real Madrid, whose attacking team scored 15 goals in their six matches, a tally which Monaco equalled at this stage.

Monaco's goalscoring rate dropped dramatically in the quarter-finals, but they still progressed. Having been held to 0-0 draw at home to Manchester United, Monaco went ahead five minutes into the second leg, as David Trezeguet scored with a thunderbolt of a long-range shot. United attacked throughout the match, but were lacking in inspiration, even after Ole Gunnar Solskjaer equalised seven minutes into the second half, and lost the tie on away goals. The all-German tie between Borussia Dortmund and Bayern Munich failed to live up to expectations. The football was dull, and the only goal was scored by Borussia Dortmund's Stephane Chapuisat as the second leg went into extra time. The other German team, Bayer Leverkusen, departed with a defeat against Real Madrid, while Juventus eliminated Dynamo Kiev, with Filippo Inzaghi (nicknamed 'Super Pippo') scoring a hat-trick in the second leg.

Juventus virtually made sure of a place in the final with a 4-1 win against Monaco in the first leg of their semi-final, as Del Piero scored a hat-trick that was comprised of a free kick followed by two penalties. Monaco won the return 3-2, but it was the Italians who took the tie, 6-4 on aggregate. The start of the first leg between Real Madrid and Borussia Dortmund at the Bernabeu was held up for an hour and a quarter, as repairs were needed to one of the goal frames, which was damaged by hooligans among the Real supporters. Borussia Dortmund were unhappy about having to play the game after this incident, and lost 2-0. A goalless draw in the return saw Real Madrid through to the final.

So Real Madrid's first European Cup final since their defeat against Liverpool in 1981 saw them face Juventus, at Amsterdam. Real were coached by Jupp Heynckes, who had played for Borussia Monchengladbach in the 1977 final. Despite leading them to the final, he was sacked a few days after the match – due to a decline in domestic form which saw Real finish fourth in the Spanish league. For Juventus, this was a third successive appearance in the final. The team selected by Marcello Lippi included four players who had appeared in both the 1996 and 1997 finals – Alessandro Del Piero, Didier Deschamps, Angelo Di Livio, and Angelo Peruzzi. Del Piero was the leading scorer in this season's competition, with ten goals.

The first half saw both teams playing open and positive football. Juventus had the better of the early play, but Real Madrid gradually gained the initiative as the half progressed. During the early part of the second half Juventus threw away two excellent chances to take the lead, with Inzaghi being the culprit each time – firstly volleying over the bar, and secondly shooting directly to Bodo Illgner, the goalkeeper. With 25 minutes left to play Real Madrid scored, with a goal that demonstrated the international nature of their team – in contrast to the all-Spanish line-up which won the 1966 final. A cross from Clarence Seedorf (a Dutchman) on the right wing found its way to Roberto Carlos (a Brazilian), whose shot deflected off a defender, Iuliano, into the path of Pedrag Mijatovic (a Yugoslav), who deftly took the ball around Angelo Peruzzi, the Juventus goalkeeper, and then clipped it into the net from a narrow angle on the left.

Juventus fought well in the remainder of the match, creating several chances, but could not avoid being defeated in the final for the second successive season, as Real Madrid held on to win the trophy for the first time since 1966. Two members of the Real team had now won the trophy with two different clubs, namely Christian Panucci (previously a winner with Milan in 1994) and Seedorf (who had won the European Cup with Ajax in 1995). Ironically the 1997-98 season, in which one tradition had been broken, with the admittance of eight teams who were not reigning national champions, ended with the revival of another tradition as Real Madrid, champions of Spain the previous season, re-asserted their place as one of the giants of the European Cup.

1997-98
First qualifying round

		1st leg	2nd leg	agg
Derry City	Maribor	0-2	0-1	0-3
Kosice	IA Akranes	3-0	1-0	4-0
Partizan Belgrade	Croatia Zagreb	1-0	0-5	1-5
Valletta	Skonto Riga	1-0	0-2	1-2
Pyunik	MTK Budapest	0-2	3-4	3-6
Crusaders	Dynamo Tbilisi	1-3	1-5	2-8
Sileks	Beitar Jerusalem	1-0	0-3	1-3
Steaua Bucharest	CSKA Sofia	3-3	2-0	5-3
Constructorul	MPKC Mozyr	1-1	2-3	3-4
Lantana	Jazz Pori	0-2	0-1	0-3
GI Gotu	Rangers	0-5	0-6	0-11
Neftchi	Widzew Lodz	0-2	0-8	0-10
Dynamo Kiev	Barry Town	2-0	4-0	6-0
Sion	Jeunesse D'Esch	4-0	1-0	5-0
Anorthosis	Kareda	3-0	1-1	4-1

Second qualifying round

		1st leg	2nd leg	agg
MTK Budapest	Rosenborg	0-1	1-3	1-4
Besiktas	Maribor	0-0	3-1	3-1
Sion	Galatasaray	1-4	1-4	2-8
Olympiakos	MPKC Mozyr	5-0	2-2	7-2
Austria Salzburg	Sparta Prague	0-0	0-3	0-3
IFK Gothenburg	Rangers	3-0	1-1	4-1
Barcelona	Skonto Riga	3-2	1-0	4-2
Brondby	Dynamo Kiev	2-4	1-0	3-4
Newcastle United	Croatia Zagreb	2-1	2-2	4-3
Feyenoord	Jazz Pori	6-2	2-1	8-3
Bayer Leverkusen	Dynamo Tbilisi	6-1	0-1	6-2
Kosice	Spartak Moscow	2-1	0-0	2-1
Steaua Bucharest	Paris Saint-Germain	3-0	0-5	3-5

Steaua Bucharest won the first leg 3-2, but were awarded the match 3-0 as Paris Saint-Germain fielded a suspended player

		1st leg	2nd leg	agg
Widzew Lodz	Parma	1-3	0-4	1-7
Beitar Jerusalem	Sporting Lisbon	0-0	0-3	0-3
Anorthosis	Lierse	2-0	0-3	2-3

Group A

Galatasaray 0 Borussia Dortmund 1
Sparta Prague 0 Parma 0
Parma 2 Galatasaray 0
Borussia Dortmund 4 Sparta Prague 1
Parma 1 Borussia Dortmund 0
Sparta Prague 3 Galatasaray 0
Galatasaray 2 Sparta Prague 0
Borussia Dortmund 2 Parma 0
Parma 2 Sparta Prague 2
Borussia Dortmund 4 Galatasaray 1
Sparta Prague 0 Borussia Dortmund 3
Galatasaray 1 Parma 1

	P	W	D	L	F	A	Pts
Borussia Dortmund	6	5	0	1	14	3	15
Parma	6	2	3	1	6	5	9
Sparta Prague	6	1	2	3	6	11	5
Galatasaray	6	1	1	4	4	11	4

Group B

Juventus 5 Feyenoord 1
Kosice 0 Manchester United 3
Feyenoord 2 Kosice 0
Manchester United 3 Juventus 2
Manchester United 2 Feyenoord 1
Kosice 0 Juventus 1
Feyenoord 1 Manchester United 3
Juventus 3 Kosice 2
Feyenoord 2 Juventus 0
Manchester United 3 Kosice 0
Kosice 0 Feyenoord 1
Juventus 1 Manchester United 0

	P	W	D	L	F	A	Pts
Manchester United	6	5	0	1	14	5	15
Juventus	6	4	0	2	12	8	12
Feyenoord	6	3	0	3	8	10	9
Kosice	6	0	0	6	2	13	0

Group C

PSV Eindhoven 1 Dynamo Kiev 3
Newcastle United 3 Barcelona 2
Barcelona 2 PSV Eindhoven 2
Dynamo Kiev 2 Newcastle United 2
PSV Eindhoven 1 Newcastle United 0
Dynamo Kiev 3 Barcelona 0
Newcastle United 0 PSV Eindhoven 2
Barcelona 0 Dynamo Kiev 4
Barcelona 1 Newcastle United 0
Dynamo Kiev 1 PSV Eindhoven 1
PSV Eindhoven 2 Barcelona 2
Newcastle United 2 Dynamo Kiev 0

	P	W	D	L	F	A	Pts
Dynamo Kiev	6	3	2	1	13	6	11
PSV Eindhoven	6	2	3	1	9	8	9
Newcastle United	6	2	1	3	7	8	7
Barcelona	6	1	2	3	7	14	5

Group D

Real Madrid 4 Rosenborg 1

Olympiakos 1 Porto 0
Porto 0 Real Madrid 2
Rosenborg 5 Olympiakos 1
Rosenborg 2 Porto 0
Real Madrid 5 Olympiakos 1
Porto 1 Rosenborg 1
Olympiakos 0 Real Madrid 0
Rosenborg 2 Real Madrid 0
Porto 2 Olympiakos 1
Real Madrid 4 Porto 0
Olympiakos 2 Rosenborg 2

	P	W	D	L	F	A	Pts
Real Madrid	6	4	1	1	15	4	13
Rosenborg	6	3	2	1	13	8	11
Olympiakos	6	1	2	3	6	14	5
Porto	6	1	1	4	3	11	4

Group E

Bayern Munich 2 Besiktas 0
Paris Saint-Germain 3 IFK Gothenburg 0
IFK Gothenburg 1 Bayern Munich 3
Besiktas 3 Paris Saint-Germain 1
Besiktas 1 IFK Gothenburg 0
Bayern Munich 5 Paris Saint-Germain 1
IFK Gothenburg 2 Besiktas 1
Paris Saint-Germain 3 Bayern Munich 1
Besiktas 0 Bayern Munich 2
IFK Gothenburg 0 Paris Saint-Germain 1
Bayern Munich 0 IFK Gothenburg 1
Paris Saint-Germain 2 Besiktas 1

	P	W	D	L	F	A	Pts
Bayern Munich	6	4	0	2	13	6	12
Paris Saint-Germain	6	4	0	2	11	10	12
Besiktas	6	2	0	4	6	9	6
IFK Gothenburg	6	2	0	4	4	9	6

Group F

Sporting Lisbon 3 Monaco 0
Bayer Leverkusen 1 Lierse 0
Monaco 4 Bayer Leverkusen 0
Lierse 1 Sporting Lisbon 1
Monaco 5 Lierse 1
Sporting Lisbon 0 Bayer Leverkusen 2
Lierse 0 Monaco 1
Bayer Leverkusen 4 Sporting Lisbon 1
Monaco 3 Sporting Lisbon 2
Lierse 0 Bayer Leverkusen 2
Sporting Lisbon 2 Lierse 1
Bayer Leverkusen 2 Monaco 2

	P	W	D	L	F	A	Pts
Monaco	6	4	1	1	15	8	13
Bayer Leverkusen	6	4	1	1	11	7	13
Sporting Lisbon	6	2	1	3	9	11	7
Lierse	6	0	1	5	3	12	1

Quarter-finals

		1st leg	2nd leg	agg
Bayer Leverkusen	Real Madrid	1-1	0-3	1-4
Juventus	Dynamo Kiev	1-1	4-1	5-2

		1st leg	2nd leg	agg
Bayern Munich	Borussia Dortmund	0-0	0-1	0-1
Monaco	Manchester United	0-0	1-1	1-1

Monaco won on away goals

Semi-finals

		1st leg	2nd leg	agg
Juventus	Monaco	4-1	2-3	6-4
Real Madrid	Borussia Dortmund	2-0	0-0	2-0

Final

May 20 1998 Amsterdam

Real Madrid 1   Juventus 0

Mijatovic

Real Madrid: Illgner, Hierro, Sanchis, Panucci, Roberto Carlos, Raul (Amavisca), Karembeu, Seedorf, Redondo, Mijatovic (Suker), Morientes (Jaime)

Juventus: Peruzzi, Torricelli, Montero, Iuliano, Di Livio (Tacchinardi), Deschamps (Conte), Davids, Pessotto (Fonseca), Zidane, Del Piero, Inzaghi

HT: 0-0

Referee: Krug (Germany)

Attendance: 48,500

The Re-branding of the Competition

The 1990s brought dramatic changes in the structure of the European Cup. A competition which had been run with a virtually unchanged format for more than 30 years was suddenly transformed. Indeed the very name of the European Cup was subject to this process, as the competition was officially re-christened the UEFA Champions League. Nevertheless the trophy awarded to the winning team each season remained the same, and traditionalists still called the competition the European Cup.

The innovations, which have continued at the start of the 21st century, began with the 1991-92 competition. The combination of an attempt by UEFA to raise extra revenue by an increase (albeit small) in the number of matches played in the competition, and the wish to head off the threat of a rival European Super League, prompted the replacement of the quarter-finals and semi-finals with two mini leagues, the winners of which met in the 1992 final. The same format was used for the 1992-93 season, and when the draw for the second of the knock-out rounds was made, UEFA coined the phrase Champions League for the league stage which was to follow it. Within a few years the UEFA Champions League became accepted as the new name for the entire competition, due to the prompting of UEFA.

Hand in hand with the renaming of the competition went a commercial onslaught by UEFA. The European Cup had always been a high-profile competition, but the new Champions League saw UEFA and the participating clubs capitalise upon the potential for vast financial gain. The main pillars of this were the introduction of corporate sponsorship, and the massive increase in the fees charged to broadcasters for the right to provide television coverage of the competition. UEFA also strengthened the identity of the competition by various means, including the introduction of a logo, the synchronised staging of matches at a set time on Tuesday and Wednesday evenings, and a fair play charter, which took its lead from FIFA's efforts in this field. In 2003 UEFA launched Champions: The Official Magazine of the UEFA Champions League, *a glossy and informative publication, which appears once every two months.*

Multi-million pound sponsorship has been agreed in recent years between UEFA and a series of corporations, including Amstel, Canon, Continental, Ford, Mastercard, PlayStation2, Philips, and Reebok. Whereas in the past television rights were negotiated individually between clubs and broadcasters, UEFA has taken control of the contracts for these. UEFA's initial strategy was to agree deals by which a single broadcaster in each of the leading European football nations (including ITV in Britain, RTI in Italy, TVE in Spain, RTL in Germany, and TF1 in France) received exclusive access to the competition for a period of several years, in return for huge payments. This approach fell foul of the European Union's free market regulations, with the result that UEFA became obliged to sell a variety of packages to competing broadcasters.

The financial explosion of the UEFA Champions League has run alongside an increasing commercialisation of football. The immediate effect of the Bosman judgement in 1995 was that UEFA were forced to drop the rule restricting each team to three foreign players per match in the European competitions, but this has been outweighed by the long-term significance of a free market in European football, in which rich clubs and their star players have profited. The top players can now command earnings of several million pounds a year. Recent years have seen the world transfer record spiral to previously unimaginable heights. In 1996 the £15,000,000 move of Alan Shearer from Blackburn Rovers to Newcastle United set a new world record. This was broken several times in the next few years, with a new high of £31,000,000 being set when Christian Vieri moved from Lazio to Internazionale in 1999. The following year Hernan Crespo's transfer from Parma to Lazio cost £35,700,000, a level that was eclipsed within weeks by the £37,400,000 move of Luis Figo from Barcelona to Real Madrid. In 2001 the current world record of £46,500,000 was set as Zinedine Zidane was sold by Juventus to Real Madrid. This staggering transfer fee was more than three times the record set by Shearer's move just five years earlier.

In the summer of 2004, UEFA proudly announced the enormous financial allocations made to the clubs that had participated in the 2003-04 Champions League. Between them the 32 clubs that featured in the group stage were rewarded with a total of almost £279,000,000 – an average of about £8,700,000 per club. The prize money was based on a combination of the progress each club made in the competition, and its share in UEFA's "market pool", the latter being derived from the value of the television contracts in the club's home country. The top three earners were all English, with Chelsea receiving £19,454,000, while Arsenal pocketed £19,110,000, and Manchester United earned £18,773,000. Monaco, the beaten finalists, were paid £17,706,000. Porto won the trophy, but only finished fifth in financial terms, with £13,244,000, due to the income from Portuguese television rights being less than that in several other countries. UEFA now predicted that prize money for the 2004-05 competition would rise to £282,000,000.

The UEFA Champions League has become the apogee of the European football market, and the earnings available to participating clubs are a massive extra incentive for success. The position has been reached where an English club would probably prefer fourth place in the Premiership, with the attendant opportunity of a multi-million pound campaign in the next season's Champions League, to winning the FA Cup, which is followed by entry to the relative backwater of the UEFA Cup.

1998-99

At the end of the 20th century the idea of a football season lasting from August to May, with a distinct summer break – albeit a break shortened by a few weeks every other year with the excitement of the World Cup or European Championship finals – was consigned to a quaint past. European football now ran for 12 months a year. The 1998-99 UEFA Champions League – the last to be completed before the turn of the Millennium – opened on July 22 1998, only nine weeks after the previous European Cup final, and just ten days after the 1998 World Cup closed, with France beating Brazil 3-0 in the final, at Paris. The World Cup finals coincided with the start on June 20 of the 1998 Inter-Toto Cup, a competition that bridged the European seasons, acting as a qualifier for the 1998-99 UEFA Cup. Amidst this blurring of the seasons, 32 of the 56 clubs competing in the 1998-99 Champions League participated in the first qualifying round. They included Celtic and Steaua

Bucharest, both previous winners of the competition, who now struggled to beat inferior opposition – St Patrick's Athletic and Flora Tallinn respectively. Celtic fell to Croatia Zagreb at the next hurdle, while Steaua lost 8-5 on aggregate to Panathinaikos. By contrast, the five former winners who entered the action in the second qualifying round – Bayern Munich, Benfica, Internazionale, Manchester United, and PSV Eindhoven – won their ties.

Olympiakos provided the big surprise of the league stage, which stretched from September to December, winning Group A, and eliminating both Porto and Ajax. Juventus struggled in Group B, drawing their first five matches before beating Rosenborg 2-0. A three-way tie on points between Galatasaray, Juventus, and Rosenborg was settled by Juventus' superior record in the matches between those teams. Real Madrid, the reigning champions, progressed as runners-up to Internazionale in Group C. The other successful runners-up were Manchester United, who finished behind Bayern Munich in Group D, but ahead of Barcelona, with whom they shared a couple of epic 3-3 draws. Arsenal, who had won the English Premiership and FA Cup double the previous season, were managed by Arsene Wenger, a Frenchman, and featured several French players. Arsenal chose to play their home matches at Wembley Stadium rather than their own Highbury ground, to allow more of their fans to attend the games, but did not benefit from the switch, putting in some indifferent performances including losing 1-0 to Lens, the unexpected French champions. Dynamo Kiev, who played some sparkling football, won Group E while Arsenal came third. Kaiserslautern were runaway winners of Group F, five points clear of Benfica.

The competition resumed with the quarter-finals in March 1999, after a three month winter break, but it was still intensely cold in the Ukraine. This factor helped Dynamo Kiev end the progress of Real Madrid. Having drawn their away leg, the Ukrainians won the return with a brace from Andrei Shevchenko. Juventus, the previous year's runners-up to Real Madrid, struggled to beat Olympiakos 3-2 on aggregate. An all-German tie saw Bayern Munich thrash Kaiserslautern – who had a player sent off in each leg – 6-0. Manchester United seized the initiative against Internazionale, winning 2-0 at Old Trafford, with Dwight Yorke twice heading in crosses from David Beckham during the first half. In the return a rearguard action gave United a deserved 1-1 draw, with Paul Scholes equalising a couple of minutes from time.

United's reward was another tie against Italian opposition. Outplayed by Juventus in their home leg, United squeezed a 1-1 draw as Ryan Giggs scored in stoppage time. In Turin, United found themselves 2-0 down, and apparently out, after only 11 minutes – both goals scored with an element of good fortune by Filippo Inzaghi. By half time United had clawed their way back into the tie, with goals from Roy Keane, their inspirational captain, and Yorke. United had levelled the aggregate score, and were even ahead on away goals. Play moved from end to end during a pulsating second half, and the tie was not finally settled until a goal by Andy Cole, six minutes from time, gave United a 3-2 win on the night. In an echo of the 1968 semi-final against Real Madrid, United's comeback had brought a 4-3 aggregate victory.

In the other semi-final, Bayern Munich similarly overcame adversity to win by the odd goal in seven, in their case against Dynamo Kiev. The Ukrainians led 2-0, and then 3-1, in the first leg, but the Germans scored twice in the last 12 minutes to level that match, and won the return with an excellent solo goal from Mario Basler. Dynamo Kiev had played some of the best football in the competition, with Shevchenko's 11 goals making him the leading scorer, but fell short of becoming the first team from the former Soviet Union to reach a European Cup final.

Manchester United and Bayern Munich met in the final at Barcelona's Nou Camp Stadium, before a crowd of 90,245, although ironically both finalists had only been runners-up in their domestic leagues the previous season. After progressing through the qualifiers, they had met in the group stage of this season's European Cup, and drawn both of their matches. Both clubs were forced to field a weakened team for the final. Bayern were without Bixente Lizarazu, a member of France's 1998 World Cup winning team, and Giovane Elber, a Brazilian, each of whom were carrying long-term injuries. United lacked Keane and Scholes, combative midfielders who were both suspended due to bookings picked up against Juventus. Keane's role as captain was filled by Peter Schmeichel, the goalkeeper, who was making his final appearance for the club. United were managed by Alex Ferguson, who had been captivated by the European Cup when he attended Real Madrid's 7-3 win against Eintracht Frankfurt, in his native Glasgow, as an 18 year-old, back in 1960. Now Ferguson had the chance to win the competition, and emulate Matt Busby, a fellow Scotsman, who had led United to victory in 1968, in their only previous appearance in a European Cup final.

Bayern's coach was Ottmar Hitzfeld, who had led Borussia Dortmund to victory in the 1997 European Cup final – after they had beaten Manchester United in the semi-final. This was their sixth final – the hat-trick of wins in the mid-1970s being followed by defeats against Aston Villa, in 1982, and Porto, in 1987. The 1999 final was being played on the anniversary of Bayern's defeat against Aston Villa. The referee, Pierluigi Collina, became the first Italian to control a European Cup final since 1991, with this being the first such contest since then that did not feature an Italian club. Collina was one of the world's most recognisable referees, with his bald head, bulging eyes, and authoritative manner.

This was one of the most dramatic finals in the history of the competition. Bayern Munich struck first, with Basler wrong-footing Schmeichel and scoring from a free kick after five minutes. Despite this setback, United remained calm, had most of the possession during the remainder of the first half, and created the better goalscoring chances. Dwight Yorke went close to scoring on 20 minutes, and United threatened twice in the last five minutes of the half – firstly with a free kick from Beckham, and then with a clever passing move that ended with Oliver Kahn, the Bayern goalkeeper, diving at the feet of Ryan Giggs.

Bayern nearly doubled their lead within two minutes of the restart, as Carsten Jancker made a powerful run into the United penalty area, followed by a shot from a narrow angle, which Schmeichel did well to push wide of the goal. Eight minutes later Manchester United in turn threatened, as a cross from Giggs on the right found Jesper Blomqvist, only for the latter to shoot over the bar from close range, as Kahn came to challenge him. United continued to enjoy the majority of play, and chances, as the second half progressed, but Bayern's occasional attacks appeared more threatening. Schmeichel was the busier goalkeeper, and had to make an excellent save to deny Stefan Effenburg with 17 minutes remaining. On 79 minutes Basler made a powerful run down the right wing, beating several United players, and then laid the ball off for Mehmet Scholl, whereupon the latter's chipped shot beat Schmeichel, but hit a post. Five minutes later Bayern hit the woodwork again, with an overhead kick from Jancker striking the crossbar during a goalmouth scramble that followed a corner. In the minutes following this second reprieve, United pushed strongly for an equaliser, but Teddy Sheringham, Yorke, and Ole Gunnar Solskjaer each failed to make the most of opportunities to score.

As the end of the scheduled 45 minutes of the second half arrived Bayern Munich still led 1-0. UEFA officials put Bayern's ribbons on the trophy, but the signal from the fourth official that three minutes of stoppage time were due gave Manchester United hope. During recent years United had scored many winning or equalising goals in the closing minutes of vital matches – indeed they had done so in the second leg of this season's quarter-final, and in both legs of their semi-final. At the start of stoppage time, United moved forward, and won a corner on the left. Schmeichel ran the length of the pitch to join the United attack in the Bayern Munich penalty area, and his presence put pressure on the opposition as Beckham's corner flew into the goalmouth.

The Bayern defence only half-cleared the corner, with the ball reaching Giggs just outside the penalty area. Giggs drove the ball back towards the goal, and Sheringham calmly slotted it, on the turn, into the bottom left-hand corner of the net. United had finally scored the equaliser that their determined pressure merited. Having simultaneously avoided immediate defeat and seized the initiative from Bayern Munich, Manchester United sensed the possibility of scoring a further, decisive, goal in stoppage time, rather than enduring the tension of extra time. United attacked again, and Solskjaer won them another corner on the left. Beckham's delivery was met at the near post by Sheringham, whose glancing header sent the ball across the goalmouth towards Solskjaer, who volleyed it into the top right-hand corner of the net. Schmeichel, who stayed in his own penalty area this time, celebrated the goal with a somersault – a moment memorably captured on television. Moments later Collina blew the final whistle, and Manchester United had suddenly won 2-1, with two goals scored in stoppage time – both by substitutes – after trailing for almost the entire match. The equaliser had been dramatic, but the way in which it was followed by a winning goal was simply sensational.

Manchester United's players and management began to celebrate their victory almost in a state of disbelief, having faced defeat only a few minutes earlier. Alex Ferguson's immediate comment to a television interviewer was "I can't believe it, I can't believe it, football, bloody hell". The Bayern Munich players reacted with equivalent despair, having lost due to a turnaround even more surprising than the latter part of the 1987 final. The United players collected their winners' medals, and the trophy was held aloft by Peter Schmeichel and Alex Ferguson. An excited Schmeichel said afterwards: "Not even Hans-Christian Andersen could have written a fairytale like that. One thing I have learned throughout my time with United is that we never give up, and we proved it tonight. You cannot get higher than this. Tonight is the night for Manchester United and champagne".

The victory was a dream finish to Schmeichel's eight-year career with United. He had established his reputation as one of the greatest goalkeepers in the world during Denmark's surprise victory in Euro '92, and been outstanding in the 2-0 win against Germany in the final. Now he had thwarted the Germans again. Although they rode their luck in the final, Manchester United were deserving winners of the competition, being unbeaten in their 13 matches, during which they scored 31 goals. They had also completed a unique treble, becoming the first English club to win the domestic championship, FA Cup, and European Cup in the same season. Besides dominating English football during the 1990s, they had been a major force in the European club competitions, winning the Cup-Winners' Cup in 1991, and showing increasing ability during a series of campaigns in the European Cup. United had now won the European Cup for the first time in 31 years, an echo of Real Madrid regaining the trophy in 1998 after a 32 year gap. This Manchester United team had reached even greater heights than their predecessors of 1968. Indeed Manchester United were soon to convert their treble into a quadruple triumph, as on November 30 1999 they beat Palmeiras, of Brazil, 1-0 in Tokyo, with a goal from Keane, to become the first English team to win the World Club Championship. Forty three years after Matt Busby had shown the foresight to lead United into Europe for the first time, they had finally won the silverware to match their claim to be the greatest club in the world.

1998-99

First qualifying round

		1st leg	2nd leg	agg
Sileks	Brugge	0-0	1-2	1-2
LKS Lodz	Kapaz	4-1	3-1	7-2
Litets	Halmstads	2-0	1-2	3-2
Grasshoppers	Jeunesse D'Esch	6-0	2-0	8-0
Celtic	St Patrick's Athletic	0-0	2-0	2-0
Kareda	Maribor	0-3	0-1	0-4
Dynamo Kiev	Barry Town	8-0	2-1	10-1
Cliftonville	Kosice	1-5	0-8	1-13
Skonto Riga	Dynamo Minsk	0-0	2-1	2-1
Valletta	Anorthosis	0-2	0-6	0-8
Beitar Jerusalem	B36 Torshavn	4-1	1-0	5-1
Dynamo Tbilisi	Vllaznia Shkoder	3-0	1-3	4-3

Dynamo Tbilisi won the first leg 1-0, but UEFA awarded the match to them 3-0 as Vllaznia Shkoder fielded an ineligible player

		1st leg	2nd leg	agg
HJK Helsinki	Erevan	2-0	3-0	5-0
Obilic	IBV Vestmannaeyjar	2-0	2-1	4-1
Zimbru Chisinau	Ujpest Dozsa	1-0	1-3	2-3
Steaua Bucharest	Flora Tallinn	4-1	1-3	5-4

Second qualifying round

		1st leg	2nd leg	agg
Rosenborg	Brugge	2-0	2-4	4-4

Rosenborg won on away goals

		1st leg	2nd leg	agg
Manchester United	LKS Lodz	2-0	0-0	2-0
Litets	Spartak Moscow	0-5	2-6	2-11
Galatasaray	Grasshoppers	2-1	3-2	5-3
Celtic	Croatia Zagreb	1-0	0-3	1-3
Maribor	PSV Eindhoven	2-1	1-4	3-5
Dynamo Kiev	Sparta Prague	0-1	1-0	1-1

Dynamo Kiev won 3-1 on penalties

		1st leg	2nd leg	agg
Kosice	Brondby	0-2	1-0	1-2
Internazionale	Skonto Riga	4-0	3-1	7-1
Olimpiakos	Anorthosis	2-1	4-2	6-3
Benfica	Beitar Jerusalem	6-0	2-4	8-4
Dynamo Tbilisi	Athletic Bilbao	2-1	0-1	2-2

Athletic Bilbao won on away goals

		1st leg	2nd leg	agg
HJK Helsinki	Metz	1-0	1-1	2-1
Bayern Munich	Obilic	4-0	1-1	5-1
Sturm Graz	Ujpest Dozsa	4-0	3-2	7-2
Steaua Bucharest	Panathinaikos	2-2	3-6	5-8

Group A

Croatia Zagreb 0 Ajax 0
Porto 2 Olympiakos 2
Ajax 2 Porto 1
Olympiakos 2 Croatia Zagreb 0
Olympiakos 1 Ajax 0
Porto 3 Croatia Zagreb 0
Ajax 2 Olympiakos 0
Croatia Zagreb 3 Porto 1
Ajax 0 Croatia Zagreb1
Olympiakos 2 Porto 1
Croatia Zagreb 1 Olympiakos 1
Porto 3 Ajax 0

	P	W	D	L	F	A	Pts
Olympiakos	6	3	2	1	8	6	11
Croatia Zagreb	6	2	2	2	5	7	8

| Porto | 6 | 2 | 1 | 3 | 11 | 9 | 7 |
| Ajax | 6 | 2 | 1 | 3 | 4 | 6 | 7 |

Group B

Athletic Bilbao 1 Rosenborg 1
Juventus 2 Galatasaray 2
Galatasaray 2 Athletic Bilbao 1
Rosenborg 1 Juventus 1
Athletic Bilbao 0 Juventus 0
Rosenborg 3 Galatasaray 0
Galatasaray 3 Rosenborg 0
Juventus 1 Athletic Bilbao 1
Rosenborg 2 Athletic Bilbao 1
Galatasaray 1 Juventus 1
Athletic Bilbao 1 Galatasaray 0
Juventus 2 Rosenborg 0

	P	W	D	L	F	A	Pts
Juventus	6	1	5	0	7	5	8
Galatasaray	6	2	2	2	8	8	8
Rosenborg	6	2	2	2	7	8	8
Athletic Bilbao	6	1	3	2	5	6	6

Group C

Real Madrid 2 Internazionale 0
Sturm Graz 0 Spartak Moscow 2
Internazionale 1 Sturm Graz 0
Spartak Moscow 2 Real Madrid 1
Internazionale 2 Spartak Moscow 1
Real Madrid 6 Sturm Graz 1
Spartak Moscow 1 Internazionale 1
Sturm Graz 1 Real Madrid 5
Internazionale 3 Real Madrid 1
Spartak Moscow 0 Sturm Graz 0
Real Madrid 2 Spartak Moscow 1
Sturm Graz 0 Internazionale 2

	P	W	D	L	F	A	Pts
Internazionale	6	4	1	1	9	5	13
Real Madrid	6	4	0	2	17	8	12
Spartak Moscow	6	2	2	2	7	6	8
Sturm Graz	6	0	1	5	2	16	1

Group D

Brondby 2 Bayern Munich 1
Manchester United 3 Barcelona 3
Bayern Munich 2 Manchester United 2
Barcelona 2 Brondby 0
Bayern Munich 1 Barcelona 0
Brondby 2 Manchester United 6
Barcelona 1 Bayern Munich 2
Manchester United 5 Brondby 0
Bayern Munich 2 Brondby 0
Barcelona 3 Manchester United 3
Brondby 0 Barcelona 2
Manchester United 1 Bayern Munich 1

	P	W	D	L	F	A	Pts
Bayern Munich	6	3	2	1	9	6	11
Manchester United	6	2	4	0	20	11	10
Barcelona	6	2	2	2	11	9	8
Brondby	6	1	0	5	4	18	3

Group E

Panathinaikos 2 Dynamo Kiev 1
Lens 1 Arsenal 1
Arsenal 2 Panathinaikos 1
Dynamo Kiev 1 Lens 1
Arsenal 1 Dynamo Kiev 1
Lens 1 Panathinaikos 0
Dynamo Kiev 3 Arsenal 1
Panathinaikos 1 Lens 0
Arsenal 0 Lens 1
Dynamo Kiev 2 Panathinaikos 1
Panathinaikos 1 Arsenal 3
Lens 1 Dynamo Kiev 3

	P	W	D	L	F	A	Pts
Dynamo Kiev	6	3	2	1	11	7	11
Lens	6	2	2	2	5	6	8
Arsenal	6	2	2	2	8	8	8
Panathinaikos	6	2	0	4	6	9	6

Group F

Kaiserslautern 1 Benfica 0
PSV Eindhoven 2 HJK Helsinki 1
HJK Helsinki 0 Kaiserslautern 0
Benfica 2 PSV Eindhoven 1
HJK Helsinki 2 Benfica 0
PSV Eindhoven 1 Kaiserslautern 2
Kaiserslautern 3 PSV Eindhoven 1
Benfica 2 HJK Helsinki 2
HJK Helsinki 1 PSV Eindhoven 3
Benfica 2 Kaiserslautern 1
Kaiserslautern 5 HJK Helsinki 2
PSV Eindhoven 2 Benfica 2

	P	W	D	L	F	A	Pts
Kaiserslautern	6	4	1	1	12	6	13
Benfica	6	2	2	2	8	9	8
PSV Eindhoven	6	2	1	3	10	11	7
HJK Helsinki	6	1	2	3	8	12	5

Quarter-finals

		1st leg	2nd leg	agg
Real Madrid	Dynamo Kiev	1-1	0-2	1-3
Manchester United	Internazionale	2-0	1-1	3-1
Juventus	Olympiakos Piraeus	2-1	1-1	3-2
Bayern Munich	Kaiserslautern	2-0	4-0	6-0

Semi-finals

		1st leg	2nd leg	agg
Manchester United	Juventus	1-1	3-2	4-3
Dynamo Kiev	Bayern Munich	3-3	0-1	3-4

Final

May 26 1999 Barcelona
Manchester United 2   Bayern Munich 1
Sheringham   Basler
Solskjaer

Manchester United: Schmeichel, G Neville, Johnsen, Stam, Irwin, Beckham, Butt, Giggs, Blomqvist (Sheringham), Yorke, Cole (Solskjaer)

Bayern Munich: Kahn, Matthaus (Fink), Babbel, Linke, Kuffour, Tarnat, Effenberg, Jeremies, Basler (Salihamidzic), Jancker, Zickler (Scholl)

HT: 0-1

Referee: Collina (Italy)

Attendance: 90,245

Alex Ferguson

The success of Jock Stein, Matt Busby, Bob Paisley, and Brian Clough in winning the European Cup, alongside numerous domestic honours, has given each of them a claim to be Britain's greatest ever club manager. In recent years their primacy has been challenged by Alex Ferguson, who has the distinction of achieving massive success in both England and Scotland, besides Europe. After taking Aberdeen to a series of honours in Scotland and Europe, Ferguson has gone on to manage a Manchester United team whose victory in the 1999 UEFA Champions League arrived during more than a decade of regular collection of trophies in the English game.

The vast success of Ferguson as a club manager contrasts with the modesty of his playing career. Ferguson was born in Glasgow, on December 31 1941, and began his football career there as an amateur with Queen's Park, while also working as a toolmaker in the Clyde shipyards. Ferguson moved to St Johnstone in 1960, and Dunfermline Athletic four years later, before being bought by Rangers for £65,000 in 1967. After two years at Rangers, during which the club did not win any honours, as Celtic dominated Scottish football at that point, Ferguson moved to Falkirk. In 1973 Ferguson joined Ayr United. Having divided his attention between football and another career at the start of his playing days, Ferguson ended his playing career at Ayr, sharing part-time football with the running of a pub.

Ferguson's managerial career began in 1974 at East Stirlingshire, followed by a quick move to St Mirren, another Second Division club, later that year. In 1977 Ferguson helped St Mirren win promotion to the Scottish Premier Division. The following year he moved to Aberdeen, replacing Billy McNeil, and began to establish his credentials as a manager. Ferguson led Aberdeen to a series of major honours. The Scottish Premier Division was won in 1979-80, 1983-84, and 1984-85. Meanwhile the Scottish Cup went to Aberdeen in 1981-82, 1982-83, 1983-84, and 1985-86 – with the League Cup also being won in the last of these seasons. Besides three seasons in the European Cup, Ferguson's Aberdeen won the European Cup-Winners' Cup in 1982-83 – beating Real Madrid 2-1 in the final – and the European Super Cup the following season. Ferguson's success at Aberdeen led to him being appointed as assistant to Jock Stein, the Scotland manager. Following the tragic death of Stein, in September 1985, Ferguson became caretaker manager, a post in which he oversaw the completion of Scotland's passage through the 1986 World Cup qualifiers. Ferguson also led his country in the finals, but Scotland returned home from Mexico without a win.

On November 7 1986 Ferguson became manager of Manchester United, following the sacking of Ron Atkinson. During the early years of his spell at the club, Manchester United were in the shadow of Liverpool, and failed to win honours. Speculation that Ferguson would be sacked was only ended by their winning the FA Cup in 1990, beating Crystal Palace in a replayed final. A year later United won the European Cup-Winners' Cup, beating Barcelona 2-1 in the final – a repeat of Ferguson's success with Aberdeen in that competition. The European Super Cup and League Cup were added to the trophy cabinet in 1991-92, but runners-up spot in the league that season left United disappointed. The following season, Manchester United won the inaugural Premier League, to become the English champions for the first time since 1967, and the days of Matt Busby. During the next decade Manchester United achieved a dominance of the English domestic game that eclipsed that of the teams managed by Busby, and matched that of Liverpool in the 1970s and 1980s. The Premier League was won again in 1994, 1996, 1997, 1999, 2000, 2001, and 2003, while the FA Cup was taken in 1994, 1996, 1999, and 2004. Having won the league and FA Cup double in both 1994 and 1996, United achieved an amazing treble in 1998-99, adding the Champions League to the Premier League and FA Cup titles that season. On top of matching the United team that won the European Cup in 1968, Ferguson's players went on to win the World Club Championship at the end of 1999.

During nearly two decades as manager of Manchester United, Ferguson has carved out a giant reputation in the English game. Besides the honours United have won with the help of his astute tactics, Ferguson's fame derives from his personality. A tense man, and compulsive chewer of gum, Ferguson tends to scowl more than he smiles. He has been a fierce defender of his players, backing them whether they are right or wrong. Eric Cantona, Roy Keane, and Rio Ferdinand have each been strongly supported by Ferguson through disciplinary problems. At the same time Ferguson has courageously dispensed with several star players whom he felt did not fit in with the development of the team. In 2003 Ferguson even went as far as selling David Beckham, at that time United's strongest player, to Champions League rivals Real Madrid. Ferguson's relations with Beckham had become uneasy, largely due to the manager's distrust of the player's celebrity lifestyle. Beckham was a product of the United youth policy, which Ferguson has revived with spectacular results. A regular succession of players have graduated from the youth team to the first team, becoming known as 'Fergie's Fledglings' – an echo of the 'Busby Babes'. Besides grooming new players, Ferguson has proved an excellent motivator of established players. One of the best examples of this is the following remark he made to the United team as they trailed 1-0 to Bayern Munich at half time in the 1999 Champions League final: "At the end of this game, the European Cup will be only six feet away from you, and you will not even be able to touch it if we lose. For many of you that will be the closest you will ever get. Don't you dare come back in here without giving your all".

Despite the consistent success of the team, Ferguson has managed to create a siege mentality at Manchester United, in which the players appear to be battling against the football authorities, errant referees, and the media, as well as other clubs. Ferguson's abrasive mind games with rival managers such as Kenny Dalglish (at both Liverpool and Blackburn Rovers), Kevin Keegan (Newcastle United), and Arsene Wenger (Arsenal) are the stuff of legend. Ferguson was due to retire at the end of the 2001-02 season, but in February 2002 he agreed an extension of his contract with Manchester United. The will to win yet more trophies continued to drive Ferguson forward as he entered his sixties.

1999-2000

This season saw a further expansion of the competition, as UEFA reacted to continuing suggestions of a rival European super league. With 71 clubs now participating, the qualifying stage was extended from two to three rounds, followed by a double group stage, initially featuring 32, instead of the previous 24, teams. The continent's strongest countries were now represented by up to four clubs each in the UEFA Champions League. The clubs benefited from extra revenue, but there was a feeling that the number of matches in the group stage had become excessive, and blunted the excitement of the competition

Chelsea, who had withdrawn from the inaugural European Cup in 1955, finally made their first appearance in the competition, 44 years later, having finished third in the Premiership. Gianluca Vialli, a winner of the European Cup with Juventus in 1996, was the player-manager of Chelsea. His squad included three other previous winners of the European Cup, namely Marcel Desailly (Marseille and then Milan), Didier Deschamps (Marseille), and Albert Ferrer (Barcelona). Chelsea's campaign began in the third qualifying round, with a 3-0 aggregate win against Skonto Riga, the Latvian champions who had unexpectedly progressed this far by thrashing Jeunesse D'Esch 10-0 on aggregate, and then beating Rapid Bucharest 5-4. Rangers made their way through the qualifiers with wins against Haka Valkeakoski and Parma. Valencia, who would eventually reach the final, began with a couple of victories against Hapoel Haifa in the last of the qualifying rounds.

In the first of the league stages Manchester United comfortably won Group D, but a 1-0 defeat away to Marseille, the runners-up, meant the end of United's unbeaten record of 18 European Cup matches, which had begun with the 1997-98 quarter-finals. Chelsea won Group H, ahead of Hertha Berlin, while Milan unexpectedly finished bottom with a single win in their six matches. Arsenal used Wembley for their home matches, just as they had the previous season, but lost there against both Barcelona and Fiorentina, the two clubs that progressed at their expense. Barcelona, who beat Arsenal 4-2 at Wembley, scored 19 goals in the course of winning four, and drawing the other two, of their games. Meanwhile Real Madrid scored 15 goals in the course of finishing top of Group E. Rangers were knocked out at this stage, finishing behind Valencia and Bayern Munich.

The first league stage was rapidly completed between mid-September and the start of November. The second stage stretched from November to March, with a lengthy winter break. Manchester United lost 2-0 against Fiorentina in their first match, but were unbeaten thereafter, and won Group B, three points ahead of Valencia. With UEFA's rule limiting clubs to three foreign players per match a thing of the past, Chelsea lined up against Lazio with three Frenchmen, two Italians, a Dutchman, a Norwegian, a Nigerian, a Romanian, a Spaniard, and a Uruguayan – but no Englishmen. Chelsea appeared to be punished for a lack of patriotism, with their 2-1 defeat against Lazio being the first they had ever experienced in a European match at Stamford Bridge. Nevertheless Chelsea advanced from Group D, just behind Lazio. Barcelona won Group A, with five wins and a draw, in which they scored 17 goals, finishing six points clear of runners-up Porto, who they beat 4-2 at home and 2-0 away. Bayern Munich won the remaining group, while Real Madrid joined them in the last eight by virtue of their head-to-head record against Dynamo Kiev.

The quarter-finals, during April, produced some excellent contests. The plum tie brought together Real Madrid and Manchester United, winners of the trophy in 1998 and 1999 respectively. After a goalless first leg, Real outplayed United at Old Trafford, building up a three goal lead by the early part of the second half – courtesy of an own goal from Roy Keane, and a brace from Raul. For the third goal Fernando Redondo produced an exquisite backheel to beat Henning Berg near the bye-line on the left, before crossing to Raul, who scored. United produced a fight-back to reduce the deficit to 3-2, with goals from David Beckham and Paul Scholes, but the Spaniards won the tie. Another clash between an English and Spanish club went the way of the latter, as Barcelona staged a comeback to beat Chelsea 6-4 on aggregate. Chelsea led 3-0 at half time in the first leg, but Barcelona pulled a goal back in the second half. In turn Barcelona established a 3-1 lead in the second leg, to take the tie into extra time. Rivaldo, who missed a penalty in the closing minutes of normal time, scored one in extra time, following which a goal from Patrick Kluivert completed Barcelona's 5-1 win on the night. Valencia beat Lazio 5-3 on aggregate, largely due to a hat-trick by Gerard in the first leg. Bayern Munich edged past Porto by the odd goal in five, to reverse their defeat in the 1987 final, with Thomas Linke scoring the decisive goal in stoppage time at the end of the second leg.

Bayern's opponents in the semi-finals, staged in early May, were Real Madrid, a team they had recently beaten 4-2 away and 4-1 at home in the second group stage. Real now put these earlier reverses behind them, controlling their home leg to win 2-0, and limiting Bayern to a 2-1 victory in Germany. The other semi-final was an all-Spanish encounter, in which Valencia upset expectations by beating Barcelona 4-1 in the first leg. Barcelona won the return 2-1, but it was Valencia who joined Real Madrid in the final.

The meeting of Real Madrid and Valencia, at the Stade de France in Paris, was the first European Cup final to be contested by two teams from the same country. Valencia, who had only appeared in the European Cup once before, back in 1971-72, and gained a place in the 1999-2000 competition by finishing fourth in the Spanish league the previous season, had become surprise finalists due to some excellent attacking football. Real Madrid had finished as runners-up, behind Barcelona, in the Spanish title race in 1998-99. They were now coached by Vicente del Bosque, who had appeared for them in the 1981 final. They began the 2000 final with four players from the team which had won in 1998, namely Roberto Carlos, Fernando Morientes, Raul, and Redondo. Fernando Hierro and Manuel Sanchis from the team of two years earlier were to appear as substitutes this time.

Real Madrid enjoyed the better of the early exchanges, but had to wait until six minutes before the interval to take the lead. A long-range free kick from Roberto Carlos was only half-blocked by the Valencia wall, and the ball fell to Nicolas Anelka, who pushed it into the path of Michel Salgado on the right-hand side of the penalty area, and the latter's cross was headed home by Morientes at the far post. Real remained the better team during the early part of the second half, and increased their lead 17 minutes after the re-start, as Steve McManaman, who had an outstanding game, drove in a shot from the edge of the penalty area. Valencia were now forced to throw men forward in search of goals, but were caught on the break 15 minutes from time, as Raul ran from inside his own half, took the ball around goalkeeper Santiago Canizares and slotted it into the empty net to complete a 3-0 victory for Real Madrid. Raul finished as joint leading scorer in this season's competition, with ten goals, alongside Mario Jardel of Porto, and Rivaldo of Barcelona, the current European Footballer of the Year, having won the award at the end of 1999. Raul had become a devastating marksman, who was set to become the modern Champions League's equivalent of Alfredo Di Stefano, at least as far as goalscoring was concerned.

The spark shown by Valencia on the way to the final had been doused by an assured performance from Real Madrid, who thereby regained the trophy they had won two years earlier. Having worn an unfamiliar black strip during the match, Real changed into their usual white to receive the trophy – ironically following in the footsteps of Barcelona, their great rivals, who had changed strips after winning the European Cup in 1992. Although Spanish clubs had dominated this season's Champions League, their national team remained under-achievers, just as they had been when Real Madrid won the first five European Cups. When the European Championship finals were staged in the Netherlands and Belgium during the summer of 2000, Spain fell in the quarter-finals, losing to France, who went on to beat Italy 2-1 in the final.

1999-2000

First qualifying round

		1st leg	2nd leg	agg
IBV Vestmannaeyjar	SK Tirana	1-0	2-1	3-1
Litets	Glentoran	3-0	2-0	5-0
Zalgiris Vilnius	Tsement	2-0	3-0	5-0
HB Torshavn	Haka Valkeakoski	1-1	0-6	1-7
Partizan Belgrade	Flora Tallinn	6-0	4-1	10-1
Jeunesse D'Esch	Skonto Riga	0-2	0-8	0-10
Sloga	Kapaz	1-0	1-2	2-2
Sloga won on away goals				
Barry Town	Valletta	0-0	2-3	2-3
St Patrick's Athletic	Zimbru Chisinau	0-5	0-5	0-10

Second qualifying round

		1st leg	2nd leg	agg
Rapid Vienna	Valletta	3-0	2-0	5-0
Anorthosis	Slovan Bratislava	2-1	1-1	3-2
Partizan Belgrade	Rijeka	3-1	3-0	6-1
CSKA Moscow	Molde	2-0	0-4	2-4
Litets	Widzew Lodz	4-1	1-4	5-5

Widzew Lodz won 3-2 on penalties

		1st leg	2nd leg	agg
Haka Valkeakoski	Rangers	1-4	0-3	1-7
Dynamo Tbilisi	Zimbru Chisinau	2-1	0-2	2-3
Dnepr Mogilev	AIK Stockholm	0-1	0-2	0-3
Sloga	Brondby	0-1	0-1	0-2
Rapid Bucharest	Skonto Riga	3-3	1-2	4-5
Besiktas	Hapoel Haifa	1-1	0-0	1-1

Hapoel Haifa won on away goals

		1st leg	2nd leg	agg
Dynamo Kiev	Zalgiris Vilnius	2-0	1-0	3-0
IBV Vestmannaeyjar	MTK Budapest	0-2	1-3	1-5
Maribor	Genk	5-1	0-3	5-4

Third qualifying round

		1st leg	2nd leg	agg
Zimbru Chisinau	PSV Eindhoven	0-0	0-2	0-2
Spartak Moscow	Partizan Belgrade	2-0	3-1	5-1
Chelsea	Skonto Riga	3-0	0-0	3-0
Rapid Vienna	Galatasaray	0-3	0-1	0-4
Fiorentina	Widzew Lodz	3-1	2-0	5-1
Aalborg	Dynamo Kiev	1-2	2-2	3-4
Rangers	Parma	2-0	0-1	2-1
Brondby	Boavista	1-2	2-4	3-6
AEK Athens	AIK Stockholm	0-0	0-1	0-1
Hapoel Haifa	Valencia	0-2	0-2	0-4
Hertha Berlin	Anorthosis	2-0	0-0	2-0
Sturm Graz	Servette Geneva	2-1	2-2	4-3
Molde	Mallorca	0-0	1-1	1-1

Molde won on away goals

		1st leg	2nd leg	agg
Lyon	Maribor	0-1	0-2	0-3
Croatia Zagreb	MTK Budapest	0-0	2-0	2-0
Teplice	Borussia Dortmund	0-1	0-1	0-2

First Group Stage

Group A

Bayer Leverkusen 1 Lazio 1
Dynamo Kiev 0 Maribor 1
Lazio 2 Dynamo Kiev 1
Maribor 0 Bayer Leverkusen 2
Lazio 4 Maribor 0
Bayer Leverkusen 1 Dynamo Kiev 1
Maribor 0 Lazio 4
Dynamo Kiev 4 Bayer Leverkusen 2
Lazio 1 Bayer Leverkusen 1
Maribor 1 Dynamo Kiev 2
Dynamo Kiev 0 Lazio 1
Bayer Leverkusen 0 Maribor 0

	P	W	D	L	F	A	Pts
Lazio	6	4	2	0	13	3	14
Dynamo Kiev	6	2	1	3	8	8	7
Bayer Leverkusen	6	1	4	1	7	7	7
Maribor	6	1	1	4	2	12	4

Group B

Fiorentina 0 Arsenal 0
AIK Stockholm 1 Barcelona 2
Arsenal 3 AIK Stockholm 1
Barcelona 4 Fiorentina 2
Barcelona 1 Arsenal 1
AIK Stockholm 0 Fiorentina 0
Arsenal 2 Barcelona 4
Fiorentina 3 AIK Stockholm 0
Arsenal 0 Fiorentina 1
Barcelona 5 AIK Stockholm 0
AIK Stockholm 2 Arsenal 3
Fiorentina 3 Barcelona 3

	P	W	D	L	F	A	Pts
Barcelona	6	4	2	0	19	9	14
Fiorentina	6	2	3	1	9	7	9
Arsenal	6	2	2	2	9	9	8
AIK Stockholm	6	0	1	5	4	16	1

Group C

Boavista 0 Rosenborg 3
Feyenoord 1 Borussia Dortmund 1
Rosenborg 2 Feyenoord 2
Borussia Dortmund 3 Boavista 1
Boavista 1 Feyenoord 1
Rosenborg 2 Borussia Dortmund 2
Feyenoord 1 Boavista 1
Borussia Dortmund 0 Rosenborg 3
Rosenborg 2 Boavista 0
Borussia Dortmund 1 Feyenoord 1
Feyenoord 1 Rosenborg 0
Boavista 1 Borussia Dortmund 0

	P	W	D	L	F	A	Pts
Rosenborg	6	3	2	1	12	5	11
Feyenoord	6	1	5	0	7	6	8
Borussia Dortmund	6	1	3	2	7	9	6
Boavista	6	1	2	3	4	10	5

Group D

Manchester United 0 Croatia Zagreb 0
Marseille 2 Sturm Graz 0
Croatia Zagreb 1 Marseille 2
Sturm Graz 0 Manchester United 3
Croatia Zagreb 3 Sturm Graz 0
Manchester United 2 Marseille 1
Sturm Graz 1 Croatia Zagreb 0
Marseille 1 Manchester United 0
Croatia Zagreb 1 Manchester United 2
Sturm Graz 3 Marseille 2
Marseille 2 Croatia Zagreb 2
Manchester United 2 Sturm Graz 1

	P	W	D	L	F	A	Pts
Manchester United	6	4	1	1	9	4	13
Marseille	6	3	1	2	10	8	10
Sturm Graz	6	2	0	4	5	12	6
Croatia Zagreb	6	1	2	3	7	7	5

Group E

Olympiakos 3 Real Madrid 3

Molde 0 Porto 1
Real Madrid 4 Molde 1
Porto 2 Olympiakos 0
Real Madrid 3 Porto 1
Olympiakos 3 Molde 1
Porto 2 Real Madrid 1
Molde 3 Olympiakos 2
Real Madrid 3 Olympiakos 0
Porto 3 Molde 1
Molde 0 Real Madrid 1
Olympiakos 1 Porto 0

	P	W	D	L	F	A	Pts
Real Madrid	6	4	1	1	15	7	13
Porto	6	4	0	2	9	6	12
Olympiakos	6	2	1	3	9	12	7
Molde	6	1	0	5	6	14	3

Group F

Bayern Munich 2 PSV Eindhoven 1
Valencia 2 Rangers 0
Rangers 1 Bayern Munich 1
PSV Eindhoven 1 Valencia 1
PSV Eindhoven 0 Rangers 1
Bayern Munich 1 Valencia 1
Rangers 4 PSV Eindhoven 1
Valencia 1 Bayern Munich 1
PSV Eindhoven 2 Bayern Munich 1
Rangers 1 Valencia 2
Bayern Munich 1 Rangers 0
Valencia 1 PSV Eindhoven 0

	P	W	D	L	F	A	Pts
Valencia	6	3	3	0	8	4	12
Bayern Munich	6	2	3	1	7	6	9
Rangers	6	2	1	3	7	7	7
PSV Eindhoven	6	1	1	4	5	10	4

Group G

Sparta Prague 0 Bordeaux 0
Willem II Tilburg 1 Spartak Moscow 3
Bordeaux 3 Willem II Tilburg 2
Spartak Moscow 1 Sparta Prague 1
Sparta Prague 4 Willem II Tilburg 0
Bordeaux 2 Spartak Moscow 1
Willem II Tilburg 3 Sparta Prague 4
Spartak Moscow 1 Bordeaux 2
Bordeaux 0 Sparta Prague 0
Spartak Moscow 1 Willem II Tilburg 1
Willem II Tilburg 0 Bordeaux 0
Sparta Prague 5 Spartak Moscow 2

	P	W	D	L	F	A	Pts
Sparta Prague	6	3	3	0	14	6	12
Bordeaux	6	3	3	0	7	4	12
Spartak Moscow	6	1	2	3	9	12	5
Willem II Tilburg	6	0	2	4	7	15	2

Group H

Chelsea 0 Milan 0
Galatasaray 2 Hertha Berlin 2
Milan 2 Galatasaray 1

182

Hertha Berlin 2 Chelsea 1
Milan 1 Hertha Berlin 1
Chelsea 1 Galatasaray 0
Hertha Berlin 1 Milan 0
Galatasaray 0 Chelsea 5
Milan 1 Chelsea 1
Hertha Berlin 1 Galatasaray 4
Galatasaray 3 Milan 2
Chelsea 2 Hertha Berlin 0

	P	W	D	L	F	A	Pts
Chelsea	6	3	2	1	10	3	11
Hertha Berlin	6	2	2	2	7	10	8
Galatasaray	6	2	1	3	10	13	7
Milan	6	1	3	2	6	7	6

Second Group Stage

Group A
Hertha Berlin 1 Barcelona 1
Sparta Prague 0 Porto 2
Porto 1 Hertha Berlin 0
Barcelona 5 Sparta Prague 0
Barcelona 4 Porto 2
Hertha Berlin 1 Sparta Prague 1
Porto 0 Barcelona 2
Sparta Prague 1 Hertha Berlin 0
Barcelona 3 Hertha Berlin 1
Porto 2 Sparta Prague 2
Hertha Berlin 0 Porto 1
Sparta Prague 1 Barcelona 2

	P	W	D	L	F	A	Pts
Barcelona	6	5	1	0	17	5	16
Porto	6	3	1	2	8	8	10
Sparta Prague	6	1	2	3	5	12	5
Hertha Berlin	6	0	2	4	3	8	2

Group B
Fiorentina 2 Manchester United 0
Valencia 3 Bordeaux 0
Bordeaux 0 Fiorentina 0
Manchester United 3 Valencia 0
Manchester United 2 Bordeaux 0
Fiorentina 1 Valencia 0
Bordeaux 1 Manchester United 2
Valencia 2 Fiorentina 0
Manchester United 3 Fiorentina 1
Bordeaux 1 Valencia 4
Fiorentina 3 Bordeaux 3
Valencia 0 Manchester United 0

	P	W	D	L	F	A	Pts
Manchester United	6	4	1	1	10	4	13
Valencia	6	3	1	2	9	5	10
Fiorentina	6	2	2	2	7	8	8
Bordeaux	6	0	2	4	5	14	2

Group C
Dynamo Kiev 1 Real Madrid 2
Rosenborg 1 Bayern Munich 1
Bayern Munich 2 Dynamo Kiev 1

Real Madrid 3 Rosenborg 1
Real Madrid 2 Bayern Munich 4
Dynamo Kiev 2 Rosenborg 1
Bayern Munich 4 Real Madrid 1
Rosenborg 1 Dynamo Kiev 2
Real Madrid 2 Dynamo Kiev 2
Bayern Munich 2 Rosenborg 1
Dynamo Kiev 2 Bayern Munich 0
Rosenborg 0 Real Madrid 1

	P	W	D	L	F	A	Pts
Bayern Munich	6	4	1	1	13	8	13
Real Madrid	6	3	1	2	11	12	10
Dynamo Kiev	6	3	1	2	10	8	10
Rosenborg	6	0	1	5	5	11	1

Group D

Marseille 0 Lazio 2
Chelsea 3 Feyenoord 1
Feyenoord 3 Marseille 0
Lazio 0 Chelsea 0
Lazio 1 Feyenoord 2
Marseille 1 Chelsea 0
Feyenoord 0 Lazio 0
Chelsea 1 Marseille 0
Lazio 5 Marseille 1
Feyenoord 1 Chelsea 3
Marseille 0 Feyenoord 0
Chelsea 1 Lazio 2

	P	W	D	L	F	A	Pts
Lazio	6	3	2	1	10	4	11
Chelsea	6	3	1	2	8	5	10
Feyenoord	6	2	2	2	7	7	8
Marseille	6	1	1	4	2	11	4

Quarter-finals

		1st leg	2nd leg	agg
Chelsea	Barcelona	3-1	1-5	4-6
Valencia	Lazio	5-2	0-1	5-3
Real Madrid	Manchester United	0-0	3-2	3-2
Porto	Bayern Munich	1-1	1-2	2-3

Semi-finals

		1st leg	2nd leg	agg
Real Madrid	Bayern Munich	2-0	1-2	3-2
Valencia	Barcelona	4-1	1-2	5-3

Final

May 24 2000 Paris
Real Madrid 3   Valencia 0
Morientes
McManaman
Raul
Real Madrid: Casillas, Salgado (Hierro), Roberto Carlos, Karanka, Campo, McManaman, Redondo, Helguera, Raul, Anelka (Sanchis), Morientes (Savio).
Valencia: Canizares, Angloma, Djukic, Pellegrino, Gerardo, Mendieta, Gerard (Ilie), Farinos, Kily Gonzalez, Claudio Lopez, Angulo.
HT: 1-0
Referee: Braschi (Italy)
Attendance: 80,000

184

2000-01

This season's competition opened with Red Star Belgrade, winners of the trophy in 1991, among the teams required to play in the first qualifying round. During the intervening years Yugoslavia had been banned from European football, due to the civil war, and then rehabilitated. After eliminating KI Klaksvik and Torpedo Kutaisi, Red Star fell to Dynamo Kiev, on away goals, in the last of the qualifying rounds. Three other former champions – Feyenoord, Internazionale, and Porto – also fell in the qualifiers. Leeds United and Rangers both progressed to the group stage, with impressive victories against Munich 1860 and Herfolge respectively.

Manchester United, who had retained the English Premiership – finishing a massive 18 points clear of runners-up Arsenal – experienced a couple of defeats in Group G, but advanced by taking second place behind Anderlecht. By contrast, Arsenal won Group B, sneaking ahead of Lazio due to a better head-to-head record. Leeds opened their matches in Group H with a 4-0 defeat against Barcelona, but recovered with a series of fine performances, including a 6-0 thrashing of Besiktas, to take second place, behind Milan. Rangers failed to advance from Group D, being eliminated by Galatasaray on head-to-head. Sturm Graz won this group despite losing 5-0 away to both Rangers and Monaco. Elsewhere Real Madrid and Valencia, the Champions League finalists in 1999-2000, both won their groups.

In the second group stage, Manchester United's play improved, and they advanced from Group A, behind Valencia on head-to-head record – with both teams being unbeaten. Arsenal also continued to progress, but only just, finishing ahead of Lyon on head-to-head, but five points behind the Group C winners, Bayern Munich. While Arsenal scored six goals at this stage, and Manchester United netted ten times, Leeds United ran up 12 goals in Group D, taking second spot behind Real Madrid. Leeds won 4-1 away to Anderlecht, with Alan Smith scoring twice, and were unlucky to lose 3-2 away to Real Madrid, for whom Raul scored a handled goal.

In Group B, Deportivo La Coruna and Galatasaray booked places in the last eight, ahead of Milan. Play in two of the matches in this group was held up by disturbing incidents. Milan's 1-0 win away to Deportivo La Coruna was achieved despite their goalkeeper Christian Abbiati being injured by a flagpole thrown from the crowd. Clashes between rival spectators caused a 20 minute delay as Paris Saint-Germain beat Galatasaray 2-0. On a brighter note, Deportivo recovered from a 3-0 deficit against Paris Saint-Germain to win 4-3, by scoring four goals in the last 35 minutes. Each of these four goals were headers, with three of them being scored by Walter Pandiani.

England had three teams in the quarter-finals for the first time, and Spain had three at this stage for a second successive season. On the other hand, there was no Italian representative in the last eight for the first time since 1987-88. Manchester United faced Bayern Munich, but could not repeat their victory in the 1999 final. At Old Trafford, Bayern won by a single goal from Sergio four minutes from time, while in Munich goals from Giovane Elber and Mehmet Scholl gave them a 2-1 win. Prior to the start of the second leg, a United fan named Karl Power, dressed in the club's kit, managed to gain access to the pitch, and join surprised players for the team photo. Arsenal were also eliminated, losing to Valencia on away goals, with the aggregate score level at 2-2. The English challenge was maintained, however, by Leeds United. They won 3-0 at home to Deportivo La Coruna, with goals from Ian Harte, Alan Smith, and Rio Ferdinand, then hung on to win the tie despite losing the return match 2-0. Real Madrid lost 3-2 away to Galatasaray, but a 3-0 win in Madrid, in which Raul scored twice, gave the Spaniards a 5-3 aggregate victory. Mario

Jardel's goal for Galatasaray in the first leg allowed him to draw level with Andrei Shevchenko, of Milan, as the season's leading scorer – with nine goals each.

In the semi-finals Leeds drew 0-0 with Valencia at Elland Road, but lost the return 3-0 – Sanchez scoring twice and Mendieta once. In the other tie, Bayern Munich beat Real Madrid, by repeating the pattern of their quarter-final against Manchester United, with a 1-0 away win being followed by a 2-1 home win. Elber scored in each leg, while Jens Jeremies netted the winner in the second leg. Real's defeat ended the possibility of the final being a repeat of their meeting with Valencia the previous season.

The final, staged in Milan, brought together the runners-up in the two preceding seasons. Bayern Munich were still managed by Ottmar Hitzfeld, who selected six players who had appeared in the 1999 final – Stefan Effenberg, Oliver Kahn, Sammy Kuffour, Thomas Linke, Hasan Salihamidzic, and Mehmet Scholl. Two other members of the 1999 team, Carsten Jancker and Alexander Zickler, would now appear as substitutes, while Giovane Elber and Bixente Lizarazu, who had missed the earlier final due to injuries, were in the starting line-up for 2001. Bayern also fielded Owen Hargreaves, a 20-year-old who had only recently found a place in the club's first team. Hargreaves, born in Canada, with an English father and a Welsh mother, would claim a place in the England team at the start of the following season, and appear in his adopted country's 5-1 win against Germany in a World Cup qualifier – at Bayern's home ground. Bayern were the reigning German champions, but Valencia had finished third in the Spanish League the previous season. Valencia were coached by Hector Cuper, an Argentinian, while their line-up featured four of his fellow-countrymen – Pablo Aimar, Roberto Ayala, Kily Gonzalez, and Mauricio Pellegrino. Both Kily Gonzalez and Pellegrino had been in the Valencia team in the final a year earlier, while three other players were making a second appearance for the club at this stage, namely Jocelyn Angloma, Santiago Canizares, and Gaizka Mendieta.

The story of the match was dominated by penalties. Mendieta gave Valencia the lead with a penalty after just three minutes. Four minutes later Bayern Munich threw away a chance to equalise, as Scholl's penalty was saved by Canizares. Bayern attacked for much of the first half, but rarely threatened to equalise. Five minutes into the second half, Dick Jol, the Dutch referee, awarded the third penalty of the match, with Bayern being the recipients. Whereas Scholl had failed in the first half, Effenberg was able to level the score at 1-1. The remainder of the second half saw cagey football from both teams, and no further goals, although Valencia's Zlatko Zahovic, on as a substitute, went close to scoring, being denied by a brilliant save from Kahn, the Bayern goalkeeper. Bayern took the play to Valencia during extra time, but the continued failure of both teams to score from open play led to the match being decided on penalties. The penalty contest started with Bayern's Paulo Sergio missing his kick. Mendieta was on target again during the shoot-out, to put Valencia ahead. Each of the next three penalties were converted, following which a sequence of three consecutive penalties were saved. This left the score at 2-2, with each team having taken four penalties. Effenberg then put Bayern ahead, and Ruben Baraja squared the score for Valencia, to take the contest into sudden death. Lizarazu and Gonzalez both scored from the respective sixth penalties. Bayern's Linke put his team back ahead, and then Kahn saved as Pellegrino took Valencia's seventh penalty of the shoot-out. A match of 17 spot kicks – three in normal time and 14 in the decider – had ended with Bayern Munich beating Valencia 5-4 on penalties.

So Valencia had lost the European Cup in two successive years, just as Juventus had in 1997 and 1998. Defeat was particularly hard for Cuper, who had been manager of Mallorca when they lost the last-ever European Cup-Winners' Cup final in 1999. Bayern Munich had won the European title for the first time in a quarter of a century, by avoiding a repeat of their defeats in the finals of 1982, 1987, and 1999. Bayern's hero was Oliver Kahn, who had kept his team level by denying Zahovic late in normal time, and saved three penalties in the shoot-out. As Bayern celebrated victory, Ottmar Hitzfeld said: "We had to suffer tremendously two years ago. We had the chance to score the second goal in Barcelona, and the ball hit a post. I know what it is like to walk off the pitch a loser. It is very bitter, but in football you get a second chance very quickly. Now the pressure to win the Champions League has been lifted, and that is a good feeling".

2000-01

First qualifying round

		1st leg	2nd leg	agg
Birkirkara	KR Reykjavik	1-2	1-4	2-6
F91 Dudelange	Levski Sofia	0-4	0-2	0-6
Haka Valkeakoski	Linfield	1-0	1-2	2-2
Haka Valkeakoski won on away goals				
KI Klaksvik	Red Star Belgrade	0-3	0-2	0-5
TNS Llansantffraid	Levadia	2-2	0-4	2-6
Shirak Gyumri	BATE Borisov	1-1	1-2	2-3
Skonto Riga	Shamkir	2-1	1-4	3-5
Sloga	Shelbourne	0-1	1-1	1-2
SK Tirana	Zimbru Chisinau	2-3	2-3	4-6
Zalgiris Kaunas	Brotnjo	4-0	0-3	4-3

Second qualifying round

		1st leg	2nd leg	agg
Anderlecht	Anorthosis	4-2	0-0	4-2
Besiktas	Levski Sofia	1-0	1-1	2-1
Brondby	KR Reykjavik	3-1	0-0	3-1
Dynamo Bucharest	Polonia Warsaw	3-4	1-3	4-7
Rangers	Zalgiris Kaunas	4-1	0-0	4-1
Haka Valkeakoski	Inter Bratislava	0-0	0-1	0-1
Helsingborg	BATE Borisov	0-0	3-0	3-0
Red Star Belgrade	Torpedo Kutaisi	4-0	0-2	4-2
Shakhtor Donetsk	Levadia	4-1	5-1	9-2
Slavia Prague	Shamkir	1-0	4-1	5-1
Shelbourne	Rosenborg	1-3	1-1	2-4
Sturm Graz	Hapoel Tel Aviv	3-0	2-1	5-1
Zimbru Chisinau	Maribor	2-0	0-1	2-1
Hajduk Split	Dunaferr	0-2	2-2	2-4

Third qualifying round

		1st leg	2nd leg	agg
Tirol Innsbruck	Valencia	0-0	1-4	1-4
Zimbru Chisinau	Sparta Prague	0-1	0-1	0-2
Brondby	Hamburg	0-2	0-0	0-2
Helsingborg	Internazionale	1-0	0-0	1-0
Besiktas	Lokomotiv Moscow	3-0	3-1	6-1
Inter Bratislava	Lyon	1-2	1-2	2-4
Anderlecht	Porto	1-0	0-0	1-0
Herfolge	Rangers	0-3	0-3	0-6
Dynamo Kiev	Red Star Belgrade	0-0	1-1	1-1
Dynamo Kiev won on away goals				
Polonia Warsaw	Panathinaikos	2-2	1-2	3-4
Leeds United	Munich 1860	2-1	1-0	3-1
Sturm Graz	Feyenoord	2-1	1-1	3-2
Dunaferr	Rosenborg	2-2	1-2	3-4

Saint Gallen	Galatasaray	1-2	2-2	3-4
Milan	Dynamo Zagreb	3-1	3-0	6-1
Shakhtor Donetsk	Slavia Prague	0-1	2-0	2-1

First Group Stage

Group A

Spartak Moscow 2 Bayer Leverkusen 0
Sporting Lisbon 2 Real Madrid 2
Bayer Leverkusen 3 Sporting Lisbon 2
Real Madrid 1 Spartak Moscow 0
Bayer Leverkusen 2 Real Madrid 3
Spartak Moscow 3 Sporting Lisbon 1
Real Madrid 5 Bayer Leverkusen 3
Sporting Lisbon 0 Spartak Moscow 3
Bayer Leverkusen 1 Spartak Moscow 0
Real Madrid 4 Sporting Lisbon 0
Sporting Lisbon 0 Bayer Leverkusen 0
Spartak Moscow 1 Real Madrid 0

	P	W	D	L	F	A	Pts
Real Madrid	6	4	1	1	15	8	13
Spartak Moscow	6	4	0	2	9	3	12
Bayer Leverkusen	6	2	1	3	9	12	7
Sporting Lisbon	6	0	2	4	5	15	2

Group B

Sparta Prague 0 Arsenal 1
Shakhtor Donetsk 0 Lazio 3
Arsenal 3 Shakhtor Donetsk 2
Lazio 3 Sparta Prague 0
Arsenal 2 Lazio 0
Sparta Prague 3 Shakhtor Donetsk 2
Lazio 1 Arsenal 1
Shakhtor Donetsk 2 Sparta Prague 1
Arsenal 4 Sparta Prague 2
Lazio 5 Shakhtor Donetsk 1
Shakhtor Donetsk 3 Arsenal 0
Sparta Prague 0 Lazio 1

	P	W	D	L	F	A	Pts
Arsenal	6	4	1	1	11	8	13
Lazio	6	4	1	1	13	4	13
Shakhtor Donetsk	6	2	0	4	10	15	6
Sparta Prague	6	1	0	5	6	13	3

Group C

Valencia 2 Olympiakos 1
Lyon 3 Heerenveen 1
Olympiakos 2 Lyon 1
Heerenveen 0 Valencia 1
Valencia 1 Lyon 0
Olympiakos 2 Heerenveen 0
Lyon 1 Valencia 2
Heerenveen 1 Olympiakos 0
Olympiakos 1 Valencia 0
Heerenveen 0 Lyon 2
Lyon 1 Olympiakos 0
Valencia 1 Heerenveen 1

	P	W	D	L	F	A	Pts
Valencia	6	4	1	1	7	4	13

Lyon	6	3	0	3	8	6	9
Olympiakos	6	3	0	3	6	5	9
Heerenveen	6	1	1	4	3	9	4

Group D

Galatasaray 3 Monaco 2
Rangers 5 Sturm Graz 0
Monaco 0 Rangers 1
Sturm Graz 3 Galatasaray 0
Galatasaray 3 Rangers 2
Monaco 5 Sturm Graz 0
Rangers 0 Galatasaray 0
Sturm Graz 2 Monaco 0
Monaco 4 Galatasaray 2
Sturm Graz 2 Rangers 0
Rangers 2 Monaco 2
Galatasaray 2 Sturm Graz 2

	P	W	D	L	F	A	Pts
Sturm Graz	6	3	1	2	9	12	10
Galatasaray	6	2	2	2	10	13	8
Rangers	6	2	2	2	10	7	8
Monaco	6	2	1	3	13	10	7

Group E

Hamburg 4 Juventus 4
Panathinaikos 1 Deportivo La Coruna 1
Juventus 2 Panathinaikos 1
Deportivo La Coruna 2 Hamburg 1
Juventus 0 Deportivo La Coruna 0
Hamburg 0 Panathinaikos 1
Deportivo La Coruna 1 Juventus 1
Panathinaikos 0 Hamburg 0
Juventus 1 Hamburg 3
Deportivo La Coruna 1 Panathinaikos 0
Panathinaikos 3 Juventus 1
Hamburg 1 Deportivo La Coruna 1

	P	W	D	L	F	A	Pts
Deportivo La Coruna	6	2	4	0	6	4	10
Panathinaikos	6	2	2	2	6	5	8
Hamburg	6	1	3	2	9	9	6
Juventus	6	1	3	2	9	12	6

Group F

Rosenborg 3 Paris Saint-Germain 1
Helsingborg 1 Bayern Munich 3
Paris Saint-Germain 4 Helsingborg 1
Bayern Munich 3 Rosenborg 1
Paris Saint-Germain 1 Bayern Munich 0
Rosenborg 6 Helsingborg 1
Bayern Munich 2 Paris Saint-Germain 0
Helsingborg 2 Rosenborg 0
Paris Saint-Germain 7 Rosenborg 2
Bayern Munich 0 Helsingborg 0
Helsingborg 1 Paris Saint-Germain 1
Rosenborg 1 Bayern Munich 1

	P	W	D	L	F	A	Pts
Bayern Munich	6	3	2	1	9	4	11
Paris Saint-Germain	6	3	1	2	14	9	10
Rosenborg	6	2	1	3	13	15	7
Helsingborg	6	1	2	3	6	14	5

Group G

PSV Eindhoven 2 Dynamo Kiev 1
Manchester United 5 Anderlecht 1
Dynamo Kiev 0 Manchester United 0
Anderlecht 1 PSV Eindhoven 0
Dynamo Kiev 4 Anderlecht 0
PSV Eindhoven 3 Manchester United 1
Anderlecht 4 Dynamo Kiev 2
Manchester United 3 PSV Eindhoven 1
Dynamo Kiev 0 PSV Eindhoven 1
Anderlecht 2 Manchester United 1
Manchester United 1 Dynamo Kiev 0
PSV Eindhoven 2 Anderlecht 3

	P	W	D	L	F	A	Pts
Anderlecht	6	4	0	2	11	14	12
Manchester United	6	3	1	2	11	7	10
PSV Eindhoven	6	3	0	3	9	9	9
Dynamo Kiev	6	1	1	4	7	8	4

Group H

Barcelona 4 Leeds United 0
Milan 4 Besiktas 1
Leeds United 1 Milan 0
Besiktas 3 Barcelona 0
Leeds United 6 Besiktas 0
Barcelona 0 Milan 2
Besiktas 0 Leeds United 0
Milan 3 Barcelona 3
Leeds United 1 Barcelona 1
Besiktas 0 Milan 2
Milan 1 Leeds United 1
Barcelona 5 Besiktas 0

	P	W	D	L	F	A	Pts
Milan	6	3	2	1	12	6	11
Leeds United	6	2	3	1	9	6	9
Barcelona	6	2	2	2	13	9	8
Besiktas	6	1	1	4	4	17	4

Second Group Stage

Group A

Valencia 2 Sturm Graz 0
Manchester United 3 Panathinaikos 1
Panathinaikos 0 Valencia 0
Sturm Graz 0 Manchester United 2
Sturm Graz 2 Panathinaikos 0
Valencia 0 Manchester United 0
Panathinaikos 1 Sturm Graz 2
Manchester United 1 Valencia 1
Sturm Graz 0 Valencia 5
Panathinaikos 1 Manchester United 1
Valencia 2 Panathinaikos 1
Manchester United 3 Sturm Graz 0

	P	W	D	L	F	A	Pts
Valencia	6	3	3	0	10	2	12
Manchester United	6	3	3	0	10	3	12
Sturm Graz	6	2	0	4	4	13	6
Panathinaikos	6	0	2	4	4	10	2

Group B

Milan 2 Galatasaray 2
Paris Saint-Germain 1 Deportivo La Coruna 3
Deportivo La Coruna 0 Milan 1
Galatasaray 1 Paris Saint-Germain 0
Galatasaray 1 Deportivo La Coruna 0
Milan 1 Paris Saint-Germain 1
Deportivo La Coruna 2 Galatasaray 0
Paris Saint-Germain 1 Milan 1
Galatasaray 2 Milan 0
Deportivo La Coruna 4 Paris Saint-Germain 3
Milan 1 Deportivo La Coruna 1
Paris Saint-Germain 2 Galatasaray 0

	P	W	D	L	F	A	Pts
Deportivo La Coruna	6	3	1	2	10	7	10
Galatasaray	6	3	1	2	6	6	10
Milan	6	1	4	1	6	7	7
Paris Saint-Germain	6	1	2	3	8	10	5

Group C

Bayern Munich 1 Lyon 0
Spartak Moscow 4 Arsenal 1
Arsenal 2 Bayern Munich 2
Lyon 3 Spartak Moscow 0
Lyon 0 Arsenal 1
Bayern Munich 1 Spartak Moscow 0
Arsenal 1 Lyon 1
Spartak Moscow 0 Bayern Munich 3
Lyon 3 Bayern Munich 0
Arsenal 1 Spartak Moscow 0
Bayern Munich 1 Arsenal 0
Spartak Moscow 1 Lyon 1

	P	W	D	L	F	A	Pts
Bayern Munich	6	4	1	1	8	5	13
Arsenal	6	2	2	2	6	8	8
Lyon	6	2	2	2	8	4	8
Spartak Moscow	6	1	1	4	5	10	4

Group D

Leeds United 0 Real Madrid 2
Anderlecht 1 Lazio 0
Lazio 0 Leeds United 1
Real Madrid 4 Anderlecht 1
Real Madrid 3 Lazio 2
Leeds United 2 Anderlecht 1
Lazio 2 Real Madrid 2
Anderlecht 1 Leeds United 4
Real Madrid 3 Leeds United 2
Lazio 2 Anderlecht 1
Leeds United 3 Lazio 3
Anderlecht 2 Real Madrid 0

	P	W	D	L	F	A	Pts
Real Madrid	6	4	1	1	14	9	13
Leeds United	6	3	1	2	12	10	10
Anderlecht	6	2	0	4	7	12	6
Lazio	6	1	2	3	9	11	5

Quarter-finals

		1st leg	2nd leg	agg
Manchester United	Bayern Munich	0-1	1-2	1-3
Galatasaray	Real Madrid	3-2	0-3	3-5
Leeds United	Deportivo La Coruna	3-0	0-2	3-2
Arsenal	Valencia	2-1	0-1	2-2

Valencia won on away goals

Semi-finals

		1st leg	2nd leg	agg
Leeds United	Valencia	0-0	0-3	0-3
Real Madrid	Bayern Munich	0-1	1-2	1-3

Final

May 23 2001 Milan
Bayern Munich 1   Valencia 1 (after extra time)
Effenberg (penalty)   Mendieta (pen)
Bayern Munich won 5-4 on penalties
Bayern Munich: Kahn, Kuffour, Andersson, Linke, Sagnol (Jancker), Hargreaves, Effenberg, Lizarazu, Scholl (Paulo Sergio), Elber (Zickler), Salihamidzic
Valencia: Canizares, Angloma, Ayala (Djukic), Pellegrino, Carboni, Baraja, Mendieta, Kily Gonzalez, Sanchez (Zahovic), Aimar (Albelda), Carew
HT: 0-1
FT: 1-1
Referee: Jol (Netherlands)
Attendance: 74,000

2001-02

The 2001-02 competition opened with a moment of glory for Barry Town, who ran up a pair of victories against Shamkir (from Azerbaijan) in the first qualifying round, to become the first Welsh club to win a European Cup tie. Barry promptly lost 8-0 away to Porto at the next stage, but in the return match they won 3-1 against the former European champions. Scotland had two teams in the competition for the first time. Rangers lost to Fenerbahce in the third qualifying round but, in a clash of former champions, Celtic beat Ajax. Elsewhere in the last of the qualifiers, Liverpool (appearing in the competition for the first time since the Heysel disaster) thrashed Haka Valkeakoski 9-1 on aggregate, with Michael Owen – who would soon be voted European Footballer of the Year for 2001 – scoring a hat-trick in the first leg. Meanwhile Red Star Belgrade were eliminated by Bayer Leverkusen, who would go on to reach the final this season.

The group stage opened on September 11, the day on which Al Queda terrorist attacks in the USA, including the destruction of the World Trade Center, killed thousands of people. That day's matches went ahead as planned, to avoid disruption at short notice, but UEFA postponed the opening games in Groups E, F, G, and H, scheduled for September 12, as a mark of respect for the victims of the tragedy.

Manchester United, who had won the English title the previous season, finished as runners-up in Group G, behind Deportivo La Coruna, to whom they lost both home and away. Arsenal squeezed through with some inconsistent performances in Group C, winning three games and losing three, and taking runners-up spot ahead of Mallorca on head-to-head record, while the group was won by Panathinaikos. Five of Arsenal's nine goals at this stage were scored by Thierry Henry, a French international who was emerging as one of the world's greatest players. Liverpool won Group B, with three wins and three draws, but only scored seven goals in the process. Celtic, like Arsenal, won and lost three times, with their spirited performances including an unlucky 3-2 defeat away to Juventus, and a thrilling 4-3 victory at home to the same opponents, but they were consigned to third place in Group E, and elimination. Celtic were managed by Martin O'Neill, who had played for Nottingham Forest in the 1980 final. Bayern Munich, the reigning champions, and Real Madrid both won their groups. Barcelona took Group F, winning five of their matches, but losing against Bayer Leverkusen, who took second spot.

The second group stage brought together Manchester United and Bayern Munich, who were meeting for the third season out of four. Both advanced from Group A, seven points clear of third-placed Boavista, drawing with each other twice on the way. Liverpool managed to advance from Group B, despite a record of one win, four draws, and one defeat – in which they scored a total of four goals – edging ahead of Roma on head-to-head record, beating them 2-0 on the last day. Gerard Houllier, the Liverpool manager, returned to the bench for that match, after being absent for five months following heart surgery. During Houllier's absence, his assistant, Phil Thompson, a winner of the European Cup as a player in 1978 and 1981, had been caretaker manager. Arsenal's progress was ended, as they finished third in Group D, won by Bayer Leverkusen. With Juventus finishing bottom of Group D, while Roma were third in Group B, Italian clubs would be absent from the last eight for a second successive season. The remaining group was won by Real Madrid, who emerged eight points ahead of runners-up Panathinaikos.

In the quarter-finals, Manchester United achieved excellent victories against Deportivo La Coruna, winning 2-0 away and 3-2 at home. Unfortunately there was a high price for this victory, as David Beckham broke a metatarsal, as a result of a rash challenge from Pedro Duscher in the second leg, and was ruled out for the remainder of United's campaign. Liverpool won by a single goal at home to Bayer Leverkusen, but collapsed to a 4-2 defeat in the second leg, with Michael Ballack scoring twice for the Germans. The big clash of the round brought together Real Madrid and Bayern Munich. After trailing for most of the match, Bayern staged a late recovery to snatch a 2-1 victory at home, but Real won 2-0 in Madrid, to end the German club's hold on the title. Meanwhile Barcelona beat Panathinaikos with a 3-2 aggregate scoreline.

Bayer Leverkusen had finished ahead of Arsenal in the second group stage, albeit without winning either match against them, before eliminating Liverpool in the quarter-finals. In the semi-finals, Bayer Leverkusen achieved another success against an English club by overcoming Manchester United on away goals. In an unfortunate coincidence, United lost Gary Neville in the first leg, as he, too, suffered a broken metatarsal. United's Ruud Van Nistelrooy, scorer of one of their goals in the first leg, finished as leading marksman in this season's Champions League, with ten goals.

The other semi-final was an all-Spanish clash, in which Real Madrid won 2-0 away to Barcelona with goals from Zinedine Zidane and Steve McManaman, before clinching a place in the final with a 1-1 draw in the return match. Even then Real players scored both goals – Raul scoring before Ivan Helguera put the ball into his own net.

The final brought together Real Madrid and Bayer Leverkusen, at Hampden Park, in Glasgow, the scene of Real's win against previous German opponents in the 1960 final. Before the match, Alfredo Di Stefano, now honorary president of Real Madrid, and some of his former team-mates staged a reunion, to recall their wonderful 7-3 victory against Eintracht Frankfurt. Whereas the attendance had been 134,000 at the 1960 final, the 2002 equivalent was 50,499 – due to the reduced capacity in what was now an all-seater stadium.

Vicente Del Bosque was still Real's coach and the team he selected included six players who had appeared in either or both of the 1998 and 2000 finals – Roberto Carlos, Helguera, Fernando

Hierro, Fernando Morientes, Raul, and Michel Salgado. The newcomers included Luis Figo, the greatest Portuguese player since Eusebio, and Zidane. While Real Madrid came to this season's Champions League as the Spanish title-holders, Bayer Leverkusen had arrived via fourth place in the previous season's Bundesliga. Leverkusen had fewer star players than Real, but their team for the final featured six players who would appear at the World Cup finals in Japan and South Korea a few weeks later – Michael Ballack, Oliver Neuville, Carsten Ramelow, and Bernd Schneider who played for Germany, Lucio of Brazil, and Yildiray Basturk of Turkey.

Real took the lead after nine minutes, as the Bayer Leverkusen defence and Hans-Jorg Butt, the goalkeeper, were caught napping. A throw-in from Roberto Carlos on the left found an unmarked Raul, whose speculative shot from wide of the goal rolled into the far corner. Stung by this, Leverkusen rallied, and equalised five minutes later, as a free kick from Schneider on the left was headed home by Lucio. The teams were evenly matched in skilful combat after the exchange of goals, until a moment of inspiration separated them a couple of minutes before half time. A cross from Roberto Carlos on the left reached Zidane, on the edge of the penalty area, a position from which the Frenchman struck a left foot volley that flew into the top left corner of the net. Zidane's stunning goal meant that Real led 2-1 at the interval.

Bayer Leverkusen pressed strongly for another equaliser during the second half, while Real concentrated on counter-attacks, the foundations for many of which were laid by Zidane. Amid committed football, several players picked up injuries, including Real's goalkeeper Cesar, who was replaced by Iker Casillas midway through the half. Casillas, aged only 20, made a series of great saves as Leverkusen laid siege to the Real goal during the last few minutes of normal time. Urs Meier, the Swiss referee, then decided upon seven minutes of stoppage time, during which Leverkusen continued to create chances. Goalkeeper Butt rushed to the opposing penalty area for a free kick, which he met with a header that flew just wide of a post. Following this Casillas made an amazing treble save from Basturk, Ulf Kirsten, and Schneider and the match ended with Real Madrid as 2-1 winners.

This had not been a spectacle in the same league as Real's win against Eintracht Frankfurt, but it was an excellent contest that deserves an honoured place in the tradition of the European Cup. Zidane's winning goal, and Casillas' goalkeeping, became instant legends, although Zidane modestly said "just instinct" when asked to explain how he had scored such a brilliant goal. So Real, in their centenary year, had won the competition for the third time in the space of five seasons and the ninth in all.

2001-02

First qualifying round

		1st leg	2nd leg	agg
Levski Sofia	Zeljeznicar Sarajevo	4-0	0-0	4-0
Linfield	Torpedo Kutaisi	0-0	0-1	0-1
KR Reykjavik	Vllaznia Shkoder	2-1	0-1	2-2
Vllaznia Shkoder won on away goals				
Sloga	FBK Kaunas	0-0	1-1	1-1
Sloga won on away goals				
VB Vagur	Slavia Mozyr	0-0	0-5	0-5
Bohemians	Levadia	3-0	0-0	3-0
Barry Town	Shamkir	2-0	1-0	3-0
Valletta	Haka Valkeakoski	0-0	0-5	0-5
F91 Dudelange	Skonto Riga	1-6	1-0	2-6
Araks	Serif	0-1	0-2	0-3

Second qualifying round

		1st leg	2nd leg	agg
Anderlecht	Serif	4-0	2-1	6-1
Shakhtor Donetsk	Lugano	3-0	1-2	4-2
Ferencvaros	Hajduk Split	0-0	0-0	0-0

Hajduk Split won 5-4 on penalties

Bohemians	Halmstad	1-2	0-2	1-4
Torpedo Kutaisi	FC Copenhagen	1-1	1-3	2-4
Omonia Nicosia	Red Star Belgrade	1-1	1-2	2-3
Haka Valkeakoski	Maccabi Haifa	0-1	3-0	3-1

Maccabi Haifa won the second leg 4-0, but they fielded an ineligible player, and the match was awarded to Haka Valkeakoski 3-0.

Levski Sofia	Brann Bergen	0-0	1-1	1-1

Levski Sofia won on away goals

Galatasaray	Vllaznia Shkoder	2-0	4-1	6-1
Porto	Barry Town	8-0	1-3	9-3
Steaua Bucharest	Sloga	3-0	2-1	5-1
Skonto Riga	Wisla Krakow	1-2	0-1	1-3
Slavia Mozyr	Inter Bratislava	0-1	0-1	0-2
Maribor	Rangers	0-3	1-3	1-3

Third qualifying round

		1st leg	2nd leg	agg
Galatasaray	Levski Sofia	2-1	1-1	3-2
Red Star Belgrade	Bayer Leverkusen	0-0	0-3	0-3
Ajax	Celtic	1-3	1-0	2-3
Shakhtor Donetsk	Borussia Dortmund	0-2	1-3	1-5
Wisla Krakow	Barcelona	3-4	0-1	3-5
Halmstad	Anderlecht	2-3	1-1	3-4
Porto	Grasshoppers	2-2	3-2	5-4
Lokomotiv Moscow	Tirol Innsbruck	3-1	0-1	3-2

Lokomotiv Moscow originally won the second leg 1-0, but the match was replayed as the referee incorrectly booked one Lokomotiv Moscow player instead of another who had already been booked, and should therefore have been sent off.

Rangers	Fenerbahce	0-0	1-2	1-2
Inter Bratislava	Rosenborg	3-3	0-4	3-7
Slavia Prague	Panathinaikos	1-2	0-1	1-3
Parma	Lille	0-2	1-0	1-2
Steaua Bucharest	Dynamo Kiev	2-4	1-1	3-5
FC Copenhagen	Lazio	2-1	1-4	3-5
Haka Valkeakoski	Liverpool	0-5	1-4	1-9
Hajduk Split	Mallorca	1-0	0-2	1-2

First Group Stage
Group A

Lokomotiv Moscow 1 Anderlecht 1
Roma 1 Real Madrid 2
Anderlecht 0 Roma 0
Real Madrid 4 Lokomotiv Moscow 0
Real Madrid 4 Anderlecht 1
Roma 2 Lokomotiv Moscow 1
Anderlecht 0 Real Madrid 2
Lokomotiv Moscow 0 Roma 1
Real Madrid 1 Roma 1
Anderlecht 1 Lokomotiv Moscow 5
Roma 1 Anderlecht 1
Lokomotiv Moscow 2 Real Madrid 0

	P	W	D	L	F	A	Pts
Real Madrid	6	4	1	1	13	5	13
Roma	6	2	3	1	6	5	9
Lokomotiv Moscow	6	2	1	3	9	9	7
Anderlecht	6	0	3	3	4	13	3

Group B

Dynamo Kiev 2 Borussia Dortmund 2
Liverpool 1 Boavista 1
Borussia Dortmund 0 Liverpool 0
Boavista 3 Dynamo Kiev 1
Boavista 2 Borussia Dortmund 1
Liverpool 1 Dynamo Kiev 0
Borussia Dortmund 2 Boavista 1
Dynamo Kiev 1 Liverpool 2
Boavista 1 Liverpool 1
Borussia Dortmund 1 Dynamo Kiev 0
Liverpool 2 Borussia Dortmund 0
Dynamo Kiev 1 Boavista 0

	P	W	D	L	F	A	Pts
Liverpool	6	3	3	0	7	3	12
Boavista	6	2	2	2	8	7	8
Borussia Dortmund	6	2	2	2	6	7	8
Dynamo Kiev	6	1	1	4	5	9	4

Group C

Schalke 04 0 Panathinaikos 2
Mallorca 1 Arsenal 0
Panathinaikos 2 Mallorca 0
Arsenal 3 Schalke 04 2
Panathinaikos 1 Arsenal 0
Schalke 04 0 Mallorca 1
Arsenal 2 Panathinaikos 1
Mallorca 0 Schalke 04 4
Panathinaikos 2 Schalke 04 0
Arsenal 3 Mallorca 1
Schalke 04 3 Arsenal 1
Mallorca 1 Panathinaikos 0

	P	W	D	L	F	A	Pts
Panathinaikos	6	4	0	2	8	3	12
Arsenal	6	3	0	3	9	9	9
Mallorca	6	3	0	3	4	9	9
Schalke 04	6	2	0	4	9	9	6

Group D

Nantes 4 PSV Eindhoven 1
Galatasaray 1 Lazio 0
Lazio 1 Nantes 3
PSV Eindhoven 3 Galatasaray 1
PSV Eindhoven 1 Lazio 0
Nantes 0 Galatasaray 1
Lazio 2 PSV Eindhoven 1
Galatasaray 0 Nantes 0
PSV Eindhoven 0 Nantes 0
Lazio 1 Galatasaray 0
Nantes 1 Lazio 0
Galatasaray 2 PSV Eindhoven 0

	P	W	D	L	F	A	Pts
Nantes	6	3	2	1	8	3	11
Galatasaray	6	3	1	2	5	4	10
PSV Eindhoven	6	2	1	3	6	9	7
Lazio	6	2	0	4	4	7	6

Group E

Rosenborg 1 Porto 2
Juventus 3 Celtic 2

Rosenborg 1 Juventus 1
Celtic 1 Porto 0
Celtic 1 Rosenborg 0
Porto 0 Juventus 0
Porto 3 Celtic 0
Juventus 1 Rosenborg 0
Rosenborg 2 Celtic 0
Juventus 3 Porto 1
Porto 1 Rosenborg 0
Celtic 4 Juventus 3

	P	W	D	L	F	A	Pts
Juventus	6	3	2	1	11	8	11
Porto	6	3	1	2	7	5	10
Celtic	6	3	0	3	8	11	9
Rosenborg	6	1	1	4	4	6	4

Group F
Lyon 0 Bayer Leverkusen 1
Fenerbahce 0 Barcelona 3
Fenerbahce 0 Lyon 1
Bayer Leverkusen 2 Barcelona 1
Barcelona 2 Lyon 0
Bayer Leverkusen 2 Fenerbahce 1
Barcelona 2 Bayer Leverkusen 1
Lyon 3 Fenerbahce 1
Fenerbahce 1 Bayer Leverkusen 2
Lyon 2 Barcelona 3
Barcelona 1 Fenerbahce 0
Bayer Leverkusen 2 Lyon 4

	P	W	D	L	F	A	Pts
Barcelona	6	5	0	1	12	5	15
Bayer Leverkusen	6	4	0	2	10	9	12
Lyon	6	3	0	3	10	9	9
Fenerbahce	6	0	0	6	3	12	0

Group G
Deportivo La Coruna 2 Olympiakos 2
Manchester United 1 Lille 0
Deportivo La Coruna 2 Manchester United 1
Lille 3 Olympiakos 1
Olympiakos 0 Manchester United 2
Lille 1 Deportivo La Coruna 1
Olympiakos 2 Lille 1
Manchester United 2 Deportivo La Coruna 3
Deportivo La Coruna 1 Lille 1
Manchester United 3 Olympiakos 0
Olympiakos 1 Deportivo La Coruna 1
Lille 1 Manchester United 1

	P	W	D	L	F	A	Pts
Deportivo La Coruna	6	2	4	0	10	8	10
Manchester United	6	3	1	2	10	6	10
Lille	6	1	3	2	7	7	6
Olympiakos	6	1	2	3	6	12	5

Group H
Spartak Moscow 2 Feyenoord 2
Bayern Munich 0 Sparta Prague 0
Spartak Moscow 1 Bayern Munich 3
Sparta Prague 4 Feyenoord 0
Feyenoord 2 Bayern Munich 2

Sparta Prague 2 Spartak Moscow 0
Bayern Munich 5 Spartak Moscow 1
Feyenoord 0 Sparta Prague 2
Bayern Munich 3 Feyenoord 1
Spartak Moscow 2 Sparta Prague 2
Feyenoord 2 Spartak Moscow 1
Sparta Prague 0 Bayern Munich 1

	P	W	D	L	F	A	Pts
Bayern Munich	6	4	2	0	14	5	14
Sparta Prague	6	3	2	1	10	3	11
Feyenoord	6	1	2	3	7	14	5
Spartak Moscow	6	0	2	4	7	16	2

Second Group Stage

Group A

Bayern Munich 1 Manchester United 1
Boavista 1 Nantes 0
Manchester United 3 Boavista 0
Nantes 0 Bayern Munich 1
Boavista 0 Bayern Munich 0
Nantes 1 Manchester United 1
Bayern Munich 1 Boavista 0
Manchester United 5 Nantes 1
Manchester United 0 Bayern Munich 0
Nantes 1 Boavista 1
Boavista 0 Manchester United 3
Bayern Munich 2 Nantes 1

	P	W	D	L	F	A	Pts
Manchester United	6	3	3	0	13	3	12
Bayern Munich	6	3	3	0	5	2	12
Boavista	6	1	2	3	2	8	5
Nantes	6	0	2	4	4	11	2

Group B

Galatasaray 1 Roma 1
Liverpool 1 Barcelona 3
Roma 0 Liverpool 0
Barcelona 2 Galatasaray 2
Liverpool 0 Galatasaray 0
Barcelona 1 Roma 1
Galatasaray 1 Liverpool 1
Roma 3 Barcelona 0
Roma 1 Galatasaray 1
Barcelona 0 Liverpool 0
Liverpool 2 Roma 0
Galatasaray 0 Barcelona 1

	P	W	D	L	F	A	Pts
Barcelona	6	2	3	1	7	7	9
Liverpool	6	1	4	1	4	4	7
Roma	6	1	4	1	6	5	7
Galatasaray	6	0	5	1	5	6	5

Group C

Panathinaikos 0 Porto 0
Sparta Prague 2 Real Madrid 3
Porto 0 Sparta Prague 1
Real Madrid 3 Panathinaikos 0
Sparta Prague 0 Panathinaikos 2
Real Madrid 1 Porto 0

Panathinaikos 2 Sparta Prague 1
Porto 1 Real Madrid 2
Porto 2 Panathinaikos 1
Real Madrid 3 Sparta Prague 0
Sparta Prague 2 Porto 0
Panathinaikos 2 Real Madrid 2

	P	W	D	L	F	A	Pts
Real Madrid	6	5	1	0	14	5	16
Panathinaikos	6	2	2	2	7	8	8
Sparta Prague	6	2	0	4	6	10	6
Porto	6	1	1	4	3	7	4

Group D

Deportivo La Coruna 2 Arsenal 0
Juventus 4 Bayer Leverkusen 0
Arsenal 3 Juventus 1
Bayer Leverkusen 3 Deportivo La Coruna 0
Juventus 0 Deportivo La Coruna 0
Bayer Leverkusen 1 Arsenal 1
Deportivo La Coruna 2 Juventus 0
Arsenal 4 Bayer Leverkusen 1
Arsenal 0 Deportivo La Coruna 2
Bayer Leverkusen 3 Juventus 1
Juventus 1 Arsenal 0
Deportivo La Coruna 1 Bayer Leverkusen 3

	P	W	D	L	F	A	Pts
Bayer Leverkusen	6	3	1	2	11	11	10
Deportivo La Coruna	6	3	1	2	7	6	10
Arsenal	6	2	1	3	8	8	7
Juventus	6	2	1	3	7	8	7

Quarter-finals

		1st leg	2nd leg	agg
Panathinaikos	Barcelona	1-0	1-3	2-3
Bayern Munich	Real Madrid	2-1	0-2	2-3
Deportivo La Coruna	Manchester United	0-2	2-3	2-5
Liverpool	Bayer Leverkusen	1-0	2-4	3-4

Semi-finals

		1st leg	2nd leg	agg
Barcelona	Real Madrid	0-2	1-1	1-3
Manchester United	Bayer Leverkusen	2-2	1-1	3-3

Bayer Leverkusen won an away goals

Final

May 15 2002 Glasgow
Real Madrid 2   Bayer Leverkusen 1
Raul   Lucio
Zidane
Real Madrid: Cesar (Casillas), Salgado, Roberto Carlos, Makelele (Conceicao), Hierro, Helguera, Figo (McManaman), Morientes, Raul, Zidane, Solari
Bayer Leverkusen: Butt, Sebescen (Kirsten), Zivkovic, Lucio (Babic), Placente, Schneider, Ramelow, Basturk, Ballack, Neuville, Brdaric (Berbatov)
HT: 2-1
Referee: Meier (Switzerland)
Attendance: 50,499

Zinedine Zidane

In 2004 Zinedine Zidane was voted the greatest ever European footballer in UEFA's massive poll of football supporters – nearly seven million people voted – and finished second behind Johan Cruyff in the companion poll of players and coaches. Winner of both the World Cup and European Championship with France, and the Champions League and World Club Championship with Real Madrid, Zidane is the complete midfielder. His touch on the ball and distribution are astounding, his runs at opposition defences are sparkling, and his tackling is solid. Zidane is also a specialist taker of penalties and free kicks. He often draws comparison with Michel Platini, his predecessor as the inspiration behind the French national team. Both players found success with Juventus, and won the European Footballer of the Year award while at that club. A passionate competitor on the football field, Zidane is a private man away from it, devoting himself to his family, and finding time to be involved in charity work in both France and Africa.

He was born at Marseille, on June 23 1972, into a family that came from Algeria, the former French colony. The Algerian team which beat West Germany in the 1982 World Cup finals included Djamel Zidane, a distant relative. As a youth, Zinedine played for a series of local teams, and was spotted by Cannes, who signed him in 1988, at the age of 16. In February 1991 Zidane, now aged 18, scored his first goal for Cannes, and was rewarded with a car, bought for him by the club president. The following year he moved to Bordeaux, where he was to spend four years, culminating in an appearance for the club in the 1996 UEFA Cup final, a defeat against Bayern Munich. In August 1994 Zidane made his debut for France, coming on as a substitute against the Czech Republic, and scoring both of his team's goals in a 2-2 draw. A couple of years later Zidane played for France at the Euro 96 finals, in England.

His talents attracted Juventus, and he moved to the Italian club in 1996. During 1996-97 Zidane played in their victories over River Plate in the World Club Championship, and Paris Saint Germain in the European Super Cup. Juventus won the Italian league that season, but lost 3-1 to Borussia Dortmund in the Champions League final. The Italian title was retained in 1997-98, but Zidane was again on the losing side in the Champions League final, as Real Madrid beat Juventus 1-0.

In the summer of 1998 France played hosts to the World Cup finals. Zidane was sent off in the 4-0 win against Saudi Arabia, for stamping on an opponent, and suspended for two matches. When he returned, Zidane put in a series of brilliant displays that were a major factor in France winning the trophy. In the final he scored two headed goals, both times getting to the ball ahead of defenders to meet a corner, to set France on their way to a 3-0 win against Brazil. 'Zizou', as he was nicknamed, had suddenly become a national hero, with many French people seeing him as an embodiment of France's multi-racial society. At the end of that year, he was voted European Footballer of the Year.

Two years later he produced some of the greatest football of his career, as France won Euro 2000. His trademark free kick opened the scoring as France beat Spain 2-1 in the quarter-finals. France beat Portugal by the same score in the semi-finals, Zidane winning the match with a golden goal in extra time, keeping his cool to score from a penalty that was delayed by several minutes of furious protest from the Portuguese. In the final, France beat Italy 2-1, with Zidane inspiring a recovery that saw them equalise in stoppage time, and then win in extra time.

Juventus had now gone into relative decline. In 1998-99 they slumped to sixth place in the Italian league, and lost to Manchester United in a Champions League semi-final. They partly recovered to finish as runners-up in the Italian League in both 1999-2000 and 2000-01, but failed to reach the last

> *16 of the Champions League in the latter season, finishing bottom of their group in the first league stage. In the summer of 2001 Zidane gave new impetus to his club career, moving to Real Madrid, for a world record fee of £46,500,000.*
>
> *At the end of his first season with Real Madrid, Zidane scored the winning goal, with a spectacular volley, as they beat Bayer Leverkusen 2-1 in the Champions League final. A few weeks later injury restricted Zidane to a single appearance in the 2002 World Cup finals, as a tired French team crashed out in the first round, failing to score in their three matches. During the remainder of 2002 Zidane played in Real Madrid's victories in the European Super Cup and World Club Championship, as they beat Feyenoord and Olimpia respectively. He won his first Spanish league title with Real at the end of 2002-03, but they fell to Juventus, his previous club, in the Champions League semi-finals.*
>
> *Zidane played in his third European Championship finals in the summer of 2004, and scored twice in stoppage time – with a free kick and then a penalty – as France dramatically beat England 2-1. France were subsequently eliminated by Greece, who went on to take the trophy. A few weeks after the tournament Zidane, who had played 93 matches for France (scoring 26 goals), announced his retirement from the international game. He reflected: "I do understand – and, anyway, everyone has been telling me – that in the public eye I have become more than a footballer, a sort of symbol for a lot of people. So, on that basis, I understand that my retirement may disappoint them. I can never thank the public enough for all the support I have enjoyed down the years, but they must realise, as I have had to, that life goes on. This is the story of sport. Every generation has to give way to the next one".*

2002-03

England's representation in the Champions League was increased from three to four clubs this season, as a result of good performances by the nation's teams in Europe during recent years. The English challenge began in the third qualifying round, with Manchester United, who had finished third in the Premiership the previous season (this being the first time since 1990-91 that the club had not been English champions or runners-up), losing 1-0 against Zalaegerszeg in Hungary, but winning the return 5-0, with Ruud Van Nistelrooy scoring twice, while Newcastle United eased past Zeljeznicar Sarajevo. At the same stage, Celtic, who were Scotland's sole entrant, lost to Basle on away goals. Meanwhile Milan, who went on to win the trophy this season, required the away goals rule to edge past Slovan Liberec, from the Czech Republic.

Arsenal, the reigning English champions, finished top of Group A, largely due to winning their first three games, following which they struggled – losing twice before finishing with a goalless draw at home to PSV Eindhoven, who ended bottom of the group. Liverpool enjoyed a couple of impressive wins against Spartak Moscow midway through Group B, but failed to win any of their other matches, and were eliminated. Manchester United were runaway winners of Group F, six points clear of Bayer Leverkusen, the team that had beaten them in the previous season's semi-finals. Bayer Leverkusen opened their campaign with a 6-2 defeat against Olympiakos, and were twice beaten by Manchester United, but won their other three matches to progress to the next stage. After they had secured their passage to the next stage, United fielded a weakened team against Maccabi Haifa – the first Israeli team to reach the group stage – and unexpectedly lost 3-0.

Newcastle United, who had previously appeared in the competition in 1997-98, were now managed by Bobby Robson, who had taken England to the 1986 and 1990 World Cup finals. Newcastle lost their first three matches, but won the next three, to finish as runners-up in Group

E, behind Juventus. Real Madrid won a group in which AEK Athens drew all six of their matches, while Barcelona won their section with six straight victories. The remaining groups were won by Internazionale and Milan.

Manchester United led the way for England in the second group stage, winning their first four matches, and emerging top of Group D, six points clear of each of the other three teams. Juventus, who lost 2-1 away to United and 3-0 at home, took second place, due to their superior head-to-head record against Basle and Deportivo La Coruna. Arsenal only managed third place in Group B. The Gunners opened with a 3-1 win away to Roma – in which Thierry Henry scored a hat-trick – but drew their next four matches, and then lost to Valencia, who won the group, ahead of Ajax. Newcastle United were also eliminated, but achieved a couple of 3-1 victories against Bayer Leverkusen – Alan Shearer scoring a hat-trick in the second of these wins – as the previous year's finalists slumped to bottom place in Group A, without winning a point. Barcelona won the group, and Internazionale joined them in the quarter-finals. Having twice beaten Legia Warsaw in the qualifiers, and then won all six of their matches in the first group stage, Barcelona won their first three matches in the second group stage. Barcelona's run of 11 successive victories was ended by a goalless draw against Internazionale. Milan won Group C, while Real Madrid only made sure of their progress by winning 1-0 away to Lokomotiv Moscow in their last match. With Borussia Dortmund finishing third in Group C, and Bayer Leverkusen last in Group A, German clubs were absent from the last eight for the first time since 1992-93.

Both Italy and Spain had three teams in the quarter-finals, while England and the Netherlands each had a single representative. Two of the quarter-finals brought together teams from Italy and Spain, with the Italians winning both of these. Juventus beat Barcelona 3-2 on aggregate, with Marcelo Zalayeta scoring the decisive goal late in extra time, while Internazionale beat Valencia on away goals. Milan beat Ajax 3-2 on aggregate, with Jon Dahl Tomasson scoring the winning goal in stoppage time at the end of the second leg, when Ajax had looked set to win the tie on away goals. This was the first time that a team from the Netherlands had reached the quarter-finals since Ajax themselves in 1996-97. Ajax were now managed by Ronald Koeman, who had scored the winner for Barcelona in the 1992 final.

Manchester United, who had reached the last eight in the European Cup for the seventh successive season, met Real Madrid in an epic tie. Real won 3-1 with an outstanding performance at the Bernabeu, with Raul scoring twice and Luis Figo once. United then won 4-3 in a brilliant, end to end, match at Old Trafford. Ronaldo scored a hat-trick for Real, and, when substituted, was applauded off the field by both sets of supporters, while David Beckham, controversially left out by United, netted twice after coming on with 20 minutes left. The outcome was that Real took the tie 6-5 on aggregate.

The result ended Manchester United's chance of appearing in a final that would be staged on their Old Trafford ground. United's Van Nistelrooy, who scored in both matches against Real Madrid, was the leading scorer, for the second consecutive season, but the number of goals he should be credited with is open for discussion. The UEFA statistics show that Van Nistelrooy scored 12 times in 2002-03, but the official figures for the Champions League exclude the qualifying matches. Some statisticians adjust the figures to include the qualifiers – aiming for consistency with the pre-Champions League era, and the full picture – giving Van Nistelrooy 14 goals for this season. That total equals the all-time record for a single season, set by Jose Altafini in 1962-63.

Real Madrid appeared set to retain the title, but they unexpectedly lost to Juventus in the semi-finals. They won their home leg 2-1, before being surprised by a superb performance from the Italians, who won 3-1 in Turin. The other semi-final brought together the two clubs from Milan, who played each other twice at the stadium they shared. Milan's home leg was a goalless draw, while Internazionale's home leg was a 1-1 draw. This meant that Milan won the tie with an away goal scored in their own stadium – a novel twist on the away goals rule.

The all-Spanish final of 2000 was followed by a meeting of two Italian clubs in the 2003 final. Juventus, the reigning Italian champions, and Milan, who had taken fourth place the previous season, faced each other at Old Trafford, in Manchester – during a time that Wembley Stadium, which had staged each of the previous European Cup finals to be played in England, was being rebuilt. The match was played on May 28, which was the date on which Milan had both lost the 1958 final and won the 1969 final. Milan were now appearing in their first final since the defeat against Ajax in 1995 – Alessandro Costacurta and Paolo Maldini remained from the team of eight years earlier. Milan were coached by Carlo Ancelotti, who had won the European Cup with them as a player in 1989 and 1990. In 2001 Ancelotti had been sacked as manager of Juventus, and replaced by Marcello Lippi, who had led Juventus to the 1996, 1997, and 1998 finals. The line-up that Lippi selected for his fourth final in charge of Juventus in the space of eight seasons included five players who had appeared for the club in previous finals – Edgar Davids, Alessandro Del Piero, Ciro Ferrera, Paolo Montero, and Alessio Tacchinardi. Juventus were, however, weakened by the absence of the suspended Pavel Nedved, from the Czech Republic, who was destined to win the European Footballer of the Year award at the end of 2003.

Milan had the better of an open first half, and got the ball into the net after eight minutes, but Andrei Shevchenko's effort was disallowed by Markus Merk, the German referee, as Rui Costa was in an offside position. Juventus went close to scoring a couple of minutes into the second half, as a corner from Del Piero was met by Antonio Conte with a flying header, but the ball hit the crossbar. As the second half progressed, the play became more cautious. The end of 90 minutes arrived with the score at 0-0. Extra time was merely a goalless stalemate, and the match had to be decided by penalties. Lippi faced a shortage of volunteers to take the minimum five penalties among the Juventus players. One of those willing to participate was David Trezeguet, but his opening kick of the penalty contest was saved by Dida, Milan's Brazilian goalkeeper. Serginho then opened Milan's account, and Antonio Birindelli equalised for Juventus with their second kick. Each of the next four penalties were saved, before Nesta put Milan 2-1 ahead with the team's fourth effort. Del Piero converted for Juventus to temporarily restore parity, but Shevchenko scored from Milan's fifth kick, to give them the match 3-2 on penalties. It was a fair outcome, as Milan had been the better team over the 120 minutes of play. Shevchenko, who had been a beaten semi-finalist with Dynamo Kiev in 1999, deserved the glory of scoring the winner in the penalty contest, as he had been the best player on the night.

This was the sixth time that Milan had won the European Cup/Champions League, in their ninth final. They had regained the trophy which they had last won in 1994, after several years of frustration, during which Real Madrid replaced them as Europe's dominant club. In the process several impressive personal records had been set. Clarence Seedorf had become the first player to win the European Cup with three clubs – the others being Ajax in 1995 and Real Madrid in 1998 – despite having a shot saved in the penalty shoot-out. Ancelotti had become only the fourth man to win the competition as both player and manager – emulating Miguel Munoz, Giovanni Trapattoni, and Johan Cruyff. Paolo Maldini had now been on the winning team for Milan in four European Cup finals – 1989, 1990, 1994, and 2003. Maldini's consistent performances for both Milan (with whom he had spent his entire career) and Italy had gained him the reputation as one of the greatest defenders in the history of football. This latest European Cup victory came 40 years after Paolo's father, Cesare Maldini, played for the Milan team which won the 1963 final, which had also been played in England.

2002-03

First qualifying round

		1st leg	2nd leg	agg
Tampere United	Pyunik	0-4	0-2	0-6
Skonto Riga	Barry Town	5-0	1-0	6-0
Portadown	Belshina	0-0	2-3	2-3
F91 Dudelange	Vardar	1-1	0-3	1-4
FBK Kaunas	Dynamo Tirana	2-3	0-0	2-3
Flora Tallinn	Apoel Nicosia	0-0	0-1	0-1
Zeljeznicar Sarajevo	IA Akranes	3-0	1-0	4-0
Hibernians	Shelbourne	2-2	1-0	3-2
Torpedo Kutaisi	B36 Torshavn	5-2	1-0	6-2
Serif	Zhenis	2-1	2-3	4-4

Serif won on away goals

Second qualifying round

		1st leg	2nd leg	agg
Zalaegerszeg	Zagreb	1-0	1-2	2-2

Zalaegerszeg won on away goals

		1st leg	2nd leg	agg
Brugge	Dynamo Bucharest	3-1	1-0	4-1
Zilina	Basle	1-1	0-3	1-4
Skonto Riga	Levski Sofia	0-0	0-2	0-2
Dynamo Kiev	Pyunik	4-0	2-2	6-2
Brondby	Dynamo Tirana	1-0	4-0	5-0
Maribor	Apoel Lefkosia	2-1	2-4	4-5
Vardar	Legia Warsaw	1-3	1-1	2-4
Boavista	Hibernians	4-0	3-3	7-3
Maccabi Haifa	Belshina	4-0	1-0	5-0
Lillestrom	Zeljeznicar Sarajevo	0-1	0-1	0-2
Hammarby	Partizan Belgrade	1-1	0-4	1-5
Sparta Prague	Torpedo Kutaisi	3-0	2-1	5-1
Serif	Graz	1-4	0-2	1-6

Third qualifying round

		1st leg	2nd leg	agg
Sporting Lisbon	Internazionale	0-0	0-2	0-2
Milan	Slovan Liberec	1-0	1-2	2-2

Milan won on away goals

		1st leg	2nd leg	agg
Rosenborg	Brondby	1-0	3-2	4-2
Shakhtor Donetsk	Brugge	1-1	1-1	2-2

Brugge won 4-1 on penalties

		1st leg	2nd leg	agg
Apoel Lefkosia	AEK Athens	2-3	0-1	2-4
Barcelona	Legia Warsaw	3-0	1-0	4-0
Levski Sofia	Dynamo Kiev	0-1	0-1	0-2
Zeljeznicar Sarajevo	Newcastle United	0-1	0-4	0-5
Partizan Belgrade	Bayern Munich	0-3	1-3	1-6
Genk	Sparta Prague	2-0	2-4	4-4

Genk won on away goals

		1st leg	2nd leg	agg
Maccabi Haifa	Sturm Graz	2-0	3-3	5-3
Celtic	Basle	3-1	0-2	3-3

Basle won on away goals

		1st leg	2nd leg	agg
Feyenoord	Fenerbahce	1-0	2-0	3-0
Zalaegerszeg	Manchester United	1-0	0-5	1-5

| Boavista | Auxerre | 0-1 | 0-0 | 0-1 |
| Graz | Lokomotiv Moscow | 0-2 | 3-3 | 3-5 |

First Group Stage

Group A

Auxerre 0 PSV Eindhoven 0
Arsenal 2 Borussia Dortmund 0
PSV Eindhoven 0 Arsenal 4
Borussia Dortmund 2 Auxerre 1
PSV Eindhoven 1 Borussia Dortmund 3
Auxerre 0 Arsenal 1
Borussia Dortmund 1 PSV Eindhoven 1
Arsenal 1 Auxerre 2
PSV Eindhoven 3 Auxerre 0
Borussia Dortmund 2 Arsenal 1
Arsenal 0 PSV Eindhoven 0
Auxerre 1 Borussia Dortmund 0

	P	W	D	L	F	A	Pts
Arsenal	6	3	1	2	9	4	10
Borussia Dortmund	6	3	1	2	8	7	10
Auxerre	6	2	1	3	4	7	7
PSV Eindhoven	6	1	3	2	5	8	6

Group B

Valencia 2 Liverpool 0
Basle 2 Spartak Moscow 0
Liverpool 1 Basle 1
Spartak Moscow 0 Valencia 3
Liverpool 5 Spartak Moscow 0
Valencia 6 Basle 2
Spartak Moscow 1 Liverpool 3
Basle 2 Valencia 2
Liverpool 0 Valencia 1
Spartak Moscow 0 Basle 2
Basle 3 Liverpool 3
Valencia 3 Spartak Moscow 0

	P	W	D	L	F	A	Pts
Valencia	6	5	1	0	17	4	16
Basle	6	2	3	1	12	12	9
Liverpool	6	2	2	2	12	8	8
Spartak Moscow	6	0	0	6	1	18	0

Group C

Genk 0 AEK Athens 0
Roma 0 Real Madrid 3
AEK Athens 0 Roma 0
Real Madrid 6 Genk 0
AEK Athens 3 Real Madrid 3
Genk 0 Roma 1
Real Madrid 2 AEK Athens 2
Roma 0 Genk 0
AEK Athens 1 Genk 1
Real Madrid 0 Roma 1
Roma 1 AEK Athens 1
Genk 1 Real Madrid 1

	P	W	D	L	F	A	Pts
Real Madrid	6	2	3	1	15	7	9
Roma	6	2	3	1	3	4	9

	P	W	D	L	F	A	Pts
AEK Athens	6	0	6	0	7	7	6
Genk	6	0	4	2	2	9	4

Group D

Rosenborg 2 Internazionale 2
Ajax 2 Lyon 1
Internazionale 1 Ajax 0
Lyon 5 Rosenborg 0
Internazionale 1 Lyon 2
Rosenborg 0 Ajax 0
Lyon 3 Internazionale 3
Ajax 1 Rosenborg 1
Internazionale 3 Rosenborg 0
Lyon 0 Ajax 2
Ajax 1 Internazionale 2
Rosenborg 1 Lyon 1

	P	W	D	L	F	A	Pts
Internazionale	6	3	2	1	12	8	11
Ajax	6	2	2	2	6	5	8
Lyon	6	2	2	2	12	9	8
Rosenborg	6	0	4	2	4	12	4

Group E

Feyenoord 1 Juventus 1
Dynamo Kiev 2 Newcastle United 0
Juventus 5 Dynamo Kiev 0
Newcastle United 0 Feyenoord 1
Juventus 2 Newcastle United 0
Feyenoord 0 Dynamo Kiev 0
Newcastle United 1 Juventus 0
Dynamo Kiev 2 Feyenoord 0
Juventus 2 Feyenoord 0
Newcastle United 2 Dynamo Kiev 1
Dynamo Kiev 1 Juventus 2
Feyenoord 2 Newcastle United 3

	P	W	D	L	F	A	Pts
Juventus	6	4	1	1	12	3	13
Newcastle United	6	3	0	3	6	8	9
Dynamo Kiev	6	2	1	3	6	9	7
Feyenoord	6	1	2	3	4	8	5

Group F

Manchester United 5 Maccabi Haifa 2
Olympiakos 6 Bayer Leverkusen 2
Maccabi Haifa 3 Olympiakos 0
Bayer Leverkusen 1 Manchester United 2
Maccabi Haifa 0 Bayer Leverkusen 2
Manchester United 4 Olympiakos 0
Bayer Leverkusen 2 Maccabi Haifa 1
Olympiakos 2 Manchester United 3
Maccabi Haifa 3 Manchester United 0
Bayer Leverkusen 2 Olympiakos 0
Olympiakos 3 Maccabi Haifa 3
Manchester United 2 Bayer Leverkusen 0

	P	W	D	L	F	A	Pts
Manchester United	6	5	0	1	16	8	15
Bayer Leverkusen	6	3	0	3	9	11	9
Maccabi Haifa	6	2	1	3	12	12	7
Olympiakos	6	1	1	4	11	17	4

Group G

Bayern Munich 2 Deportivo La Coruna 3
Milan 2 Lens 1
Deportivo La Coruna 0 Milan 4
Lens 1 Bayern Munich 1
Deportivo La Coruna 3 Lens 1
Bayern Munich 1 Milan 2
Lens 3 Deportivo La Coruna 1
Milan 2 Bayern Munich 1
Deportivo La Coruna 2 Bayern Munich 1
Lens 2 Milan 1
Milan 1 Deportivo La Coruna 2
Bayern Munich 3 Lens 3

	P	W	D	L	F	A	Pts
Milan	6	4	0	2	12	7	12
Deportivo La Coruna	6	4	0	2	11	12	12
Lens	6	2	2	2	11	11	8
Bayern Munich	6	0	2	4	9	13	2

Group H

Lokomotiv Moscow 0 Galatasaray 2
Barcelona 3 Brugge 2
Galatasaray 0 Barcelona 2
Brugge 0 Lokomotiv Moscow 0
Galatasaray 0 Brugge 0
Lokomotiv Moscow 1 Barcelona 3
Brugge 3 Galatasaray 1
Barcelona 1 Lokomotiv Moscow 0
Galatasaray 1 Lokomotiv Moscow 2
Brugge 0 Barcelona 1
Barcelona 3 Galatasaray 1
Lokomotiv Moscow 2 Brugge 0

	P	W	D	L	F	A	Pts
Barcelona	6	6	0	0	13	4	18
Lokomotiv Moscow	6	2	1	3	5	7	7
Brugge	6	1	2	3	5	7	5
Galatasaray	6	1	1	4	5	10	4

Second Group Stage

Group A

Bayer Leverkusen 1 Barcelona 2
Newcastle United 1 Internazionale 4
Internazionale 3 Bayer Leverkusen 2
Barcelona 3 Newcastle United 1
Barcelona 3 Internazionale 0
Bayer Leverkusen 1 Newcastle United 3
Internazionale 0 Barcelona 0
Newcastle United 3 Bayer Leverkusen 1
Barcelona 2 Bayer Leverkusen 0
Internazionale 2 Newcastle United 2
Bayer Leverkusen 0 Internazionale 2
Newcastle United 0 Barcelona 2

	P	W	D	L	F	A	Pts
Barcelona	6	5	1	0	12	2	16
Internazionale	6	3	2	1	11	8	11
Newcastle United	6	2	1	3	10	13	7
Bayer Leverkusen	6	0	0	6	5	15	0

Group B

Roma 1 Arsenal 3
Valencia 1 Ajax 1
Ajax 2 Roma 1
Arsenal 0 Valencia 0
Arsenal 1 Ajax 1
Roma 0 Valencia 1
Ajax 0 Arsenal 0
Valencia 0 Roma 3
Arsenal 1 Roma 1
Ajax 1 Valencia 1
Roma 1 Ajax 1
Valencia 2 Arsenal 1

	P	W	D	L	F	A	Pts
Valencia	6	2	3	1	5	6	9
Ajax	6	1	5	0	6	5	8
Arsenal	6	1	4	1	6	5	7
Roma	6	1	2	3	7	8	5

Group C

Milan 1 Real Madrid 0
Lokomotiv Moscow 1 Borussia Dortmund 2
Borussia Dortmund 0 Milan 1
Real Madrid 2 Lokomotiv Moscow 2
Real Madrid 2 Borussia Dortmund 1
Milan 1 Lokomotiv Moscow 0
Borussia Dortmund 1 Real Madrid 1
Lokomotiv Moscow 0 Milan 1
Real Madrid 3 Milan 1
Borussia Dortmund 3 Lokomotiv Moscow 0
Milan 0 Borussia Dortmund 1
Lokomotiv Moscow 0 Real Madrid 1

	P	W	D	L	F	A	Pts
Milan	6	4	0	2	5	4	12
Real Madrid	6	3	2	1	9	6	11
Borussia Dortmund	6	3	1	2	8	5	10
Lokomotiv Moscow	6	0	1	5	3	10	1

Group D

Basle 1 Manchester United 3
Deportivo La Coruna 2 Juventus 2
Juventus 4 Basle 0
Manchester United 2 Deportivo La Coruna 0
Manchester United 2 Juventus 1
Basle 1 Deportivo La Coruna 0
Juventus 0 Manchester United 3
Deportivo La Coruna 1 Basle 0
Manchester United 1 Basle 1
Juventus 3 Deportivo La Coruna 2
Basle 2 Juventus 1
Deportivo La Coruna 2 Manchester United 0

	P	W	D	L	F	A	Pts
Manchester United	6	4	1	1	11	5	13
Juventus	6	2	1	3	11	11	7
Basle	6	2	1	3	5	10	7
Deportivo La Coruna	6	2	1	3	7	8	7

Quarter-finals

		1st leg	2nd leg	agg
Real Madrid	Manchester United	3-1	3-4	6-5
Internazionale	Valencia	1-0	1-2	2-2
Internazionale won on away goals				
Ajax	Milan	0-0	2-3	2-3
Juventus	Barcelona	1-1	2-1	3-2

Semi-finals

		1st leg	2nd leg	agg
Real Madrid	Juventus	2-1	1-3	3-4
Milan	Internazionale	0-0	1-1	1-1
Milan won on away goals				

Final

May 28 2003 Manchester
Milan 0   Juventus 0 (after extra time)
Milan won 3-2 on penalties
Milan: Dida, Costacurta (Roque Junior), Nesta, Maldini, Kaladze, Gattuso, Pirlo (Serginho), Rui Costa (Ambrosini), Seedorf, Shevchenko, Inzaghi
Juventus: Buffon, Thuram, Tudor (Birindelli), Ferrera, Montero, Tacchinardi, Davids (Zalayeta), Camoranesi (Conte), Zambrotta, Del Piero, Trezeguet
Referee: Merk (Germany)
Attendance: 63,300

2003-04

UEFA changed the format again for the 2003-04 season. The second group stage was dispensed with, being replaced by an extra knock-out round. The alteration reduced the excessive group matches, which had caused the competition to lose some focus in recent seasons, and pleased those nostalgic for the old knock-out European Cup. Another innovation – destined to last a single season – was the introduction of the silver goal rule as a means to settle drawn ties within extra time, replacing the use of the away goals rule within the added 30 minutes. Silver goal was a modification of the golden goal rule, used in some competitions, but not the Champions League, which stipulated that the first goal to be scored in extra time would win a match. The silver goal rule decreed that if one team was ahead at the end of the first 15 minute period of extra time, the match would end at that point. Whereas the golden goal was a single goal, under silver goal conditions more than one goal could be scored. Indeed it was possible for both teams to score the same amount of goals in the first 15 minutes, following which the match could be decided by further goals in the second 15 minutes – or penalties if extra time failed to split the teams.

The challenge from the British Isles opened with Chelsea, Celtic, and Rangers negotiating their way out of the qualifying stage. Newcastle United failed to join them in the group stage, as they were beaten by Partizan Belgrade on penalties, while Barry Town, Glentoran, and Bohemians made early exits. Benfica were the only former champions to fall in the qualifying stage, losing 4-1 on aggregate to Lazio.

Group E brought together Manchester United and Rangers, the reigning champions of England and Scotland respectively. United won both of the matches between the two teams, and topped the group, ahead of Stuttgart, while Rangers finished bottom. Arsenal won Group B in mixed fashion, failing to achieve a victory in any of their first three matches, but winning each of the remainder, including a brilliant 5-1 thrashing of Internazionale in Milan – Thierry Henry scoring twice, Frederik

Ljungberg, Edu, and Robert Pires once each. Another impressive English victory in Italy saw Chelsea beat Lazio 4-0, on their way to the top spot in Group G, while each team had a player sent off – Glen Johnson of Chelsea, and Sinisa Mihajlovic of Lazio. Celtic finished third in Group A, behind Lyon and Bayern Munich. Milan's defence of the title opened with them winning Group H, despite home defeats against both Brugge and Celta Vigo. In Group C, Monaco ran up an amazing 8-3 victory at home to Deportivo La Coruna, in which Dado Prso, a Croatian, scored four goals. Fifteen days earlier, the first match between the clubs, in Spain, had seen Deportivo win by a single goal. Both clubs eventually advanced from the group.

The 16 teams that emerged from the group stage moved into what UEFA, rather awkwardly, called the first knock-out round. Manchester United were now eliminated by Porto, a defeat that ended their run of reaching the quarter-finals each season from 1996-97 onwards. Porto won 2-1 at home, but United led for most of the match at Old Trafford, and looked set to take the tie on away goals, until Costinha equalised in the final minute. United's goal was scored by Paul Scholes, who later had a goal incorrectly disallowed for offside. Arsenal beat Celta Vigo 3-2 and 2-0, with Edu scoring twice in the first leg, while Henry did likewise in the return. Chelsea squeezed past Stuttgart by a single goal, an own goal scored by Fernando Meira. In the strongest tie of the round, Real Madrid accounted for Bayern Munich in a close contest, drawing 1-1 away, and then winning 1-0 at home. The elimination of both Bayern Munich and Stuttgart meant that no German club reached the last eight for a second successive season. There were mixed fortunes for the Italian clubs which had contested the 2003 final, as Milan beat Sparta Prague, but Juventus lost to Deportivo La Coruna. A double French success saw Lyon and Monaco beat Real Socieded and Lokomotiv Moscow respectively, with Monaco winning their tie on away goals.

Arsenal and Chelsea faced each other in the quarter-finals, with this being the first all-English tie in the European Cup since Nottingham Forest beat Liverpool at the start of the 1978-79 season. The first leg, at Chelsea's Stamford Bridge ground, was a 1-1 draw. Arsenal took the lead late in the first half at Highbury, through Jose Antonio Reyes (recently bought from Seville) but Chelsea staged a great fightback in the second half to win 2-1, with goals from Frank Lampard and Wayne Bridge. Elsewhere there were a couple of big surprises. Monaco lost 4-2 away to Real Madrid, but a 3-1 win in the return saw Monaco through on away goals, for the second successive round. Fernando Morientes, who was ironically on loan from Real Madrid, scored for Monaco in both legs. Morientes would finish the season as the Champions League's leading scorer, with nine goals. Deportivo La Coruna staged an even more dramatic comeback, losing 4-1 away to Milan before winning 4-0 at home. Porto continued their progress, with a win and a draw against Lyon.

In the semi-finals, Monaco won 3-1 at home to Chelsea, despite having Zikos sent off early in the second half, when the score was 1-1. Monaco won by raising their game, while Chelsea lost their shape, due to some ill-judged substitutions by Claudio Ranieri, their Italian coach. Back in London, Chelsea temporarily undid the damage, by moving into a two goal lead on the night, but Monaco fought back to draw the match 2-2, and win the tie 5-3 on aggregate. As in the quarter-finals, Fernando Morientes scored for Monaco in each leg. Defeat was a bitter blow for Chelsea, who had spent heavily on new players, trying to buy success, since the club was acquired by Roman Abramovich, a Russian multi-millionaire, in a surprise takeover the previous year. The other semi-final was a tight contest, in which Porto beat Deportivo La Coruna by a single goal – a penalty from Derlei in the second leg.

Monaco and Porto met in the final, at Gelsenkirchen, thus ending the dominance of Spain, Italy, Germany, and England, who had provided all of the teams that contested the seven finals from 1996-97 through to 2002-03. If the Netherlands were to be added to make the big four countries into a group of five, then Monaco and Porto were the first outsiders to reach the final since Marseille in 1993. Monaco were aiming to become the second French representatives to win the competition by emulating Marseille. Although Monaco is an independent principality, geographically situated within France, the club which take their name from the tiny territory play in the French league. They had finished as runners-up in France the previous season, behind Lyon. Monaco were coached by Didier Deschamps, winner of the trophy with Marseille in 1993 and Juventus in 1996. Porto were coached by Jose Mourinho, who had led them to both the Portuguese title and the UEFA Cup the previous season – the latter being won with a thrilling 3-2 victory against Celtic in the final. Porto's team for the final included six players who would feature for Portugal when their nation staged the European Championship finals a few weeks later – Ricardo Carvalho, Costinha, Deco, Paolo Ferreira, Maniche, and Nuno Valente. Portugal were to reach the Euro 2004 final, only to lose 1-0 against Greece, the surprise winners of the tournament.

The Champions League final began quietly, with few chances created by either team in the opening stage. Midway through the first half Prso came on as substitute for Monaco, replacing the injured Ludovic Giuly. Monaco had slightly the better of the early play, but it was Porto who took the lead, six minutes before half time, as Carlos Alberto, a 19-year-old Brazilian, scored with an opportunist volley. Monaco pressed hard during the second half, and created a series of goalscoring chances, but were caught out by Porto, who increased their lead with a breakaway goal 20 minutes from time. Dmitri Alenichev, who had arrived as a substitute for Carlos Alberto 12 minutes earlier, ran down the left wing, and then passed to Deco, who wrong-footed the retreating Monaco defenders with a fine shot from the edge of the penalty area. Four minutes later, another Porto attack down the left ended with Derlei feeding Alenichev, who drove the ball home from close range. This completed a 3-0 win for Porto, whose superiority over Monaco grew as the match progressed.

Porto thus regained the trophy they had previously won by beating Bayern Munich in the European Cup final 17 years earlier. After the match Jose Mourinho said: "I told my players before the game that we would never forget this day – even when we are very old – so they had better make sure the memories they took away were good. Now, as a manager, I want to do more. I have given my utmost for Porto, and I feel proud of what I have done here, but a few months ago I said that the country in which I would like to work is England. I have not changed my mind".

Mourinho arrived in England a few days later, to become the manager of Chelsea, with Abramovich having sacked Claudio Ranieri, despite the latter having taken the club to the Champions League semi-finals, plus second place in the Premiership, this season.

2003-04

First qualifying round

		1st leg	2nd leg	agg
Pyunik	KR Reykjavik	1-0	1-1	2-1
Serif	Flora Tallinn	1-0	1-1	2-1
HB Torshavn	FBK Kaunas	0-1	1-4	1-5
BATE Borisov	Bohemians	1-0	0-3	1-3
Vardar	Barry Town	3-0	1-2	4-2
Grevenmacher	Leotar	0-0	0-2	0-2
Glentoran	HJK Helsinki	0-0	0-1	0-1
Sliema Wanderers	Skonto Riga	2-0	1-3	3-3
Sliema Wanderers won on away goals				
Omonia Nicosia	Irtysh Pavlodar	0-0	2-1	2-1
Dynamo Tbilisi	SK Tirana	3-0	0-3	3-3
SK Tirana won 4-2 on penalties				

Second qualifying round

		1st leg	2nd leg	agg
MTK Budapest	HJK Helsinki	3-1	0-1	3-2
Pyunik	CSKA Sofia	0-2	0-1	0-3
FBK Kaunas	Celtic	0-4	0-1	0-5
Leotar	Slavia Prague	1-2	0-2	1-4
Serif	Shakhtor Donetsk	0-0	0-2	0-2
Zilina	Maccabi Tel-Aviv	1-0	1-1	2-1
Bohemians	Rosenborg	0-1	0-4	0-5
Maribor	Dynamo Zagreb	1-1	1-2	2-3
CSKA Moscow	Vardar	1-2	1-1	2-3
Rapid Bucharest	Anderlecht	0-0	2-3	2-3
Partizan Belgrade	Djurgardens	1-1	2-2	3-3
Partizan Belgrade won on away goals				
Wisla Krakow	Omonia Nicosia	5-2	2-2	7-4
FC Copenhagen	Sliema Wanderers	4-1	6-0	10-1
SK Tirana	Graz	1-5	1-2	2-7

Third qualifying round

		1st leg	2nd leg	agg
Vardar	Sparta Prague	2-3	2-2	4-5
MTK Budapest	Celtic	0-4	0-1	0-5
Rangers	FC Copenhagen	1-1	2-1	3-2
FK Austria	Marseille	0-1	0-0	0-1
Brugge	Borussia Dortmund	2-1	1-2	3-3
Brugge won 4-2 on penalties				
Shakhtor Donetsk	Lokomotiv Moscow	1-0	1-3	2-3
Lazio	Benfica	3-1	1-0	4-1
Dynamo Kiev	Dynamo Zagreb	3-1	2-0	5-1
Rosenborg	Deportivo La Coruna	0-0	0-1	0-1
Grasshoppers	AEK Athens	1-0	1-3	2-3
Zilina	Chelsea	0-2	0-3	0-5
Celta Vigo	Slavia Prague	3-0	0-2	3-2
Partizan Belgrade	Newcastle United	0-1	1-0	1-1
Partizan Belgrade won 4-3 on penalties				
Galatasaray	CSKA Sofia	3-0	3-0	6-0
Anderlecht	Wisla Krakow	3-1	1-0	4-1
Graz	Ajax	1-1	1-2	2-3

Group Stage

Group A

Lyon 1 Anderlecht 0
Bayern Munich 2 Celtic 1
Celtic 2 Lyon 0
Anderlecht 1 Bayern Munich 1
Anderlecht 1 Celtic 0
Lyon 1 Bayern Munich 1
Celtic 3 Anderlecht 1
Bayern Munich 1 Lyon 2
Anderlecht 1 Lyon 0
Celtic 0 Bayern Munich 0
Lyon 3 Celtic 2
Bayern Munich 1 Anderlecht 0

	P	W	D	L	F	A	Pts
Lyon	6	3	1	2	7	7	10
Bayern Munich	6	2	3	1	6	5	9
Celtic	6	2	1	3	8	7	7
Anderlecht	6	2	1	3	4	6	7

Group B

Dynamo Kiev 2 Lokomotiv Moscow 0
Arsenal 0 Internazionale 3
Internazionale 2 Dynamo Kiev 1
Lokomotiv Moscow 0 Arsenal 0
Lokomotiv Moscow 3 Internazionale 0
Dynamo Kiev 2 Arsenal 1
Internazionale 1 Lokomotiv Moscow 1
Arsenal 1 Dynamo Kiev 0
Lokomotiv Moscow 3 Dynamo Kiev 2
Internazionale 1 Arsenal 5
Dynamo Kiev 1 Internazionale 1
Arsenal 2 Lokomotiv Moscow 0

	P	W	D	L	F	A	Pts
Arsenal	6	3	1	2	9	6	10
Lokomotiv Moscow	6	2	2	2	7	7	8
Internazionale	6	2	2	2	8	11	8
Dynamo Kiev	6	2	1	3	8	8	7

Group C

AEK Athens 1 Deportivo La Coruna 1
PSV Eindhoven 1 Monaco 2
Monaco 4 AEK Athens 0
Deportivo La Coruna 2 PSV Eindhoven 0
Deportivo La Coruna 1 Monaco 0
AEK Athens 0 PSV Eindhoven 1
Monaco 8 Deportivo La Coruna 3
PSV Eindhoven 2 AEK Athens 0
Deportivo La Coruna 3 AEK Athens 0
Monaco 1 PSV Eindhoven 1
AEK Athens 0 Monaco 0
PSV Eindhoven 3 Deportivo La Coruna 2

	P	W	D	L	F	A	Pts
Monaco	6	3	2	1	15	6	11
Deportivo La Coruna	6	3	1	2	12	12	10
PSV Eindhoven	6	3	1	2	8	7	10
AEK Athens	6	0	2	4	1	11	2

Group D

Juventus 2 Galatasaray 1
Real Sociedad 1 Olympiakos 0
Olympiakos 1 Juventus 2
Galatasaray 1 Real Sociedad 2
Galatasaray 1 Olympiakos 0
Juventus 4 Real Sociedad 2
Olympiakos 3 Galatasaray 0
Real Sociedad 0 Juventus 0
Olympiakos 2 Real Sociedad 2
Galatasaray 2 Juventus 0
Juventus 7 Olympiakos 0
Real Sociedad 1 Galatasaray 1

	P	W	D	L	F	A	Pts
Juventus	6	4	1	1	15	6	13
Real Sociedad	6	2	3	1	8	8	9
Galatasaray	6	2	1	3	6	8	7
Olympiakos	6	1	1	4	6	13	4

Group E

Rangers 2 Stuttgart 1

Manchester United 5 Panathinaikos 0
Panathinaikos 1 Rangers 1
Stuttgart 2 Manchester United 1
Stuttgart 2 Panathinaikos 0
Rangers 0 Manchester United 1
Panathinaikos 1 Stuttgart 3
Manchester United 3 Rangers 0
Stuttgart 1 Rangers 0
Panathinaikos 0 Manchester United 1
Rangers 1 Panathinaikos 3
Manchester United 2 Stuttgart 0

	P	W	D	L	F	A	Pts
Manchester United	6	5	0	1	13	2	15
Stuttgart	6	4	0	2	9	6	12
Panathinaikos	6	1	1	4	5	13	4
Rangers	6	1	1	4	4	10	4

Group F

Real Madrid 4 Marseille 2
Partizan Belgrade 1 Porto 1
Porto 1 Real Madrid 3
Marseille 3 Partizan Belgrade 0
Marseille 2 Porto 3
Real Madrid 1 Partizan Belgrade 0
Porto 1 Marseille 0
Partizan Belgrade 0 Real Madrid 0
Marseille 1 Real Madrid 2
Porto 2 Partizan Belgrade 1
Real Madrid 1 Porto 1
Partizan Belgrade 1 Marseille 1

	P	W	D	L	F	A	Pts
Real Madrid	6	4	2	0	11	5	14
Porto	6	3	2	1	9	8	11
Marseille	6	1	1	4	9	11	4
Partizan Belgrade	6	0	3	3	3	8	3

Group G

Sparta Prague 0 Chelsea 1
Besiktas 0 Lazio 2
Lazio 2 Sparta Prague 2
Chelsea 0 Besiktas 2
Chelsea 2 Lazio 1
Sparta Prague 2 Besiktas 1
Lazio 0 Chelsea 4
Besiktas 1 Sparta Prague 0
Chelsea 0 Sparta Prague 0
Lazio 1 Besiktas 1
Sparta Prague 1 Lazio 0
Besiktas 0 Chelsea 2

	P	W	D	L	F	A	Pts
Chelsea	6	4	1	1	9	3	13
Sparta Prague	6	2	2	2	5	5	8
Besiktas	6	2	1	3	5	7	7
Lazio	6	1	2	3	6	10	5

Group H

Milan 1 Ajax 0
Brugge 1 Celta Vigo 1
Celta Vigo 0 Milan 0

```
                    Ajax 2 Brugge 0
                    Ajax 1 Celta Vigo 0
                    Milan 0 Brugge 1
                    Celta Vigo 3 Ajax 2
                    Brugge 0 Milan 1
                    Ajax 0 Milan 1
                    Celta Vigo 1 Brugge 1
                    Milan 1 Celta Vigo 2
                    Brugge 2 Ajax 1
```

	P	W	D	L	F	A	Pts
Milan	6	3	1	2	4	3	10
Celta Vigo	6	2	3	1	7	6	9
Brugge	6	2	2	2	5	6	8
Ajax	6	2	0	4	6	7	6

First knock-out round

		1st leg	2nd leg	agg
Stuttgart	Chelsea	0-1	0-0	0-1
Porto	Manchester United	2-1	1-1	3-2
Real Sociedad	Lyon	0-1	0-1	0-2
Celta Vigo	Arsenal	2-3	0-2	2-5
Bayern Munich	Real Madrid	1-1	0-1	1-2
Sparta Prague	Milan	0-0	1-4	1-4
Deportivo La Coruna	Juventus	1-0	1-0	2-0
Lokomotiv Moscow	Monaco	2-1	0-1	2-2

Monaco won on away goals

Quarter-finals

		1st leg	2nd leg	agg
Porto	Lyon	2-0	2-2	4-2
Real Madrid	Monaco	4-2	1-3	5-5

Monaco on away goals

		1st leg	2nd leg	agg
Chelsea	Arsenal	1-1	2-1	3-2
Milan	Deportivo La Coruna	4-1	0-4	4-5

Semi-finals

		1st leg	2nd leg	agg
Monaco	Chelsea	3-1	2-2	5-3
Porto	Deportivo La Coruna	0-0	1-0	1-0

Final

May 26 2004 Gelsenkirchen

Porto 3   Monaco 0

Carlos Alberto

Deco

Alenichev

Porto: Vitor Baia, Paulo Ferreira, Jorge Costa, Ricardo Carvalho, Nuno Valente, Pedro Mendes, Costinha, Maniche, Deco (Pedro Emanuel), Carlos Alberto (Alenichev), Derlei (McCarthy)

Monaco: Roma, Ibarra, Rodriguez, Givet (Squillaci), Evra, Cisse (Nonda), Bernardi, Zikos, Giuly (Prso), Rothen, Morientes.

HT: 1-0

Referee: Nielson (Denmark)

Attendance: 53,053

2004-05

The 50th season of the European Cup/Champions League brought together 72 teams from 48 countries – with Andorra, Kazakhstan, Liechtenstein, and San Marino being the only members of UEFA not represented. Five of the sixteen clubs that had featured in the inaugural European Champion Clubs' Cup of 1955-56 also appeared in the UEFA Champions League of 2004-05, namely Anderlecht, Djurgardens, Milan, PSV Eindhoven, and Real Madrid. Meanwhile 12 of the 16 countries represented in 1955-56 maintained their record of participation in every season of the European Cup/Champions League – Austria, Belgium, Denmark, France, Germany/West Germany, Hungary, Poland, Portugal, Scotland, Spain, Sweden, and Switzerland. The 2004-05 competition was played in a very different Europe from that in which the European Cup had been launched half a century earlier. The divisions of the Cold War had ended during the intervening period, and the dominant political theme in early 21st century Europe was the development of the European Union. At the start of 2002, the majority of the member states, but not the United Kingdom, switched from their national currencies to the new Euro. May 2004 brought a major expansion of the European Union, with the accession of ten states, mostly from eastern Europe, increasing the membership to a total of 25 countries.

Shelbourne, from the Republic of Ireland, enjoyed a good run in the qualifying stage, eliminating KR Reykjavik and Hajduk Split, and then holding Deportivo La Coruna – semi finalists the previous season – to a goalless draw, before losing the return 3-0. Liverpool were grateful for Steven Gerrard's two goals away to Graz in the qualifying round as they lost 1-0 at home. Two goals from new signing Alan Smith helped Manchester United through qualifying, too, but Rangers were eliminated. Benfica and Red Star Belgrade, former winners of the competition, also departed in the qualifiers. Real Madrid, who finished fourth in the Spanish league the previous season, opened their Champions League campaign with a 5-1 aggregate win against Wisla Krakow with Fernando Morientes (later to join Liverpool) and Ronaldo each scoring twice.

Porto's defence of the trophy began in Group H, where they were paired with Chelsea, the club to which Jose Mourinho, their manager, had moved at the end of the previous season. Porto needed a late winner from Benni McCarthy against Chelsea in their last match to reach the next stage, a point ahead of CSKA Moscow. It was the Londoners' only defeat in the group. Arsenal, unbeaten in their 38 Premiership games the previous season, drew four games, and won two, in Group E, to finish ahead of PSV Eindhoven on head-to-head record. Manchester United emerged as runners-up in Group D, behind Lyon with Ruud Van Nistelrooy scoring eight of United's fourteen goals, including all four in the 4-1 win against Sparta Prague. Van Nistelrooy did not score any other goals in this season's competition, but he finished as the leading scorer, for the third time in four seasons. Wayne Rooney, who emerged as a star for England in the Euro 2004 finals at the age of eighteen, following which he was bought by Manchester United from Everton for £25,000,000, netted a hat-trick in his Champions League debut, as Fenerbahce were beaten 6-2. United's 2-1 win against Lyon was achieved in Alex Ferguson's 1000th match as manager of the club. Liverpool squeezed into the knock-out stage, a second half comeback bringing a 3-1 win against Olympiakos in their last match, with their third, and decisive, goal being scored by Gerrard, with a twenty five yard shot four minutes from time. This was just enough to make Liverpool runners-up in Group A, ahead of Olympiakos on head-to-head, but a couple of points behind Monaco, while Deportivo La Coruna finished bottom of the group, without scoring a goal.

All four English teams thus advanced, but Celtic finished bottom of their group, which was won by Milan, while Barcelona were runners-up. Besides Milan, two other Italian clubs, Internazionale and Juventus, won a group, but Roma exited in disgrace. Roma's first match, at home to Dynamo Kiev, was abandoned at half time by Swedish referee Anders Frisk after he was struck by an object thrown from the crowd. UEFA subsequently awarded the match to Dynamo Kiev, appearing in the competition for a twelfth successive season, with a 3-0 scoreline. Roma took only a single point in the group, which was won by Bayer Leverkusen, ahead of Real Madrid on head-to-head record.

Following the winter break, the highlight of the first knock-out round was the clash between Chelsea and Barcelona. Back in 2000 Jose Mourinho had been an assistant coach for the Catalan club when they eliminated Chelsea. Now he led Chelsea against the Spaniards. The Londoners took a first half lead at the Nou Camp, as a cross from Damien Duff was deflected into his own net by Barcelona's Juliano Belletti but early in the second half Chelsea's Didier Drogba was sent off and Barcelona gained control, going on to win 2-1, with goals from Maxi Lopez and Samuel Eto'o. The match was surrounded by acrimonious exchanges between Mourinho and Frank Rijkaard, the Barcelona coach. Mourinho accused Rijkaard of intimidating referee Frisk at half time. Amid the ensuing recriminations, Frisk announced his retirement from refereeing, having received death threats from Chelsea supporters. In the second leg Chelsea rushed to a 3-0 lead in the first twenty minutes only for Ronaldinho to inspire a Barcelona revival. He pulled a goal back with a penalty and reduced the deficit on the night to 3-2 before half time, with some deceptive footwork and a brilliant shot from the edge of the penalty area. The aggregate score was now level, with Barcelona ahead on away goals. Barcelona held the initiative for most of the second half, but a headed goal from John Terry fourteen minutes from time gave Chelsea a 4-2 win, and a 5-4 aggregate success, although referee Pierluigi Collina failed to spot a foul by Ricardo Carvalho on Barcelona goalkeeper Victor Valdes as Terry's header went past him.

Luis Garcia scored three times as Liverpool progressed with a pair of fine 3-1 wins against Bayer Leverkusen – reversing the defeat against the German club in 2002. But Arsenal performed badly in losing 3-1 away to Bayern Munich and although they won the return at Highbury it was by a single goal from Thierry Henry. Manchester United, appearing in the Champions League for the ninth successive season, departed with a pair of 1-0 defeats against Milan. Both Milan's goals were scored by Hernan Crespo, an Argentinian on loan from Chelsea. Porto's run was ended by Internazionale, with Adriano scoring a second leg hat-trick. Monaco, the previous season's runners-up, also departed, losing to PSV Eindhoven. Juventus eliminated Real Madrid, with Marcelo Zalayeta scoring the decisive goal four minutes from the end of extra time. Lyon surprised Werder Bremen with a 3-0 win in Germany, and won the return 7-2 – Sylvain Wiltord scored a hat-trick in the latter match.

In the quarter-finals, Chelsea disposed of Bayern Munich, winning 6-5 on aggregate. They took control of the tie with a 4-2 win at Stamford Bridge, in which Frank Lampard scored twice. A solid performance during most of the return match saw Chelsea through to the last four, although a couple of late goals left Bayern as 3-2 winners of the game. The draw brought together Liverpool and Juventus, for their first meeting since the 1985 final before which 39 Juventus fans died. Both clubs made gestures of friendship and the games passed without incident. A great display from Liverpool gave them a 2-1 win at home, with goals from Sami Hyppia and Luis Garcia, while staunch defending by Liverpool in the return led to a 0-0 draw. Milan and Internazionale met twice at the stadium they shared, just as they had in 2003. Milan won their home leg 2-0, and were leading 1-0 in the second leg when the match was abandoned by Markus

Merk as Internazionale supporters threw firecrackers on to the pitch. One hit Milan goalkeeper Dida and UEFA subsequently awarded the second leg to Milan 3-0 and fined Internazionale £132,000. They were also ordered to play their next four home matches in European competition behind closed doors. In the remaining quarter-final, PSV Eindhoven beat Lyon on penalties, after a pair of 1-1 draws.

Having faced Arsenal in the previous season's quarter-finals, Chelsea now met Liverpool in the semi-final. The first leg, at Stamford Bridge, was tense and goalless while Liverpool took the lead three minutes into the second leg in controversial circumstances. A pass from Steven Gerrard found Milan Baros, whose run was blocked by Petr Cech, the Chelsea goalkeeper. The ball was hooked towards goal by Luis Garcia and appeared to have crossed the line before William Gallas cleared it. Lubos Michel, the Slovakian referee, awarded a goal on the basis of a judgement from his assistant, but it was not certain from television replays that the whole of the ball had crossed the line. On the other hand, if the goal had not been awarded, it appeared likely that the referee would have awarded Liverpool a penalty, and sent off Cech for a foul on Baros. Chelsea controlled the remainder of the play, but their football lacked the quality which had made them English champions for the first time since 1955 – a title confirmed in the interval between the Champions League matches against Liverpool – while Liverpool defended with great strength. The referee added six minutes of stoppage time at the end of the second half, and in the last of these minutes Chelsea's Eidur Gudjohnsen hit a powerful shot just inches wide of a post. In the other tie, Milan won 2-0 at home to PSV Eindhoven. The Dutch club built up a two goal lead in the return, and extra time beckoned, until Massimo Ambrosini scored a decisive goal for Milan in stoppage time. PSV in turn scored during the remainder of stoppage time, but their 3-1 win was not enough, as Milan progressed on away goals, with the aggregate score level at 3-3.

The final was played on May 25, the anniversary of Liverpool's win in 1977, before a crowd of 69,600, who had paid prices ranging from 50 Euros (about £34) to 150 Euros (about £103) for their tickets. Liverpool were managed by Rafael Benitez, a Spaniard who had led Valencia to win both the Spanish league and the UEFA Cup the previous season. Benitez had brought several Spanish players to Anfield, but more importantly, he had restored the tactical strength that had often been missing at Liverpool during recent years. A series of gritty displays, with solid defending and spells of inspired attack, had seen Liverpool through to the Champions League final, despite uneven form in the domestic game. Appearing in their first final since 1985, and the Heysel disaster, Liverpool were attempting to add to the European titles they had won in 1977, 1978, 1981, and 1984. The club had not actually won the English title since 1990, and had scraped into the Champions League by finishing fourth in the Premiership at the end of the 2003-04 season. Milan – reigning Italian champions, having finished eleven points clear of runners-up Roma in Serie A the previous season – had an even better record in the European Cup/Champions League than Liverpool, having won the trophy six times, and been runners-up three times. They were coached by Carlo Ancelotti, who had led them to victory in the final a couple of years earlier, and retained Dida, Gennaro Gattuso, Paolo Maldini, Alessandro Nesta, Andrea Pirlo, Clarence Seedorf, and Andrei Shevchenko from the team that had beaten Juventus. Shevchenko, who had scored the winning penalty in the 2003 final, won the European Footballer of the Year award at the end of 2004.

Milan took the lead in the 50th final after just 50 seconds, as a free kick from Andrea Pirlo on the right flank was met in the penalty area by Paolo Maldini, who scored with a volley. Maldini, aged 36, thereby became the oldest player ever to score in a final – this was his seventh final.

After an attacking flurry from Liverpool in the next few minutes, Milan took control of the play, with some superb passing and movement.

Seven minutes before half time Liverpool had a good appeal for a penalty when Nesta appeared to use his arm to block the ball as Luis Garcia ran into the penalty area, but Manuel Mejuto Gonzalez, the Spanish referee, waved play on. Milan immediately counter-attacked, with Kaka running at the Liverpool defence, and finding Shevchenko, whose cross was turned into the net by Crespo. Milan struck again a couple of minutes before the interval, with an outstanding goal, as a long range pass from Kaka found Crespo, who chipped the ball over the advancing Jerzy Dudek to give Milan a 3-0 half time lead.

The Italian club resumed their dominance at the start of the second half, and Dudek had to make a great save at full-stretch to deny Shevchenko. But eight minutes after the re-start Gerrard scored, meeting a cross from John Arne Riise on the left with a powerful header. This was the start of a remarkable Liverpool recovery, inspired by Gerrard, their captain and midfield dynamo. Two minutes later Vladimir Smicer scored with a 20 yard shot, to further reduce the deficit. Following this Gerrard was brought down by Gattuso as he ran towards goal, and Liverpool were awarded a penalty. Xabi Alonso's attempt was parried by Dida, but the Liverpool player drove the loose ball into the roof of the net. A trio of goals in the space of just six minutes had brought Liverpool level at 3-3. They continued to take the game to Milan, but the Italians soon regained their composure. With twenty minutes remaining an error by Dudek allowed Shevchenko a chance, but Liverpool's Djimi Traore cleared the effort off the goal-line. The remainder of the second half saw a continuation of the thrilling football, with both teams creating several chances, but there were no further goals.

The game therefore moved into extra time. Liverpool's exertions in the second half had left some of their players feeling drained, and they struggled during the added 30 minutes, as Milan regained the initiative. A tactical reorganisation had seen Gerrard filling in at right back, from where he made several telling interceptions while the only other English player in the Liverpool line-up, Jamie Carragher, performed brilliantly in defence, despite needing treatment for cramp. Dudek, from Poland, was also inspired, and made an amazing double save from Shevchenko a couple of minutes from the end of extra time, as Liverpool held out to reach a penalty contest.

As the players prepared for the penalties, Carragher suggested to Dudek that the goalkeeper attempt to distract the Milan penalty takers, just as Bruce Grobbelaar had done when Liverpool beat Roma in the 1984 final. Dudek put on an even more theatrical display than Grobbelaar, alternating the wobbly legs routine with some wandering up and down the goal-line, and the waving of his arms. This had the desired effect, as Serginho put Milan's first kick over the bar, following which Dudek saved from Pirlo. Dietmar Hamman and Djibril Cisse scored from Liverpool's first two kicks. Tomasson scored to get Milan off the mark, following which Dida saved from Riise. Kaka scored from the next penalty, to put Milan level at 2-2, but Liverpool still had a kick in hand. Smicer scored to restore Liverpool's lead. Milan's fifth penalty was taken by Shevchenko, and saved by Dudek. Liverpool had won the penalty contest 3-2, to complete their transformation of the match.

Besides the quality of the play, and the drama, the 2005 final was notable in other respects. With the match having kicked off at 9.45pm local time, the penalty contest which decided the outcome was not completed until half an hour after midnight. The six goals made this the highest scoring final since Benfica beat Real Madrid 5-3 in 1962, while Liverpool were the first team ever to win the final after trailing by three goals – albeit with the aid of a penalty contest. Milan could count themselves unlucky to lose a final in which they had scored three goals – a fate previously experienced by Stade de Reims in 1956, Eintracht Frankfurt in 1960, and Real Madrid in 1962. Indeed Milan were the first beaten finalists to score more than one goal since Real Madrid 43 years earlier.

Steven Gerrard collected the trophy, to the cheers of about 30,000 Liverpool fans who had made the long journey to Turkey, and summed up the victory by saying: "Milan outplayed us in the first half, but ours was a terrific second half performance. 3-0 down at half time and I thought I was going to be in tears at the final whistle, but every one of us deserved this. We were all gone in extra time, cramping up, but we kept going and I'm just on top of the world. The fans are the twelfth man, they deserve this as much as the players. All credit to Benitez, he wouldn't let us put our heads down. He told us the game wasn't over and we knew if we got an early goal, we were back in it. This is the best feeling of my life".

The following evening an estimated 500,000 people gathered on the streets of Liverpool, as the team took a bus tour of the city to display the trophy. Having won the competition for a fifth time, Liverpool had been awarded permanent possession of the current trophy, the fifth club to be accorded this honour, the others being Real Madrid (on their sixth title in 1966), Ajax plus Bayern Munich (as they each completed a hat-trick of titles in the 1970s), and Milan (when they were champions for a fifth time in 1994). Although Liverpool had the European trophy, and a place in the forthcoming Club World Championship, it appeared they would not defend their trophy as they had finished only fifth in the 2004-05 Premiership. The Football Association had announced that as usual England's entrants in the 2005-06 Champions League would be the first four in the Premiership, Chelsea, Arsenal, Manchester United, and Everton. Liverpool and the Football Association lobbied UEFA, and on June 10 UEFA announced that Liverpool would be allowed to defend their title provided they started in the first qualifying round.

The 2005 final was a fitting a climax to the fiftieth season of the European Cup/Champions League. The competition continued to provide football of the highest quality, that fascinated millions of people throughout Europe. Twenty one years after their success in 1984, Liverpool had won the trophy again. This echoed the revivals in recent years from Real Madrid, Manchester United, Bayern Munich, Milan, and Porto – fellow giants of European football who had regained the continental title after long spells of frustration. The dramatic contest between Liverpool and Milan demonstrated why football is the beautiful game, and maintained the best traditions of the European Cup/Champions League.

2004-05

First qualifying round

		1st leg	2nd leg	agg
KR Reykjavík	Shelbourne	2-2	0-0	2-2
Shelbourne won on away goals				
Skonto Riga	Rhyl	4-0	3-1	7-1
Flora Tallinn	Gorica	2-4	1-3	3-7
Linfield	HJK Helsinki	0-1	0-1	0-2
Pobeda	Pyunik	1-3	1-1	2-4
Serif	Jeunesse D'Esch	2-0	0-1	2-1
Georgia Tbilisi	HB Torshavn	5-0	0-3	5-3
Sliema Wanderers	FBK Kaunas	0-2	1-4	1-6
Siroki Brijeg	Neftchi	2-1	0-1	2-2
Neftchi won on away goals				
Gomel	SK Tirana	0-2	1-0	1-2

Second qualifying round

		1st leg	2nd leg	agg
Pyunik	Shaktor Donetsk	1-3	0-1	1-4
Apoel Nicosia	Sparta Prague	2-2	1-2	3-4
Rosenborg	Serif	2-1	2-0	4-1
Young Boys Berne	Red Star Belgrade	2-2	0-3	2-5
Gorica	FC Copenhagen	1-2	5-0	6-2
Neftch	CSKA Moscow	0-0	0-2	0-2
MSK Zilina	Dynamo Bucharest	0-1	0-1	0-2
HJK Helsinki	Maccabi Tel-Aviv	0-0	0-1	0-1
Skonto Riga	Trabzonspor	1-1	0-3	1-4
Brugge	Lokomotiv Plovdiv	2-0	4-0	6-0
SK Tirana	Ferencvaros	2-3	1-0	3-3

Ferencvaros won on away goals

		1st leg	2nd leg	agg
Hajduk Split	Shelbourne	3-2	0-2	3-4
Djurgardens	FBK Kaunas	0-0	2-0	2-0
WIT Georgia	Wisla Krakow	2-8	0-3	2-11

Third qualifying round

		1st leg	2nd leg	agg
Graz	Liverpool	0-2	1-0	1-2
Juventus	Djurgardens	2-2	4-1	6-3
Ferencvaros	Sparta Prague	1-0	0-2	1-2
Rosenborg	Maccabi Haifa	2-1	3-2	5-3
Bayer Leverkusen	Banik Ostrava	5-0	1-2	6-2
CSKA Moscow	Rangers	2-1	1-1	3-2
Shaktor Donetsk	Brugge	4-1	2-2	6-3
Dynamo Kiev	Trabzonspor	1-2	2-0	3-2
Red Star Belgrade	PSV Eindhoven	3-2	0-5	3-7
Dynamo Bucharest	Manchester United	1-2	0-3	1-5
Basle	Internazionale	1-1	1-4	2-5
Benfica	Anderlecht	1-0	0-3	1-3
Shelbourne	Deportivo La Coruna	0-0	0-3	0-3
PAOK Salonika	Maccabi Tel-Aviv	0-3	0-1	0-4

Maccabi Tel-Aviv won the first leg 2-1, but PAOK Salonika fielded an ineligible player, and the match was awarded to Maccabi Tel-Aviv 3-0.

		1st leg	2nd leg	agg
Gorica	Monaco	0-3	0-6	0-9
Wisla Krakow	Real Madrid	0-2	1-3	1-5

Group Stage

Group A

Liverpool 2 Monaco 0
Deportivo La Coruna 0 Olympiakos 0
Monaco 2 Deportivo La Coruna 0
Olympiakos 1 Liverpool 0
Liverpool 0 Deportivo La Coruna 0
Monaco 2 Olympiakos 1
Deportivo La Coruna 0 Liverpool 1
Olympiakos 1 Monaco 0
Monaco 1 Liverpool 0
Olympiakos 1 Deportivo La Coruna 0
Deportivo La Coruna 0 Monaco 5
Liverpool 3 Olympiakos 1

	P	W	D	L	F	A	Pts
Monaco	6	4	0	2	10	4	12
Liverpool	6	3	1	2	6	3	10
Olympiakos	6	3	1	2	5	5	10
Deportivo La Coruna	6	0	2	4	0	9	2

Group B

Bayer Leverkusen 3 Real Madrid 0
Roma 0 Dynamo Kiev 3
Match abandoned with Dynamo Kiev leading 1-0. Match awarded to Dynamo Kiev 3-0.
Dynamo Kiev 4 Bayer Leverkusen 2
Real Madrid 4 Roma 2
Real Madrid 1 Dynamo Kiev 0
Bayer Leverkusen 3 Roma 1
Dynamo Kiev 2 Real Madrid 2
Roma 1 Bayer Leverkusen 1
Real Madrid 1 Bayer Leverkusen 1
Dynamo Kiev 2 Roma 0
Bayer Leverkusen 3 Dynamo Kiev 0
Roma 0 Real Madrid 3

	P	W	D	L	F	A	Pts
Bayer Leverkusen	6	3	2	1	13	7	11
Real Madrid	6	3	2	1	11	8	11
Dynamo Kiev	6	3	1	2	11	8	10
Roma	6	0	1	5	4	16	1

Group C

Ajax 0 Juventus 1
Maccabi Tel-Aviv 0 Bayern Munich 1
Bayern Munich 4 Ajax 0
Juventus 1 Maccabi Tel-Aviv 0
Juventus 1 Bayern Munich 0
Ajax 3 Maccabi Tel-Aviv 0
Bayern Munich 0 Juventus 1
Maccabi Tel-Aviv 2 Ajax 1
Juventus 1 Ajax 0
Bayern Munich 5 Maccabi Tel-Aviv 1
Ajax 2 Bayern Munich 2
Maccabi Tel-Aviv 1 Juventus 1

	P	W	D	L	F	A	Pts
Juventus	6	5	1	0	6	1	16
Bayern Munich	6	3	1	2	12	5	10
Ajax	6	1	1	4	6	10	4
Maccabi Tel-Aviv	6	1	1	4	4	12	4

Group D

Fenerbahce 1 Sparta Prague 0
Lyon 2 Manchester United 2
Manchester United 6 Fenerbahce 2
Sparta Prague 1 Lyon 2
Sparta Prague 0 Manchester United 0
Fenerbahce 1 Lyon 3
Manchester United 4 Sparta Prague 1
Lyon 4 Fenerbahce 2
Sparta Prague 0 Fenerbahce 1
Manchester United 2 Lyon 1
Fenerbahce 3 Manchester United 0
Lyon 5 Sparta Prague 0

	P	W	D	L	F	A	Pts
Lyon	6	4	1	1	17	8	13
Manchester United	6	3	2	1	14	9	11
Fenerbahce	6	3	0	3	10	13	9
Sparta Prague	6	0	1	5	2	13	1

Group E

Panathinaikos 2 Rosenborg 1
Arsenal 1 PSV Eindhoven 0
PSV Eindhoven 1 Panathinaikos 0
Rosenborg 1 Arsenal 1
Rosenborg 1 PSV Eindhoven 2
Panathinaikos 2 Arsenal 2
PSV Eindhoven 1 Rosenborg 0
Arsenal 1 Panathinaikos 1
Rosenborg 2 Panathinaikos 2
PSV Eindhoven 1 Arsenal 1
Panathinaikos 4 PSV Eindhoven 1
Arsenal 5 Rosenborg 1

	P	W	D	L	F	A	Pts
Arsenal	6	2	4	0	12	7	10
PSV Eindhoven	6	3	1	2	7	8	10
Panathinaikos	6	2	3	1	11	8	9
Rosenborg	6	0	2	4	6	13	2

Group F

Celtic 1 Barcelona 3
Shaktjor Donetsk 0 Milan 1
Barcelona 3 Shaktjor Donetsk 0
Milan 3 Celtic 1
Milan 1 Barcelona 0
Shaktjor Donetsk 3 Celtic 0
Barcelona 2 Milan 1
Celtic 1 Shaktjor Donetsk 0
Milan 4 Shaktjor Donetsk 0
Barcelona 1 Celtic 1
Shaktjor Donetsk 2 Barcelona 0
Celtic 0 Milan 0

	P	W	D	L	F	A	Pts
Milan	6	4	1	1	10	3	13
Barcelona	6	3	1	2	9	6	10
Shaktjor Donetsk	6	2	0	4	5	9	6
Celtic	6	1	2	3	4	10	5

Group G

Valencia 2 Anderlecht 0
Internazionale 2 Werder Bremen 0
Werder Bremen 2 Valencia 1
Anderlecht 1 Internazionale 3
Anderlecht 1 Werder Bremen 2
Valencia 1 Internazionale 5
Werder Bremen 5 Anderlecht 1
Internazionale 0 Valencia 0
Anderlecht 1 Valencia 2
Werder Bremen 1 Internazionale 1
Valencia 0 Werder Bremen 2
Internazionale 3 Anderlecht 0

	P	W	D	L	F	A	Pts
Internazionale	6	4	2	0	14	3	14
Werder Bremen	6	4	1	1	12	6	13
Valencia	6	2	1	3	6	10	7
Anderlecht	6	0	0	6	4	17	0

Group H

Paris Saint-Germain 0 Chelsea 3

Porto 0 CSKA Moscow 0
CSKA Moscow 2 Paris Saint-Germain 0
Chelsea 3 Porto 1
Chelsea 2 CSKA Moscow 0
Paris Saint-Germain 2 Porto 0
CSKA Moscow 0 Chelsea 1
Porto 0 Paris Saint-Germain 0
CSKA Moscow 0 Porto 1
Chelsea 0 Paris Saint-Germain 0
Paris Saint-Germain 1 CSKA Moscow 3
Porto 2 Chelsea 1

	P	W	D	L	F	A	Pts
Chelsea	6	4	1	1	10	3	13
Porto	6	2	2	2	4	6	8
CSKA Moscow	6	2	1	3	5	5	7
Paris Saint-Germain	6	1	2	3	3	8	5

First knock-out round

		1st leg	2nd leg	agg
Real Madrid	Juventus	1-0	0-2	1-2
Porto	Internazionale	1-1	1-3	2-4
Barcelona	Chelsea	2-1	2-4	4-5
Werder Bremen	Lyon	0-3	2-7	2-10
Liverpool	Bayer Leverkusen	3-1	3-1	6-2
PSV Eindhoven	Monaco	1-0	2-0	3-0
Manchester United	Milan	0-1	0-1	0-2
Bayern Munich	Arsenal	3-1	0-1	3-2

Quarter-finals

		1st leg	2nd leg	agg
Liverpool	Juventus	2-1	0-0	2-1
Lyon	PSV Eindhoven	1-1	1-1	2-2

PSV Eindhoven won 4-2 on penalties

		1st leg	2nd leg	agg
Chelsea	Bayern Munich	4-2	2-3	6-5
Milan	Internazionale	2-0	3-0	5-0

Second leg abandoned with Milan leading 1-0. Match awarded to Milan 3-0.

Semi-finals

		1st leg	2nd leg	agg
Milan	PSV Eindhoven	2-0	1-3	3-3

Milan won on away goals

		1st leg	2nd leg	agg
Chelsea	Liverpool	0-0	0-1	0-1

Final
May 25 2005 Istanbul

Liverpool 3	Milan 3 (after extra time)
Gerrard	Maldini
Smicer	Crespo 2
Xabi Alonso	

Liverpool won 3-2 on penalties
Liverpool: Dudek, Finnan (Hamann), Hyppia, Carragher, Traore, Gerrard, Xabi Alonso, Luis Garcia, Riise, Baros (Cisse), Kewell (Smicer)
Milan: Dida, Cafu, Stam, Nesta, Maldini, Gattuso (Rui Costa), Seedorf (Serginho), Pirlo, Kaka, Shevchenko, Crespo (Tomasson)
HT: 0-3
FT: 3-3
Referee: Manuel Mejuto Gonzalez (Spain)
Attendance 65,000